D0450391

UTSA
Memorial Fund
in memory of

Luther Nichols Grimes, Sr.

From a Gift
to UTSA by

the donors to the
UTSA Memorial Fund

America's Germany

WITHDRAWN
UTSA LIBRARIES

America's Germany

John J. McCloy and the
Federal Republic of Germany

THOMAS ALAN SCHWARTZ

Harvard University Press
Cambridge, Massachusetts
London, England
1991

To my family

Copyright © 1991 by the President and Fellows of Harvard College
All rights reserved
Printed in the United States of America
10 9 8 7 6 5 4 3 2 1

This book is printed on acid-free paper, and its binding materials
have been chosen for strength and durability.

Library of Congress Cataloging-in-Publication Data

Schwartz, Thomas Alan, 1954–
America's Germany : John J. McCloy and the Federal Republic of
Germany / Thomas Alan Schwartz.
p.   cm.
Includes bibliographical references and index.
ISBN 0-674-03115-6 (alk. paper)
1. United States—Foreign relations—Germany (West) 2. Germany
(West)—Foreign relations—United States. 3. McCloy, John J., 1895–
4. European Economic Community. 5. European federation.
6. Germany—History—Allied occupation, 1945– 7. United States—
Foreign relations—1945–1953. 8 United States—Foreign
relations—1953–1961. I. Title.
E183.8.G3S513 1991
327.73043—dc20
90-39849

**Library
University of Texas**
at San Antonio

Contents

Preface   *ix*

1   The Making of a High Commissioner   *1*

2   Changing of the Guard   *29*

3   Avoiding the Fate of Weimar: The Petersberg Protocols   *57*

4   Monnet and the Schuman Plan   *84*

5   The Dilemmas of Rearmament   *113*

6   Dealing with the Past: Moral Integration   *156*

7   Ties That Bind: Economic Integration   *185*

8   The Skeleton Key: Military Integration   *210*

9   How Free Should the Germans Be? Political Integration   *235*

10 The New Look: Eisenhower and Dulles, 1953–1955   *279*

Conclusions: European Unity, Dual Containment,
and the American "Empire"   *295*

Abbreviations   *312*

Selected Bibliography   *313*

Notes   *321*

Index   *395*

Illustrations

Map of Germany and Europe after 1945   *34*

Following page 184:

McCloy as Assistant Secretary of War. *Harris and Ewing, Truman Library*

McCloy in Tunisia, March 1943. *U.S. Army, Eisenhower Library*

Andrei Gromyko, Henry Stimson, and McCloy at Potsdam. *McCloy family*

Cologne at the end of the war. *German Information Center*

Berlin: Brandenburg Gate, May 8, 1945. *German Information Center*

Averell Harriman, McCloy, and David Bruce. *McCloy family*

The three Allied High Commissioners signing the Occupation Statute. *McCloy family*

Konrad Adenauer asserting his Teppichpolitik. *German Information Center*

"Reconstruction in Berlin with Marshall Plan assistance." *German Information Center*

McCloy touring the Farbwerke-Hoechst plant. *McCloy family*

Rebuilding the Volkswagen plant in Wolfsburg. *German Information Center*

Kurt Schumacher addressing a rally in Berlin. *UPI/Bettmann Newsphotos*

Harry S Truman, McCloy, and Dean Acheson. *Abbie Rowe, National Park Services*

Jean Monnet. *UPI/Bettmann Newsphotos*

General Thomas Handy, General Dwight D. Eisenhower, and McCloy. *UPI/Bettmann Newsphotos*

"Hold It, Please." Political cartoon. *Copyright 1951 by Herblock in The Washington Post*

Anthony Eden, Konrad Adenauer, Dean Acheson, and Robert Schuman at the signing of the contractual agreements, May 1952. *German Information Center*

McCloy and Dean Acheson following the signing of the contractual agreements. *McCloy family*

John and Ellen McCloy leaving Germany. *McCloy family*

John Foster Dulles and Konrad Adenauer. *German Information Center*

Frankfurt before and after its rebuilding. *German Information Center*

McCloy, Gerald Ford, and Walter Scheel, June 1975. *German Information Center*

Preface

On a bright, crisp March afternoon in 1989 more than five hundred friends and associates of the man once dubbed the "Chairman of the Establishment" gathered in Park Avenue's Brick Presbyterian Church to pay tribute to John J. McCloy. McCloy's death at ninety-three brought to an end an extraordinary career in law, finance, and government, and symbolized the passing of an era. The dignitaries in attendance—Richard Nixon, Henry Kissinger, Cyrus Vance, Paul Volcker, Charles Mathias, David Rockefeller, James Baker, McGeorge Bundy—were a tribute to this modest man who, as Kissinger reminded the congregation, had never held a Cabinet-level position and had not held a permanent public office for the past three decades. Perhaps most impressive were the representatives from the Federal Republic of Germany, among them the former President, Karl Carstens, and the former Chancellor, Helmut Schmidt. Schmidt praised McCloy as "our very reliable friend," who had "rendered outstanding service to the world at large and Germany in particular." In a voice filled with emotion, he told a story about Abraham Lincoln to express his own understanding of McCloy's achievement as High Commissioner in postwar Germany. Advised to "destroy" his enemies, Lincoln responded, "Am I not destroying my enemies when I make friends of them?"

Four decades earlier few would have imagined a scene in which a German leader would quote an American President in tribute to an American statesman. In a May 1949 profile of McCloy, then newly appointed as American High Commissioner for Germany, the *New*

York Times commented, "There are many, indeed, who believe that peace in this age depends on the way American leadership is exercised in the boiling cauldron of postwar Germany." Having fought two wars within less than a quarter-century, American leaders were justly nervous about Germany's position at the center of the Cold War with the Soviet Union. Would a divided Germany trigger conflict between the superpowers? Would an upsurge of German nationalism and a desire for reunification jeopardize the peace and stability of Europe? Could the Continent recover and be defended without German participation? If Germany's revival was necessary to Europe's defense, how could the United States reconcile the concerns of its Allies, Great Britain and France, with such a potentially dangerous policy? How should America deal with the legacies of Nazism and encourage the creation of a healthy German democracy? In view of all these dilemmas and the many powers and interests at work in Central Europe, few observers were optimistic about the chances for peace. As one expert on Germany told a reporter for *Time* magazine, "Whenever you think you have the answer to a German problem, you have to box the compass to see how it checks with all the major forces. You usually wind up finding that you've boxed yourself—and have to start over."

This book is a study of American policy toward the Federal Republic of Germany during the period 1949–1955, with special emphasis on the years 1949–1952, when John J. McCloy was High Commissioner and the major directions of that policy took shape. Two distinct stories unfold here, though they become closely intertwined. The first concerns the personal role of McCloy, a man who was one of the most important, if least well known, of the "Founding Fathers" of postwar American internationalism. By training and cultivation, McCloy represented the best and worst of the values and beliefs of a generation of American foreign policy leaders; and he brought to Germany the historical experience, ideological perspective, and strong sense of American mission that characterized these men. His prestige within the American government gave him a degree of power in shaping policy toward Germany that was unique to this period. He played a major part in all the important decisions concerning Germany, and his role in implementing these decisions affected their outcome.

The second story is that of the birth and development of the Federal Republic of Germany, a new state in an old nation, given its second opportunity in the twentieth century to create a viable democracy.

The dramatic events of late 1989 and 1990, with the collapse of the
Berlin Wall, the disintegration of East Germany, and the Kohl-
Gorbachev agreements on the admission of a reunited Germany into
NATO, have all served to underscore the impressive political and
economic success of the Federal Republic. But in 1949 this new
Germany's leaders faced the challenge of providing a better life for a
people traumatized by fascism and war, while at the same time trying
to survive in a Europe torn between the two superpowers. The German Chancellor, Konrad Adenauer, sought to establish the prestige
and legitimacy of his government under the watchful supervision of
the Allies. The German economy, still limited by Allied controls and
prohibitions, was only beginning to revive, and the country's formerly
powerful Wehrmacht had ceased to exist.

This study chronicles these two intersecting histories, in which an
American leadership elite, filled with the sense of self-confidence and
historical mission that had been forged in World War II, supervised
the birth of a new republic. *America's Germany* describes a unique
period in the relationship between the two countries, a period when
both were transformed. The two nations forged an extraordinary range
of connections and linkages—political, economic, military, and cultural—as the Federal Republic became a part of the Western "club"
and the "new" Europe, all within the environment of the short-lived
and paradoxical "American Empire."

American historians, as Lloyd Gardner has recently reminded us,
are now using the term "empire" to describe America's postwar expansion, even though "we are still very far from agreed about the
circumstances of its creation, and its purpose." To the extent that
America ruled an empire after 1945, John J. McCloy was one of its
most distinguished "proconsuls," and the Federal Republic of Germany one of its most important "provinces." This book, I hope, will
contribute to our understanding of the postwar American Empire, or
as Charles Maier once called it, "the empire that dare not speak its
name." The major sources for this book are the diplomatic records of
the United States, the Federal Republic of Germany, Great Britain,
and to a far lesser extent, France. These have been supplemented by
a range of private sources, including the records of important members
of the High Commission and of the German industrial concerns affected by American policies. Interviews with surviving policymakers
of all four nations have added further information. Through the use

of this multi-archival approach, which attempts to explain American policies and their results from different national perspectives, I hope to fill a gap in the broader international history of the United States in the twentieth century, often called the American Century.

Professor Ernest R. May has watched over this project from the beginning, and his intellectual guidance has been invaluable. I also owe an intellectual debt to Professor Charles S. Maier, whose ideas have greatly influenced my approach to this topic. Responsibility for the content of this work rests with me alone, but I should like to thank the following scholars for their advice, assistance, and support: Thomas Alpert, Günter Bischof, Alan Brinkley, Richard Chriss, Gitta Frank, Norbert Frei, John Gillingham, Guido Goldmann, Henning Gutmann, Peter Hayes, Jeffrey Herf, Michael Hogan, Max Holland, Richard Hunt, Robert Johnson, Daniel Klingensmith, Wolfgang Krieger, Jennifer Laurendeau, Melvyn Leffler, Geir Lundestad, Fran MacDonnell, Gregory Mark, Forrest Pogue, Aviel Roshwald, Andrew Saxe, James Shenton, Mark Spaulding, Melissa Stockdale, Thomas Sugrue, Marc Trachtenberg, and Robert Wampler. Very special thanks go to Maureen McPeak, Mary Malbon, and Marie Miller.

John J. McCloy was always willing to help me with this project, and I am sorry that he did not live to see it published. Edward J. Reilly, one of Mr. McCloy's most distinguished partners at Milbank Tweed, has offered so much assistance that I find it difficult to thank him enough. I also thank Ellen Z. McCloy and John J. McCloy II for permission to use several photographs of their father. The Amherst College Archives has granted me permission to quote from the McCloy diary, and Shepard Stone has allowed me to quote from his own private papers.

Among my innumerable debts to archivists, I must single out the helpful staff of the Truman Library, especially Elizabeth Safly and Dennis Bilger, and, at the National Archives, Sally Marks, Kathy Nicastro, Will Mahoney, and David Pfeiffer.

Generous financial assistance from the Social Science Research Council and the Harry S. Truman Institute's Scholar's Development Award gave me the time to turn my dissertation into a book. The Charles Warren Center at Harvard provided me with an office and the opportunity to test my ideas in association with other scholars.

Dr. Karl Kaiser of the Deutsche Gesellschaft für Auswärtige Politik provided me with a place to work during my trips to Bonn. Ernst and Maria Giesen offered me the warm hospitality of their home in Cologne.

At Harvard University Press the manuscript has received the professional consideration and care of Aida Donald and Elizabeth Suttell, as well as the expert copyediting of Dorothy Whitney.

My sister, Mary Guinan, has sustained my morale during endless revisions of the manuscript. My wife, Amy Helene Kirschke, came into the project at a later stage, but she helped prepare the final draft and has given me the love, support, and encouragement without which it would have been impossible to finish.

1

The Making of a High Commissioner

When he was appointed High Commissioner in May 1949, John J. McCloy, Wall Street lawyer and President of the World Bank, remarked, "There's some destiny about all this business—Germany seems to dog my footsteps." McCloy had good reason to believe this. He had been raised in a German-American household, had fought against Imperial Germany in the First World War, married into a prosperous German-American family, successfully sued the German government in the 1930s, and helped run the War Department against Germany in the Second World War, devising at the end the policies that would guide the occupation. But McCloy's career was not only the story of one American's involvement with issues relating to Germany. His rise to prominence within the American foreign policy Establishment provides a unique perspective on the historical experience, values, and beliefs of a generation of leaders, the "Founding Fathers" of American internationalism. Those of McCloy's generation were, as Dean Acheson later put it, "present at the creation," having the opportunity to leave their imprint on the world during the era when the United States was the world's first political, economic, and military superpower.[1]

From Market Street to Wall Street, 1895–1940

John Snader McCloy was born on March 31, 1895, in Philadelphia, the second son of John Jay McCloy and Anna May Snader. (He later changed his middle name to honor his father.) Though McCloy often referred to being born "north of Market Street, on the wrong side of the tracks," his family background was solidly middle class. His father's family was of Scotch-Irish ancestry, his mother's Pennsylvania "Dutch," or German. Both families had emigrated to America before the Revolution and settled in eastern Pennsylvania. The senior Mc-Cloy, a claims officer for Penn Mutual Life Insurance Company, was an ambitious man with little formal education but a love of the classical languages and literature. He taught himself Latin, and even assisted in a translation of the *Aeneid* and other, more obscure Latin poems. He regretted not knowing other languages and wanted both his sons to have a classical education, telling his wife on his deathbed, "Have John study Greek." John Jay McCloy was only thirty-nine years old when he died of heart failure in 1901.

Her husband's death was the second major tragedy for Anna McCloy. Her older son, William, had died of diphtheria eighteen months earlier, leaving her alone with young Jack. After these tragedies Anna McCloy returned to her parental home and, along with her two sisters Sadie and Lena, went to work to support the extended family. Anna was a strong-willed and stubborn woman, determined that her son would have every opportunity for education and social advancement. Her work opened some of these doors, in a quite literal sense. She was a beautician—"did heads," as McCloy later recalled—and in those days before beauty parlors she carried her equipment to the homes of her clients. Many of these women were married to Phila-delphia's doctors, lawyers, and businessmen, and Anna McCloy rec-ognized the advantage of these contacts. She arranged jobs for Jack as a "chore boy" in her clients' fashionable summer camps in the Adirondack Mountains, saying that she wanted her son to escape Philadelphia for the "strenuous life" of the outdoors. She also insisted that he learn tennis, a favorite sport of the wealthy, even providing him with the used racket of a client's son. (McCloy went on to become an accomplished player.) As a result of observing the prominence and power of lawyers, Anna McCloy decided her son would become one.[2]

Anna also wanted him to have an education that would enable him to compete with the best. Her frugality enabled her to pay for private schools—first Maplewood, a Quaker school, and then Peddie, a prep school in rural Hightstown, New Jersey. Faithful to his father's dying wish, McCloy studied Greek, even winning the Greek prize. (Later in life he commented that the best way to get a calm start for a hard day at the office was to read a bit of Greek on the subway.) Though he did well enough academically, Jack's great love was sports. Heeding the admonition of one of his coaches, John Plant, that he should always challenge himself to do better, to compete with those of superior skill and intellect, to "run with the swift," Jack became an accomplished athlete. Despite the cruel side of this competitiveness—after having flinched at a tackle in a football game, he found his jersey marked with a yellow streak—he conformed to Plant's credo with unrestrained enthusiasm. He was determined to succeed, to study longer, run faster, and try harder than those who "were better than I."[3]

In September 1912 McCloy entered Amherst College in Massachusetts, a small, distinguished liberal arts school. He worked hard at Amherst, ultimately graduating with honors, and supported himself by waiting on tables and tutoring. Among his favorite subjects were Greek and history; and one teacher, Frederick Thompson, inspired him to take a lifelong interest in the Civil War. Among his friends was Lewis W. Douglas, the son of a wealthy Arizona mine owner, who would later become Ambassador to Great Britain when McCloy was High Commissioner. The two young men shared a love of sports, and both supported the Allied cause and attended the Plattsburg army camps. But in one respect they were quite different. Douglas was often self-righteous, and he carried on "agonizing moral debates with himself over issues and decisions." McCloy, on the other hand, was prepared to compromise and conciliate rather than to take strong moral—and isolating—positions.[4]

The outbreak of war in Europe in 1914 had a decisive effect on McCloy's career. The President of Amherst, Alexander Meikeljohn, and a substantial part of the student body favored American neutrality. McCloy, who favored "preparedness," joined with three other Amherst men in the summer of 1915 to take part in the first military training camps at Plattsburg, New York. Led by prominent New York lawyers and bankers—men such as Elihu Root, Henry Stimson, Grenville Clark, and Leonard Wood—the "Plattsburg movement" had roots in the Progressive tradition, which held that those who were most privileged should serve the state and society. Defending the camps against charges of militarism, the liberal journal *New Republic* maintained that they sought "to civilize the American military system," arguing that citizens would not become "automatons" but rather that soldiers would become citizens. Decrying the self-interest and selfishness which many saw as their "rights," the journal warned of "national disintegration" and emphasized the need to cultivate the "responsibilities of citizenship."[5]

The Plattsburg movement embodied some of the contradictions inherent in Progressivism. Although it preached the unifying and democratizing effects of military service in assimilating immigrants and bridging class differences, the participants were overwhelmingly wealthy, white, educated Protestants. Whatever the contradictions, the camps had a powerful and lasting effect on the men who served in them. They were "a kind of secular retreat for a generation (in which) the upper-class elite underwent a conversion experience of patriotism, individual responsibility, and collective action." Many Plattsburgers became prominent leaders, exalting "the principle of federal control in military matters" and believing that the American nation could come of age only when its government was strong enough to harness and direct the energies of all its citizens.[6]

McCloy participated enthusiastically in the Plattsburg camps. Despite his German heritage, he shared the general sympathy for the Allies and was outraged over such German actions as the invasion of Belgium and the sinking of the *Lusitania*. But he also admitted that one reason to go to Plattsburg was that "all the right people went." The summer camps in which he had been a chore boy were not very different from this new form of camp. At Plattsburg he distinguished himself as a marksman, winning top honors in 1915 and tying with Douglas in 1916. Military training gave McCloy a greater maturity and self-confidence and offered him the valuable experience of command. He learned to ride, studied military science, and gained "a certain recognition" from his commanders.[7]

After graduating from Amherst in 1916 McCloy entered Harvard Law School. But when the United States declared war in April 1917, he received notice to report to Plattsburg the following month. After a short time there, he was transferred to Fort Ethan Allen in Vermont, where the training was rigorous and demanding even for a Plattsburger. He wrote his mother that "the work is getting more and more complicated . . . We have exams each day in the stuff and I am not getting along any too well in them." Hoping to go overseas quickly, McCloy took a commission as a provisional second lieutenant. He was assigned to a field artillery brigade as an operations officer and arrived in France in July 1918. His unit saw limited action at the front between the Moselle River and Verdun, and after the armistice he joined the American Army of Occupation at Trier.[8]

McCloy, who liked being a soldier, developed a respect for and rapport with soldiers that would prove important later in his career. It was an exciting time for him, a time of increasing recognition and success. At Fort Ethan Allen, McCloy came to the attention of General Guy H. Preston, a crusty old Cavalry officer. Preston admired the young officer's determination and perseverance, observing once that McCloy finished a ride with his pants soaked in blood, enduring the pain without complaint. Preston later recalled, "I said to myself that any son of a bitch who could keep riding with that much pain must be a damn good officer." Under Preston's sponsorship McCloy rose to the rank of captain. Through Preston, McCloy met General Pershing, as well as such future leaders as George Marshall, Colonel William "Wild Bill" Donovan, and Douglas MacArthur. Preston was so pleased with his young aide's performance that he wanted McCloy to take a permanent Army commission.[9]

McCloy was never part of the "lost generation"; he did not experience the disillusionment of many veterans of the Great War. His views were similar to those of another veteran who wrote that a "lot of people were like myself and enjoyed the war . . . The things I loved about it . . . are apparently essential to any happiness." These things were a "close association with large numbers of one's fellow men in a common purpose, the chance to put forth intensive and disinterested effort in a cause greater than one's personal concerns, economic equality, freedom from economic worries, and adventure." That the war did not make the world "safe for democracy" did not detract from these feelings. And in McCloy's case the war had provided an opportunity to show leadership qualities and receive recognition.[10]

McCloy returned to the United States and Harvard Law School in the fall of 1919. He later characterized the move from Amherst to Cambridge as like "going from the Greek provinces to the metropolis of Athens." His mother moved to Cambridge so that she could share an apartment with him while he completed law school. Her savings and earnings supplemented McCloy's scholarship, as did his fees for teaching handball and squash. Living with his mother must not have been easy for the twenty-five-year-old veteran. Neither were his classes. After "having commanded a field artillery battery in the greatest war in history," sitting in a classroom seemed "dull." But McCloy's intellectual competitiveness was stimulated by Harvard Law School, which was in a period of "intellectual brilliance": the Socratic method had just been introduced, and the faculty included such men as Roscoe Pound, Samuel Williston, and Felix Frankfurter. The school was intensely competitive, with a third of the class dropping out before completing a degree. McCloy, who felt "somewhat out of [his] depth at the Law School," did not break into the top echelon of his class by making the prestigious *Harvard Law Review.* After McCloy gained fame, Felix Frankfurter, who always knew the brighter and more socially prominent students in his classes, could not remember having taught him at Harvard.[11]

After graduating in 1921 McCloy unsuccessfully sought a job in Philadelphia. A friend of his mother and a leader of the Philadelphia bar, George Wharton Pepper, advised him to go to New York. There he quickly got a position with the Wall Street firm of Cadwalader, Wickersham, and Taft. New York was replacing London as the center of world finance, and Wall Street law firms were expanding quickly to meet the new demands. Cadwalader gave McCloy important responsibilities, such as representing the Lackawanna Steel Company in the 1922 sale of its properties to Bethlehem Steel. But McCloy was still looking about for other, more challenging opportunities. His friend and classmate Donald Swatland, a brilliant lawyer who had graduated first in McCloy's Harvard class, encouraged his interest in the firm of Cravath, Henderson, and deGersdorff (later Cravath, Swaine, and Moore). Although it was one of Wall Street's oldest and most distinguished firms, Cravath was more open to men with talent and ability who lacked a special family background, social status, or wealth. McCloy joined the firm as an associate on December 1, 1924.[12]

As a new law clerk McCloy became heavily involved in cases concerning the reorganization of the Western railroads. The work required long and grueling hours on the part of both partners and clerks, but McCloy performed well. There were even fleeting moments of fame. In 1926 he and Swatland worked on a purchase plan for the Chicago, Milwaukee, and St. Paul Railroad. When they organized a temporary holding company in Delaware, McCloy was designated President. Newspapers published the picture of America's youngest railroad president, even as the holding company was being dissolved.[13]

McCloy's capacity for hard work and his initiative led Cravath to send him to Europe. There he provided the legal assistance needed in issuing securities for European municipalities, power companies, and agricultural associations. In the aftermath of the war Europe required American capital to rebuild, and many of Cravath's clients provided it. The young lawyer lived for almost a year in Italy, where Cravath was advising the government. He also traveled to France, Germany, and Greece and came to know the Frenchman Jean Monnet, who worked for the investment house Blair and Company, one of Cravath's clients. Although America had rejected the League of Nations, McCloy was becoming an internationalist who recognized the interdependence of the American and European economies and the potential leadership role of the United States.[14]

These years were more important for establishing McCloy's reputation on Wall Street than for shaping his ideas about foreign policy. He was never to become known as a brilliant lawyer or outstanding litigator. Rather his stature rested on qualities of character and personality. Most important were his extraordinary vitality and his capacity for hard work. Yet McCloy did not devote all his energy to the practice of law. He consciously cultivated a range of interests: from attending operas at the Met to perfecting his tennis game at the West Side Tennis Club, he sought to become a well-rounded "generalist." He collected books, especially first editions, and maintained an interest in history, poetry, and the classics. His outdoor interests, especially hunting and fishing, brought him many friends among bankers and businessmen, as well as a better understanding of their professional needs and concerns. Affable and optimistic in demeanor, democratic and unpretentious in his approach to people, McCloy became a skillful negotiator who could arrange compromises among conflicting claims and help antagonists reach satisfactory settlements. He believed all conflicts were negotiable as long as each side tried to view the problem "objectively"—a word which McCloy used frequently and which embodied his essential pragmatism and interest in results. He delighted in accomplishment, arranging settlements, finalizing mergers, and avoiding the courtroom. He wanted to become what senior partner Paul Cravath described as a "lawyer of affairs," a man possessed not of "brilliant intellectual powers" but of a "sound sense of proportion" in judging and evaluating cases.[15]

Yet in some respects McCloy's success on Wall Street came because he fitted the mold. He was a man who got along. Even his physical appearance—round, open face and short, stocky body—lacked sharp edges. His affability and graciousness were genuine, but they also reflected an eagerness to please and a willingness to conform that made him an unlikely defender of principle or unpopular causes. He tended to take the moderate and centrist approach to questions, both when it was right and when it was desperately wrong. He could be more "establishment" than the Establishment in his moderation and pragmatism.

In 1929, the same year he became a partner in the Cravath firm, McCloy ran into his former Amherst classmate Lewis Douglas, traveling with his wife, Peggy, on an eastbound train to New York. Douglas was by then a Congressman from Arizona, a rising star in the Democratic party. He introduced McCloy to his wife's older sister, Ellen Zinsser, the daughter of a prominent German-American family. Ellen's grandparents had come from Germany in 1848, and German traditions (including the language) were maintained in the household. The Zinsser family had achieved recognition: her father was the owner of a chemical factory, and his brother, Hans Zinsser, a professor of bacteriology at Harvard and a well-known author. Ellen, a graduate of Smith College, was an intelligent and strong-willed woman, with a clear sense of the importance of family. After a yearlong courtship that included many outings at the Zinsser home, the two were married on April 25, 1930. For a rising lawyer like McCloy, Ellen was the perfect wife. She deferred to his career, caring for their two children, running the household during his frequent absences, and participating in numerous volunteer and charitable organizations. Like McCloy's mother, Ellen was ambitious for him, encouraging him to seek greater opportunities and challenges, and insisting that he receive proper professional and financial recognition. McCloy's marriage to Ellen was of inestimable importance; she gave him the love, stability, and security he needed, as well as encouragement and unflinching support in his career. He became devoted to her, and he never underestimated her contribution to his success.[16]

On their wedding day McCloy and Ellen set sail for Paris, where he was to take charge of the Cravath office. During the following year in Europe, McCloy began a decade-long involvement with the Black Tom case, a case which proved to be the springboard to his career in government. On July 30, 1916, a thundering explosion at the Black Tom munitions depot had rocked lower Manhattan. German sabotage was suspected, but definitive proof was lacking. After the war a number of American firms, including Bethlehem Steel (an important Cravath client), filed claims with the German-American Mixed Claims Commission. Despite some incriminating evidence provided by British intelligence, the German government denied responsibility. When the case came before the International Court at The Hague, McCloy attended the proceedings as an observer. Following the Court's finding that the United States had not proved the responsibility of any German agent, McCloy spent several months in France and Germany investigating and seeking new material. When he returned to America in 1931, he plunged actively into the investigation.[17]

For the next ten years, as America coped with the Great Depression, McCloy was preoccupied with the Black Tom case, traveling from Dublin on the west to Warsaw in the east, interviewing Irish republicans, Czarist exiles, and German spies. He negotiated with such Nazi notables as Rudolf Hess and Hermann Göring, and was even invited to spend an afternoon in Hitler's private box at the 1936 Olympic games. McCloy worked virtually around the clock during the summer of 1938, drafting the major brief for the Claims Commission. In June 1939 the Commission held for the plaintiffs. It found that the evidence, much of which McCloy had assembled, established German responsibility for the Black Tom explosion and other acts of sabotage. The case dragged on another year and a half until the Supreme Court upheld the decision, and then the American claimants received $26 million in damages, with Bethlehem Steel receiving $2 million.[18]

The Black Tom case was one of the most celebrated and spectacular in modern international law. Cravath's official history noted that "in size of recovery and duration of the litigation it far exceeded the *Alabama* claims after the Civil War." For McCloy it was a distinctly personal achievement. As the coordinator of more than twenty lawyers representing different clients, he had "tirelessly fitted the vast mosaic together." Recognizing that he had borne "the laboring oar" on the legal work in the case, the Cravath partners voted McCloy a special distribution.[19]

The Washington Years, 1940–1949

McCloy's triumph in the Black Tom case was the high point of his legal career, but the war in Europe cast a shadow over his success. With the fall of France and the battle of Britain, Nazi Germany threatened America's geographical isolation and security. McCloy joined William Allen White's Committee to Defend America by Aiding the Allies, an organization which lobbied for more American support for Britain. True to his Plattsburg beliefs, he was also active in encouraging legislation for the Selective Service Act, which Congress passed in September 1940. A more significant opportunity to serve came when President Roosevelt made the Republican elder statesman Henry Stimson the new Secretary of War. Stimson needed assistants, and he had met McCloy during the Black Tom litigation. In Stimson's view, McCloy knew "more about subversive German agents in this country I believe than any other man." To McCloy, Stimson was a symbol of Wall Street's more noble traditions of public service. In October 1940 Stimson asked McCloy to come to Washington and act as a special consultant on German espionage. A few months later he became the Assistant Secretary of War.[20]

Ironically for a lifelong Republican, McCloy's move to Washington began a career of service to Democratic Presidents. Except for the Black Tom case, much of his legal practice in the 1930s had involved defending corporations against the Justice Department, the New Deal regulatory agencies, and Congressional investigations. McCloy traced his political views to his father and grandfather, both admirers of Lincoln, and adhered to the liberal Republicanism associated with such men as Wendell Willkie and Thomas Dewey. Although he accepted a role for the federal government in "certain important social fields" and was flexible in his definition of these responsibilities, he remained fundamentally conservative, an unabashed elitist in a time of egalitarian fervor. He felt it was "important to keep a force opposed to the monolithic state." A strong defender of the "incentive and initiative of free enterprise," McCloy feared that its "destruction" by the New Deal would "bring everything down to a low undistinguished level of life." He even labeled some New Dealers "totalitarians," and he resented those aspects of Roosevelt's policies which he thought emphasized class divisions. He told Dean Acheson, a conservative Democrat, that the "contrasts" in Roosevelt's leadership "amazed" him. "The destroyer deal [of 1940] was a stroke of real statesmanship," but a Roosevelt speech to the Teamsters' Union "might just as well have been written by [Leon] Blum" (the French Socialist leader). In McCloy's view Roosevelt resembled Blum in his "ridiculous" argument "that every element in the country, except labor, must make sacrifices in order to defend the country."[21]

The doubts McCloy may have had about Franklin Roosevelt and the New Deal were quickly overcome by his association with Henry Stimson, who had served as Secretary of War for President Taft and as Secretary of State for President Hoover. The seventy-three-year-old Stimson, who was to become a "hero-statesman" to McCloy, brought to the Administration the Establishment tradition of a strong, activist American foreign policy. The founder of this tradition had been Elihu Root, the Secretary of State for William McKinley and Theodore Roosevelt and Stimson's own hero-statesman. (Stimson kept Root's published works in his office.) The Establishment embraced a broad spectrum of beliefs, but it was united by the conviction that the United States had certain national interests, above partisan political considerations, which it had to defend. One of these, as McCloy once put it, was "that the security and democratic welfare of Europe were essential to the security and welfare of the United States." Stimson led the fight for a military draft and believed that the United States required a strong military, based on universal service. At the same time Establishment leaders feared that creation of the powerful state necessary for the conduct of foreign policy might threaten the economic and personal liberties they enjoyed. For this reason they preferred the easy movement from private and corporate life into government service, and back again, to the creation of a powerful and professional civil service similar to that of European countries. By shuttling between private and public roles, they hoped to control the new state they were creating.[22]

Stimson and McCloy warmed to each other almost instantly. Stimson developed a paternal feeling for McCloy, whose wide-ranging knowledge, "enormous energy," and "unquenchable optimism" brought renewed vitality to the War Department. The elder statesman recognized quickly that this "very useful and energetic man" could be groomed in the Root-Stimson tradition, and that McCloy's dynamism would give a strength to Stimson's ideas that he himself could no longer provide. For his part McCloy respected Stimson as a man of great integrity and courage whose experience had given him a broad and "objective" understanding of the national interest. Stimson had what Felix Frankfurter called "moral authority" that McCloy greatly admired. Both men loved the outdoors, hunting, and the "lonely appeal of the wilderness." Enjoying Stimson's confidence and trust, McCloy could behave in Washington not only as Stimson's "eyes and ears" but also as an independent actor in policy questions.[23]

Stimson's War Department was a nerve center of wartime Washington, and McCloy worked with an elite group. Robert Lovett of Brown Brothers, Harriman, a major New York financial house, was Stimson's other Assistant Secretary, handling primarily the problems of the Air Force. Judge Robert Patterson, a New York lawyer, was Under Secretary, dealing with problems of procurement. McCloy's job placed him "at all the points of the organizational chart where the lines did not quite intersect." Among these were the Army's dealings with Congress, the Joint Chiefs, and civilians, both American and those in Allied and enemy countries. McCloy found himself in the middle of bureaucratic battles that challenged his ability to achieve consensus. As a "troubleshooter" he sought to find the ground for compromise among different agencies, services, and even, at times, among the Allies. One of his principal achievements was the creation of the State-War-Navy Coordinating Committee, the forerunner of the National Security Council. Although rarely the originator of ideas, McCloy got things done, and he "took a consuming delight in the successful operation" of government. With an "acute sense for the location of real influence," the Assistant Secretary was involved in so many decisions that Stimson once wondered whether "anyone in Washington ever acted without having a word with McCloy."[24]

McCloy's varied involvements validated Stimson's claim. Before the United States entered the war, he was Stimson's representative on Capitol Hill, lobbying legislators on behalf of Lend-Lease. He slept on a cot in the office of the Foreign Relations Committee throughout the debate, always prepared to answer questions and pressure wavering Senators. His earlier friendship with Jean Monnet led him to pass on Monnet's phrase "arsenal of democracy" to Felix Frankfurter, who passed it on to the White House. McCloy oversaw the plans for the new Pentagon building, bargaining with the White House to gain approval of the project. He handled the administrative details of the Army's training program, and he helped create the unit that later broke the Japanese intelligence codes.

The Black Tom case also shaped McCloy's early activities in the War Department. In his original report to Stimson about the possibility of another campaign of German sabotage, McCloy said that Germans had told him they "did not contemplate any sabotage in the United States" unless America was "clearly about to enter the war." They added, however, that if the United States became involved, "they had plans for a much more effective campaign than had ever been put into action in the last war." Although McCloy took this threat "with a grain of salt," he proposed to prevent such activity with both carrot and stick. One way to avoid sabotage in factories was "good working conditions, high pay, [and] good recreational facilities," which would make it "more difficult for the Germans to get their 'stooges.'" McCloy also thought that the United States would be justified in going beyond the law, if necessary, to combat "the machinations of German agents . . . who seek to interrupt production of vitally needed defense material." In early 1941 he engaged in a running dispute with the Department of Justice and Attorney General Robert Jackson over the War Department's concern that some "labor leaders were financed by foreign sources" and were encouraging disturbances and strikes. In Jackson's view, McCloy believed that "investigators should be unrestrained in wire tapping, in stealing of evidence, in conducting unlimited search and seizures, use of dictaphones, etc., etc." McCloy even suggested the creation of a "suicide squad" to carry out such investigations. Jackson objected strongly to such "lawless methods" and the anti-labor bias of the investigation, reminding McCloy that the man who "today will rifle your desk for me, tomorrow will rifle mine for someone else." At this point McCloy backed away from his original demands, assuring Jackson that he did not "question the wisdom of your decisions" and understood "there is a real problem and, perhaps, the only solution is via legislation." Still McCloy's enthusiasm for such extralegal approaches reveals the degree to which "national security" already inclined him to sanction what he himself described as "quite distasteful means" to combat foreign threats.[25]

McCloy's sense of urgency about the war effort was matched by his emphasis on "preparedness." His speeches reveal a view of recent history similar to that of other leaders of his generation—the so-called Establishment view, which would shape American foreign policy for the next decades. He told an Amherst alumni audience in June 1941 that Americans had ignored events "eloquent of future disaster" in Manchuria, Ethiopia, Austria, and Czechoslovakia. Shortly after Pearl Harbor he told another audience that it was "amazing" that "no act of aggression by Germany or Japan in the twenties and the thirties aroused us." McCloy's experience had convinced him of the dangers of a militarily weak and unprepared America and of the need for "eternal vigilance" against aggression. He believed that "there is no war to end all wars. No war to make the world forever safe." This commitment to preparedness, to keeping America from slipping back into the isolation and unpreparedness of the 1920s and 1930s, shaped his subsequent foreign policy perspective.[26]

After Pearl Harbor McCloy's duties and responsibilities increased exponentially. For a short time he wanted to leave the War Department and return to active service, but Stimson persuaded him to remain. As Stimson's liaison with the State Department and the Joint Chiefs of Staff, he influenced foreign policy as well as the planning of most of the major campaigns on both fronts. He was involved in strictly military questions as well, such as encouraging the use of spotter planes to guide artillery. He toured all the theatres of operation, once even demonstrating the use of a bazooka to puzzled GIs. He worked closely with General George Marshall, a man who, in McCloy's opinion, "came as close, if not closer to touching the mantle of greatness than anybody that I've ever come in contact with, in and out of the Army." In assisting Marshall, McCloy dealt with such thorny issues as racial segregation within the Army, chairing the Advisory Committee on Negro Troop Policies that was known as the McCloy Committee. McCloy resisted the demands of civil rights activists for a quick end to segregation. He told one leader, "Frankly I do not think that the basic issues of this war are involved in the question of whether colored troops serve in segregated units or in mixed units, and I doubt whether you can convince people of the United States that the basic issues of freedom are involved in such a question." He argued that if the United States lost the war, the lot of the black community would be far worse, and that blacks should give unstinting support to the war effort in anticipation of the benefits of victory. But black leaders, who remembered this argument from World War I, continued to protest racial segregation, often comparing it with Nazi practices. Gradually McCloy came to see the Army's use of segregated units as detrimental to "military efficiency," and his committee recommended that "black troops not be wasted by leaving them to train endlessly in camps around the United States." In March 1944 the committee recommended that black units be introduced into combat; and McCloy defended their performance to a skeptical Stimson, who continued to insist that such units required white officers. Before McCloy left office in November 1945, he advocated ending racial segregation and quotas on blacks in the military. Characteristically he defended his views not on moral grounds, but in the interest of military efficiency.[27]

The most controversial role McCloy played in wartime policy concerned the government's decision to "relocate" and intern almost 120,000 Japanese-Americans who lived on the West Coast. Anti-Japanese sentiment in that area had a long history. In 1908 political pressures from Western states had led to the famous Gentleman's Agreement, which restricted Japanese immigration, and in 1924 came complete prohibition. Japanese immigrants were barred from American citizenship, though their children, the Nisei, were citizens by birth. When the success of Japanese farmers led to intense economic rivalry, California prohibited Japanese immigrants from owning land. Hostility increased further as Imperial Japan began its expansion into China and Southeast Asia. The attack on Pearl Harbor, coupled with the rapid, startling string of Japanese victories in the Pacific, the appearance of Japanese submarines off the West Coast, reports of Japanese "sabotage" at Pearl Harbor, and rumors of ship-to-shore signaling, triggered near hysteria. Congressional delegations from the Western states, politicians such as California Governor Culbert Olson and Attorney General Earl Warren, and journalists such as Walter Lippmann demanded action against Japanese-Americans to secure the West Coast against "fifth-column" sabotage. General John DeWitt, the Army commander in the region, supported their demands. The small Japanese minority, racially identifiable, culturally distinct, and concentrated in specific areas, had almost no defenders.[28]

Although McCloy shared the general prejudice against the Japanese, his support for internment resulted mainly from his earlier experience with espionage and subversion. He accepted the widely held belief, later proved false, that a fifth column of Japanese-Americans in Hawaii had assisted in the attack on Pearl Harbor; and after the destruction of the U.S. fleet in Hawaii he could foresee the possibility of Japanese military action against the West Coast. Though initially hesitant to back internment, he told Attorney General Biddle at a meeting on February 1, 1942—in words that he might have used with Biddle's predecessor, Robert Jackson—that "if it is a question of the safety of our country [and] the constitution . . . why the constitution is just a scrap of paper to me." Three days later McCloy decided to support internment after reading an "apocalyptic" note from his aide, General Allen Gullion, who reported from the West Coast: "If our production for war is seriously delayed by sabotage in the West Coastal states, we very possibly shall lose the war . . . From reliable reports from military and other sources, the danger of Japanese inspired sabotage is great." McCloy believed that the "urgency" of the situation prevented making an individual determination of the loyalty or disloyalty of every Japanese-American, and in those circumstances drastic action was justified. He then had to convince Stimson, who worried that a decision for internment would tear a "tremendous hole in our constitutional system." Yet Stimson also believed that the Japanese "racial characteristics are such that we cannot understand or trust even the citizen Japanese."[29]

On February 19, 1942, President Roosevelt signed Executive Order 9066, which gave the Secretary of War the power to exclude all persons, citizens and aliens, from designated areas. McCloy used his energy to make the program run smoothly. In June the removal of Japanese-Americans was almost completed, and he praised the "skill, speed, and humanity" with which the Army had handled the evacuation. Despite his key role in supporting the internment program, he often spoke for moderation in its application, particularly after the U.S. victory at Midway had eliminated any immediate military danger to the West Coast. He was also influential in establishing a voluntary combat team of Nisei soldiers, seeing in military service a way for Japanese-Americans to reassure their fellow citizens of their loyalty. (Later the Presidential Commission which condemned internment called this action "the first significant step to end detention.") McCloy also strongly insisted, against General DeWitt's opposition, that Nisei soldiers be allowed to return to California and the exclusion zone. In addition, the War Department set up a loyalty review program which allowed for the release of some internees. By the spring of 1943 McCloy, along with General Marshall and Secretary Stimson, had concluded that there was no longer any justification for the program. As McCloy himself noted, "social considerations rather than military ones" were determining the "total exclusion policy." Those "social" considerations were political, for California voters had defeated Governor Olson after he suggested that the Japanese be allowed back. President Roosevelt, always sensitive to such matters, maintained the exclusion order until December 1944, immediately after the presidential election. In that same year McCloy had played a major role in defending the program when it was challenged before the Supreme

Court. And finally, in 1981, as one of the last living decision makers, he vigorously defended Roosevelt's decision before a Presidential Commission and argued against compensation for surviving internees.[30]

Another controversial issue in which McCloy was involved had to do with bombing the extermination camp of Auschwitz. By early 1944 Allied officials had obtained reliable information about the Nazi death camps, and Jewish organizations were urging military action against them. McCloy was one of the officials to whom such requests were made. Like many others in the Administration, however, he believed that "the most effective relief which can be given victims of enemy persecution is to insure the speedy defeat of the Axis." McCloy told the Jewish agencies that bombing the death camps was "impracticable" and would divert forces from "decisive operations elsewhere." He also maintained that bombing the camps would kill only Jews and "might provoke even more vindictive acts by the Germans," though critics later asked what "more vindictive acts" were possible.[31]

Recent research makes it clear that, contrary to McCloy's argument, the Allied bombers could have reached Auschwitz and the rail lines leading to the camp any time after June 1944. In fact Allied bombers hit targets only a few miles from there during August, September, and December. Although a direct raid on the camp would have killed some inmates, it would also have slowed the killing process, perhaps sparing some 400,000 Hungarian Jews. (Nazi determination to kill the Jews makes this a point of some controversy.) Why did McCloy and the War Department show a reluctance to act? Like many other Americans, McCloy seems never to have grasped either the urgency of the crisis or the moral issues at stake, and for bureaucratic reasons he was reluctant to push the military to undertake an unwanted mission. Despite appeals from Jewish friends like Nahum Goldmann, McCloy pushed the matter aside, telling Goldmann that "any decision as to the targets of bombardments in Europe" was in the hands of the British. To most American policymakers, European Jews, because they were not American citizens, were not their responsibility. McCloy's behavior reflects this attitude.[32]

McCloy may also have recalled the exaggerated atrocity stories of World War I. In December 1944, in a conversation with Leon Kubowitzki of the World Jewish Congress, McCloy asked, "Tell me the truth. Do you really believe that all those horrible things happened?"

Kubowitzki could only note, "His sources of information, needless to say, were better than mine. But he could not grasp the terrible destruction." Indeed nothing in McCloy's experience had prepared him to confront the enormity of the Nazi crimes, and he, like other American leaders, failed to give them the attention and action they deserved.[33]

McCloy's role in the Auschwitz case reflects the single-minded emphasis on military victory that permeated the War Department. He shared the determination of men such as Stimson, Marshall, and Eisenhower that America should strive for the quickest and most direct military victory over the Axis. For this reason he became a leading advocate of the Second Front strategy and pushed for a cross-Channel invasion of Europe. He supported Eisenhower's agreement with the Vichy collaborator Admiral Jean Darlan, to insure the safe landing of American troops in North Africa. After Darlan's assassination, McCloy visited North Africa and met his successor, General Henri Giraud, explaining to him the necessity for repealing various anti-Semitic Vichy decrees and working with General Charles de Gaulle's Free French movement. McCloy respected Giraud as a military professional but doubted his political judgment and ability. These doubts were encouraged by McCloy's friend Jean Monnet, who was an influential French representative in wartime Washington. Monnet followed McCloy to North Africa, where McCloy had arranged for his protection. Refusing the entreaties of both Giraud and de Gaulle for unqualified support, Monnet, with American backing, managed to bring about the minimal cooperation between the two leaders that was necessary for military action. With the formation of the French Committee of National Liberation, Giraud's authority faded rapidly, and de Gaulle emerged as the symbol of the French resistance.[34]

Many in Washington greeted this development with anger and disdain. Both President Roosevelt and Secretary of State Cordell Hull despised de Gaulle, and they saw in his pretensions to power a danger to their vision of postwar Europe. McCloy, however, came to accept de Gaulle as the symbol of the resistance and the choice of the French people. Influenced in part by Monnet, in part by his own understanding of Europe, he believed the reemergence of a powerful and stable France was in the American national interest. Noting that "Europe is not Anglo-Saxon by a long shot," McCloy wrote Eisenhower that "we gain . . . by incorporating the French more closely into our effort." He strongly supported recognizing de Gaulle's Committee as the responsible government of France after the liberation. At one Cabinet meeting McCloy's strong endorsement of de Gaulle infuriated the President. (Harry Hopkins scrawled in his notes, "One more crack from McCloy to the Boss about de Gaulle and McCloy leaves town.") Although McCloy shared with Stimson a certain distrust of the General's intentions, his judgment proved more realistic than Roosevelt's and Hull's hopes for an alternative.[35]

McCloy displayed a similar realism in addressing the question of Germany's future. In August 1944 as Allied armies neared Germany and the question of occupation policy became acute, a bitter controversy erupted within the American government. The Secretary of the Treasury, Henry Morgenthau, condemned the handbook prepared by the Army as guidance for American and British officers involved in military government, referring to it as a "soft policy" which would allow the Germans to pay reparations and "wage a third war in ten years." He objected to the handbook's call to provide for the "gradual rehabilitation of peacetime industry and a regulated economy" and for a restoration of Germany's civil service. Forwarding extracts to Roosevelt, Morgenthau told him that nobody "has been studying how to treat Germany roughly along the lines you wanted." FDR ordered the handbook withdrawn, commenting, "It is of the utmost importance that every person in Germany should realize that this time Germany is a defeated nation." He did not "want to starve them to death," but they should only be fed "three times a day with soup from Army soup kitchens." Further, he insisted that it be "driven home to the German people" that their "nation has been engaged in a lawless conspiracy against the decencies of modern civilization."[36]

With the President's support Morgenthau and the Treasury Department prepared their own plan (the Morgenthau Plan) for the occupation, which called for dividing Germany into a northern and a southern state and awarding the Saar to France and East Prussia and Silesia to Poland and Russia. The Morgenthau Plan demanded the summary execution of leading Nazi war criminals, as well as strict decentralization of the German government. In its most controversial passage, it recommended that the Ruhr, "the cauldron of wars," should not only "be stripped of all presently existing industries but so weakened that it can never again become an industrial area." The population in this region should be encouraged to migrate or "transfer to new occupations having no military potential."[37]

Secretary Stimson vehemently opposed Morgenthau's ideas. From his experience as Secretary of State in the early 1930s, he was convinced that a more generous treatment of Germany's economic and political grievances after World War I would have strengthened democratic forces within the country. The Morgenthau approach struck him as worse than the Versailles Treaty, more inhumane and vindictive, and likely to lead to further conflict. Although Stimson wanted Nazi war criminals to be punished, the accused should have "an opportunity for a hearing and for counsel." Stimson argued that the destruction of the Ruhr would lead to starvation and unrest in Germany and Europe as a whole. In eloquent memoranda, drafted by McCloy, he stated that the Morgenthau Plan's "enforced poverty" "destroys the spirit not only of the victim but debases the victor." Finally, he compared the Plan to Germany's ruthless occupation policies: "it would be a crime against civilization itself."[38]

Despite this plea, Stimson and McCloy lost their initial battle with Morgenthau over occupation policy. Morgenthau traveled alone with the President to the Quebec Conference in September 1944 and presented his ideas to the British there, offering Treasury's support for continuing Lend-Lease and suggesting to Prime Minister Winston Churchill and his adviser Lord Cherwell that England would gain additional export markets from the destruction of German industry. Churchill at first resisted, arguing that he did not want to chain himself to "a dead Hun." But Morgenthau's financial inducements led him to embrace the Plan and even to contribute the term "pastoral state" as a description of Germany's future. But Morgenthau's success was short-lived. When the Plan was leaked to the press after the President's return to Washington, public opposition quickly changed Roosevelt's mind. By the end of September the President admitted to Stimson that he had "pulled a boner" with the Plan, and had no idea how he could ever have approved it. Later in October, as the Allied drive into Germany stalled, FDR refused to make any final decision on occupation policy, telling Cordell Hull, "I dislike making detailed plans for a country which we do not yet occupy."[39]

The controversy between Stimson and Morgenthau placed McCloy in an awkward position. He strongly supported Stimson, though he questioned whether the Soviet Union should partake in an international trusteeship over the Ruhr. At the same time, he was on good personal terms with Morgenthau and agreed with him on the necessity for a vigorous "denazification" policy. McCloy's principal concern was to provide some "practical" guidance to Eisenhower on military government. The War Department also wanted to limit the Army's involvement in the economic and social problems of postwar Germany, with a view toward insuring only a brief period of military government and a rapid return to civilian control. Indeed McCloy turned down Roosevelt's suggestion that he take charge of the situation in 1945 as "High Commissioner." Because he believed that only a soldier would have the authority to deal with the "disaster" conditions in Germany, he suggested that FDR appoint General Lucius Clay instead.[40]

McCloy's concern about a "practical" directive was a major reason for doubting the efficacy of the Morgenthau Plan. After hearing the results of the Quebec Conference, he told Secretary of the Navy James Forrestal that "the Army's role in any program would be most difficult because the Army, by training and instinct, would naturally turn to the re-creation of order as soon as possible, whereas under [the Morgenthau Plan] they apparently were to encourage the opposite." Roosevelt's change of heart after Quebec opened the possibility for compromise, and McCloy played a key role in finding the middle ground. The resulting directive, known as JCS 1067, eliminated any reference to the "pastoralization" of the German economy, but stressed that the military governor should not take any steps to "rehabilitate" the German economy. It also put great weight on the "denazification and demilitarization" goals of American policy. McCloy obtained an important concession for the War Department in the provision allowing the military commander to act if the purposes of the occupation were threatened by "disease and unrest." Although McCloy was not completely happy with JCS 1067, he thought it was the only "realistic solution." In January he wrote the American Ambassador in London that JCS 1067 was "a pretty good base on which you can negotiate [with the British] an overall plan for the interim period." McCloy never thought of JCS 1067 as a permanent policy, but considered that its harshness reflected the fact that as long as Germany continued to resist, conditions in the postwar period "are going to be very bad."[41]

On the question of how to treat the Nazi leaders, McCloy opposed Morgenthau's proposal for summary executions. He shared Stimson's view that some form of international trial was more in keeping with "Anglo-Saxon" tradition. When the Anglo-Saxon British supported summary executions, McCloy went to London to argue the case for trials. He told them that "political action" against Nazi criminals would be a "retrogression" to the Napoleonic era. "The Nazi crimes were profound and widespread and they demanded trial and punishment as all crimes, no matter how clear, do." McCloy echoed Stimson's argument that a trial might have lasting significance: "if all the main United Nations participated, it would give a serious precedent that might operate as an added deterrent to waging aggressive war in the future." The British hesitated to reject Washington's preference, and thus the concept of trials for war criminals became a part of Allied policy. Whatever flaws the Nuremberg trials had, they did prevent the "mood of vengeful anarchy" from getting out of control. They also produced a comprehensive and thorough record of Nazi crimes and atrocities that made any repetition of the "stab-in-the-back" or "war guilt" controversies of the interwar period impossible.[42]

In April 1945 McCloy traveled to the front to observe the defeat of Germany and prepare the way for military government. With many commanders predicting continued German resistance, McCloy was struck by the magnitude of the problems faced by the occupying armies. The enormous number of displaced persons, the breakdown in transportation and communication, and the scale of destruction moved him deeply. After seeing the rubble of Cologne, he commented in his diary, "No one of Germany's enemies could wish for a more complete sight of destruction." McCloy doubted whether Germany could ever fully recover, for "all Europe hates her and harbors well seated grudges." He still feared the "vigor" of the Germans and agreed with General Kenneth Strong about the need to "root out the scientists and the General Staff people." Worried about the internal weakness of France, McCloy suggested taking into France one or two million German immigrants "to invigorate the country." After all, he told one French leader, "the Germans had made good citizens in the U.S. in the main and they were a source of much of our strength."[43]

When he returned to America, McCloy recorded two major impressions from the trip. The first was of "the power and professional skill of the American Army," though he thought "it is probably just as well that we do not realize how very strong we are." The second impression was of "the complete social, political and economic collapse of Middle Europe and the great and terrible complexities it brings." In considering this collapse, McCloy was disheartened by what he saw as the tendency to "give way to each Russian advance—she has greatly prevailed in many places and on many issues." Yet McCloy had not given up hope for cooperating with the Soviets. The true "test" of American statesmanship, he wrote in his journal, was whether "in spite of what all speak of [as] the rudeness and crudities of Molotov and some of the Russians, we go on working out intelligently the issues which arise between us." The problem would become more acute in "that cockpit of our policy in Germany before we emerge on a sound working base."[44]

McCloy accompanied the American delegation and the new President, Harry Truman, to the Potsdam Conference in July 1945. (The new Secretary of State, James Byrnes, had told Truman that no one in the government knew more about Germany than McCloy.) McCloy's ideas on how to treat Germany were similar to those he had advocated in Stimson's name. In his diary he listed a three-step plan: "a) strike down Germany's war-making machinery to a peace-time economy basis by removals and destruction; b) Punish the Nazi war criminals promptly and vigorously; c) Do our utmost to enable the German to build himself up again morally and politically and economically to a position of stability."[45]

McCloy hoped America's German policy would constitute part of an overall foreign policy "as strong and appealing as the Russian." He regretted that "we are so hesitant about setting up our idealogy [*sic*] against hers." In keeping with his pragmatic orientation, he was willing to deal with the Soviets in terms of a clear recognition of "spheres of influence." Unlike Stimson, who worried that "until there is a more general acceptance by the Russians of the concept of liberty of the individual, we shall always be distrustful of each other," McCloy noted in his diary, "Personally I think they have their political religion and we have ours." He thought it best "to have a clear line of distinction [with the Soviets] and negotiate across that line." For this reason he favored each power taking reparations from Germany from its own occupation zone. This would be preferable to "the constant distrust and difficulty we would have with the Russians over their being in our zones, knowing what goes on and we not being in theirs." Despite his distrust of the Soviets, McCloy respected them as adversaries; he was impressed by the "intelligence" of their negotiators—"they are sharp thinkers and firm."[46]

His return to Berlin depressed McCloy: "the misery of the place and the conflict between the East and the West hangs over you all the time." He was not particularly impressed by President Truman. "He is a simple man, prone to make up his mind quickly and decisively, perhaps too quickly—a thorough American." The President's advisers, men like Byrnes and Admiral Leahy, struck him as "not a particularly intellectually-minded group," and he wondered how "enlightened" their policies would be. McCloy left Potsdam early to review the situation in Germany, pushing the Army officers to pursue denazification and demilitarization. He encouraged General Lucius Clay to continue his constructive policies, but advised him against seeking a revised policy directive to replace JCS 1067. McCloy thought the "disease and unrest" clause would prove flexible enough to allow Clay to cope with most of the major problems he faced in the German economy.[47]

After Potsdam, McCloy took another around-the-world trip, stopping at points in Europe and Asia to review American policy. On his return he told a select New York audience that "the outstanding impression that I bring back with me is the global character of all the problems that face the world." McCloy found himself discussing the same problems—"economic dislocation, currency problems, relations with Russia, coal, fuel, transportation"—everywhere he went. Certainly everyone was concerned about America's relations with Russia, and McCloy labeled this the "A-1 priority job for the statesmen of the world to work out." He was also struck by the "terrifyingly high" prestige of the United States. The world looked to America for "leadership," as "the one stable element . . . around which they can get back to decent living." American leadership was necessary "to bring this world, which is so out of joint, into some semblance of balance again." In his journal he was more emphatic: "We can influence [the world] in a way that no other country can—Russia's concepts and example will wilt before ours, if we have the vigor and farsightedness to see our place in the world."[48]

McCloy was an early apostle of what the historian Daniel Yergin has called the "gospel of national security." He recognized that the European-centered international system had collapsed and that the two superpowers, America and Russia, dominated world politics. Given his experience during the 1930s, McCloy thought the appeasement of totalitarian states encouraged aggression, and that in the modern world even events in far-off lands—Manchuria or Czechoslovakia—were of immediate concern to the United States. But for America's voice to be heard—and reckoned with—its military must not be allowed to collapse into the disrepair and weakness of the interwar period. With Stimson he advocated the continuation of the draft and the eventual adoption of universal military training. "It is mainly in our strength and steadfastness of purpose that the future peace of the world lies—and we must never forget it."[49]

McCloy also recognized that the rapid advance of technology had "altered the very nature of war." In the next conflict, he told a national radio audience in November 1944, "war will come suddenly from the air and we will be the first attacked." The wars he had witnessed had begun with the use of cavalry and ended with the atomic destruction of two cities. Thanks to technological advances, he had been able to range around the world on his airborne inspection trips "as casually as an alderman touring [his] ward." The picture he saw—of a small, interdependent world whose parts faced much the same problems and looked to America for leadership—demanded from the American people "a new kind of internationalism and sophistication, and from the government a new efficiency." For if the rest of the twentieth century was to be the American Century, this nation would have to transform its government, its military, and perhaps most important, its own self-image and understanding.[50]

With his sense of America's new responsibilities and its opportunities for leadership, McCloy hesitated to return to the "humdrum things" of private life at the end of the war. In his diary he confessed that he "would like to be able to work at a job which would enable me to give a good support to my family and still not be completely removed from world affairs—not a very easy combination." But after the defeat of Japan he told Secretary of the Interior Harold Ickes that he had "exhausted all his savings to make up the difference between his living expenses [in Washington] and his salary." Supporting his mother and two aunts, and with two young children, McCloy looked back to corporate law. Despite an offer from President Truman to become Ambassador to Moscow, he wanted to return to the Cravath firm. But the senior partner, Robert Swaine, refused to recognize McCloy's wartime position as a reason for promotion: He told McCloy in effect that "plenty of good men stayed at Cravath during the war." McCloy briefly considered an offer to become president of his alma mater, Amherst College, but he "doubted whether he could tolerate the traditional alumni attitude." Finally the Wall Street law firm of Milbank, Tweed, Hope, and Hadley, a firm connected with the Rockefellers and the Chase Bank, offered to make McCloy a "name partner," and he joined them in January 1946. Milbank assured McCloy, as he wrote Dean Acheson, of its "readiness to arrange things so that I could . . . take on outside public work." McCloy closed his letter to the Under Secretary of State by wistfully commenting, "I miss it all very much."[51]

Whatever his financial problems, McCloy found the exercise of power exciting and alluring, and soon he accepted Acheson's invitation to serve on the Acheson-Lilienthal Committee formed to draft a plan for the international control of atomic energy. During the Potsdam talks, when McCloy had heard a description of the first test of the atomic bomb, he had noted, "You can let your mind roam on this thing until it floats off into space. It makes this little drama here seem rather inconsequential." After the bomb was used against Hiroshima, he wrote, "May it mark the end rather than the beginning of further destruction on earth." (At a White House meeting on June 18, 1945, McCloy had raised the possibility of modifying the demand for un-conditional surrender from Japan by allowing the retention of the Emperor, a position that might have made it unnecessary to use the bomb.) Finding the Acheson committee's work "fascinating," he wrote to Felix Frankfurter: "I have begun to get a glimpse of what it is all about." He agreed with the Acheson-Lilienthal report recommending an "international authority" to control atomic weapons.[52]

McCloy remained active in the public sector after the Acheson committee disbanded. Looking for a greater challenge, he found it at the International Bank for Reconstruction and Development, known as the World Bank. Established by the Bretton Woods agreement of 1944, the World Bank was designed as a "lending agency" through which prosperous countries, primarily the United States, could aid war-torn and underdeveloped lands. But as of February 1947 the Bank had made no loans, had no recognized procedures for processing loan applications, and had raised no funds. Because of dissension on the international board of directors and the efforts of the American director, Emilio Collado, to control the Bank's policy, the first presi-dent, Eugene Meyer, resigned in December 1946. As a result the Bank had almost no standing within the American financial community.

Washington looked to McCloy to establish the Bank's reputation on Wall Street and to make it an effective part of the "economic diplomacy" of the Truman Administration. McCloy initially refused the position, but he finally accepted it after being assured of "the power of management to manage." Collado resigned and was replaced by McCloy's handpicked man, the Vice Chairman of Chase, Eugene Black. For the next two years McCloy ran the Bank with little concern for the directors, treating them "with a brusqueness verging on contempt" and keeping them in the dark on loan negotiations. To McCloy this was simply approaching problems "on the basis of an objective, nonpolitical analysis of the issues involved rather than as a result of political compromises." Others were less convinced. When McCloy lined up with the directors for a farewell picture, one official joked, "Why don't the members pose with their rubber stamp in their hands?"[53]

This criticism notwithstanding, McCloy's vigorous presidency settled the basic question of authority within the Bank, giving management the initiative in operations and loans and establishing the Bank's credibility on Wall Street. McCloy's political connections served him well in obtaining legislation across the United States that made the Bank's bonds eligible for legal investment. Only a few months after his appointment he successfully floated the Bank's first bond issue of $250 million to American investors. His authority also made it possible to coordinate the Bank's activities with other American policy initiatives. Though he argued that there would be no "political loans," he defined these as loans inconsistent with American foreign policy goals. Before the Marshall Plan took effect, the Bank stepped in to provide limited assistance to European countries in their reconstruction projects. One of McCloy's first priorities was a $250 million loan to France, followed by smaller loans to the Netherlands, Denmark, and Luxembourg. Yet at the same time a loan to Poland was canceled because of the "uncertain political conditions" in that Eastern European country.[54]

McCloy's fundamental concern was the health of the Western European economy. He gave strong support to the Marshall Plan, working publicly and privately for its adoption. He also believed that a "Coal Authority" for the entire Ruhr region, patterned on the interstate authorities in the United States, was necessary for European recovery. Compared with the "wasteful" national projects the Bank supported, such an "Authority," which "could borrow money, operate and develop mines, and allocate production," would be far more efficient and could have the "greatest single bearing on the whole European problem." McCloy's idea of a "Ruhr Coal Authority" initially surfaced in the form of the International Authority for the Ruhr

(IAR), established in early 1949. The IAR was largely a concession to the French, to guarantee adequate supplies of Ruhr coal for their steel industry. But many Americans held out the hope that it could become something more—the first building block in regional economic integration.[55]

Called in to provide advice during the Berlin Blockade, McCloy remained in close touch with Administration thinking about the future of Europe. Toward the end of 1948 he used his position to stress the necessity for "unified thinking, planning, and action in the best interests of Western Europe as a whole." The ultimate answer to Europe's problems, in McCloy's view, might be "complete economic union." He added that "this cannot be accomplished without political union as well." Although he did not want to put "undue emphasis" on this "ultimate objective," his conviction of the economic necessity of such a union decisively affected his outlook and policies on Germany.[56]

The Presidency of the World Bank enhanced McCloy's stature in Washington, giving him another success in the world of banking that confirmed his reputation as a man who could get things done—quietly, efficiently, and in line with the overall foreign policy of the country. As World Bank President he was in touch with the major problems of the postwar political economy: the need to reestablish Europe's production and trade, to encourage modernization and create new markets in the developing world, and to avoid the lending problems of the interwar era. McCloy called the Bank "a postgraduate lesson in the flow of mankind's economic bloodstream," and his experience there caused him to look more deeply into the economic causes underlying international stability or instability.

By early 1949 McCloy had settled into the presidency of the Bank, though his strained relations with the directors had whetted his interest in another position. At fifty-four he was an enormously vital, energetic man whose confidence and optimism seemed to increase with age. Photographs, which show him in a fashionable double-breasted suit, always rumpled, reveal broad shoulders, a strong athletic physique, and dark brown eyes. The only sign of age was his balding pate and graying hair. As one associate described him, "Jack McCloy was a fundamentally happy man." Despite his achievements, reporters still found him "one of the most unostentatious and modest men in government," whose easygoing manner and personable disposition "cloaked a healthy and aggressive spirit of competition." Unsentimental and pragmatic, he seemed the ideal man for a challenging job.[57]

2

Changing of the Guard

Shortly after his stunning election victory in November 1948 President Truman summoned former Under Secretary of State Dean Acheson to his Blair House Office. The two made an unlikely pair: the short, bespectacled Midwestern politician who had been thrust into the Presidency by FDR's death; and the tall, debonair Washington lawyer, whose bristling mustache and caustic wit symbolized the Eastern Establishment. Yet Truman valued loyalty of the kind that Acheson had demonstrated when, alone among Administration officials, he had met the President's train after the Democratic Party's drubbing in the 1946 Congressional elections. Truman told Acheson that because of General Marshall's recent illness and Under Secretary Robert Lovett's frail health, the Department of State needed new leadership, and he wanted Acheson to be Secretary of State. Acheson accepted the offer, agreeing to keep the news secret for the next month. The demands of his other work and a difficult confirmation hearing meant that he arrived on the job in January 1949 without "any thorough advance briefing on the exact nature and state of the work in process—and of the problems too." One of the thorniest problems was Germany.[1]

American Policy toward Germany and the Appointment of McCloy

When Acheson took office, Germany was the "cockpit" of American policy, as McCloy had called it, and the central battlefield of the Cold War. Tensions between East and West had existed ever since the Potsdam Conference of 1945. Although the Big Three had agreed that an Allied Council based in Berlin (later called the Allied Control Commission) should treat the occupied country as an economic unit, they had also agreed that each occupying power should take most of its reparations from its own zone, thereby undermining the unity principle. This agreement resolved the U.S.-Soviet dispute over reparations, in which the United States had wanted Germany's import-export program to be settled before reparations, while the Soviets had wanted reparations to take priority. In addition, each country began to implement its own version, in its own zone, of what it meant to "democratize and denazify" Germany. In 1945 the Soviets were the most energetic actors, undertaking a social transformation along Stalinist lines. They created "anti-fascist" political parties, launched sweeping land reforms, expropriated major industries, and stripped their zone of virtually all movable capital. Western suspicions grew as the Soviets began to restrict contact with Eastern Germany.[2]

In addition to the superpower conflict, divisions among the Western Allies, domestic politics in the United States, and German political and economic conditions had an impact on policy toward Western Germany. The major figure on the American side was the Military Governor, General Lucius Clay, "an intense and disciplined Army technocrat" whose imperious personality hid his sensitivity to Washington's criticism and his concern for the welfare of "his" Germans. Clay quickly recognized the leeway provided him by the "disease and unrest" clause of JCS 1067. He believed that his first responsibility was to get Germany "on its feet," thus reducing the cost of occupation to the American taxpayer. The destruction of Germany—Berlin, Cologne, and other cities in ruins; bridges, housing, and railways destroyed; acute food shortages; and industrial production at a standstill—impressed him deeply. He recognized that creating a democratic and economically stable state would help guarantee the peace. He also believed that only if Germany were treated as an economic unit could recovery and therefore reparations begin. France's refusal to cooperate in setting up central German agencies frustrated him; the State Department's refusal to pressure the French irritated him even more. In May 1946 Clay suspended reparations deliveries from the American zone to all recipients, to "force a decision on economic unity." Although he may have intended to exert pressure on the French as much as the Soviets, the State Department saw his actions as a chance to put "Soviet protestations of loyalty to Potsdam to first test and fix blame for the breach of Potsdam on [the Soviets] in case they fail to meet the test."[3]

Confronted with the continuing deadlock in the Allied Control Commission, in July 1946 Secretary of State James Byrnes invited the others to merge their zones with the American sector in order to create an economic union. The French and Soviets balked at the idea; only the British, financially weakened by the strain of feeding their heavily populated zone, accepted. In September Secretary Byrnes spoke publicly in Stuttgart, affirming an American commitment to German economic recovery and reassuring Europeans that the United States would "continue our interest in the affairs of Europe and the world . . . As long as there is an occupation army in Germany, American armed forces will be part of that occupation army." The Stuttgart speech, often regarded as a turning point, confirmed the policy toward Germany that Clay had already initiated.[4]

The process of economic recovery in Germany was painfully slow. The harsh winter of 1946-47 nearly reduced the country to starvation, and the merger of the American and British zones into "Bizonia" at the end of 1946 had little positive impact. The Western Allies saw that they had underestimated the dependence of Europe's economy on Germany, both as a producer and a market. In February 1947 former President Herbert Hoover, who had headed a governmental mission to Germany, concluded: "We can keep Germany in these economic chains but it will also keep Europe in rags."[5]

The proclamation of the Marshall Plan in June 1947, calling for a massive and coordinated plan for European economic recovery, broke the stalemate. American insistence on the inclusion of the West German economy within the Plan compelled France to recognize that Washington "would not agree to [a] system of allocations of German resources . . . which would postpone German recovery until full recovery [of] other countries has been assured." To encourage French acquiescence, Washington reiterated its assurances that it would maintain its forces in Europe until peace was secured. Washington also agreed to set up an international control agency for the Ruhr which would make it impossible for Germany to use its heavy industry for military purposes. The Americans rejected French calls for permanent limits on Germany's industrial capacity, hoping that the Ruhr Authority would provide for "a larger degree of Western European cooperation and economic integration" and a "more efficient utilization of the Ruhr resources . . . for the common good." The Ruhr Authority, they said, was not meant to be "punitive."[6]

After the decision had been made to take Germany into the Marshall Plan, the Western Allies agreed at the London Conference in June 1948 to begin the establishment of a West German government. They also agreed to restrict that government's powers with an Occupation Statute specifying those matters over which the Germans would have authority. The Soviets reacted bitterly to these policies, arguing that the West was dividing Europe and planning to include a German state in its aggressive alliance. In February Soviet support for a Communist coup in Czechoslovakia had produced anxiety throughout Europe, and the war scare of February-March further encouraged movement toward an Atlantic alliance. When, on June 20, Operation Bird Dog, the Allied currency reform in West Germany, went into effect, the Soviets began to restrict access to Berlin. Four days later they cut overland routes between West Germany and West Berlin and shut off electricity to the city. The Berlin Blockade had begun.

The Berlin Airlift—fleets of American and British transport planes that carried twenty-five hundred tons of food and fuel daily to the people of Berlin—was the Allied response to the blockade. Divided Berlin became the main battlefield of the Cold War, a crucial symbol to both sides. The struggle over the city helped to change American perceptions of the Germans, whose determination to resist the Soviet action evoked widespread admiration. America's sense of the "enemy" began gradually to move eastward from Germany to the Soviet Union. The irony of this change was not lost on the American Ambassador to Moscow and former General, Walter Bedell Smith, who told the State Department in September 1948, "Our present hysterical outburst of humanitarian feelings about the [Germans] keeps reminding me that just 3½ years ago I would have been considered a hero if I had succeeded in exterminating those same Germans with bombs." The Berlin airlift, which successfully avoided direct conflict with the Soviet Union, was one of America's first triumphs in the Cold War.[7]

The blockade and the united Allied stand in Berlin, however, did not signal an end to the Allies' disagreements over Germany's future. Their differing constitutional principles and economic policies, as well as the security fears of the French, stalled attempts to issue an Occupation Statute and establish a West German government. A frustrated Clay cabled Washington: "I thought we crossed the Rubicon at [the]

London [Conference], but it looks like we sat down in the middle of the stream." Along with the Allied quarrels went increasingly bitter disputes within the American government over the proper approach to Germany. The Economic Cooperation Administration (ECA), the agency responsible for administering Marshall Plan assistance, wanted to treat Germany within a European framework of economic recovery, while Clay insisted that he should administer Germany as a separate and special recipient of American funds, solely responsible to Congress. Despite several conferences with Averell Harriman, the special representative of ECA in Paris, Clay refused to compromise. He was convinced that ECA intrusions into his authority would mean that "military government may no longer have the authority and prestige which makes successful administration possible."[8]

At the same time, Clay's own military government was coming under increasing criticism. Despite signs of economic recovery—German industrial production soared from a low of 34 percent (of the 1936 figure) in early 1947 to almost 90 percent of that figure in 1949—Congressional conservatives blasted continued dismantling and the limits placed on industrial production. Other Congressmen charged that the military government had failed to break up German cartels. Liberals, attacking the "denazification" program as a complete failure, pointed to former Nazis who had been restored to their old jobs, especially teachers and members of the civil service. Even war criminals had their supporters: Senator Joseph McCarthy led an investigation into charges of physical abuse and torture of German prisoners accused in the Malmedy massacre case. And scandals involving the black market and coffee smuggling fed the notion that military governors were living in luxury amid desperate German poverty. By the beginning of 1949 the necessity for a fresh American initiative in Germany was clear.[9]

When Acheson took office in 1949, his first concern was the negotiations for the North Atlantic Treaty, which had stalled when France insisted that Italy be included. Acheson had no clearly defined plan for dealing with the "German problem," although he shared the State Department's view that because France was America's most important Continental ally, its legitimate security concerns must be honored. Skeptical about creating a West German state, he did not rule out some type of four-power arrangement despite his distrust of the Soviets. In order to work toward a decision, Acheson proposed,

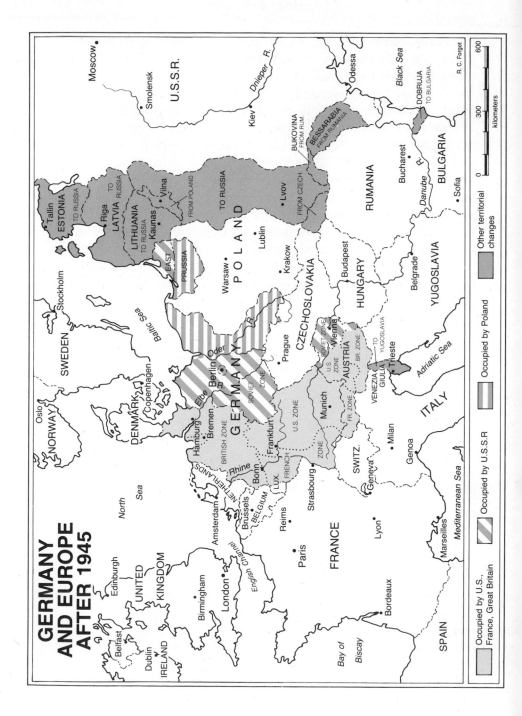

GERMANY AND EUROPE AFTER 1945

R. C. Forget

Occupied by U.S., France, Great Britain

Occupied by U.S.S.R.

Occupied by Poland

Other territorial changes

0   300   600
kilometers

with the President's approval, that the State Department prepare a paper on German policy for presentation to the National Security Council (NSC), where sharp differences of opinion were already evident. He selected George Kennan, the Director of the Department's Policy Planning staff, to chair a subcommittee on Germany and to provide him with policy choices.[10]

Over the next two months Kennan's review of German policy produced a "positive maelstrom of drafts and counterdrafts, conferences, informal discussions and special studies." At the center of this maelstrom was Kennan himself, the young, brilliant, often erratic Soviet specialist whose famous "X" article of 1947 had given the "containment" policy its name. Kennan was no stranger to Germany. He spoke the language fluently, had served there in 1939, and had been interned there after war was declared. As early as March 1946 he had favored carrying the process of partition, begun by the Russians with their amputation of the lands of Eastern Germany, to "its logical conclusion." That meant "walling off" Western Germany and "integrating" it into an "international pattern of western Europe rather than into a united Germany." Kennan feared that the West's attempt to negotiate a united "rump Germany west of the Oder-Neisse" would leave the country open to Russian political domination, although his reference to the Oder-Neisse boundary indicates that his concept of Western Germany included the Soviet zone. In 1948, however, Kennan turned about and took a different tack. He saw the Berlin Blockade as a desperate step by the Soviet Union to hold on to what it had, not as a harbinger of further expansion. Tito's challenge to Stalin's rule in June 1948 also indicated the potential for fragmentation of Stalin's Eastern European empire. These two developments, coupled with Kennan's belief that the Germans would never accept partition, led him to sponsor "Program A" as an approach to a four-power settlement, calling for internationally supervised elections, a provisional German government, the abolition of zonal boundaries, and the simultaneous withdrawal of occupation forces to specified garrison areas. Kennan proposed this program as an alternative to the creation of a divided Germany with a separate West German state, which would only freeze the division of Europe, preclude the loosening of Moscow's grip on Eastern Europe, and result in further instability and war.[11]

As chairman of the National Security Council subcommittee, Kennan worked to establish a new relationship between Germany and its

European neighbors. He argued that "there is no solution of the German problem in terms of Germany; there is only a solution in terms of Europe." Although the Europeans themselves must create a Europe which could "absorb" Germany, Kennan believed the United States could give strong support to such a unity movement. It would be dangerous to establish a separate West German government, which would surely become the focus of nationalist and irredentist sentiment. It would seek to play off East against West and would damage American relations with the Allies, especially the French. To maintain America's freedom of action, Kennan urged that the Allies create a provisional administration in Western Germany over which they could retain absolute authority.[12]

Although the cogency of these ideas impressed Acheson, he found the conclusions vague and unclear. How, in practical terms, could Germany be "Europeanized"? If a united Europe had to include everything west of the Soviet border, did that mean that the United States would have to wait for Soviet withdrawal from the Eastern countries before "integrating" Germany into Europe? If the French were distraught over a West German state, what would be their reaction to a reunified Germany, even under Allied controls? Was it possible to establish a provisional arrangement in Germany without creating an expectation of eventual self-government?[13]

Kennan believed that the main reason for favoring a West German state at the London Conference had been to force the Russians to come to the bargaining table, and that if they did come, the United States should negotiate a four-power treaty. Above all else Kennan wanted to avoid freezing the division of Europe. But the other members of the NSC subcommittee accepted that division as inevitable and thought the United States should seek the "closest association" of a West German government with the Western European community. Robert Murphy, Clay's political adviser, argued that it would be less difficult to "integrate" a "West" German state than a united Germany into Europe, as well as being more acceptable to the French. An integrated West German state, politically stable and economically prosperous, would also exercise a "magnetic" attraction on Eastern Germany and "make even more difficult Soviet control of that area." From this perspective the United States, by adhering to the London formula, could acquire not only an "integrated Germany" but a weapon in the Cold War. It could then offer the Russians a four-power meeting to arrange the integration of the Soviet zone into Western Germany.[14]

If Kennan's Program A had been vague about how to "Europeanize" the Germans, Murphy's "magnet" theory of reunification failed to spell out how economic pressure would loosen Soviet control. In fact Murphy was pessimistic about the chances for a settlement, expecting that the best possible result would be the peaceful coexistence of East and West Germany in a divided Europe. His argument had the advantage of drawing on a developing transnational coalition of political forces which, for a variety of different and sometimes contradictory reasons, was willing to accept the existing division of Germany.[15]

The most important members of this coalition were the British and the French. Both worried that any four-power arrangement in Germany which required an American troop withdrawal would have disastrous consequences for their own national security. Both viewed Soviet power in Eastern Europe as a threat—less in terms of direct invasion than in the encouragement it gave to local Communist parties to engage in subversion and stimulate unrest. The problem was especially troublesome in France, whose well-organized Communist party was slavishly obedient to Moscow. French leaders, fearing the Americans would adopt a military strategy that would again "liberate" them from, rather than deter, a Russian invasion and internal uprising, lamented, "Next time you'll liberate corpses!" Paris cooperated secretly with General Clay on a plan to defend Western Europe along the Rhine and even allowed the U.S. Air Force to stockpile supplies on French territory. For both Britain and France, keeping the Americans in Europe was of critical importance.[16]

Both the French and the British wanted the opportunity to discuss the German question when they assembled in Washington in early April 1949 to sign the Atlantic Pact treaty. Initially Acheson opposed this, but the French Foreign Minister, Robert Schuman, and the British Foreign Secretary, Ernest Bevin, insisted that he reconsider. At the same time Acheson received secret indications from his United Nations envoy, Philip Jessup, that the Soviets were prepared to bargain over Berlin by proposing to lift the blockade in return for a meeting of the Council of Foreign Ministers (CFM). Within the American government, too, both the Army and the ECA encouraged Acheson to discuss the German question with the Allies, hopeful that a settlement would help resolve the bureaucratic battles at home.[17]

In mid-March Acheson agreed to put German questions on the agenda for the Washington meeting, triggering a flurry of diplomatic activity. Foreign Minister Schuman arranged to meet secretly with

General Clay in Paris. Despite the frequent French protests against Clay's policies during the previous four years, Schuman agreed wholeheartedly with the General's plea that "now is the time for a rapprochement with Western Germany and the French should take the lead in this effort." In the course of their long conversation, Schuman and Clay cut through the wide array of disagreements between the French and the Americans, agreeing on the desirability of a shorter and simpler occupation statute and of fewer but more essential controls on German industry, and setting conditions for joining the French zone with Bizonia. Clay characterized the conversation as being the "most satisfactory which he had ever had with any French official."[18]

At the end of March George Kennan returned from a tour of Germany and Europe, reporting to Acheson that the French, as they had told Clay, were willing to resolve quickly the disagreements over an Occupation Statute and the Bonn Constitution. Although he still had hopes for his Program A as the best long-term solution, Kennan had been surprised to find the West German leaders largely pro-Western and conciliatory rather than virulently nationalistic. He advised Acheson to assist these leaders, thereby avoiding the mistakes of the interwar period, when the West, after refusing concessions to pro-Western Germans, had ultimately yielded to their aggressive nationalistic successors. After receiving Kennan's report, Acheson approved the final draft of a subcommittee paper which recommended creating a West German state. On March 31 he informed the President of his policy approach to Germany, which embodied a simplified Occupation Statute, a stronger German central government, and the transfer of authority from military governors to civilian high commissioners—all combined with an offer to the Russians of a CFM meeting. With this "two-track policy" the Secretary hoped to proceed with the creation of a West German state while still holding open the possibility of a four-power agreement.[19]

Acheson presided over the signing of the North Atlantic Treaty on April 4, 1949, marking a decisive break in the long history of America's isolationism and its refusal to join "entangling" alliances. The NATO treaty also made possible the Washington Agreements on Germany, signed only four days later. The French, who considered NATO a guarantee against German as well as Russian aggression, abandoned their policy of delay and allowed the movement toward a West German state to proceed. The only significant modification of the London formula came in the Occupation Statute. Instead of specifying every power or function that was reserved for the Germans and every one that was reserved for the Allies, the Western powers decided to reserve "supreme authority" in Germany for themselves. They also kept their primary responsibility for certain "select" and undefined areas—foreign affairs, demilitarization, control over the Ruhr, restitution, reparations, decartelization, deconcentration, displaced persons, refugees, foreign trade and exchange, the security of Allied forces, respect for the new constitution or Basic Law, and war criminals. This change puzzled and angered the Germans, and it led Clay to accuse Washington of turning the new German state into a "colony." But the revision also held open the possibility of eventually including the Soviet zone. To this extent, the new arrangement met Kennan's criteria for retaining control while making possible a four-power agreement and German reunification.[20]

At first it seemed as if the Soviets might respond to the implicit Western offer. The Washington Agreements and the final proclamation of the German Basic Law on May 8 coincided with secret talks in Paris between the Americans and Russians over ending the Berlin Blockade, which had not only proved to be a costly failure and a propaganda disaster for the Russians but had also produced difficulties in East Germany. The Russians offered to sacrifice their position on the currency issue and end the blockade in return for minimum concessions from the West—a cessation of the West's counter-embargo of goods and a reconvening of the CFM in Paris.

Although Acheson held open the prospect for an accord based on Kennan's Program A, European concerns constrained American policy. Kennan's ideas were leaked to the press shortly before the Paris talks began, and they received a cool reaction from the British and French foreign offices. One official said that "if there was one thing likely to frighten the French out of their new found solidarity with the Western powers, it was a proposal to liberate the bulk of Germany from Allied occupation before a peace treaty was signed." To the French the Washington arrangements were only possible for a divided Germany; a reunited country required tighter controls. Within the American government General Bradley, Chairman of the Joint Chiefs of Staff, argued against Kennan's withdrawal plan, saying that it would place American forces in indefensible port cities while putting Soviet forces only a few hundred miles east of their current position. General

Clay, too, cabled angrily that "if the West Germans heard of these [proposals], they would throw up their hands and quit." Clay was certain, however, that British and French opposition would prevent this "buffer state" approach: "Thank God, we have British and French allies who will never buy this one." American occupation forces, though providing no real military security in the event of Soviet attack, created what Clay termed "security against fear." The Kennan Plan did raise fears among the West Germans, who opposed an Allied withdrawal. After a trip to Germany, Bevin told Ambassador Lewis Douglas that the leaders of the Social Democratic Party (SPD) and the Christian Democratic Union (CDU) "reminded him of members of his old Dock Workers Union who used to tell him not to sell them out just before he went into wage negotiations with employers."[21]

After the Allies rejected the Kennan Plan as the basis for negotiations, Acheson was concerned that Soviet enticements might break the united front. The Soviets might exploit inter-Allied differences over certain issues, such as the control of German industry, which divided the United States and France. But the Russians were unwilling to move from their opposition to the London arrangements and from their insistence on continuing tight control over East German political and economic life. The Paris talks, as Acheson described them, were "completely sterile." These talks, which clearly revealed the rigid Soviet position, marked a turning point for him. Giving up hope of an East-West settlement until after the Western powers had strengthened their position and achieved greater unity, he shifted his emphasis from Germany to "Europe." As he put it, "If the Soviet price for reunification of Germany imperiled or destroyed prospects for the future of Europe, then the price should not be paid."[22]

The possible appointment of John J. McCloy as the first High Commissioner had a positive influence on the inter-Allied and American bureaucratic impasse over Germany. If the State Department was to accept responsibility for Germany, Acheson wanted to be sure that the new High Commissioner was a man with whom the Department could deal. The Army wanted General Mark Clark, who had been Military Governor of Austria, but the State Department considered him another "brass hat," a man insensitive to the larger political implications of the German task. Averell Harriman's name also surfaced as a possible High Commissioner, indicating the importance which the Marshall Plan administration attached to Germany. As it happened, however, late in March after McCloy had turned down an offer from the new Secretary of Defense, Louis Johnson, to become his Under Secretary, he went to James Webb, Acheson's deputy, and made clear his interest in the German position provided his authority and independence were recognized.[23]

For Acheson, a McCloy appointment could solve a number of problems at once. Although the two were not close friends, their general ideas about foreign policy and America's role in the world were strikingly similar. McCloy's ties to Jean Monnet and his frequent support of French interests made him acceptable to Paris. The Army, whose massive presence in Germany guaranteed it a veto over the selection, enthusiastically approved the former Assistant Secretary of War. McCloy's liberal Republican credentials helped with Congress, keeping policy toward Germany a bipartisan affair. Ellen McCloy's German ancestry and fluency in the language would also assist her husband in personal diplomacy, an important part of the High Commissioner's job.[24]

Yet, when McCloy recognized that the State Department was interested in him, he began to express reservations. He was worried about providing care for his two aunts and elderly mother. He also wanted to insure that Eugene Black, whom he had selected as the American director at the World Bank, would become his successor as president. Most important, he wanted to secure his own authority as the undisputed civilian chief in Germany. From his brother-in-law, Lewis Douglas (the Ambassador to Great Britain), McCloy had learned of the conflicts between General Clay, Washington, and the Marshall Plan administrators. On April 30, after gaining Acheson's full support, McCloy met with the President. During the meeting he insisted on a "free hand in picking people" and asked that "no substantial decisions on Germany" be made "without consultation with me." Finally, he gained Truman's approval of his request for authority over ECA in Germany, without which he would have been prepared to refuse the position.[25]

McCloy recognized that control over Marshall Plan funds was critical to the prestige and authority of the High Commissioner. As the Allies turned over more authority to the Germans, ECA funds would become a major lever with which to exercise influence. Since its creation ECA had battled to have its own man in Germany, completely independent of the Military Governor or High Commissioner. The agency feared that the merger of its authority with either of these positions would subject ECA to certain Allied policies, such as placing limits on German industry, that were unpopular with Congress. But when ECA's leaders, Paul Hoffman and Averell Harriman, learned that the new High Commissioner was likely to be McCloy, they retreated without a fight, telling the State Department that McCloy could "write his own ticket." Thus his "two-hat" authority as High Commissioner and head of ECA was assured. In his agreement with Truman McCloy had also made sure that he would be responsible directly to the President, not the Secretary of State, a distinction which indicated that this position was not simply a new form of ambassadorship. As Acheson later recalled, McCloy was "very wise" in securing his "sacred charter of authority" before agreeing to accept the post.[26]

McCloy as Military Governor

McCloy's departure for Germany coincided with a brief period of optimism during the Cold War. Although the Paris talks had failed, Washington was pleased with the unity the Western powers had displayed. The Americans thought this unity might eventually force the Soviets to retreat from Germany, where, as Acheson put it, the West was about to embark on a "new era" of relations with its former enemy and a new offensive in the struggle for the "soul of Europe." As part of this new era, McCloy arrived in Germany on July 2, 1949, assuming the office of Military Governor. As soon as a German Government had been formed—an election campaign was still under way—he would become High Commissioner. Though he had once called the job of Military Governor the closest thing to a "Roman proconsulship" the modern world afforded, McCloy did not intend to exercise such power. Rather his first assignment was to dismantle the large and costly apparatus of military government, which had entered into almost every aspect of German life. McCloy hoped to set a new tone for the occupation, one of friendship and equality rather than arrogance and superiority. He ordered the removal of all signs on American homes proclaiming "no entrance to German civilians," and he insisted that U.S. officials study the German language. He saw his mission as directed toward the Germans, rather than toward treating Germany as a mere battlefront in the Cold War—as a job of political persuasion and public relations rather than political and social reform.[27]

Following the pattern of his World Bank experience, McCloy took his own "team" with him to Germany. He placed Chauncey Parker, a former Cravath lawyer and World Bank aide, in charge of reorganizing and reducing the staff of the Military Governor. Faithful to the concept of serving as a "shadow" government, McCloy wanted a "Cabinet" consisting of the heads of the High Commission's departments— economic affairs, political affairs, public affairs, military security, labor, intelligence, administration, general counsel, the executive secretariat, and the field division. Allowing each department wide discretion, the High Commissioner's office would simply coordinate their activities and contacts with the Germans. McCloy also gave Parker carte blanche to proceed with the reduction in personnel mandated by Congressional budget. These cuts occasioned some sharp internal controversy, but McCloy himself displayed little interest in the details of administrative organization.[28]

McCloy's top staff was composed almost entirely of new men. Within a few months the High Commission "Cabinet" shrank to a small circle of key advisers. Among the most important was Benjamin Buttenwieser, a New York investment banker and longtime friend of McCloy's, who was appointed Assistant High Commissioner with special responsibility for financial questions. McCloy valued Buttenwieser's energy and knowledge and stood by him when he was attacked because of his wife's involvement in the defense of Alger Hiss. For his General Counsel, McCloy brought over Robert Bowie, a Harvard law professor who had served in Germany briefly under General Clay. Bowie's razor-sharp mind and skill in negotiations made him McCloy's most important and influential adviser, especially on matters relating to European integration. McCloy also placed considerable emphasis on his Public Affairs Department. When his first choice as head, Ralph Nicholson, a Southern newspaper publisher, did not work out, McCloy recruited Shepard Stone, an editor of the Sunday *New York Times,* who had earned a doctorate at the University of Berlin. Stone's knowledge of Germany and his contacts with Germans attracted McCloy's respect, and Stone's department flourished.[29]

McCloy's new team operated under a new policy directive as well. Drafted by the State Department's newly created Bureau of German Affairs, this lengthy document covered the whole range of responsibilities of the American High Commission in Germany (HICOG). The directive stressed the importance of an "economically stable Germany" with close ties to the other states of Western Europe. Germany would be "fully integrated into the common structure of a free Europe." Under the revised Occupation Statute agreed upon in Washington, the Allies had a vaguely defined but essentially unlimited authority to intervene in German decision making. The Department hoped, however, that the High Commissioner would regard the exercise of direct power as "temporary and self-liquidating in nature." It preferred a more subtle exercise of American influence, operating through behind-the-scenes persuasion rather than by the public exercise of the High Commissioner's power. The directive also noted that Germans would "share in due time as equals in [a free Europe's] obligations, its economic benefits, and its security," a formulation which deliberately left the door open to some form of German contribution to defense. As the Department put it when questioned by McCloy, "The plain fact is that we do not know what role it may be possible to permit to Germany in the Western security system a year from now, and we will have to play this one by ear as time goes on."[30]

The formal policy directive, intended in part for public consumption, was not a complete guide to American policy in West Germany. The aim of that policy was to restore limited self-government and responsibility to the Germans, as well as encourage conditions conducive to political and economic stability. Yet both Acheson and McCloy believed that unless the French cooperated, the restoration of Germany might destroy Western unity. Only a Franco-German rapprochement could guarantee a strong Europe capable of resisting Soviet domination. For this reason Acheson emphasized that France should exercise leadership on German issues. In October 1949 he told the American ambassadors in Europe that "France and France alone can take the decisive leadership in integrating Western Germany into Western Europe." French action was essential "if Russian or German, or perhaps Russian-German domination [of Europe] is to be avoided." McCloy, who fully supported the Secretary's views, told every German political figure he met that the first priority of the new republic should be reconciliation with France. In one of his first interviews in Germany he said that the "military vacuum created by a disarmed Germany can and must be filled by a strong French nation."[31]

Most Americans believed that Germany would inevitably revive, no matter what policy the Western allies followed; the real question was how the Europeans, especially the French, would react to its revival. Would they again attempt to control and repress Germany, thereby giving strength to nationalist and radical forces within the country, which might then look eastward? Or would France be more conciliatory, acknowledging a major German role in Europe and dealing with its former enemy on terms of equality? Both Acheson and McCloy recognized the political weakness of France's Fourth Republic, with its shifting coalitions and frail executive. Still, Acheson knew that American support would be a powerful aid to Foreign Minister Schuman, who could use it against his domestic opponents. Schuman could tell them that because Germany's restoration was inevitable, France should seize the initiative offered by the Americans to "integrate" the new Federal Republic into Europe.[32]

This basic policy orientation provided no master plan, but it did provide a spirit for America's German policy and for its demands on the leaders of the other European countries. The transnational political coalition could work only if moderate French politicians like Schuman acted with a strength and boldness which they had seldom shown before. From the new German political leadership the policy required moderation and understanding toward France, a nation whose sensitivities were easily aroused. From both the United States and Britain the policy demanded patience with the instability of French governing coalitions and a refusal to curry favor with the Germans. To succeed, such a policy would require enough unity among the Western Allies to ward off Soviet threats and enticements, including the constant offers of German reunification. And finally, the policy would have to endure the vicissitudes of overheated political debates in the United States, where a new interest in Asia and an undercurrent of neo-isolationism threatened to predominate.

Denazification and the Rebirth of German Politics

McCloy returned home briefly after his first month in Germany, to report on his impressions and recruit more administrators. As soon as he arrived in Washington, journalists asked about the reports of a revival of nationalism and neo-Nazism in Germany. McCloy surprised them with his confidence and optimism: "There is enough sense of freedom and decency in the German people on which, given time, there can be built a healthy and peaceful state." He added a paraphrase of one of Stimson's favorite expressions: "You must give the Germans the feeling that they are being trusted, or they will never trust themselves." McCloy went on to make a national radio address, assuring the American people that although many former Nazi followers had regained their jobs, this did not warrant fears of a "rebirth of Nazism." He asked them to recognize the long tradition of "blind obedience" to the state in Germany, which had limited resistance to the Nazis. Finally he criticized the press for its "scandal-spot" coverage of neo-Nazi incidents, such as the painting of swastikas in cemeteries and the wild comments of extremist politicians.[33]

The question of a neo-Nazi and nationalist revival dominated much of the press coverage of McCloy's years in Germany. This was inevitable, since the horrors of the death camps had seared the conscience of the West. But the Nazi revival story was often the only one reporters were looking for, and it was a story their readers expected. Theodore White, later the chronicler of American presidential campaigns, confessed in his memoirs, "When I arrived in Bonn in February of 1949, I knew a new German government was forming, and if I could expose any taint of sin or Nazism in these new constitution-framers, it would make an exciting story." White was surprised when he was unable to find the makings of a "Fourth Reich," but other reporters were convinced it lurked somewhere, waiting to be exposed.[34]

What had existed, and could still be detected, was the enthusiastic support of millions of Germans for the Nazi regime. Although the first Americans to enter Germany had joked about how hard it was to find a Nazi, in 1949 the Allies recognized how widespread and deep the regime's support had been. Some 12 million Germans out of a prewar population of 80 million had been members either of the party or of one of its numerous organizations. The American program of denazification, hammered out in the War Department under McCloy's supervision, was more extensive and sweeping than those of the other Western powers. This program sought "the elimination of active Nazis from public and quasi-public office and from positions of importance in private enterprise." By May 1949, when the program came to an official end, 13.4 million Germans over eighteen in the American zone had registered, and of that number nearly 3.7 million had been charged with various offenses. Of this total, following the amnesties and the trials by German courts, nearly 130,000 were found to be "offenders" of various categories; 147,000 were declared either ineligible to hold public office or restricted in employment; and for 635,000 others various sentences were meted out, including assignment to labor camps, confiscation of property, and fines.[35]

However impressive these numbers are, they conceal major inequities and injustices. American officials, particularly in the military and intelligence communities, spirited out of Germany people who could be of use to them regardless of their wartime activities—men like General Reinhard Gehlen, Klaus Barbie, and the German rocket scientists. The other Allies acted with similar expediency. The Soviets used denazification to eliminate "class enemies," placing emphasis on the "owners of businesses, public officials, and persons in important private positions," while those former Nazis who joined the official Socialist Unity Party were eligible for immediate rehabilitation. The French, who considered almost every German a Nazi, adopted a similar rule of expediency. Only 17,000 denazification proceedings were held, and Nazi managers in the Saar were kept on the job to produce the coal France needed. Britain's program was similar to America's; but though their zone had a larger population, the British conducted a fraction of the trials—only 22,296 compared with the 169,282 in the American zone.[36]

The sheer size of the American denazification effort—requiring one of the most extensive legal procedures ever undertaken—would have strained the capacity of even the most experienced bureaucrats. The American officials were not of that quality. Clay recognized this and turned the program over to the Germans in 1946. Under German administration there were often sharp inequities, with severe treatment being given to the "little Nazis" while their "respected superiors" escaped punishment. The fact that almost every civil servant and industrial manager was in the criminal category added further confusion. With the renewed emphasis on economic recovery, many of these returned to their jobs in 1947 and 1948. When critics charged that "re-nazification" was going on, McCloy admitted in a national radio address in August 1949 that "some 30 percent" of the positions in government and industry were occupied by former Nazi followers.[37]

McCloy acknowledged the limits to denazification created by changes in American policy and the encouragement of economic recovery. He found it "ridiculous" to think that all those people could be excluded from the community, and he emphasized that people must be judged by their "present attitudes." The High Commission's Office of Political Affairs, which examined the re-nazification charge, concluded that "there is no organized movement to plant former Nazi activists as such in key positions." Yet the Office also noted that "the average German cannot, will not, and could not be expected to regard mere membership in, or even open devotion to, the party in the days of its domination, as a crime or even as something that detracts from his neighbor's character." This popular distaste for the denazification program intensified as the drive for economic recovery began. Under the original American proceedings, some 80 percent of the schoolteachers and 50 percent of the doctors in the American zone lost their jobs. Germany's enormous human capital, "the men of brains, skill, and competence," were crucial to its recovery, and excluding them made sense only if Germany was to be denied that recovery.[38]

A contemporary study of denazification argued that "the removal and exclusion program was too massive and might have preferably and more rapidly been dealt with from the top down." The legacy of denazification had important consequences for West German society and contributed to the political upheavals of the late 1960s and the 1970s. For American policymakers in 1949, however, the failure of denazification created concern about the political reliability of the new Germany. Shortly before McCloy arrived in Germany, intelligence analysts had predicted a "nationalist revival," and the tone of the German election campaign of 1949 provided superficial evidence for this judgment. Both major parties, the conservative CDU and the socialist SPD, criticized the Allied powers, occasionally indulging in rhetoric that sounded to foreign ears like the anti-Versailles and nationalist speeches of the 1920s. The smaller parties were even worse offenders, and the lifting of controls allowed some unrepentant Nazis and their sympathizers to surface. Still this was not the significant feature of the 1949 campaign. In the midst of a largely cynical and apathetic population, a group of German politicians, mostly middle-aged and older, sought to restore a functioning democracy to Germany. Theodore White later wrote that it was as if the Anglo-American presence "had magnetized and drawn out of the wreckage of German politics a collection of waifs, strays, victims, outcasts, and resistants to Hitler's politics," men "more devoted to liberty, republicanism, and democracy even than ourselves." No two men better symbolized these old Weimar politicians, as well as the conflicts and contradictions of the new Germany, than Konrad Adenauer of the CDU and his arch-rival, Kurt Schumacher, leader of the SPD.[39]

Konrad Adenauer was seventy-three when he became the first Chancellor of postwar Germany. His doctor thought he could rule for at least one year, or maybe two. Most thought he would be at best a transitional leader or, at worst, another mediocre leftover from Weimar. In his campaign appearances and speeches he reminded reporters of "a wrinkled mummy breaking into voice." "A stiff old man, [he] walked as if his legs were hinged by rusting joints," and his "austere, almost forbidding appearance" was marked by "high almost mongoloid cheekbones." Despite his long political career Adenauer was still a fairly obscure figure within Germany: according to a public opinion poll only a third of all West Germans knew who he was. No one expected that this man would dominate German political life for the next fourteen years.[40]

Konrad Adenauer was born in 1876 in Cologne, the center and capital city of the Rhineland. After acquiring a university degree in law, he began his political career in the Catholic Zentrum party, whose religious base cut across the class and social cleavages of Imperial Germany. Through the Zentrum he rose quickly to become Oberbür-germeister (mayor) of Cologne in 1917. He exercised his authority autocratically, dedicating himself to making "Holy Cologne" one of the most beautiful and powerful cities in Germany. His achievements included the greenbelt of parkland around the city and the revitalization of the university and its institutes.[41]

Adenauer served as mayor during one of the Rhineland's most chaotic political periods, the Allied occupation after World War I. His political maneuvers opened him to charges of being a Rhineland separatist, secretly working to detach the region from Germany and bring it under French rule. He did favor both a close relationship with France and the separation of the Rhineland from Prussia, the Protestant state which had dominated Imperial Germany. His strong Catholicism and his glorification of Charlemagne's Holy Roman Empire made him a so-called West German, an individual convinced of the cultural and spiritual superiority of Western Europe over the militaristic and Protestant East. Yet Adenauer's policies during these years were not so much parts of a predetermined plan as the outcome of his reactions to external events and pressures. In the confusing circumstances of military occupation, labor unrest, and economic collapse, he defended the interests of the Rhineland and his own personal power with all the intellectual cunning and craftiness at his disposal. When the crisis was over, he reconciled himself easily to the Weimar Republic, almost becoming Chancellor in 1926. Instead, he was reelected mayor of Cologne in 1929.[42]

As a conservative Catholic, Adenauer bitterly opposed the Nazis, seeing in them the same godless, socialist danger he saw in the communists. In March 1933, two months after Hitler's seizure of power, the Nazis forcibly "retired" Adenauer. He was imprisoned for a few days after the Roehm purge in 1934 and arrested again after the failed coup of July 20, 1944. During these years he received financial help from Dannie Heinemann, an American banker and electrical engineer who had met Adenauer before the First World War. Thus Adenauer slipped into the obscurity of retirement, occupying himself with his gardening, listening to music, and presiding over his large family. His first wife, Emma Weyer, who had come from a prominent Cologne family, had died in 1916 after bearing him three children. With his second wife, Gussie Zinsser, he had four more children. It was through her that Adenauer was distantly related to Ellen Zinsser, McCloy's wife.[43]

When the American Army entered Cologne in March 1945, Adenauer was appointed mayor. But because the city was in the British occupation zone, he soon faced a different group of superiors who were less pleased with his conservative politics and who fired him on the grounds of "inefficiency." Ironically this did Adenauer more good than harm. It weakened charges that he was a "collaborator" and gave him freedom from administrative tasks so that he could devote himself to organizing the Christian Democratic Union, the interdenominational party which succeeded the Zentrum. The party program called for a system of economic planning and control through corporative organs and under the supervision of a parliament. Adenauer's political maneuvering moved the loosely organized party to the right, and eventually he became its leader.[44]

Before the first postwar election Adenauer's CDU had embraced the concept of a Soziale Marktwirtschaft (social market economy), an economic program proposed by Ludwig Erhard which combined free markets with the welfare state. Supported by the Americans, Erhard, an obscure economics professor from Bavaria, had enjoyed a meteoric rise to fame after 1945. As Director of Economic Administration for Bizonia, he was determined to abolish the remaining controls over the German economy. Erhard also emphasized increasing Germany's production and export capability, in sharp contrast to the Third Reich's autarchy and Lebensraum. Although the CDU recognized the initial popularity of Erhard's program, its left wing retained influence and continued to support such concepts as codetermination for workers in major industries and public ownership of heavy industry.

The Federal Republic's first election was in reality the "last election of the Weimar era," with a large number of parties competing and the vote fragmented among them. The CDU won a narrow victory, receiving less than one-third of the total vote. Though its support for "free enterprise" earned it the reputation of being the "American party," Adenauer resisted American suggestions that he form a broad coalition government with the Social Democrats, who had come in second with just under 30 percent of the vote. To protect his concept of a free economy, Adenauer built a "small coalition" with the Free Democratic Party (FDP) and the small, nationalistic German Party (DP). The FDP supported free markets and had close ties to big business. It was more nationalistic than the CDU, and it supported a strong central government. These smaller parties pulled Adenauer's coalition to the right both on economic issues and on questions relating to Germany's Nazi past, taking an "unreconstructed" attitude toward war crimes and restitution to Germany's victims. This coalition, which held only a narrow majority in the Bundestag (the new German parliament), provided Adenauer with a one-vote margin at his election as Chancellor in September 1949.[45]

Adenauer entered office with many strong convictions. One of his central insights was that foreign policy and domestic policy were so intertwined as to constitute a single problem. He wrote in his memoirs, "As long as we were only an object in the policies of other powers, domestic policy and the solution of our own social problems was difficult." Success in foreign policy—for example, ending the limitations on Germany's industrial production—would help solve such domestic problems as unemployment. Much more important, practical success in bringing about higher living standards and full employment would give his government a prestige and legitimacy with the German people which the Weimar Republic had never achieved. Gaining respect for the Federal Republic in international forums would also translate into greater strength for a democratic government at home.[46]

Another of Adenauer's convictions was that a rapprochement with

France was a necessity for the new German state, both to shape its character and to strengthen Western Europe against the Soviet Union. He recognized that American involvement in Western Europe, which was necessary for its defense, was linked to an improvement in German-French relations. A good relationship with France, he told his Cabinet, was the basis of his American policy. Adenauer's turn westward, however, opened him to the charge that he was abandoning those Germans who were still under Soviet rule. He saw the problem differently. If West Germany's only aim were to be reunification, this would eventually dictate a compromise acceptable to the Soviet Union, but it would also mean the withdrawal of American forces, which would inevitably be followed by Soviet hegemony over Western Europe. Whether this hegemony would mean a communist state in Germany was unclear, but the existence of strong Communist parties in France and Italy led Adenauer to fear that German democracy might eventually crumble.[47]

Integration with the West not only provided a strategy for Germany's rehabilitation; it also provided protection against a renewal of German aggression. Here Adenauer's third conviction came into play. His attitude toward his own people was tinged with skepticism and doubt. He feared the lack of moderation in Germans, their tendency to oscillate between the extremes of arrogance and deep depression, and their propensity for nationalistic "romanticism." At an early Cabinet meeting he expressed outrage at some of the "pan-German" and nationalist speeches given during the first days of the Bundestag. Though he sympathized with the plight of the refugees from the East, he emphasized the destructive effect of such speeches on Western public opinion. He coldly told his ministers, "We must be absolutely clear about the reality of the situation." The anchoring of a German state within the West was a defense against the possible resurgence of nationalism and irredentism, a development which Adenauer expected and feared.[48]

These three principles constituted a "map" for Adenauer's approach to issues, a way of dealing with the complex questions he would face. Nevertheless, under the pressure of circumstances and for reasons of political expediency, he could and did act contrary to them. He was a political pragmatist whose understanding of politics as the art of the possible distinguished him as a leader. As the first Chancellor of the Federal Republic of Germany, he continually tested the limits of his power, always seeking more room to maneuver between the conflicting demands of the Allies and the diffuse political forces within his coalition. Certainly he had structural advantages that Weimar politicians had lacked. Both the "constructive no-confidence" provision—whereby a government could not be voted out of office without its successor's possessing the necessary majority—and the 5 percent rule—which limited representation in parliament to parties acquiring at least 5 percent of the vote—were designed to strengthen the stability of ruling coalitions. But in 1949 it was by no means clear that structural remedies would save German democracy from another round of paralysis and self-destructive behavior.[49]

Adenauer recognized quickly the advantage he gained from the leader of the opposition, Kurt Schumacher. One irony of the postwar period was that a man like Schumacher, a heroic survivor of the concentration camps, could become a threat to the Western Allies. The State Department called him "the one man menacing the unity of Western Europe." A fellow Socialist, the President of France, Vincent Auriol, saw Schumacher as an "arrogant Prussian nationalist," and André François-Poncet, the French High Commissioner, called him a "Hitler of the left."[50]

Kurt Schumacher was born on October 13, 1895, in the town of Kulm on the Vistula River, south of Danzig, only twenty miles from the border with Imperial Russia. Just as Adenauer embodied many characteristics of the Rhinelanders, from his accent to his prejudices, so Schumacher represented the Germans of West Prussia: the border Germans. His warnings about the Soviet Union echoed that area's historic belief that it had to protect Western civilization from Slavic barbarism, and his anticlericalism reflected the belief of Protestant Germans that the Polish majority in their midst were dominated by a reactionary Catholic clergy. Even his interest in a new German army showed traces of the Prussian military spirit.[51]

Schumacher's father was a small businessman, and he grew up in fairly comfortable circumstances. His education was interrupted by the outbreak of war in August 1914. He enlisted in November, and less than a month later, when fighting on the Russian front, he lost his right arm. After his recovery, he made his way to Berlin to study for a doctorate. He regarded the city as his new home, and it was there that he joined the SPD in January 1918. It was also in Berlin that he acquired the passion for politics which was to engross him for the rest of his life.[52]

Schumacher's talent as an orator was the key to his rapid rise within the SPD. His speeches, marked by intellectual depth and political passion, kept audiences spellbound for hours. His speaking style— energetic and emotional, accented by his piercing eyes and emphatic one-armed gestures—made him a sought-after speaker at party rallies. He soon became one of the SPD's leading personalities, despite an aggressive political style that made him known as the "man with one arm and a dozen elbows." Schumacher was elected to the Reichstag in September 1930, the same election in which the Nazis made their first significant showing. A scathing and effective opponent of the Nazis, he called National Socialism an appeal to the "innere Schwei-nehund" (the "intrinsic evil") in man. The ridicule which he heaped on the brownshirts made him a target for arrest in 1933 only a few weeks after Hitler came to power.[53]

The Nazis imprisoned Schumacher in Dachau, the main concentra-tion camp for political opponents. Testimony from other survivors after the war led one biographer to write, "Schumacher's courage, intellect and incorruptibility commanded respect and admiration in a community in which these qualities were in short supply." He assisted sick and starving inmates and maintained his friendships with "non-Aryan" and Jewish prisoners despite punishment. Though the Nazis tortured him severely, they never broke his spirit. When he was re-leased in 1943, he was expected to die quickly. One friend described him as "a pitiful walking cadaver, with ulcers, yellowing stumps for teeth, flickering eyesight . . . and a developing thrombosis in his left leg." Schumacher lost his leg in 1948, and he required an assortment of pain-killers for other ailments. But despite all he had suffered, he recovered enough to emerge in 1945 as the most prominent German leader in the Western zones.[54]

Schumacher's greatest triumph in the immediate postwar period was preventing the merger of the SPD and the German Communist Party (KPD). Under Soviet pressure such a merger had already taken place in East Germany. To Schumacher, however, the Communists were nothing more than "a red-lacquered second edition of the Nazis." He refused to accept the argument that Communists and Socialists were "ideological brothers." "Yes," he would say sarcastically, "like Cain and Abel." When, with strong British support, he succeeded in preventing the merger, he became a political hero to the Social Dem-ocrats in Western Germany. From then on, his leadership of the SPD, the strongest political party, boasting organizational cohesiveness and working-class support, was never seriously challenged.[55]

Nevertheless, Schumacher's relations with the Western powers were difficult and frequently strained. The Americans in the military government were suspicious of the tight control he exercised over his party. When his insistence on more power for the central government threatened the talks on the Bonn constitution, General Clay labeled the SPD a "totalitarian party" and urged a policy of no concessions. Washington rejected this recommendation, but Clay delayed announcing the American concession until the last possible moment, hoping in vain to avoid giving Schumacher a public victory over the Allies. During the 1949 electoral campaign Schumacher's passionate anti-dismantling speeches angered the Western powers, including even the sympathetic British. When the SPD was narrowly defeated, he blamed the British, arguing that if Bevin had only halted dismantling, the SPD would have triumphed.[56]

Schumacher's expectation of victory was so certain that the electoral defeat dealt him a crushing blow and increased his bitterness toward the "usurper," Adenauer. As leader of the opposition his political behavior reflected his ideological convictions and understanding of Germany's recent history. An emphatic patriot and nationalist, he considered himself first and foremost a *German* socialist. Believing that the restoration of German unity must be the paramount goal, he opposed a close relationship with France, which always sought to "keep Germany down, to paralyze it, to make it impotent." In a twist on the "magnet" theory of reunification, Schumacher contended that close integration with the West could turn Germany into a "clericalist and capitalist state" and make it less attractive to Protestant and socialist East Germany. Along with many others in the European Left, Schumacher hoped Germany could find a "third way," somewhere between Soviet communism in the East and American capitalism in the West.[57]

Schumacher, like Adenauer, anticipated a revival of German nationalism, but he hoped to capture that sentiment for Social Democracy. He believed that the millions of refugees from the Eastern territories would support this new nationalism and that the SPD could steer their resentment into "progressive" channels. Like Adenauer, he expected events to follow a pattern similar to that of the interwar period, but his conclusions were based on a Marxist interpretation of the period. He thought that Erhard's free-market economic policies would cause an increasing polarization of German society, with a small elite at the top and a broad stratum of workers and the lower middle class at the bottom, and he interpreted the increase in unemployment and inflation following the currency reform as signals of the coming crisis of German capitalism. Still, the SPD's domestic program was comparatively moderate. It called for a full employment policy, socialization of key industries and raw materials, and more state planning and control of investment, a program similar to that of the British Labour Party.[58]

Many foreign observers took a jaundiced view of both Adenauer and Schumacher, seeing them as leftovers from earlier eras: Adenauer as a man from the Wilhelmine age and Schumacher, with his Marxist ideology and speeches about class conflict, as a relic of the 1920s. Schumacher's nationalist rhetoric struck a raw nerve in foreigners still traumatized by Hitler, and they hoped for a rapid transition of power in both political parties. To them the confrontation between Adenauer and Schumacher symbolized the unresolved tensions at the heart of postwar Germany. What balance could be achieved between the pursuit of ties with the West and the hope of reunification with East Germany, between free-market capitalism and state-sponsored socialism, between Germany as an integral part of the Western world and Germany as a bridge between East and West? No German leader was completely free to answer these questions; the constraints of the four-power occupation and the weight of the German past would have restricted any Chancellor. But in 1949 the Federal Republic of Germany at least had a voice, and how it would address these matters would decisively influence relations with the new Allied High Commission, as well as the future course of German politics.

3

Avoiding the Fate of Weimar: The Petersberg Protocols

On September 21, 1949, Konrad Adenauer, the new federal Chancellor of Germany, ascended the steep hill outside Bonn known as the Petersberg on his way to the white mansion at the top. This mansion, once a hotel where British Prime Minister Neville Chamberlain had stayed, had become the headquarters of the Allied High Commission, and Adenauer had been called there to receive a parchment copy of the Occupation Statute, the document which defined the limits placed on the new Bonn government. Contrary to American wishes, Adenauer had opposed an elaborate ceremony. He took along only a few of his Cabinet ministers, careful not to create the impression that his Cabinet selections required Allied approval. Once inside the mansion, he was instructed to stand before the three High Commissioners and, after the proclamation of the Occupation Statute, to step forward onto the carpet on which the three were standing. But when André François-Poncet, the French High Commissioner, came forward before the proclamation to shake the Chancellor's hand, Adenauer seized the opportunity to step onto the carpet, symbolically asserting equality with the Commissioners. The Teppichpolitik (carpet policy) greatly impressed his ministers, who later remembered him as the "Victor of the Scene."[1]

This story, which Adenauer told in his memoirs, illustrated his insistence that the Allies grant Germany a position of equality among the Western nations. Granting such a demand would be particularly difficult for France, where the wounds of war were deep. (But Adenauer, who had vivid memories of the invective hurled at leaders of the Weimar Republic as the "Versailles traitors," wanted the Allies to accord his government political respect. McCloy would recall later that he himself had learned a lesson from the Chancellor in how to guard the "dignity of defeat."[2]

The First Weeks of the High Commission

Political divisions in and in relation to Germany were expressed not only in the Adenauer-Schumacher rivalry but among the Western Allies themselves. Both the British and French had distinctive attitudes toward Germany, formed by their experience with the Weimar Republic and the Third Reich. Although both wanted the Americans to guarantee the security of Western Europe, both also sought to preserve as much independence as possible from the United States and to prevent hasty American actions from endangering their security. Germany was to prove a testing ground for Allied unity.[3]

The British and the French viewed the post of High Commissioner as of critical diplomatic importance. Although McCloy was hardly a novice in German affairs, his Allied counterparts had had more diplomatic experience than he and were more familiar with German history and with the condition of the country in 1949. General Brian Robertson, the British High Commissioner, was the only original military governor to remain after the proclamation of the Occupation Statute. Like McCloy, Robertson had experienced the first occupation of Germany in 1918, as an aide-de-camp to his father, the commander-in-chief of the British army in the Rhineland. During the Second World War he had handled important supply operations but had not seen combat. In August 1945 he was named chief of staff of the British zone in Germany, and almost immediately the bulk of the administrative and diplomatic problems devolved upon him. He became Military Governor late in 1947. A slow, deliberate, self-disciplined man, Robertson's temperament and conservatism allowed him to work effectively with Adenauer even though he represented the Labour government, which was linked with the SPD. Because of his cooperation with Adenauer in the British zone before 1949, Robertson was closer to the Chancellor than the other two High Commissioners.

In June 1950 Robertson was replaced by Sir Ivone Kirkpatrick, a professional diplomat who had served in the British Embassy in Berlin during the 1930s. Although both Robertson and Kirkpatrick tended to reflect the views of the British Foreign Office, British policy was directed by Foreign Secretary Ernest Bevin, a former trade unionist and strong anti-communist, who remained skeptical about the Germans and wanted the Allies to keep a close watch on the emerging Federal Republic.[4]

The French High Commissioner was André François-Poncet, a diplomat, scholar, and writer. His knowledge of Germany and the Germans was so thorough that he intimidated some American officials. As a youth he had studied in Germany, learned to speak the language without accent, and acquired a lifelong interest in German literature. After compiling a brilliant record at the Ecole Normale Supérieure, he had accepted a professorship at the Lycée de Montpellier, planning to make a study of the classical German novel. The outbreak of World War I interrupted these plans. François-Poncet served at the front for two years and then entered the diplomatic service. During the occupation he served in both the Rhineland and Berlin before becoming economic adviser to General Degoutte in the Ruhr. Through marriage François-Poncet had acquired substantial holdings in the French steel industry, and it was as a defender of that industry that he began his political career in the 1920s. He distinguished himself as a parliamentary spokesman for conservative causes and an opponent of organized labor. In 1931 he was appointed Ambassador to Germany, where he remained until 1938.[5]

François-Poncet's role in Germany during the 1930s remains controversial. As a strong advocate of closer industrial ties between Germany and France, he proposed a new international cartel in heavy industry. Not only was he one of the few diplomats who could speak directly to the Führer, but he was also conceded to be "the only foreign diplomat who enjoyed Hitler's liking and respect." Although some observers, including the American Ambassador, William Dodd, thought François-Poncet was "not far from being a fascist," the Frenchman argued in his memoirs that he was only playing a role, and that "as a liberal and humanist" he had found National Socialism "revolting." Above all François-Poncet considered himself a realist. He had been "tough" toward the Weimar Republic, but he could reconcile himself to Nazi Germany's commanding position in Europe if Hitler pursued his goals peacefully and allowed France a position in his "New Order." Even after the Munich Conference, François-Poncet argued that "Franco-German relations . . . were like a lottery in which France had to try her luck." He still believed Hitler "was inspired by a sincere though 'intermittent' desire for an understanding." After the outbreak of war the Frenchman finally turned against Hitler, but he was not arrested until 1943. He was interned by the Germans until May 1945.[6]

After the war François-Poncet found a forum for his views on Germany in the conservative newspaper *Le Figaro*. Like General de Gaulle and other French conservatives he stressed the necessity of confederation for Germany: "To make it into a unitary Reich is to perpetuate the work of the Nazis. To make it into a federal state is to follow in the tracks of the Weimar Republic or Bismarck's Empire; the two precedents are equally unsatisfactory." With the exception of a special control for the Ruhr, François-Poncet wanted the individual states to be the centers of power in a confederated Germany. He suggested an alliance between France and those German states with which France had economic and geographical connections. In 1948 he became an adviser to the new Foreign Minister, Robert Schuman, himself a border politician (born in Lorraine) and committed to Franco-German reconciliation. François-Poncet accompanied Schuman on a trip to Germany, staying on as an observer at the German Constitutional Assembly. His deputy commissioner, Armand Bérard, was also a professional diplomat who had served in Germany during the 1930s.[7]

By the time he was appointed High Commissioner, François-Poncet had accepted the goal of "integrating" Germany into the West, arguing that "Europe can recover only to the extent to which Germany can be interested in both the recovery and the solidarity of the West" against the Soviet threat. He favored a tougher line toward Germany than his own Foreign Minister, however, and his speeches and pronouncements often took the form of warnings to the Germans. At one of the first meetings of the High Commission he told Adenauer, "We do not wish to be forced to use sharp measures against you but wish to help you fulfill your tasks . . . this new Republic is our child. You are living in . . . a controlled and watched liberty." This mistrust on the part of the French High Commissioner increased the tension at early meetings of the Allied High Commission (AHC), where it was obvious that the lectures on German behavior were being given by the weakest Allied power, the only one that the Germans had defeated.[8]

French reservations about the new Germany played an important role in the first crisis faced by the AHC—the devaluation of the deutsche mark (DM). On September 18, 1949, Great Britain devalued the pound sterling by 30 percent. This devaluation, indicative of British financial weakness, nevertheless promised to be a short-term boon for British exporters. Countries within the sterling bloc soon followed the British lead, while France devalued the franc by 22.5 percent. Germany's major trading rival was Great Britain, and the devaluation posed a challenge to Ludwig Erhard's free-market experiment as well as to the authority of the new Adenauer government. The crisis is also an interesting case study of McCloy's influence on the Germans and his use of American power to promote "European" solutions.[9]

There were good reasons for Germany to match the British action. Two-thirds of West Germany's exports went to the sterling area. In Erhard's view a strong export industry was essential to the survival of a market-oriented economy. Even before World War II Germany had needed to export to feed its growing population. The division of Europe, the loss of the agricultural lands in the East, the huge increase in population resulting from the arrival of expellees and refugees, and the destruction caused by the war made the need for foreign trade even more striking. The Federal Republic was only beginning to regain markets it had lost during the war; it could not afford to let the British gain an effective price advantage.[10]

Yet there were more compelling reasons to avoid a sharp devaluation like Britain's. Germany was already running a heavy import surplus, two-thirds of which came from the dollar area. A 30 percent devaluation would sharply increase that, put further pressure on the value of the currency, and increase the cost of living. Erhard told the Americans that "the impact of a 30 percent devaluation on the social position of a German worker would be greater than the Government is prepared to face." The only way for the German government to offset the increased prices would be to increase its subsidies of foodstuffs. To conservative German leaders, who had experienced two periods of inflation in one generation, nothing seemed worse than the risk of starting an inflationary wage-price spiral. They also worried that the devaluation would further decrease the willingness of Germans to save, which was already badly shaken by past experiences with runaway inflation. For these reasons the Germans ruled out the 30 percent choice and debated whether a 20 or 25 percent devaluation was more appropriate. The United States and Britain were prepared to accept either figure.[11]

The French government, however, did not consider the devaluation of the DM a matter to be decided by the Germans alone. Since the currency reform of June 1948 French anxiety over the German economic revival, particularly in heavy industry, had increased. The chief concern was the price of German coal, on which French steel production was heavily dependent. As was the practice in some other countries, notably Great Britain, West Germany sold coal to domestic consumers at a lower price than it was sold abroad. Consequently the chief consumers, the German steel manufacturers, had a competitive advantage over the other steel producers in Europe who required German coal. Its price in France was already 30 to 40 percent higher than the German domestic price, and a sharp devaluation would further increase the disparity. In the fall of 1949 it was also expected that there would soon be a glut of steel on the world market. The French feared that their increased steel production facilities, created by their Planning Commissariat after the war, would find it difficult to compete with the Germans. As a result, the French attempt to create an "economic balance of power" in Western Europe would fail.[12]

The devaluation crisis paralleled the bitter disputes of the interwar era, especially the economic nationalism that followed the Great Depression, while economic rivalries heightened political tensions and stifled the cooperative instincts of the Western European leaders. In McCloy's words, the "old fears of domination of the Ruhr in Europe's economy arose with great vehemence and force." This time, however, the American government had both the power and the will to mediate, and if necessary, impose a solution. McCloy's actions in the devaluation crisis reflected this new determination.[13]

Before the German Cabinet met, Erhard told a group of Allied officials that the government would propose a 20 percent rate of devaluation. But when the Cabinet did meet—on September 21, 1949—Erhard's proposal encountered powerful resistance. Hermann Abs, not a Cabinet member but a prominent banker and the head of the Reconstruction Finance Corporation, insisted that 20 percent was not a large enough devaluation, and that it would hurt export industries and create unemployment. He said that the government could control food prices by importing more food from the sterling area countries, or by using Marshall Plan funds as subsidies. His arguments convinced Adenauer and the rest of the Cabinet of the need for the steeper devaluation of 25 percent.[14]

In making this decision Adenauer ignored a warning that the French did not want the Germans to devalue the DM more than the franc. The next day the French Prime Minister, Henri Queille, called in the American Ambassador, David Bruce, to complain about American policy. The French were angry over what they perceived as the "special relationship" between the "Anglo-Saxon" powers, which excluded French leaders from consultations preceding Allied decisions. The devaluation of the DM, along with the division of Marshall Plan aid and the devaluation of the pound, was the "straw to break the camel's back." Queille, who assumed that the Americans had dictated the 25 percent devaluation to the Germans, insisted that the French would not allow any devaluation unless a single price was set for German coal—the same for domestic use as for export. Later he instructed François-Poncet to use the AHC's authority to delay the German action.[15]

Adenauer was outraged at the High Commission's refusal to accept his Cabinet's decision. He either did not comprehend or did not take seriously the French concerns, but rather saw in the Commission's veto a perpetuation of the "Frankfurt regime," by which he meant the direct American contacts with, and penetration of, the German authorities set up in Bizonia, such as the Frankfurt Economic Council and the Bank Deutscher Länder. Adenauer saw these contacts, especially that with Erhard, as discrediting the Bonn government. He believed that the Allies, who knew that Erhard favored the 20 percent rate, were supporting him and trying to overturn the Chancellor's decision. "The Frankfurt regime is over," Adenauer told the Cabinet. He refused to back down from the 25 percent figure even after McCloy informed him that Marshall Plan funds could not be used as subsidies for food prices.[16]

At the September 24 meeting of the High Commissioners, François-Poncet threatened to appeal any Allied decision contrary to French wishes, thus invoking a three-week delay provided for in the Washington Agreements and sending the matter to the individual governments for decision. McCloy pressed instead for immediate action, warning that "if the governments are called in on the first test . . . it would be better to recall the High Commissioners and replace them with Low Commissioners, leaving the running of Germany to Paris, London, and Washington." After observing the Quai d'Orsay's tight control over François-Poncet's negotiating leverage, McCloy decided to try to bring the parties together through personal diplomacy. Over the next five days he shuttled between Berlin, Frankfurt, Bonn, and Paris, in an attempt to resolve the dispute.[17]

The first order of business was to obtain concessions from the Germans. Despite the late hour of McCloy's call, Adenauer was impressed by his willingness to "come down from the Petersberg" to see him at his home in Rhöndorf. McCloy told Adenauer that he was anxious to reach an agreement, and that he had no desire to force anything on anyone. Adenauer was prepared to accept the 20 percent devaluation, but he resisted lowering the export price of coal. Such a change in trade practices, Adenauer told McCloy, should be a part of an overall "new order" in European commerce.[18]

With Adenauer's position in mind, McCloy went to Paris. Although François-Poncet had suggested his visit, the all-day session at the Quai d'Orsay, at which both Prime Minister Queille and Finance Minister Petsche were present, did not result in an agreement. The French would accept the 20 percent rate, but they wanted a commitment from the Americans favoring an end to the dual pricing of coal. McCloy was willing to give a general promise to study that problem, but he refused to commit the United States to any action before the study was completed. Despite the ECA's dislike of dual pricing, Averell Harriman backed McCloy's approach to the French.[19]

At that point McCloy cabled Acheson in Washington, asking him to tell Schuman that the French "will not win by delay." He even urged Acheson to threaten that if the French appealed the AHC decision, the United States might insist on a devaluation greater than 20 percent. Acheson went to Schuman, telling him that McCloy had been working so hard on devaluation that he had not slept for seventy-two hours. Pointing out that McCloy was taking "a broad and European view" of the matter, Acheson urged Schuman to show more flexibility. Later he assured Schuman that "the future of Western Europe depended upon the establishment of understanding between the French and the Germans; that this could only be brought about by the French, and only as fast as the French were prepared to go; and that therefore the role of the U.S. and U.K. in this matter was to advise and assist the French and not put them in the position of being forced reluctantly to accept American or U.K. ideas."[20]

Although Schuman may well have wondered whether the American pressure to agree on devaluation accorded with Acheson's soothing words, he conveyed Acheson's views to the French Cabinet and urged them to compromise. But first he suggested to Acheson that the two of them make a private deal, excluding the Allied High Commission, to eliminate dual pricing. Acheson pointedly refused, telling Schuman that "it was the policy of our Government to give Mr. McCloy the fullest discretion." This strengthened McCloy's position with his French counterparts, who realized then that his actions had Washington's support. At the AHC meeting on September 27 McCloy finally obtained agreement on the 20 percent rate. He continued to refuse to oppose dual pricing, worried that a commitment to do so would lead to a British protest. After an adjournment to allow François-Poncet to consult with his government, the French conceded. The AHC agreed on the 20 percent rate, and gave a general understanding to "eliminate discriminatory practices and dumping" and protect the interests of coal-importing countries by reducing the disparity between the domestic and export price of German coal. Germany went along by lowering the export price of coal by 20 percent.[21]

The next day the High Commissioners held a tense meeting with the Chancellor. Adenauer was angry that he had not been consulted before the final agreement was announced. He had already publicly challenged the right of the AHC to set the rate of the DM, and François-Poncet immediately criticized him for this. To defuse the tension McCloy sought to convince Adenauer of the urgency of the problem, which required swift action to prevent losses to German exporters. Adenauer pleaded with the High Commissioners not to damage the prestige of his government by such cavalier treatment, saying that the Allies had to give up their "Frankfurt" habits and deal with his government as the only representative of Germany. If they did not accord respect to Bonn, the German people would never do so.[22]

After the meeting McCloy admitted to his staff that his procedures for contacting the Germans had been "somewhat crude," especially the "late in the middle of the night visits I paid Adenauer." Criticism in the German press reinforced the perception that the AHC had simply "informed" the German government of its decision, issuing a Diktat that had to be obeyed. Newspapers emphasized that this treatment not only discredited Adenauer, whose political position was far from secure, but also invited comparisons with the East zone, where the Soviets were about to embark on a new initiative.[23]

Throughout the summer of 1949 the Soviet Union had continued to denounce the West for planning to divide Germany. But this propaganda could not conceal a similar process under way in its own zone, designed to give East Germany a separate government, a police force, and most important, an "alert police" known as the Bereitschaften. The size of this special force was estimated at 50,000, and its members underwent military-style training. (The creation of such a force followed a pattern similar to that in other Soviet-dominated East European countries.) The early land reform and socialization measures had dictated a separate development for the Russian zone, and this process accelerated in 1948 and 1949. The creation and mobilization of a wide range of political organizations to represent various groups, such as former soldiers, women, and youth, followed the Soviet model. Finally on October 7, 1949, the German Democratic Republic (GDR) was founded.[24]

The founding of the GDR did not mean the Soviets had abandoned their interest in a reunified Germany. Americans thought the Russians were "riding two horses—Bolshevization of their own zone and winning all of Germany," a policy that was the reverse of the U.S. concept of Germany as a "magnet" to the East. Stalin's speech congratulating the founders of the GDR was remarkable for its conciliatory tone. Despite Soviet wartime propaganda, which had portrayed the Germans as savages, the Russian leader said that both peoples had suffered "the greatest losses" and understood the need for "peace and democracy." The founding of the GDR was a "turning point in history," putting an end to the animosity which had existed between the peoples of Germany and their neighboring states. Stalin's conciliatory approach indicated that the Soviets hoped to exploit German desires for reunification, opening the possibility of another Rapallo (the German-Soviet agreement of 1922). McCloy thought that the Russians had acquired some important propaganda tools in the creation of East Germany. They could exploit the appeal of Berlin as the capital city of a new Germany, in sharp contrast to the provincial town of Bonn which Adenauer's government had chosen. The potential for unlimited trade with the East compared favorably with the problems to be faced in seeking to regain markets in the West. And the German "dream of unity" was still powerful. McCloy, who characterized the East-West confrontation in Germany as the "struggle for the soul of Faust," speculated that the Russians "may be planning to make East Germany their major satellite."[25]

Yet McCloy underestimated the constraints that were laid on Soviet policy toward East Germany, which were similar to those placed on the United States by the Franco-German antagonism. One of the first actions of the East German government, undoubtedly encouraged by the Soviets, was to recognize the Oder-Neisse boundary with Poland, a decision deeply resented by Germans expelled from the region and distasteful to other Germans as well. Throughout the early 1950s Soviet policy would fluctuate between appeals for reunification and actions which made reunification unappealing to the Western Germans. This fluctuation did not mean, however, that the Western Allies could discount the impact of the Soviet approach, for the West German populace overwhelmingly supported a foreign policy emphasizing reunification.[26]

Despite his original intention to concentrate on improving Germany's relations with France, McCloy found himself increasingly concerned with East-West tensions. He urged a reluctant Adenauer to show more interest in the divided city of Berlin, whose economic plight in the post-blockade period verged on disaster. On this issue Adenauer joined forces with the French High Commission to block an SPD-sponsored measure to include Berlin in the Federal Republic as a Twelfth Land (or state in the federation). To the French, Berlin represented the evils of a centralized German state as well as the spirit of Prussian militarism. Adenauer worried that making Berlin the Twelfth Land would put the Federal Republic in conflict with the Soviet Union. He also knew that including an SPD-dominated Berlin in the Bundestag would weaken his majority. After an AHC meeting in which Adenauer had engaged in a series of angry exchanges with François-Poncet, the French High Commissioner could still say of the Chancellor's Berlin policy, "Dr. Adenauer seems to be reasoning this problem with a cool head." Despite strong sympathy for Berlin, the United States was reluctant to intervene in any area about which the French and Germans could agree.[27]

East-West rivalry and the problem of Franco-German cooperation provided the backdrop for the High Commission's review of the continued dismantling of German industry. Both the legacy of the interwar period and the controversy over the Morgenthau Plan helped shape the postwar policy of dismantling German industries. It was the widely held perception of American leaders, particularly President Truman and Secretary of State Byrnes, that the post-Versailles policy of taking reparations from current production had been a costly failure, in which American loans had financed Germany's payments to the other European countries. Truman was resolved to prevent this, and the Potsdam Treaty specified that capital equipment, rather than goods from current production, would constitute the main source for reparations. The framers of the Morgenthau Plan argued that Germany had created an "excessive" industrial base, and that these "war industries," particularly steel, synthetic oil, and rubber, had facilitated German aggression and expansion. To determine the plants "in excess" of what Germany needed to restore a standard of living "not exceeding" her neighbors, and to identify those plants whose "sole" function was "war production," the Allied Control Council in March 1946 agreed on a "level-of-industry" plan for all Germany. The Allies were to dismantle, as payment for reparations, those plants in excess of the permitted level.[28]

Four-power cooperation on the level-of-industry plan broke down during 1946, when the Soviets refused to provide any accounting of the capital equipment they removed from their zone. According to several Soviet defectors, the policy of removing equipment proved counterproductive, for the German machinery was often damaged by the time it reached the Soviet Union. By the end of 1946 the Russians had largely shifted to a policy of taking reparations from current production, which often led to Soviet ownership of East German factories. At the same time, the Soviets stepped up their propaganda about the Ruhr and the importance of four-power control over the heartland of German industry.[29]

This change in Soviet policy paralleled the shift in Allied thinking. In the absence of a four-power agreement the United States and Great Britain decided on an upward revision of the permitted level of industry for Bizonia, with the result that on the October 1947 lists the number of plants to be dismantled was reduced from 1500 to 859. The production limit for steel was raised from 5.8 million to 11.1 million tons, a figure which corresponded to 50 percent of the remaining capacity, while in the consumer goods section all production ceilings were lifted. Moreover, in the new Prohibited and Limited Industries (PLI) plan it was pointed out that "an orderly and prosperous Europe requires the economic contribution of a stable and productive Germany." The inauguration of the Marshall Plan raised further questions concerning the wisdom of continuing the dismantling program, which contradicted and worked against the Plan's goal of rebuilding Europe. This contradiction could be understood only in terms of the Europeans' continuing fear of Germany and their hope that the limits placed on its "dangerous" heavy industry would redirect its economy toward "peaceful" light industries and the production of consumer goods.[30]

Even after the reduction in number of plants, influential groups continued to urge a halt to dismantling. An ECA Industrial Advisory Committee composed of American businessmen recommended the retention of 167 of the 381 plants it had studied. German workers in the Ruhr clashed with British soldiers who were defending dismantling operations, the first significant defiance of Allied rule. American critics of the Truman Administration saw in dismantling an indication of the ineptitude of the President's foreign policy. In April 1949, during the discussions that led to the Washington Agreements, American leaders wanted a still sharper reduction in dismantling. Besides agreeing on an International Authority for the Ruhr (IAR), the Western Allies set new limits and production quotas for German industry, thus saving 159 of the 167 plants specified by the ECA Committee. Most of the eight plants that were excluded (at French insistence) were steel production facilities, including the August-Thyssen works in Duisburg, one of Germany's most modern plants. At the same time the Allies affirmed their determination to continue dismantling the remaining plants. Here a "package deal" was clear: the French had given way on the creation of a West German state in return for the security provided by the continuing controls on German industry.

The Allies may have thought that the Washington Agreements would close the book on dismantling, but the Germans sought to pry it open. Dismantling was a major issue in their 1949 election campaign, and it increasingly triggered German resentment and anger. As the Allies accelerated the dismantling program, protests grew in scope and intensity, including threats against those German workers who worked for the Allies. The Germans saw dismantling as not only a wasteful policy but a cause of their poverty and unemployment. They suspected that the motivation for most dismantling was a desire to limit competition, not a desire for security or reparations. They particularly suspected the British, in whose zone most of the dismantling took place. Many Americans had the same suspicion, though recent studies have supported the view that security rather than economic competition was the principal motive for the policy.[31]

Germans of all political stripes entreated McCloy to do something about dismantling. On September 13, when he was in Bonn for the inauguration of the German President, Theodor Heuss, he received separate visits from Adenauer and Schumacher. Both urged that the "painful subject" of dismantling be discussed by the Foreign Ministers, then meeting in Washington. Each leader stressed that this would create a good atmosphere in which the new German government could begin its work. Adenauer feared that continued dismantling would provide the extreme right with a new slogan, which it would use against his government in a manner resembling the attacks on the Weimar regime. He noted that the workers, whether rightly or wrongly, did see dismantling as an economic policy directed against German competition. Schumacher, emphasizing the consequences of unemployment resulting from dismantling, urged that the Allies halt the program until further studies could be made.[32]

McCloy reminded each leader of the sufferings and consequent concern of the victims of German aggression, and of the bitterness harbored by many. Observing that each leader underestimated Allied security concerns, he suggested that "cooperation in the erection of a new democratic state" might bring an end to dismantling. Angered by Schumacher's willingness to act with the Communists and place the dismantling issue first on the agenda of the Bundestag, McCloy threatened that "anything suggesting a test of strength particularly at the outset of the new government could only have one result as far as the Allies were concerned."[33]

But despite his anger, McCloy was affected by this bipartisan appeal. Shortly after arriving in Germany he had told his friend Eric Warburg that the Allies should carry the dismantling program to completion, treating the Germans as the Romans had by "breaking their spears and swords right in front of them." But after the two leaders' visits he changed his views and sent Acheson a memorandum indicting the dismantling policy. Arguing that the German agitation was "not inspired by Nazi influences," McCloy pointed out that it came largely from the left and center of the German political spectrum. After stating that the "abrasive character" of the dismantling policy was endangering other, more important occupation policies, McCloy added "that we [should] avoid the mistakes that we made after Weimar where we were rather hasty to give up to the wrong government things we had long begrudged to a better one."[34]

McCloy did not argue for unreciprocated concessions on the part of the Allies. The Germans should give "some assurances as to cooperation" on security, perhaps "in terms of internationalizing some of the properties." German approval of the Ruhr Agreement would also indicate a cooperative attitude. While still supporting the dismantling of "all war plants and . . . the destruction or removal of all machinery which can be used for war-making purposes," he urged concessions in such areas as steel and synthetic fuels. He also hoped Allied action toward Western Germany might offset whatever concessions the Russians might offer East Germany.[35]

Spurred on by McCloy, Acheson raised the subject of dismantling at his meetings with Bevin and Schuman. Referring to increasing public criticism of the policy in the United States, where the Senate had approved yet another review of dismantling, Acheson admitted that he had hoped "that dismantling would have been concluded by now." But both Bevin and Schuman held firm on the issue, wishing to wait until the policies of the new German government had become clear. Schuman accused the German leaders of trying to deceive and divide the Allies. He insisted on continued firmness toward the German demands, saying that "the German government is always making claims, and that if we accept the present claims, they would only make new ones." The meeting ended with a vague decision to review the issue at the next conference of Foreign Ministers.

For the fledgling Adenauer government, a halt to dismantling remained a priority. Adenauer compared the issue with the Versailles Treaty in being the "best propaganda for unbounded nationalism." On October 3, 1949, he sent his first proposal to the AHC. Condemning the accelerated dismantling of the August-Thyssen works and the Gelsenberg-Benzin installation, Adenauer appealed for an immediate halt to the process, along with negotiations between his government and the AHC. He emphasized his willingness to work out a solution to the reparations problem which would satisfy Allied claims but not damage the economy of Germany or imperil the development of democracy. Although he had as yet not concrete proposal to offer, he assured the Allies it was being "worked out."[36]

McCloy and Robertson (the British High Commissioner) informed Adenauer that one roadblock to ending dismantling was the lack of a convincing German proposal. McCloy even told one German industrialist that he doubted whether the Adenauer government was "strong enough" to make a politically acceptable proposal. Responding to the challenge, Adenauer made his first attempt in a letter to the AHC dated October 10. Although he still wanted an overall halt to dismantling, the Chancellor limited his proposal to the Thyssen facility. He suggested two alternatives to dismantling it, both designed to satisfy the demand for reparations. The first was to create a new company to control the Thyssen works, giving shares in its ownership to those countries that were entitled to reparations. The second alternative was that the same countries should receive new goods from the current production of the Thyssen works. Adenauer ended his letter by complaining about the increased tempo of dismantling at the plant, lamenting that he would soon be faced with a "fait accompli."[37]

A few days later, at a meeting with the High Commissioners, Adenauer departed from his specific proposals to urge that the United States use its financial power to force France and Germany together. America should invest directly in French industry in order to allow the French to invest in German industry. "Common economic interests are the best basis for cooperation between nations," Adenauer argued, adding that this had also been his goal in the 1920s. McCloy replied that American economic pressure could produce resentment, and that investment was not enough to bring about Franco-German cooperation. As if to confirm McCloy's point, Adenauer and François-Poncet clashed sharply over other issues. Adenauer criticized France for missing a chance to promote peace in 1918 by pursuing "a senseless and misguided separatist policy." (Given Adenauer's own flirtation with separatism, this comment was certain to provoke the French.) François-Poncet, angrily noting the nationalist tone of the speeches in the Bundestag, commented, "You have caused us the greatest disappointment, disillusionment, and bitterness." Later in the month Adenauer lashed out at the Allies for their "lack of understanding of the German mind," and for repeating the same mistakes they had made at Versailles. François-Poncet fired back, citing nationalist articles in the

German press and telling the Chancellor that "not enough attention is paid to enlightening the German people." He added bitterly that "the entire situation harkens back twenty years."[38]

As Adenauer searched for a proposal, the campaign in the United States against dismantling neared its peak. It had begun less than a year after the war ended, with conservative Republicans, former isolationists, Quakers, pacifists, and pro-German groups in the Midwest leading the fight. This pro-German orientation on the part of many conservatives was linked to their distrust of England and its "socialistic policies." They argued that dismantling would bankrupt the American taxpayer, and that England was holding down German industry for its own selfish reasons. If the campaign against dismantling had remained the preserve of conservative Republicans, it could hardly have succeeded. But through the astute efforts of two American lobbyists in Washington, John and Joan Crane (a married couple on the staff of a conservative Senator, George Malone of Nevada), this campaign spread across the political spectrum. Aided by information and funds supplied by Hans-Günther Sohl, a former top manager of Vereinigte Stahlwerke who had been put in charge of the Thyssen works, the Cranes launched a campaign in the leading newspapers and magazines on the East Coast. They supplied material to the *New York Daily News, Newsweek,* the *Wall Street Journal,* and other smaller journals, which published stories emphasizing both the destructive character of dismantling and its cost to the American taxpayer. Joan Crane lobbied vigorously in both the State Department and Congress, providing officials with information on the speeded-up pace of dismantling and the need for an immediate change. Her biggest success came in October 1949: first a bipartisan petition against dismantling was signed by forty-four Senators, twenty-six Republicans, and eighteen Democrats; then on October 17 a Senate resolution against the policy only narrowly missed approval. Policymakers both in the United States and abroad carefully monitored the Congressional actions. Paul Hoffmann, the head of ECA in Washington, put his weight behind a change in policy. He wrote Acheson, "The American people, originally quite content with the April [1949] agreements, are now growing restive, and this creates a difficult situation for both of us, which we can not ignore."[39]

While Hoffmann and Congress were turning up the heat on the State Department, McCloy's public statements and interviews were stirring up a storm in European capitals. Once McCloy decided that dismantling was a destructive policy, he used his position to stimulate public debate on the subject. In a newspaper interview on October 9, 1949, he urged an end to "aimless dismantling" and advocated a new international control over the Ruhr to ensure Western Europe's security. He also suggested that Germany's remaining reparations might be met through current production. When the British protested, he issued the following disclaimer: "My personal view does not favor a cessation of dismantling unless and until guarantees as to security and reparations can be given by Germany sufficiently strong to justify it." Only a week later he told the London *Times* of his hope that dismantling might be ended if the Germans gave their wholehearted support to the Ruhr Authority, adding that the Authority itself could be expanded to cover all Western European heavy industry. He felt that any sort of "grand international cartelization" could be prevented by insisting that industries operate under the principle of "competitive and unrestricted free enterprise." A few days later McCloy went to Paris and presented the same idea to the French.[40]

The British were furious about McCloy's public statements. They thought his suggestion of reparations from current production not only echoed Russian methods in East Germany but also recalled the unhappy experience after World War I. Such a scheme would also allow the Germans to import more raw materials from the United States and would require an increase in their share of Marshall Plan aid. McCloy's statements supported the German argument that the Ruhr Authority "discriminated" against them by controlling only the Ruhr. The Germans, the British said, would now refuse to join the IAR until it was enlarged to cover other industrial areas, an undesirable and unlikely possibility. The British concluded their message to the State Department by noting that these "personal views" of McCloy were not only ruinous to Allied unity but also encouraged the Germans to play the Allies off against each other.[41]

Despite all that had happened—the German proposals, Congressional pressures, and McCloy's statements—Acheson remained calm during the dismantling agitation. The State Department tried to restrain McCloy, asking him to remember that "nothing must be done which could give rise to the inference U.S. is seeking to impose a solution on French or British." Since the PLI Agreement was "one of the basic security arrangements underlying the Washington agree-

ments . . . we cannot yield to German pressure on question of security." Reminding McCloy that the French saw the Washington
Agreements as a package deal, the State Department feared that "our
difficulties" with the French "will be intolerable if they believe we are
seeking to withdraw from our part of the bargain, particularly as
regards security." Acheson himself did not anticipate any new developments on the issue until January. On October 27, in fact, he told
the President that he wanted to take a vacation during the first two
weeks of November, and Truman readily approved.[42]

The Secretary of State's vacation did not come off as planned. On
October 25, 1949, Adenauer told his Cabinet he had reluctantly concluded that the Germans must offer to join the Ruhr Authority. The
Americans attached a great deal of importance to German cooperation,
and this cooperation might gain important concessions for Germany.
Then Adenauer drafted a short letter to the High Commission, in
which he stated Germany's willingness to participate in any organization which served to control Germany's "war potential," admitting
that its steel production did pose a question of security to its neighbors. Next Adenauer launched a personal campaign to sway German
and American opinion. In an interview in *Die Zeit* he made three
important statements: improving Germany's relations with France was
the Angelpunkt (cardinal point) of his foreign policy; the security
question was the Kernfrage (essential question) of Franco-German
relations; and despite the various obstructions raised against cooperation, such as the status of the Saar, Germany must recognize that
France feared a revival of German nationalism. Only a few days later
in an interview with the *Baltimore Sun,* one of President Truman's
favorite papers, Adenauer suggested that France should own 40 percent of the German steel industry, and that this investment should be
supported by American capital. He wanted the President to know that
he agreed with Acheson and McCloy, and that his own fundamental
goal was Franco-German reconciliation.[43]

At the same time that Adenauer was recognizing the importance of
the security issue, the British were coming under pressure from the
United States and Germany. To Foreign Secretary Bevin the actions
of Congress and McCloy's statements indicated that the Americans
were putting the blame for the Allied policy on the shoulders of the
British and were currying favor with the Germans. This angered Bevin,
who was also receiving disturbing reports from his own High Com-

missioner. At a rally on October 21 in Bochum, the heart of the Ruhr, August Schmidt, head of the miners' union, had proclaimed that no "decent German" should take part in dismantling operations. Fearful of more clashes between British troops and German workers, Bevin worried that Schmidt's implied threats would prevent the British from finding workers to carry out their policy. This would be a humiliating defeat for the Allies, comparable to that resulting from the passive resistance of German workers during the French occupation of the Ruhr in the 1920s. On October 28 Bevin cabled Schuman and Acheson, urging that the Foreign Ministers meet for an immediate review of dismantling. The fall in Allied prestige had resulted from "the fact that our joint policy in Germany has not been properly coordinated and proclaimed." This was the time to act together to bolster the Adenauer government and associate "Germany closely with the Western world."[44]

Acheson, who recognized Bevin's message as an aid to ridding himself of an irritant in Congress, urged another Foreign Ministers' meeting. In a letter to Schuman he expressed his concern that "events were taking control, and that in the last analysis the problem was whether we could move shoulder to shoulder fast enough to lead and not be controlled by events which were taking on an all too familiar pattern." The pattern Acheson saw was similar to that which was causing French worries about developments in Germany, but his solution was altogether different. Rather than showing the Germans "unbending firmness," he argued that "the 1920's teach us that we must give genuine and rapid support to those elements now in control of Germany if they are to be expected to retain control." He added that "extremist views and weakening of the allegiance to democratic principles will come if these parties and their supporters are not strengthened." Moreover, Allied vacillation might encourage the Germans to turn to the Soviet Union, a country which Acheson believed was encouraging "anti-democratic and aggressive tendencies" in Germany. But he again stressed that the Allies should only move as far as France would allow. He did not want to "add to his [Schuman's] problems," but it seemed that this was "the time for French initiative and leadership of the type required to integrate the German Federal Republic promptly and decisively into Western Europe."[45]

In preparing the American position for the Paris meeting, McCloy recommended to Acheson that the three powers approve a broad negotiating strategy for the High Commission to implement. He thought the "crux of the matter" was the August-Thyssen works, because allowing this plant to remain open meant a "substantial increase in the permissible production of primary steel point on which French are exceptionally sensitive." McCloy urged Acheson to insist that the Allied strategy be "something more than a mere surrender to German agitation on dismantling." It should be "evidence of the continuity of our policy respecting the development of the West German state." The State Department agreed that any solution "should not only be acceptable to the Federal Government of Germany but should be of such a character as to enhance the prestige of that Government vis-à-vis dissident and anti-democratic elements within Germany." Although some American officials, including President Truman, worried about retaining a steel production capacity in Germany in excess of the quota, the State Department argued that the anticipated glut of steel meant that such facilities would not be used in the near future. The State Department acknowledged the "special interests" of the British and French, but argued that "we can, perhaps, bring a certain detachment to the treatment of German problems which it is difficult for other peoples to attain."[46]

When the Paris talks began on November 9, 1949, American "detachment" was perceived by the British to mean a disregard for their interests. Early in the talks Bevin attacked McCloy for using "pressure tactics." With characteristic aplomb, Acheson defused the tension with a quote from the Book of Common Prayer: "The contemplation of our misdeeds is grievous unto us and the burden of them is intolerable." Schuman quickly interjected that the same prayer was in the Catholic rituals. The tension broken, Bevin laughed and said that as a "bush Baptist" he had never heard that particular prayer. The rest of the conference, which Ivone Kirkpatrick later described as an "exceedingly difficult meeting," revealed Schuman's deep concern over Germany's retention of excess steel capacity, a situation that had both security and economic dimensions. Acheson tried to ease his concerns by agreeing not to raise the German steel quota above 11.1 million tons of production and also promising that Marshall Plan assistance would not be used to rebuild partially dismantled plants. Schuman was pleased with the capacity the Allies had already dismantled— about six hundred industrial plants—as well as the Anglo-American promise to continue dismantling "war plants." Finally the French agreed to a compromise. The Allies would spare the August-Thyssen works, but the Watenstedt-Salzgitter plant—formerly the Hermann-Goering works—would remain on the list, even though its dismantling would mean laying off between three and four thousand workers. The Foreign Ministers gave the High Commissioners a list of specific plants whose "reprieve" they could grant in return for German willingness to join the Ruhr Authority and to cooperate with the Military Security Board (MSB), the Allied agency which enforced the demilitarization of Germany. If the Germans would also agree to accept the Allied programs of decartelization and civil service reform, more concessions would be possible. To assist the High Commissioners, the Foreign Ministers decided to keep all these decisions secret.[47]

After the meeting McCloy persuaded Acheson to accompany him to Bonn. The Secretary of State became the first foreign statesman to visit the new German capital and hold talks with both Adenauer and Schumacher. The remarkable contrast, in content, tone, and atmosphere, between the conversations with the two German leaders had important implications for American policy. Adenauer began by telling Acheson that the German nation was in a state of "mental instability" resulting from the events of the past thirty-five years. The only way to guide the population through the next few years would be to maintain the closest possible links with the West. Adenauer referred to an old German proverb which showed that Germans "take on the color of the wall," or tend to conform to their environment. The integration of Germany into Western Europe would make the Germans "Europeans," allowing for the "rebirth of Europe" and a real and lasting reconciliation with France. Alluding to German history, Adenauer stressed the differences between East and West Germany: the influence of Roman and Christian culture throughout the centuries had tied West Germans closer to France and Western Europe, while Eastern Germany looked to Russia. He concluded by contrasting his own conciliatory attitude with the nationalism of the SPD, adding that "in Dr. Schumacher, the Secretary would meet a typical East German."[48]

Adenauer's comments on the instability, divisions, and weaknesses of the German people were remarkably candid, but they were also a clever attempt to appeal for American support. Acheson was clearly impressed. He stressed the need for Adenauer to work harmoniously with the High Commissioners, to which the Chancellor responded that working with McCloy, who had such a "warm-hearted under-standing of German problems," would never be difficult. Acheson then emphasized the need for progress in Franco-German reconcilia-tion, to keep the American public interested in Europe. If Western European countries cooperated with each other, Americans would be willing to assist Europe both politically and economically. Adenauer said he understood this, but reminded Acheson of the German fear that Russia would assert its domination after America withdrew. He promised Acheson that he would use his power to bring Germany into the circle of the West European nations.[49]

Acheson later wrote that during his talk with Adenauer he had begun to feel that he could rely on the German government to make important concessions when these were necessary for the success of American policy. "There seemed to me a feeling that [the Germans'] hope lay with America . . . that we could do more with the Germans than the French or British could." Even McCloy's "high praise" of Adenauer "had not prepared me for views from the head of the German Government which raised such hope for a new day in Eu-rope." In fact these feelings had not come to Acheson immediately. Never one for immediate conversions, he took actions during the next few months, on issues such as the Saar, that reflected a continued mistrust of Germany. Still, he did sense in the Chancellor a man with whom he could deal, one who wanted to tie his country's and his own political fortunes to the successful consolidation of an American-led Western alliance. And recognizing that Adenauer was still a politically obscure and untested figure, Acheson sought to build up the Chan-cellor's stature with the German people. On the way to the Bonn train station after their meeting, when Acheson saw that a large and excited crowd had gathered, he took the reluctant Chancellor into the middle of it in the manner of an American politician searching for votes. The cheers for America moved even Acheson, who had faced hostility from critics at home. As he later remarked, "things like that do affect one's judgment as much as things you read in cablegrams."[50]

Acheson's affection for Adenauer became even more solid after he met Kurt Schumacher. Schumacher began their talk with a series of rapid-fire, aggressive questions that revealed his dislike for the secrecy still surrounding the Paris talks. When he denounced Adenauer's gov-ernment as unrepresentative of the German people, Acheson re-sponded that a great many Americans had thought the same about

President Truman before the elections of 1948. Then Acheson, urging the SPD leader to adopt a more moderate tone, suggested a bipartisan foreign policy. But Schumacher, although assuring Acheson that the SPD opposed the Russians and not the Western occupation powers, continued to speak with a political passion that ruffled the normally unflappable Secretary. In Acheson's view Schumacher combined a "harsh and violent nature with nationalistic and aggressive ideas"; he was "a fanatic of a dangerous and pure type . . . as long as he was in command of the Social Democratic Party it was going to be hopeless."[51]

While in Germany Acheson also affirmed McCloy's position there. He told the German leaders that McCloy spoke with "the complete confidence and full support of the President of the United States and his Secretary of State," adding that "when anyone speaks for the United States in Germany, it will be Mr. McCloy."[52]

The positive atmosphere created by Acheson's visit carried over into the negotiating sessions between the High Commissioners and Adenauer. At the first session on November 15 Robertson, that month's chairman of the AHC, told Adenauer the results of the Paris meeting, emphasizing the Allied hope that Germany would join more of the international organizations and would limit further dismantling. McCloy added that while many of the PLI limits and quotas remained, and the Allies still "did not aim at increasing the German economic potential . . . neither was it intended to fix the present state of affairs for all eternity." From the perspective of the Western Allies McCloy's words were not particularly well chosen, for they seemed to invite further challenges from Germany. But they revealed McCloy's frustration with the Allies' restrictive approach to Germany's future and the hope that a positive solution, stressing European cooperation and economic growth, would replace the negative strategy.[53]

The High Commissioners also asked Adenauer to state whether his government was ready to join the Ruhr Authority. At that point the Chancellor appeared to back off from his previous commitment by raising doubts about Article 31 of the Ruhr Statutes. This article seemed to him to give a "blank check" to any decisions of the IAR, and Germany could not agree to that. Some wording should be added to the agreement that would bring Germany into the Authority but at the same time allow it to work for the revision of the IAR statutes. Rejecting Adenauer's interpretation of the article, the Allies insisted that the Germans must not attempt to attach conditions to their membership. As Robertson put it, accession to the Ruhr Statute was "the essential condition" of a settlement.[54]

After his first meeting with the AHC Adenauer reported to the Bundestag on his negotiations. The Social Democrats vigorously opposed joining the Ruhr Authority, maintaining that it was too high a price to pay for a halt to dismantling. Adenauer's answer was typical of his pragmatic and realistic approach to foreign policy. Responding to the SPD's specific suggestion that the Allies must give Germany its sovereignty before the Federal Republic made any concessions, he asked bluntly, "Who, after all, do you think has lost the war?" Adenauer realized, however, that the SPD's rhetoric would help his position with the Commissioners; and when he next met with the AHC, he stressed the paradoxical difference between the late 1940s and the 1920s, for the nationalists were now on the left in the Bundestag, not on the right.[55]

Although Adenauer's stand against nationalism impressed them, the Allies wanted him to act more decisively against the remaining "authoritarian" and "Bismarckian" influences in German public life. McCloy, who admitted that this "was a matter hard to put into words," stressed the American interest in civil service reform, which would reduce the elite status of the German civil service. He approved of Adenauer's policy of bringing the "little Nazis" back into the community, but reminded him that Americans were worried about former Nazis regaining positions of influence.[56]

Although Adenauer formally agreed to cooperate with civil service reform, he himself was quite willing to use civil servants who had worked in the Third Reich. He attached enormous importance to restoring Germany's prestige in the West, but his understanding of how to purge Germany of "authoritarianism" or to limit the influence of "former Nazis" was quite different from McCloy's. Adenauer saw a sharp distinction between Germany's authoritarian traditions and the particular evil of Nazism, and he insisted that he could not govern effectively without the use of former civil servants, even those who had cooperated with Nazi policies. Later in his term he appointed Hans Globke as his State Secretary, despite the fact that Globke had helped write the infamous Nuremberg laws. To Adenauer, resistance to the Nazis would have been either very exceptional behavior or the product of a wishful re-creation of the past. He had far less faith than

McCloy in the "other Germany" of the July 20 plot against Hitler, skeptically noting that "in the plot of 20th July more people have had their finger than actually live in Germany." Although Adenauer had never had any sympathy with Nazism, his cynical outlook on human nature inclined him to a more lenient view of those who had served the Nazi state. McCloy later compared Adenauer's attitude to that of Abraham Lincoln and his hopes for Reconstruction after the Civil War. The Chancellor did not want "to divide the German people irrevocably" into "sheep and goats."[57]

Adenauer played for time. He knew that the stronger his own position became, the less the Allies were likely to "rock the boat" with such issues as civil service reform. Unfortunately, his approach simply postponed that problem until the time when a new generation of Germans would challenge the forgiving attitude toward collaboration that Adenauer represented.

The final agreement, known as the Petersberg Protocols, followed the Foreign Ministers' guidelines. In return for German cooperation with the Ruhr Authority, the MSB, and the decartelization and de-mocratization policies, the Western Allies spared eleven synthetic oil and rubber plants and seven steel plants, and stopped all dismantling in Berlin. In a separate protocol they relaxed shipbuilding restrictions. Germany was also permitted to open consulates abroad, setting up a bureau in Bonn to direct them. To Adenauer the agreement repre-sented a "great step forward" in his policy of "cooperation based on mutual trust" and the integration of Germany into "the orbit of Western Europe." It was the first success of his "fulfillment policy," or as he described it, "making the necessary possible."[58]

The Petersberg Protocols, which were adopted only two months after the proclamation of the Occupation Statute, were a tribute to the Adenauer government's ability to turn its original weakness into strength. But although they ended an outdated and destructive policy, the Protocols stirred up controversy throughout Germany. Adenauer's triumphant unveiling of the agreement to the Bundestag on November 24 led to a bitter debate in which the SPD attacked the Allies for pursuing a policy in favor of big business which served to "prop up an authoritarian Adenauer regime" rather than "allow it to be replaced by a democratic regime." The Socialists had been outmaneuvered, and they resented Adenauer's success. Schumacher was particularly angered by the policy of the trade union leader, Hans Böckler, who, despite his opposition to the Ruhr Authority, supported Adenauer's agreement. When Adenauer suggested that perhaps the SPD "preferred" continued dismantling to an agreement negotiated by its political opponents, Schumacher shouted that Adenauer was the "Chancellor of the Allies." Pandemonium broke out in the Bundestag, and Schumacher had to be suspended for twenty sessions. Coverage of the incident in the international press gave the impression of instability, weakness, and division in the young republic.[59]

McCloy quickly stepped in to encourage a settlement. He met privately with representatives of both parties, reminding them of the importance to Germany of cultivating American public opinion, which could have a positive influence on economic aid. He suggested a compromise whereby Schumacher would apologize to Adenauer and have his suspension lifted and Adenauer would retract his statement about the SPD and dismantling. But the damage had been done. Over the next few weeks Adenauer's refusal to submit the Protocols to the Bundestag for approval, along with Schumacher's insistence that an SPD government would not consider itself bound by any agreement, brought back memories of an authoritarian and unreliable Germany. As the State Department analyst in Bonn wrote, "Truth is that Adenauer with his age and dictatorial tendencies and Schumacher with his sensitivity and excitability are problem children for their respective parties." The day after the Adenauer-Schumacher confrontation, the British High Commissioner stated firmly, "We are not expecting that this agreement should be regarded as a stepping stone for further demands." Yet the parliamentary conflict and the need for Germany's continuing revival would quickly put such firmness to the test.[60]

4

Monnet and the Schuman Plan

The Petersberg Protocols did not pacify West Germany: German leaders continued to demand changes in Allied policy. Uncertainty over the direction to be followed by the Federal Republic contributed to the general sense of drift among American policymakers in early 1950, touched off by the Soviet atomic test and the fall of China in late 1949. Despite the successes of the Marshall Plan, the Berlin Blockade, and NATO, American leaders were deeply concerned that, as Acheson told McCloy, the United States had allowed its "great advantages" to slip away. Somehow America needed to come up with a "new approach" to "recapture the initiative" from the Soviet Union. Washington perceived a Europe in which British detachment, French neutralism, and the German resurgence seemed destined to allow the pattern of the interwar years to repeat itself. As a result, American attention turned to the problem of alliance consolidation, to building a position of strength within the West in order to oppose Soviet aims more successfully. Only in the light of this atmosphere of pessimism and uncertainty is it possible to understand the powerful support which American leaders gave to the Schuman Plan of May 1950, a proposal they viewed as the "most important act of Western statesmanship since the launching of the Marshall Plan."[1]

Germany at the Crossroads

A British diplomat captured succinctly the dilemma which the Western Allies faced in their treatment of Germany when he wrote, "It will not be pleasing or easy to treat Germany as a partner and equal, but we cannot have it both ways." The Western powers, he concluded, would have to make Germany "a full member of the club and reconcile ourselves to seeing her smoking a large cigar in front of the fire in the smoking room." This problem—accepting Germany as a member of the Western "club" despite European fear and resentment—bedeviled Allied-German relations. It influenced McCloy's efforts to improve his political relationship with Chancellor Adenauer after agreement had been reached on the Petersberg Protocols. When McCloy returned to the United States in early 1950 to defend his policies and testify before Congress, he became acutely aware of the concern about Germany. American observers complained that developments there were taking on a familiar pattern, that nationalism was reasserting itself, and that the Germans would never change and could not be trusted. Although McCloy had the power to "crack down" on Germany, he resisted the demands to do so, knowing that such action would undermine Adenauer, and argued that the best way to approach the Germans was "to encourage the positive affirmative elements, and there are many fine elements among them." He believed that "at this stage of history there is a better chance to influence the German mind than there has been for a century." Adenauer, for his part, pursued his goal of Western integration with an urgency and insistence that made the Allies uncomfortable. He proposed dramatic actions, such as the political unification of France and Germany and the convening of a European parliament to draft a constitution. And he used the media, especially the American newspapers, to insist that the Allies must act quickly to bring Germany into the West as an equal and respected partner, to prevent a resurgence of nationalism that would endanger Western Europe's security and invite Soviet expansion.[2]

Despite the similarity in goals, the McCloy-Adenauer relationship remained fragile. Adenauer complained bitterly about criticism from the High Commission, asserting that it undermined his stature with the German people. He himself criticized McCloy for not consulting him about Allied plans for Germany, which he took, with good reason, as continuing evidence of his exclusion from the Western "club." McCloy, who disliked the Chancellor's extreme partisanship and autocratic style of governing, hinted at the desirability of a grand coalition of the CDU and SPD, a political change which would have replaced Adenauer. In a long private conversation held in April 1950, the two men revealed their suspicions and doubts with surprising frankness. The specific problem, German entry into the Council of Europe, proved less important than the larger issues that came up. The Chancellor informed McCloy that the Germans saw on one side a weak, disarmed Western Europe disunified and plagued with crises, while on the other side they saw the powerful, unified bloc of Russia and its satellites, rearming rapidly. Many Germans, especially certain industrialists, were saying that it would be more advantageous to look for markets in the East than in the West. Others advocated a neutral policy for the Federal Republic. Referring to the talk of a new German nationalism, Adenauer told McCloy that such nationalists would seek support from the Soviet Union. He concluded that the United States must act decisively to offset weakness in the West.[3]

The Chancellor's complaints, and especially his reference to a possible German-Soviet understanding, raised sensitive issues. McCloy insisted that the Germans must not create the impression that they were delaying their entry into the Council of Europe because they were hoping for some gesture from the Soviets that could be used as a bargaining chip with the West. Such an attempt to play off East against West renewed memories of Germany's earlier Schaukelpolitik (seesaw policy) and destroyed the trust between Germany and the West that was essential for progress in European integration. McCloy also warned Adenauer that any thought of a neutral policy was chimerical, since the Soviets would never respect German neutrality. He counseled Adenauer to be more patient, to understand that the Federal Republic would have to be accepted in European affairs as "the weight of 48 million Germans" made itself felt. As a final warning McCloy raised the possibility of America's reverting to isolationism, especially if the American people thought that the Europeans would not put aside their differences in order to resist the Soviet Union.[4]

These sensitive issues—a revival of German nationalism and Schaukelpolitik, the possibility of neutralism, a German-Soviet alliance, a return to American isolationism—reflect how strongly the interwar experience continued to dominate the thoughts of policymakers as they tried to break out of history's grasp. Why had these concerns become more acute by early 1950? The first reason was Adenauer's desire to strengthen the German government. He was determined to prove that Schumacher had been wrong in saying that he was the "Chancellor of the Allies." Although his perception of the interests of the Federal Republic differed from Schumacher's, the Chancellor expressed those interests with a conviction and persistence that unsettled the Allies, who had grown accustomed to more deference from "their" Germans. Despite his agreement to cooperate with the rest of the dismantling process, he continued to press publicly for an end to the program. He provoked foreign criticism by singing the third verse of the controversial "Deutschland über alles" at a political rally, arguing that he did not want the song to become "the property of the nationalists." He urged continually that the Western powers show respect for his government as the only legitimate representative of German interests.[5]

The second reason for concern resulted from the ending of most Allied censorship, which allowed nationalist and neo-Nazi ideas to be expressed. Two members of Adenauer's Cabinet, Thomas Dehler and Hans-Christoph Seebohm, delivered fiery nationalist speeches, denouncing the Western Allies for Germany's troubles and blaming them for the rise of Hitler. Sensational reports of a secret military organization, the Brüderschaft, fueled concerns about the nationalist activities of former Wehrmacht soldiers. A Bundestag deputy from the German party publicly questioned whether the Holocaust had occurred. The *New York Times* obtained a HICOG confidential report entitled "Nationalism in Western Germany," which painted a picture of political apathy and indifference and concluded that "the struggle for the mind of Germany has only begun and is far from won." Such developments led Congress to approve an investigation into U.S. policy and the growth of nationalism in the Federal Republic.[6]

But the most worrisome problem came not from the speeches of a few politicians or from HICOG's reports, but from issues that were strikingly reminiscent of those of the interwar era. The most important of these was the future of the Saar, a question which mingled national sentiment with concrete political and economic interests.

Located on the German-French border, the Saar was a small, minerally rich region only slightly larger than Rhode Island. Historically a center of dispute between Germany and France, it had reverted to provisional French control after the war. Germany's economic revival after the currency reform dramatically increased pro-German sentiment within the region, threatening to undermine Franco-German rapprochement. Only a few days before Robert Schuman's first official visit to Bonn in January 1950, Paris revealed that France and the Saar planned to open talks on new economic and administrative treaties.

The most important provisions would give France a fifty-year lease on the Saar coal mines and integrate the Saar railways into the French system. To German leaders this was clear evidence that the French were setting up a fait accompli before the peace treaty was signed, to insure an economic integration of the Saar which would make permanent its political detachment from Germany. Encouraged by his industrialist supporters and egged on by Schumacher's denunciation of the accords as creating a new "Alsace-Lorraine," Adenauer not only raised the issue with Schuman, surprising and angering him, but also sought McCloy's intervention. After insisting that he did not consider the Saar important to Germany in the long run and cared little about the railroads or the administrative arrangements, he said, however, that the French action would weaken German territorial claims in the East and could ignite nationalist sentiment. Adenauer impressed McCloy with his "sincerity," especially in suggesting some type of "international" arrangement for the Saar; but Acheson, who remained unmoved, strongly rebuked the Chancellor for taking this position, noting that French control of the Saar was one of the "consequences" of the war that the Germans had started.[7]

Acheson's rebuke calmed the waters temporarily, but the issue emerged again at the beginning of March, when Paris finalized its agreement with the Saar. The treaties insured that the Saar's coal mines and railroads would continue to operate under French control. When Adenauer protested the accords and announced that his government would not join the Council of Europe, American leaders were dismayed. They thought of the Council, a consultative and largely symbolic organization based in Strasbourg, as "one of the many forces working for Western unity" and saw German membership as a way of "enmeshing" the Federal Republic in another international organization. After Adenauer realized that German membership in the Council had taken on symbolic significance in the United States, he attempted to bargain for more concessions, insisting that the Federal Republic must be invited to join the Council before it could apply for membership. This led François-Poncet to complain, "You always want other people to make gestures." The Chancellor shot back that "if it had not been for the Saar, an invitation would not have been necessary." Adenauer got his invitation on April 1, 1950, but when he discovered that the Council had also invited the Saar to join with the same "associative" status, he reacted indignantly, telling an interviewer that Germany would not join without further concessions and complaining, "Time and again I have put out my hand to France only to have it spurned." François-Poncet was so angry at the Chancellor that he told his deputy that Adenauer should resign. Ultimately Adenauer's demands for further concessions were unsuccessful, and in early May he asked for and received his Cabinet's approval for German membership in the Strasbourg organization.[8]

Political tensions over the Saar and the Council of Europe were aggravated by the issue of German reunification. Kurt Schumacher raised the unity question during the Bundestag debate on Germany's entrance into the Council. Viewing his own commitment to reunification as of paramount importance—"We cannot regard as a friend of the German people anyone whose political actions deny or hinder German unity"—Schumacher and the SPD opposed membership on the grounds that it would mean abandoning East Germany. Other prominent voices joined the Socialist leader's. Pastor Martin Niemöller, a courageous foe of Hitler and influential leader of the Protestant Church, criticized both the Allies and Adenauer for their lack of action on German reunification. Niemöller's charge reflected his suspicion that the Chancellor's Catholicism accounted for his indifference toward German unity, for East Germany was heavily Protestant. The Americans and British were particularly sensitive to this issue, fearing that "West Germany will not become either a firm or responsible member of an integrated Western Europe, unless and until it is convinced that Western Europe is interested in the unification of Germany, and that integration with Western Europe does not, therefore, connote a writing off of the East." McCloy insisted that "we must get the western Germans more on the offensive against the eastern Germans," even though Adenauer was "not interested in the question, and again the French are reluctant to move in this direction." It was not until March 22, 1950, that the Adenauer government proposed a plan for free elections in all Germany, three weeks after the first American proposal had been made and two months after the East German regime had announced its own unity referendum.[9]

These political questions were inextricably linked to a series of economic concerns. The interwar era had demonstrated that economic instability and hardship in Germany would fuel political extremism and nationalist agitation. Yet the dilemma of the moment was that economic hardship might fuel nationalism, but a rapid resurgence of

Germany's economic power would certainly create political insecurity in Britain and especially in France. In early 1950 the Federal Republic presented a strange mixture of economic weaknesses and strengths. Germany's industrial production had reached prewar levels, but its problems were so great that McCloy's economic adviser described the country "as flat on its ass." Most American officials doubted whether it could achieve "viability" by 1952, the cutoff date for Marshall Plan assistance. The most serious problem was unemployment, which hit a postwar high of 12.2 percent of the labor force, or more than two million workers in the first quarter of 1950. The lack of investment capital and the severe housing shortage also posed such difficulties that some Allied officials worried about the unfavorable comparison with East Germany. One British study concluded that even though the standard of living in the East lagged behind that of the Federal Republic, East Germany had two advantages: "tolerable housing conditions for everyone and security against unemployment." Almost a third of the jobless in the Federal Republic were refugees from the "lost territories," a political consideration that was not lost upon Allied policymakers. The number dramatically increased in March, following the expulsion of an additional 125,000 Germans from the Oder-Neisse area of Poland. This led the British High Commissioner to conclude: "This is a Russian trick to upset the economy of Western Germany." The Allies feared that unless the refugees were integrated into West Germany's economy and society, they would constitute a source of political extremism and would support irredentist adventures.[10]

Because of the perceived dangers of a weak German economy, the American High Commission wanted the Adenauer government to act more aggressively on economic policy. In dealing with these issues McCloy's role as head of ECA in Germany afforded him more leverage with the Germans than either the French or the British possessed. The ECA Agreement, which Germany had signed in December 1949 (the Federal Republic's first treaty with a foreign country), allowed the first significant release of counterpart funds into the capital-starved German economy. (Counterpart funds were those local currency funds generated through the sale of Marshall Plan commodities. The United States and the recipient country together determined how these funds would be used.) As required by ECA rules, late in the 1949 German government submitted a memorandum proposing a plan for the utilization of Marshall Plan assistance. This, however, turned out to be less a plan than a lament. It blamed Germany's economic problems on Allied policies, singling out the influx of refugees and pointing to the industrial limits and prohibitions on German economic activity. The Germans saw Allied agencies, such as the Military Security Board, as forms of "industrial espionage" and sought ways to circumvent them. They also argued that German unemployment was largely "structural" in nature and could not be reduced through government policies. The memo, which was utterly pessimistic, was intended not only as a technical analysis but also as an appeal for a greater share of Marshall Plan assistance.[11]

The American response, which leaked to the press in what came to be known as the "war of the memoranda," sharply criticized the "laissez-faire and defeatist attitude" embodied in the German plan and urged a "careful expansionary monetary and fiscal policy." American policymakers, who regarded questions of economic policy as technical rather than political, valued flexibility. Many Americans in Germany, including McCloy, while sympathizing with Ludwig Erhard's vision of a German economy with more competition, an export orientation, and less government tutelage, considered some forms of planning and control essential in a modern economy, especially when that economy relied on American assistance. Within Adenauer's government, Erhard and the members of the smaller coalition parties resisted the American demands, arguing that expansionary credit measures would cause inflation and damage the value of the currency. To deal with the American critique and obtain the release of more counterpart funds, Adenauer proposed a modest job-creation program. He pointedly assured the Allies that he was "not another Brüning"—a reference to the last Weimar chancellor, whose harsh deflationary policies had undermined the political stability of the republic. The tension eased, but the Americans still felt that the Adenauer government was not acting vigorously enough to solve Germany's economic problems.[12]

The differing American and German views on economic policy resulted in more political conflict over the German income tax law in April 1950. At McCloy's insistence the AHC provisionally vetoed a tax reform measure, passed by the Bundestag, that was designed to encourage capital formation by lowering taxes proportionately more for upper-income than for lower-income groups. American officials estimated that this reform would increase Germany's budget deficit by DM 800 million, raising it to DM 1 billion, a deficit that American aid would have to cover. McCloy feared Congress would find it difficult to accept such a German proposal. Adenauer decided to turn the veto of the tax law into an occasion for a public protest against Allied interference, and a group within his Cabinet even urged resignation. Reason prevailed, however, and the Chancellor agreed to submit a luxury tax bill to make up for any loss of revenue.[13]

Germany's growing trade deficit also caused concern among American policymakers. Marshall Plan officials in Washington, in accord with Erhard and other German leaders, had encouraged a substantial liberalization of Germany's trade policies. Indeed ECA Washington believed that Germany should serve as a model of the American concept of free trade for other countries in Western Europe. The initial results, however, did not please many HICOG officials, who watched as Germany's balance of payments deficit ballooned to $1.1 billion in 1949 and the country was flooded with "luxury imports" from its European neighbors. Although some wanted the Bonn government to reintroduce import controls, German leaders complained that other Western nations had not yet matched their measures of liberalization. The trade deficit also led to increasing complaints in Germany about the loss of its prewar markets. Some important voices, such as the *Frankfurter Allgemeine Zeitung,* urged more trade with the Soviet Union and Eastern Europe. McCloy told a British official that the "Russians are offering the Germans a market from Poland to the Pacific," and that "many Germans have always believed that the natural market of Germany lay in the South and East." To American leaders this posed the clear danger of directing Germany's political orientation away from the West. One intelligence report used a comparison that American leaders could readily understand: "The man whose business or job depends largely or partly on friendly relations with the USSR is not likely to vote Communist for such a reason, but he is not unlikely either to be affected by his actual economic dependence in a way that is not basically different from the manner in which the Marshall Plan has influenced public opinion in Western Europe."[14]

Unemployment, budget deficits, and trade with the East were minor concerns to Allied officials compared with their worry about Germany's coal and steel production. More than any other issue the future of heavy industry and the Ruhr reminded observers of the pattern of events after World War I. These memories—the French occupation of the Ruhr to insure coal deliveries, the German hyperinflation which followed, the subsequent role of the Ruhr in Hitler's war effort—influenced all discussion and thinking about these issues. In the Petersberg Protocols the Allies had allowed West Germany to retain considerable unused steel production capacity in the Ruhr, far exceeding the German production quota of 11.1 million tons per year. By 1950 the demand for steel had begun to slacken in Western Europe, and production had fallen off in France and Belgium. By contrast, the combination of pent-up demand and underutilized capacity led to an expansion of steel production in West Germany and the reentry of German steel exports into European markets. The Germans signaled in their ECA plan that they would challenge the limits and quotas placed on their industries by the Allies.[15]

In addition to considering the quota, the High Commission was also finishing its work on a new law which would define and regulate the position of the coal and steel industry in West Germany. Since 1945 the Allies had sought to transform Germany's heavy industry, debating programs of nationalization, deconcentration, and international control and limitation. They sought a "New Order" which would alter the patterns of ownership, the internal structure, and the labor relations of these vital industries. When the British and Americans ran Bizonia, they decided on Law 75 as the instrument for decentralizing and returning these industries to German control. After the merger of Bizonia with the French zone, the law was to be renegotiated and reissued under a new number. Both the quota issue and the new law raised a dilemma for the Allied leaders, who sought a way for German coal and steel, the sinews of military power and economic strength, to contribute to the West's strength rather than to undermine its unity and stability.[16]

In the weeks before the May conference of Foreign Ministers in London, the Americans increasingly inclined toward liberalizing the Allied controls. In April 1950 Acheson informed Foreign Minister Schuman that the United States would side with Britain on the central issue still in dispute on the new Law 27—the ownership of the Ruhr industries. Though each country had its own preference—the United States for private ownership, the British for nationalization—the Anglo-Saxon powers were prepared to allow a "freely elected German government" to decide the question of ownership. Acheson explained that the West could not "risk the possibility of serious political and economic disturbances in Germany" by overthrowing a commitment already made in Law 75. Although the Secretary did not raise the subject of steel production limits, the French knew that McCloy had criticized them as shortsighted and increasingly irrelevant, arguing that a "progressively liberalized western European economy has little to fear and much to gain from [a] strengthened and more productive German economy," because it would provide the "basis for firm establishment [of] democratic government in western Germany." He added, "What German democracy needs and has never had is success in the eyes of the German people." Although controls on German shipbuilding or steel production might have seemed "logical in the context of postwar international cooperation" with the Soviet Union, they made no sense in the "divided world" of Cold War Europe, only alienating Germans who might otherwise support the West. In McCloy's view, the fear of a revived and powerful Germany was preventing the pursuit of a peaceful and cooperative Germany.[17]

To French leaders the American position was a clear indication that their own policy on the Ruhr was nearing collapse. The IAR was increasingly being seen as "a white elephant." With a total budget of less than $300,000 and no statistical services, it had no direct authority over the German government, but could act only through the AHC, where the real power remained. Since the Ruhr Authority had been designed to insure French access to scarce Ruhr coal—two-thirds of the coking coal requirements of the French were met by Ruhr deliveries—a growing surplus of coal in early 1950 left the agency without any real function. France, which had hoped to change the balance of economic power in Europe by creating a larger steel industry than Germany's, found itself still dependent on the Ruhr but without any real voice in the future of this pivotal region.[18]

Domestic politics in the United States increased the pressure on Acheson to devise new policies. Under attack for the "loss of China" and his "defeatist" approach, the Secretary of State had become the lightning rod for domestic critics. His defense of Alger Hiss after the latter's conviction for perjury further inflamed his opponents. McCarthy's charge that there were Communists in the State Department appealed to millions of Americans searching for an explanation of the Cold War and the expansion of Soviet power. This atmosphere, together with the various political and economic issues, the sense that some action was needed to prevent a repetition of the interwar era, and the perception of being at an important historical turning point, created a belief among Americans, expressed strongly by McCloy, that there was an "urgency in the situation" which led them to look for "some imaginative and creative policy which will link Western Germany more firmly into the West and make the Germans believe their destiny lies this way." McCloy himself wanted, and spoke publicly for, "prompt action" to create a politically "united Europe" as the only lasting solution to the German problem. He urged Acheson to tell the French that "we view the Federation of Europe as a vital cornerstone upon which our whole fundamental policy rests and that the barriers to effective progress along this line rest primarily in the French attitude toward Germany." He concluded that "to secure the peace of Europe, Germany and France must come to a peaceful and harmonious settlement of their difficulties and develop a progressive and common policy in Europe."[19]

Nevertheless, as the May meeting of Foreign Ministers approached, neither London nor Washington was prepared to offer any new or startling proposals about Germany. The British only planned to propose the lifting of a few controls, mainly those dealing with political matters. Acheson remained skeptical about the drastic schemes of political confederation being discussed in the State Department and was not prepared to propose any new organization, such as a North Atlantic Union. He did, however, plan the "re-introduction of Germany into community life," a task calling for the "sacrifice of purely national interests." He concluded that "no harder enterprise than this has ever been undertaken jointly by a group of nations," a statement indicative of the lingering uneasiness over accepting Germany into the Western alliance.[20]

The lack of Anglo-American initiatives, coupled with the signal from the United States that it would welcome action, provided an opening for French leadership. Jean Monnet sensed this opportunity and offered France an alternative to its failed policies.

Jean Monnet

In May 1950 neither the Americans nor the British expected the French government to take a major foreign policy initiative. The British Foreign Office, studying France's world role in late 1949, concluded that with its myriad problems—"muddled politics, a weak economy, poor armed forces"—France was "not much" use to Britain.

The strength of neutralist sentiment, expressed in the pages of *Le Monde,* along with the continuing hold of the Communist party over the working class, weakened successive French governments. France was unable to prevent the creation of a new German state, and her restrictive policies toward Germany continued to meet defeat. Even as sympathetic an observer as the American lawyer George Ball commented that the mood in France reflected a "resurgence of introspection, a slackening of vitality, and the insidious exhumation of old, dark rivalries, fears, and complexes." Before the May Conference the Quai d'Orsay had no new strategy to deal with the Ruhr question. The only idea Prime Minister Bidault planned to present concerned an "Atlantic High Council for Peace," a loosely structured organization which, he promised, might someday embrace Germany.[21]

Into this vacuum stepped Jean Monnet, a man whose influence remains impossible to measure but difficult to underestimate. To General de Gaulle, his great rival and critic, Monnet was "the inspirer with his panacea called fusion," a man whose actions conformed to Washington's interests, not those of Paris. In a recent historical treatment of the period, Alan Milward caustically refers to Monnet as "an assiduous self-publicist and a remarkable collector of disciples." But for a "self-publicist" Monnet is little known, and although he did have many "disciples," these were not spineless figures but some of the most distinguished American and European statesmen of the era. For that reason, and because he played such an important role in influencing his friend, John McCloy, this brandy salesman from France deserves special attention.[22]

Jean Monnet was born in the small French town of Cognac on November 9, 1888. Cognac was a village concerned with brandy, and Monnet's grandfather had established a thriving family business in this profitable liquor. Monnet left school at sixteen and began training for the business. Prior to the First World War he spent most of his time traveling the world, especially the English-speaking countries, selling his father's brandy. He acquired both a cosmopolitan attitude and a perfect knowledge of English, including British and American idioms and a New England accent. His friend André Fontaine observed that Monnet's "education, far from being classical, was personal and pragmatic. He knows more English words than he does French." Indeed Monnet came to admire and respect the "Anglo-Saxon" mentality and temperament that so confused, and at times angered, his countrymen.

His personal wealth always gave him independence, and it endowed him with a self-confidence, persistence, and even boldness that would wear down his opposition.

Physically unfit for military service in the First World War, Monnet was well qualified for the role he played—working on the inter-Allied purchasing enterprises designed to make the best use of scarce resources. It took almost three years to bring some direction to this war effort, but the Allied Maritime Transport Executive played an important role in the final year of the war. It also gave Monnet a strong conviction that international cooperation was the key to solving problems, and that such cooperation required governments strong enough to plan and direct economic policy as well as bend private interests to cooperative goals. After the war Monnet became Deputy Secretary-General of the League of Nations and worked on such problems as the Saar and Silesia. Among the Americans he met at Versailles was the international lawyer and diplomat John Foster Dulles, with whom he was to maintain a lifelong friendship. Dulles served as Monnet's lawyer later in the 1920s when both had returned to private life. (Monnet would later say, with great acuity, that "nothing important is done in the United States without lawyers.")

In 1923 Monnet abruptly resigned from the League in order to return to Cognac and rescue the faltering family business. Two years later, with that accomplished, he joined Blair and Company of New York, an investment bank which specialized in loans to governments and national banks seeking to stabilize their currencies. Under the Blair aegis Monnet worked to stabilize both the Polish and Rumanian currencies. During this time he acquired a remarkably large circle of important and powerful American friends, many of whom were engaged in overseeing the enormous financial investments American banks were making in Europe. Not least among these friends was the Cravath lawyer Jack McCloy.

Monnet's work during the interwar period and his extensive knowledge of the United States and the American mentality made him the perfect choice to plead French military needs to the American government during the late 1930s. Many of the East Coast lawyers and bankers Monnet had known earlier worked for Roosevelt's wartime government. Monnet pushed hard for France and Britain to develop a joint plan for the purchase of American aircraft. Unfortunately these airplanes did not arrive until shortly before the fall of France and were of no consequence in the battle. During the crisis of spring 1940 Monnet was the prime mover behind Churchill's unsuccessful offer of a political merger of Britain and France, a plan designed to sustain France's will to resist.

After June 1940 Monnet did not join de Gaulle's Free French movement, but rather returned to Washington, working for the British. He pushed upon his American associates the necessity of converting America into the "arsenal of democracy." Through his friendship with Roosevelt's adviser Harry Hopkins, Monnet also convinced the President to announce in his 1941 inaugural address the seemingly absurd goal of producing fifty thousand planes a year. During this period Monnet and McCloy, then Assistant Secretary of War, grew to be close friends and collaborators. In November 1941 McCloy wrote Judge Frankfurter that "[Monnet] has been responsible more than anyone connected with the British mission . . . for the orientation of the men he comes in contact with in the War Department to the primary task which the United States must perform if it is to act effectively in the war . . . Monnet is the only one . . . who talks and presses to the point almost of irritation the broad picture of the United States obligation. He thinks on the basis of wide experience with the men of influence in three governments . . . and the quality and plane of his thinking shows it." Though Monnet's friendship with McCloy was genuine, it clearly allowed him to influence important personages within the American government, thus obtaining a voice for French interests that conventional diplomacy did not provide.[23]

After the Allied landings in North Africa, Monnet returned to the French political scene, going to Algiers in January 1943. With French unity as his overriding objective, he worked to effect a compromise between General Giraud and de Gaulle's Free French, and to obtain American support for the arrangement. This fragile coalition did not last, for de Gaulle rapidly emerged as the major leader of the Free French Movement. Although Monnet probably anticipated this development, his mediation efforts earned him the enduring suspicion of de Gaulle, who saw him as the "inspirer" of the coalition effort. Yet the General had a certain grudging respect for Monnet and sent him back to Washington in late 1943 as the representative of the French Committee of National Liberation, hoping that his American friendships could bring more aid to France. He was, as André Kaspi has called him, "the minister of Franco-American relations," and his efforts helped lead to the American decision, reached in summer 1944, to recognize the Free French as the interim government of the liberated country. After liberation de Gaulle turned to Monnet for ideas on France's economic rehabilitation. In virtually his last act as head of the French Provisional Government, the General appointed Monnet head of the Commissariat-General of the French Modernization and Investment Plan. For the next five years Monnet and his men practically ran the economy of France as the governments of the Fourth Republic came and went with depressing frequency.[24]

The "Monnet plan" for the modernization of France called for the active involvement of the state in planning and coordinating the investment of funds in France's infrastructure as well as its heavy industries, especially steel. Although some American critics saw the plan as a dangerous move toward "socialism," Monnet's goal was to associate "economic interests in a process of collective problem solving," an approach which drew much of its inspiration from the American wartime planning experience. Robert Nathan, the principal outside consultant for Monnet's plan, was the former chairman of the planning committee of the War Production Board and deputy director of the Office of War Mobilization. Monnet, who believed in persuasion rather than compulsion, was certain that modernization was more "a state of mind than a matter of equipment," pointing out that a farmer on a tractor "thinks differently" from one using a horse. Above all Monnet wanted to sell to French business leaders "a dynamic attitude toward economic development inspired by America's example." Without such an approach he feared that France would slip into permanent economic backwardness and dependence and "inevitably become like Spain."[25]

Postwar France was a bitterly divided country, torn by class, regional, and political conflicts. In this situation it was difficult for successive governments to demand financial sacrifices by way of taxes, and this weakness contributed to a serious problem of inflation. One key to Monnet's power was that he could rely heavily on the assistance of the United States and his important American friends for the financial means to launch his initial plan. Loans from the State Department's Export-Import Bank and from the World Bank under McCloy, totaling almost $900 million, allowed Monnet's Commissariat "to facilitate the restoration, reconstruction, and modernization of the French economy." When the Marshall Plan came into existence,

Monnet was also able to use its counterpart funds for the objectives of his plan. Such Americans as Ambassador David Bruce and the Treasury Department's William Tomlinson helped convince Washington that investing counterpart funds in the Monnet plan was not inflationary. In 1949 some 90 percent of the French Modernization Plan's resources came from the Marshall Plan. Monnet believed that American support for France had helped give a sense of confidence and buoyancy to the entire economy.[26]

By the late 1940s Jean Monnet had become a man of enormous influence among Western leaders. Largely unknown to the general public, he was called the "most mysterious major public figure of modern times." His quick intelligence, indefatigable optimism, and curious single-mindedness impressed all those who dealt with him. He possessed a sharp sense of the location of power and was ruthless in reaching key figures. After listening to an American journalist discuss a problem, Monnet exclaimed, *"Exacte!* But *dites-moi,* on whose table should I pound to get the decision?" His willingness to allow others, especially politicians, to garner public acclaim for his ideas also accounts for his great influence. Monnet's skill was "recognizing a valid idea, knowing the men to whom it could be sold, sensing the time they needed it, and locating the technicians who could make the idea work." French leaders also recognized that his understanding and cultivation of influential Americans was unmatched. "This short, dumpy man, whose balding head, solid face and sharp nose" seemed to epitomize a French peasant, was more effective than any other Frenchman in communicating with Americans. McCloy greatly admired Monnet's willingness to spare himself "no indignity or rebuff" in his pursuit of his goals. It was through his friendship with McCloy that Monnet came to exercise a profound influence on America's German policy.[27]

On a trip to the United States in 1948 Monnet was feted by some of Washington's most influential figures. He was anxious to "check from the outside the views that I have now formed during these last two years here . . . of the character and temperament of my countrymen, a judgment and opinion which certainly differ from those I had in the past." Monnet believed even more strongly than before that the French must be prepared to shed their nationalist and protectionist outlook of the past and "turn their efforts into a truly European effort." Despite his own success in getting American financial support,

Monnet feared that the growth of European economic and military dependence on America would have harmful effects on both parties. He believed that a united Europe could act as a moderating force in international relations and might serve to defuse the Cold War between the United States and the Soviet Union. Only a "federation of the West," including Britain, would "enable us to solve our problems quickly enough, and finally prevent war." For France to reestablish its importance in world affairs, it had to lead the way toward a united Europe. But although Monnet was certain about this grand idea, the specific steps to reach it, including such vital questions as the future role of Germany, remained vague and unclear.[28]

The economic dynamism of postwar America impressed Monnet, but it also posed a challenge to Europe. Monnet was fascinated by "the flexibility and breadth of [America's] markets compared with Europe's markets." He believed that much of America's economic growth, technological advancement, and personal opportunity came from its single, enormous, Continental market. Looking to the future, Europe's only hope of competing successfully rested on the creation of a similar mass market. Monnet became as fervent as many of the American Marshall Plan administrators in his advocacy of trade liberalization within Europe. He also accepted the importance of competition in encouraging production and higher living standards. Hoping to transform "an old-fashioned capitalism into a means of sharing among citizens the fruits of their collective effort," he believed that an abundance of goods and a unified mass market would stimulate productivity and help Europe escape the "civil wars" of class and national conflicts.[29]

Early in 1950, however, Monnet grew pessimistic about the international situation and the future of France and Western Europe. British resistance frustrated his hopes that the Organization for European Economic Cooperation (OEEC) would serve as the nucleus for a strong European federation. After the Saar dispute Monnet feared "history [was] repeating itself," particularly in the failure of the Schuman-Adenauer talks. German demands to increase the steel quota were another troubling sign. Monnet warned Schuman that even though France would resist the demand, the Americans, including his friend McCloy, would insist on the change, and France would have to concede. Monnet knew that French steel production was leveling off and even falling, while Germany's economic superiority rested "on

her ability to produce steel at a price that France cannot match."
Unless France came up with a new approach that would attract American support, the future might bring a bleak scenario reminiscent of the interwar period: "Germany expanding; German dumping on export markets; a call for the protection of French industry; an end to trade liberalization; the re-establishment of prewar cartels; perhaps, eastward outlets for German expansion, a prelude to political agreements; and France back in the old rut of limited protected production." This scenario took on added probability in the atmosphere of the Cold War, in which Germany had become "a prize" to both superpowers.[30]

Monnet recognized that Germany's heavy industry was at the center of France's fears, for both political and economic reasons. Coal and steel "were at once the key to economic power and the raw materials for forging weapons of war." Consequently they had "immense symbolic significance." Monnet knew that many American leaders, and especially McCloy, were in favor of some type of "internationalization" of heavy industry and would welcome any step in that direction. Significant forces within Germany, both the Adenauer government and private groups of industrialists, had also signaled their desire for some accommodation with France in the realm of heavy industry. One German proposal, presented at a November 1949 meeting with the French, called for a customs union between the two countries, and the German industrialists even told their French counterparts that Germany's need for investment funds would never be met unless France's security could be guaranteed.[31]

Monnet knew that conditions were ripe for a new French initiative. In the short term, a proposal would secure the future of the Monnet Plan, which had wagered heavily on an expansion of French steel production, especially through the building of continuous wide-strip rolling mills. These plants, which produced flat products such as sheet metal, were considered the engines of national growth. An increase in Germany's steel production quota without easier access for France to the German market might jeopardize whatever chance France had to become Europe's foremost steel producer. In the long term, Monnet wanted to reassert French leadership on European issues, and believed that this could be accomplished by transforming the Franco-German problem into a European problem. Drawing on his World War I experience, he wanted some type of coal and steel "pool" to be set up between France and Germany. Because he wondered if this could be done in the context of international law, he presented the problem to Paul Reuter, a law professor from eastern France, who sketched the details of a "High Authority" for coal and steel. Along with two other aides, Pierre Uri and Etienne Hirsch, Monnet fleshed out the proposal. He insisted that the new institution should require some sacrifice of national sovereignty, and that its decisions would be binding on both nations. It would have the power to equalize certain economic factors in France and Germany, such as the taxes imposed on steel and coal, transport charges, social security and other labor costs, production quotas, and financial compensation for price differentials; and it would be able to rationalize the industry and set up a reemployment fund for displaced workers. The goal was to create a single, unified market for coal and steel, not as a cartel would—by dividing the market and assigning fixed percentages of a fixed production level to the various companies—but by eliminating the barriers to competition and encouraging production to meet the needs of a larger market. The primary responsibility of the representatives of each country on the High Authority would be to increase production and raise living standards. Finally, the Germans would have "equality" in making decisions.[32]

The proposed High Authority had functions that were not unlike those of earlier international syndicates, and to some extent it resembled a "government-sanctioned supercartel." One of the central differences was that the Monnet proposals "brought institutions and practices into the sphere of public policy which up to then had been conducted only semi-officially or privately." The public character of the High Authority was a guarantee against the private abuses of a cartel, as well as a guarantee that the essentially political objective of the proposal, the achievement of progress toward Franco-German rapprochement, would always predominate.[33]

Monnet took his plan to Bernard Clappier, Schuman's principal private secretary, who shared Monnet's desire to break with the protectionist policies of the past. Clappier enjoyed Schuman's full confidence and told Monnet that the Foreign Minister was searching for an initiative to present in London. Schuman had been "obsessed" since September 1949 with finding a proposal on Germany that could respond to Acheson's insistence that France take the lead in insuring Germany's integration into Western Europe. Informed of McCloy's position on Germany's production quotas, Schuman suspected that if France was not forthcoming the United States might propose the abolition of the Ruhr Authority. And Monnet's proposal afforded Schuman other political advantages. Unlike Bidault's Atlantic High Council idea, it gave the Foreign Minister a face-saving way out of inevitable defeat on the Law 27 question concerning the ownership of the German coal and steel industry. The proposal promised to defuse the Saar question, to further Franco-German cooperation, and to restore France to its former position of leadership in Europe.[34]

Despite the principle of "equality" embodied in the proposal, Schuman told his Cabinet, it would retain the German steel quota, the Ruhr Authority, and the application of Law 27 to the German companies. Both Schuman and Monnet believed that once equal competitive conditions were established, France's Lorraine steel industry would predominate. They reassured the Americans that they did not intend to choke off the German steel industry's development, pointing out that France would have to accept a 20 percent reduction in its own coal industry. But the proposal contained an implicit political deal: France would become Europe's major steelmaker and Germany its source of coal. Looking toward the future, the coal and steel pool offered protection against competition from the United States; at the very least it guaranteed a type of "industrial balance of power" between the two Western European countries.[35]

In an atmosphere of secrecy within the French government Monnet and Schuman worked out the final details of what was to be known as the Schuman Plan. They consulted neither the French steelmakers, the coal industry, nor the career diplomats of the Quai d'Orsay. Because it would have been risky to try for Cabinet approval without first getting American support, they sought the views of one person outside France—Dean Acheson, who was coming to Paris before the London meeting to clear up some bilateral matters with the French. On May 7, the day of his arrival, Schuman called on him at the American Embassy. Acheson's initial reaction to Schuman's "casual" presentation was fear that the proposal would result in a giant cartel. He remembered the steel cartel of the 1920s, which had once been heralded as the beginning of an "Economic United States of Europe," and which would certainly not command support in America. Acheson's negative reaction pained Schuman, who had tried to stress the political nature of the proposal and its implications for Franco-German relations. Acheson's protest, however, forced the French to add a stronger anti-cartel statement to their plan. To reassure Acheson, McCloy also went to Paris to discuss the proposal with Monnet. He was delighted with it because it followed his own suggestions for the "internationalization" of European heavy industry. Although McCloy helped remove some of Acheson's worries, the Secretary still feared the plan might disguise a French effort "to secure detailed control over investment policies and management" of the Ruhr coal and steel industry. But by the time the London Conference began, he had swallowed whatever doubts he still had and become an enthusiastic supporter, terming the plan a "major contribution toward the resolution of the pressing political and economic problems of Europe."[36]

The Schuman Plan

American foreign policy leaders greeted the Schuman Plan with unrestrained delight. President Truman echoed Acheson's praise, calling it "an act of constructive statesmanship." Monnet's friend John Foster Dulles, the foreign policy adviser of the Republican party, cabled Acheson that the proposal was "brilliantly creative and could go far to solve the most dangerous problem of our time, namely the relationship of Germany's industrial power to France and the West." Like many others, he was surprised that the French had had the courage to propose it. Averell Harriman of ECA thought it "the most important step towards the economic progress and peace of Europe since the original Marshall speech." Senator J. William Fulbright, who had sponsored resolutions aimed at "encouraging" European unity, hoped that Acheson would "pledge our support and cooperation in every way possible." David Bruce, the Ambassador to France, noted "the profound psychological implications" of the plan, in that "France, the natural leader of continental civilization, had emerged from her lethargy and spirit of defeatism and had once again erected a standard to which her neighbors could rally." Even important critics such as Walter Lippmann applauded the proposal. Although a few raised the cartel issue, this objection was drowned in the wave of public and private enthusiasm. An article in *Time* claimed that in the pervasive atmosphere of gloom about Europe and its defense the Schuman Plan was "a gust of fresh wind into a musty study long unused." *Newsweek* echoed that view: "A world accustomed to looking on all problems as unsolvable was literally staggered by the common sense of the French proposal."[37]

Ironically the Schuman Plan, though a French initiative, gave a new coherence and direction to American policy on Germany, steering it into closer alignment with French concerns. The British, who realized that the Americans would join the French in treating the Schuman Plan as the next step toward the integration of Germany, on which all other steps had to wait, found themselves pushed to the side. Acheson, referring to statements by High Commissioner Robertson expressing British displeasure over Allied vetoes of German laws, pointedly criticized British "free-wheeling" within the High Commission. McCloy stated his conviction that the German "internal situation is the key to peace" and that HICOG must retain its power to ensure "democratic development in Germany." And although British Foreign Secretary Bevin wanted to grant greater freedom to the Germans, the Franco-American bloc prevailed. Ultimately the Foreign Ministers agreed to establish the Inter-Governmental Study Group (ISG) in London, made up of representatives of each foreign office, to review the Occupation Statute and suggest changes; but they declared that controls would only be eased in accord with the "rate at which Germany advances toward a condition in which true democracy governs and the just liberties of the individual are assured."[38]

The new American alignment with France manifested itself most strikingly in the policies of McCloy and the American High Commission. When Monnet went to Bonn to present the Schuman Plan to the AHC, McCloy, who was chairman that month, greeted the Frenchman warmly and indicated that the High Commission was anxious to achieve results on the Schuman Plan. Monnet stressed the plan's political importance, especially its potential to further Franco-German reconciliation as well as to benefit the European economy. At the end of his presentation General MacReady, the British Deputy High Commissioner, raised an important legal point. Since the German coal and steel industry was under Allied authority, should not a representative of the High Commission attend the talks? Monnet, who had already experienced British coolness toward the proposal, sensed immediately that if the AHC were admitted, the British government might undermine the talks, and, indeed, the Allied presence might encourage a future German government to repudiate the treaty as a Diktat of the occupation powers. Monnet argued, therefore, that "given the scope

of the commitments Germany will be undertaking in the Schuman
Plan Treaty, it is vital that no one in the future should be able to claim
that they were not freely accepted." McCloy gave his strong support
to Monnet's position, arguing that the significance of the occasion
justified extraordinary methods. The AHC did approve direct talks,
and as the meeting closed McCloy praised the proposed High Authority as similar to American creations such as the New York Port
Authority and the Niagara Authority.[39]

American support for the plan was also a central consideration to
Adenauer, who quickly let it be known that he considered the proposal
"an enormous success" for his own policies, "inasmuch as it corre-
sponds so exactly with [my] frequently publicized views." Adenauer
suspected that although the "initiative is apparently purely French . . .
Acheson is the real instigator." When Monnet met with Adenauer,
however, he found the Chancellor, whose "attitude was still marked
by long years of hard negotiation and wounded pride," suspicious of
French intentions and motives. But during the course of their talk
Adenauer relaxed and agreed not to appoint a German industrialist as
chief negotiator, but rather to select someone with a broader political
outlook and to oversee the negotiations himself. Eventually Adenauer
appointed Walter Hallstein, a relatively unknown professor of law,
who would become an influential adviser and advocate of European
integration.[40]

The Schuman Plan also affected America's German policy. Earlier
in the year McCloy had argued that America must adopt a timetable,
ranging from eighteen months to two years, for phasing out occupation controls. Although he still held to this view, his public speeches
grew more cautionary. When the German government and press speculated about a quick end to occupation controls, McCloy told Germans that "large and thoroughgoing measures" were still needed to
reform their politics and society, and that the United States would
remain an "active" influence "for some time." In another interview he
estimated that the occupation would last "another five years," a statement at odds with his private judgment but, ironically, an accurate
prediction. "The longer the barrel of the gun, the more accurate the
shot," McCloy reminded one reporter. He stressed again that the
Germans did not "understand that other countries still distrusted them
and at times feel towards them a resistance not far short of revulsion."[41]

In June 1950 McCloy advocated the Schuman Plan when speaking to a prominent group of Ruhr industrialists in Düsseldorf. Encouraging the industrialists to expand their exports, he at the same time warned them against looking toward markets in the East and reminded them that for other countries "the Ruhr is a symbol of industrial capacity devoted to aggression." To regain the confidence of the world, he urged them to cooperate with the implementation of Law 27, saying, "Since the policy behind this law is now settled, it is clearly in the interest of everyone to carry it out promptly." After making it clear that the United States would support the Schuman Plan to the fullest, he concluded, "It is a political and economic fact of the first magnitude that France has proposed the idea and Germany has accepted it."[42]

Following McCloy's speech the industrialists asked a number of tough and unfriendly questions, taking the opportunity to "rub something under McCloy's nose." Theodor Goldschmidt of Essen's Chamber of Commerce raised the problems of refugees and high occupation costs and passionately criticized the Allied decisions made at Yalta and Potsdam. McCloy replied angrily: "Don't forget who started the war. Whether or not you gentlemen here are responsible personally for it, remember the war and all the misery that followed it—including your own—was born and bred in German soil and you must accept responsibility." One industrialist, lamenting the outcome of the meeting, warned his fellow businessman that "dealing in politics might well be left to the federal government, parliament, and political meetings." McCloy's speech put the industrialists on notice that both Law 27 and the Schuman Plan would be implemented together, a procedure which the French also favored. The meeting also highlighted the continuing mistrust which existed between the American High Commission and the German industrial leadership, a suspicion rooted in the belief that the industrialists had played a pivotal role in Hitler's dictatorship and still preferred an authoritarian government to a democratic one. Nevertheless, the meeting did indicate that McCloy was willing to open a dialogue with these leaders, hoping to enlist their cooperation in furthering the American goals of Western security, European integration, and democratic development in Germany.[43]

Although the Schuman Plan drew together the American, French, and German governments, it divided them from the British government and the German socialists. London's policy, which one British journal described as "petulant isolationism" from the Continent, was a great disappointment to the Americans. Looked at objectively, Britain's reaction to the Schuman Plan reveals the basic principles of its postwar foreign policy. The primary aim of British policymakers was to cultivate their "special relationship" with the United States. Although Britain and America were bound together naturally by language, ideology, and cultural heritage, "at the heart of the special relationship was Britain's need for American protection and America's need for Britain as an essential junior partner in the containment of the Soviet Union." The British also used this special relationship to restrain what they saw as the extremes in American foreign policy, the oscillation from naive isolationism to extreme anti-communism and overcommitment. Finally, the special relationship, by compensating for Britain's own economic weakness after the war, allowed it to have an "independent" foreign policy with the assistance of the United States. As Sir Orme Sargent put it, Britain was to "have a policy of [its] own and try to persuade the United States to make it *their own*."[44]

Although the special relationship was central to British policymakers, it did not imply doing America's bidding, especially in Europe and Germany. In late 1949 and in 1950 Americans such as McCloy, David Bruce, and Lewis Douglas lamented the decline in British power but remained convinced that the "key to European integration is the United Kingdom." Officials in the State Department's Bureau of German Affairs believed that the United States had to find a way of "freeing the UK so as to allow her to become a Continental power," since without British support the French would never act to integrate the Federal Republic into Western Europe. But Foreign Secretary Bevin, while aware that the Americans wanted British cooperation with Europe, also believed in maintaining a strong, independent Britain. "Fundamentally," as Bevin's biographer, Alan Bullock, has noted, "Bevin saw the search for a distinctive European identity as incompatible with the Atlantic pattern of Western Union," while the Americans and the French saw the two as "complementary." Bevin believed that the best solution for the problem of Germany's integration into the West was an "Atlantic Community," which would bind the United States and Britain to Continental Europe and thereby possess enough strength to offset any German inclination to deal with the Soviets. Western Europe on its own was simply too weak to contain a revived Germany. France in particular was regarded by the British as "built on sand," a country with a "defeatist attitude," an increasingly neutralist sentiment, and an army suffering from "a lack of finance, poor training, and a demoralizing war in Indochina." In addition, the Commonwealth continued to play a large role in British thinking about the world. The remarkable success of the Colombo Conference early in 1950 contributed to Bevin's doubts about closer European ties. In fact Bevin assured Commonwealth members that European cooperation would not be allowed to undermine the Commonwealth relationship.[45]

The Schuman Plan took British policymakers completely by surprise. They had expected nothing more than Bidault's Atlantic High Council, and Bevin's shock and dismay at being excluded from the advance notice given to Acheson led him to accuse Acheson of joining in a "conspiracy." Although the ailing Foreign Secretary eventually cooled down, he told the other ministers at the London Conference that the Schuman Plan posed a problem for the "planned economy" and "full employment" policies of Britain. Monnet's insistence that all members had to accept the supranational principle as a non-negotiable basis for the talks increased British concerns. The British "fundamental fear" was that "by joining the Schuman Plan, they [would] expose their internal position to external forces which might impair their ability to plan and which might possibly interfere with their program for eternal full employment." In more colloquial terms, Sir Oliver Franks told Acheson that the British could not "buy a pig in a poke."[46]

British refusal to join the Schuman Plan led to bitterness and suspicion among the Americans and Europeans. McCloy suspected that the British were trying to sabotage the talks through "the imputation of sinister motives to the Germans." Along with some American observers, Adenauer believed that Britain had reverted to its older policy of trying to "divide the rule" in dealing with France and Germany, and that it actually feared the efforts of the two to achieve greater unity. Monnet, for his part, suspected that the British had written off Continental Europe, expecting that none of the countries would have the means or ability to resist Soviet aggression. "She therefore does not wish to let her domestic life or the development of her resources be influenced by any views other than her own, certainly not by continental views." In response the Labour party's Executive Committee issued a statement on European unity that was strongly critical of the Schuman Plan. John Strachey, the Minister of War, condemned the plan as a "plot" against Socialism and declared that the British Labour movement was "not going to have any bogus federation of Western Europe."[47]

Despite this heated rhetoric the British were extremely sensitive to the charge of "sabotage" in their approach to the Schuman Plan, both because of the importance they attached to Franco-German coopera-tion and because of the importance the Americans ascribed to the plan. Whitehall officials agreed in July 1950 that Britain should not do anything to hamper a rapprochement between France and Ger-many. Nevertheless, Britain's failure to join the plan and the Labour party's attacks on it probably did influence the German Social Dem-ocrats. The SPD had already decided to oppose German entry into the Council of Europe, arguing that it would lead to membership in NATO and rearmament, as well as deepen the division of Germany. The timing of the Schuman Plan, and its French authorship, imme-diately provoked Schumacher's suspicions. Privately he argued that the plan had been designed by the French to seal the division of Germany. He also feared that the plan was intended to consolidate and strengthen private control of heavy industry, producing a "Europe of the managers" rather than a democratic and socialist Europe. Pub-licly, however, he did not close the door to approval of the plan, though his conditions were left vague and subject to change.[48]

Schumacher remained cool despite strong pressures from other Eu-ropean socialist parties, from more moderate SPD leaders, and from the German trade unions. All the other West European socialist parties and the non-communist trade unions embraced the plan, and they criticized their German comrades for hesitating. To the other Socialists the unity of Europe was more important than the unity of Germany. There were even some dissenters within the SPD. Willy Brandt, a young deputy from Berlin, argued that the party should "warmly welcome" a proposal which brought a true "Europeanization" of heavy industry. A number of the SPD mayors, including Max Brauer of Hamburg, Ernst Reuter of Berlin, and Wilhelm Kaisen of Bremen, also expressed more conciliatory sentiments toward the Western in-tegration efforts of the Allies. If Germany could not enter the Council of Europe, Kaisen asked plaintively, "Where else shall we go?" Schu-macher had already stated that he wanted nothing to do with the East or a policy of neutrality. Kaisen's question was a blunt way of asking the SPD leader for a realistic alternative.[49]

The organization of German trade unions, the DGB, also broke with Schumacher's opposition stance. After the adoption of the Petersberg Protocols, Schumacher knew that Hans Böckler and the DGB would not automatically follow the SPD's lead. He explained bitterly to other party members that Böckler recognized Adenauer's need for union support and wanted to exploit this power. Another SPD member lamented, "At no time since 1875 have we had so little influence over the unions." Although the unions had joined the SPD in opposing Erhard's economic policies, they refused to do so on foreign policy issues. The French trade unionists were also effective in persuading their German comrades of the merits of the Schuman Plan. They argued that Monnet's proposed High Authority would engage in more planning than had occurred under Erhard's policies. The new arrangements would be compatible with government ownership, for the French coal industry was already nationalized. Consequently the DGB, although expressing some reservations about the High Commission's Law 27, came out initially in favor of the Schuman Plan.[50]

The dramatic effects of the Schuman Plan were evident during the debate in Bonn over German entry into the Council of Europe. Adenauer again stressed the political importance of the Schuman proposal, noting "there is no better way of dispelling French doubts about the German people's love of peace than to bring together the two countries' coal, iron, and steel which are ever the mainstay of rearmament." When the Bundestag voted 220 to 152 to accept the Council's offer of associate membership, it was the first major success for Adenauer's European policy.[51]

To American leaders like McCloy the Schuman Plan marked a break from a pattern which had closely resembled the interwar era. With U.S. encouragement the leaders of France and Germany were finally attempting to end a long "civil war" that had twice brought American soldiers to Europe. The Schuman Plan gave renewed energy to America's European policy, providing the next step after the Marshall Plan. Yet the Schuman Plan could not change the fact that a new threat to Europe's peace had come into prominence, the Soviet Union, and that despite its economic recovery Western Europe had still not come to terms with its security problems. In June 1950 events in a small Asian country would act as another catalyst, speeding the process of German recovery and challenging the new European policy of the United States.

5

The Dilemmas of Rearmament

Although the Schuman Plan offered the promise of ending the Franco-German impasse, the shadow of the Cold War continued to hang over Western Europe. The increasingly bitter struggle between the United States and the Soviet Union dominated the discussion of all issues, including the future of Germany. In 1949 the creation of both the North Atlantic Alliance and the FRG raised the question of Germany's military potential in the Cold War, leading the Parisian editors of *Le Monde* to comment that "the rearming of Germany is contained in the Atlantic Pact like the yolk in the egg." In fact, despite the "logic of the situation," which called for the re-creation of a German military, the issue of German rearmament touched a sensitive nerve in all the Western democracies and spawned one of the most significant crises in the history of NATO. To understand this crisis requires an awareness of the political atmosphere of the West in 1950, when the perception of the increasing Soviet threat, the sense of Western weakness, and a stunning surprise attack in Northeast Asia led the Western Allies, particularly the United States, to endorse the rearming of a nation and people against whom they had fought two of history's greatest wars.[1]

Soviet Challenge and Western Response

To American leaders the events of late 1949, particularly the explosion of a Soviet nuclear device and the fall of China, brought fear that "the Soviet assessment of the correlation of forces" would change in a direction unfavorable to the West. The Soviet test shattered the hopes which the United States had placed in its nuclear monopoly. As early as October 1949 General Omar Bradley told Congress that Soviet possession of the bomb would make impossible any operation similar to the Normandy landings used to liberate Europe. Intelligence analysts predicted that the Soviets would soon have a stockpile of two hundred atomic bombs and an air force capable of delivering them. Because mutual deterrence, or, as Bradley called it, "atomic deadlock," seemed likely by the mid-1950s if not earlier, American attention shifted back to the conventional balance of forces.[2]

Allied leaders firmly believed that they faced an overwhelming Soviet conventional superiority. They credited the Russians with some 175 divisions while NATO could dispose of only 12, including 2 American divisions doing occupation duty in Germany. Historians now dispute the Soviet figures, arguing that many of their divisions were only paper units consisting of a skeleton headquarters staff. But even though the figure of 175 was an exaggeration, the Soviet Union did maintain more than "thirty elite divisions" in Eastern Europe after World War II, a "ready-made spearhead" for an invasion of Western Europe. Although these forces may originally have served only a policing function, Stalin may have intended to counter the American nuclear threat with a threat to use them to occupy Western Europe. In any case, the perception that the Soviet Union was fast acquiring a nuclear delivery capability made these Red Army forces seem an increasingly ominous presence.[3]

Soviet policies in Germany did little to minimize Allied concerns. Early in 1950 both the British and the Americans worried over substantial increases in the numbers and level of military equipment being supplied to East Germany's Bereitschaften. Most Western analysts believed that these forces were intended primarily for internal use, but the build-up appeared to go beyond those needs and to fit into a larger Soviet program begun in 1949 to strengthen the armies of the East European satellites. The Soviets also continued to pressure the Western position in Berlin, periodically obstructing Western access to the city. These actions contributed to the political uncertainty and economic distress of the city, where unemployment stood at close to 40 percent and investment capital remained difficult to attract. In May 1950 the Communist authorities staged a massive youth rally in Berlin, bringing some 400,000 blue-shirted members of the Freie Deutsche Jugend to the city. Although Allied fears of an attempt to "overthrow the legal Berlin government by violence" proved groundless, the rally demonstrated a sense of strength and purpose among the Communists that contrasted sharply with the West's disunity and disorganization. American leaders, who had developed strong emotional ties to Berlin during the blockade, were particularly sensitive to Soviet intimidation of this "beleaguered beachhead in a hostile Red Sea." McCloy explained that in Berlin "you take in the fear and the pressure of this great force that is coming from the East," and that unless the Allied powers developed more strength the Western position there and indeed throughout Germany would be lost.[4]

The West's response to Soviet military strength was slow and "leisurely." Although warning of the possible dire consequences of inaction, American and Allied officials not only retained the "confidence that time was on the side of the Alliance" but regarded the rebuilding of Europe's defenses as "a gradual process that would develop slowly but steadily in such a way that equilibrium with the Soviet bloc could be achieved painlessly and almost imperceptibly." NATO was, as Paul Nitze put it, "a North American political commitment to the defense of Europe rather than a framework for a military organization." The European allies resisted diverting resources from domestic reconstruction and economic recovery in order to increase the pace of their military programs. In the United States the Truman Administration kept a tight ceiling on the defense budget, setting a total of a little over $11 billion as the "upper limit" of what the economy could bear. Congress was also reluctant to appropriate money for military assistance to the Allies. By April 1950 only $42 million of the $1.3 billion promised by the United States under the Military Development Assistance Plan had actually been spent.[5]

Corresponding to the minimal defense efforts of the United States and its allies was a NATO military strategy that made the organization a "promise-of-liberation alliance." Few doubted the conclusion of the Joint Chiefs of Staff that if a major war broke out, the Soviet Union could immediately "overrun Western Europe, with the possible exception of the Iberian and Scandinavian Peninsulas." Military planners, therefore, prepared for an orderly evacuation of NATO forces, with the hope of holding the line at the Pyrenees. The Western Allies trusted that the American nuclear deterrent would persuade the Russians to avoid a conventional assault that might kill American soldiers. The Americans would act as a "tripwire" for the deterrent. In defending the American strategy to a skeptical Adenauer, McCloy emphasized that the "presence of one battalion" of American soldiers was Germany's best guarantee of security. McCloy harbored his own private doubts about this assertion, but George Kennan remained convinced that "two high-quality Marine divisions" were sufficient to support America's containment policies.[6]

In the months immediately preceding the Korean War a countervailing trend appeared, encouraged by a loose conspiracy of leaders in Washington who disapproved of the attitude of complacency toward Western defense. Late in January 1950, when President Truman approved the development of the hydrogen bomb, he also directed Secretary of State Acheson and Secretary of Defense Johnson to undertake a "general re-examination of this country's strategic plans and its objectives in peace and war." The result was a policy paper, NSC-68, which called for the "rapid build-up of political, economic, and military strength in the free world." Arguing that this "Republic and its citizens" stood "in greater jeopardy than ever before in our history," NSC-68 sounded the clarion call of the Cold War, insisting that Americans must recognize it as "a real war in which the survival of the free world is at stake." To do so would require a massive increase in America's defense spending, totaling some $40 billion— more than a threefold increase over the Truman Administration's proposed $12.5 billion. NSC-68, however, was stalled in the bureaucracy. After receiving it President Truman kept it under advisement, at least until he could acquire more information from the Bureau of the Budget about the costs involved.[7]

The German Rearmament Issue before the Korean War

NSC-68, mirroring the indecision within American leadership circles, did not suggest a clear position on German rearmament. Although the document called for an American build-up, it only speculated that it might be "desirable for the free nations . . . to conclude separate arrangements with Japan, Western Germany and Austria, which would enlist the energies and resources of these countries in support of the free world." The chief reason for this cautious stance was that German rearmament was perceived as one of the greatest *dangers* to the Western alliance, raising the possibility of a new German militarism, a German-Soviet arrangement, and the death of German democracy. The rearmament issue also created divisions across national lines as loose trans-national coalitions appeared on both sides of the question. These coalitions were, in part, the product of different professional concerns, representing the military and strategic as opposed to the political and economic view of the question. But they also represented different views of the German past and future, and leaders struggled with the problem of exorcising old demons without creating new ones.

Foremost among the members of the pro-rearmament coalition was Konrad Adenauer, who saw rearmament both as a solution to Ger-many's military insecurity and as a way to acquire a stronger bargaining position with the Western powers. Only days after the Petersberg agreements had been concluded in December 1949 Adenauer told a reporter from the *Cleveland Plain Dealer* that because the Allies had disarmed Germany, they had the duty to provide for its security. After dismissing the idea of recruiting Germans for the Allied armies, Ad-enauer expressed interest in establishing German armed forces under a European command. Off the record he told the reporter that "the Germans are the only people who can stop the Russians," but that with the passage of time German soldiers were forgetting their military skills. "If the Allies wait too long . . . it may be too late [for them] to be of immediate use to defend Germany against Russia."[8]

The *Plain Dealer* interview created a storm of controversy, but this did not shake Adenauer's interest in a "German contingent inside a European army or under a European command," in which the Ger-mans would serve under conditions of "equality." Adenauer always saw Germany's military contribution to the West in relation to the political strength it would bring to his government. He belonged "to that patrician class of Rhineland bourgeoisie who have always resented the supremacy and intrusion of the Prussian officer class," and he had no particular fondness for Germany's military traditions. (He once referred to the East German forces as recruited from the Prussians, "the most obstinate and stubborn elements" in Germany.) Adenauer realized, however, that military circles in the West looked on German manpower as the only means of defending Europe, and that this offered him another route to the restoration of German sovereignty and even to membership in NATO.[9]

Although his political concerns were paramount, the Chancellor also worried about the security of the young republic. He disputed McCloy's assurance that Germany was well protected by a single

American battalion, arguing that an American strategy that relied so heavily on airpower to attack Soviet cities would not stop the Red Army from overrunning Western Europe. Indeed Adenauer often compared atomic weapons to poison gas, a weapon whose usefulness would disappear once the other side acquired it. A Soviet occupation of Western Europe, with its purges and deportations, would make eventual liberation by the Americans unlikely. Why liberate a "dead continent"? Adenauer asked rhetorically. He also considered the possibility of an attack by the East German Army to "liberate" the Western zones, and he worried that he would become Europe's "Chiang-Kai-shek." Reports from his military adviser, the former General Gerhard Graf von Schwerin, painted a bleak picture of Soviet forces reaching the Rhine within days of an attack. Neither American atomic weapons nor the American military assistance program would prevent West Germany from becoming little more than a strategic "buffer zone" for the Western powers. Only a significant contribution of German forces, which Schwerin estimated at ten to twelve divisions, could provide some deterrent to a Russian invasion.[10]

Concern about the conventional balance was the key reason that made both American and British military leaders support German rearmament. In April 1950 the American Joint Chiefs of Staff reported that "from the military point of view, the appropriate and early rearming of Western Germany is of fundamental importance to the defense of Western Europe against the USSR." A few weeks earlier the British Chiefs of Staff had concluded that Western Europe was "indefensible without German manpower." They were concerned, however, about the effects of German rearmament on France and recommended a gradual approach involving the creation of a German "gendarmerie," a police force that could serve as an interim solution to the problem. The Americans displayed less political sensitivity. Pressed by Truman's budget cuts and distrustful of the fighting ability and even the loyalty of the conscripts in the French Army, the U.S. Army looked on Germany as an untapped source of manpower, a strongly anti-communist nation whose men had had "practical fighting experience against the Soviet Army." Estimating this manpower pool at between three and four million, the Army believed they could be "fit for combat after a relatively short period of refresher training." Since the first phase of a war with Russia would "unquestionably be fought on German soil," German technical knowledge of the terrain and combat conditions would be an important advantage. Although conceding that German rearmament "would give a *coup de grace* to possible Franco-German rapprochement," the Americans believed that the advantage of German soldiers, whose "fighting ability is judged to be among the highest in the world," would outweigh the political fallout.[11]

The American Army made little headway in convincing the State Department or High Commission to support its view. The British Chiefs, on the other hand, found an ally in the British High Commission, which had previously opposed rearmament. What precipitated the change was an incident in early March 1950 when German police failed to defend British dismantling teams from hostile demonstrators at the Salzgitter steel plant. British troops restored order, but the High Commission was appalled by the political aftermath. When Robertson complained to Adenauer about the poor performance of the local German police, the Chancellor blamed the violence on East German agents who had crossed the poorly guarded zonal border, and he reminded Robertson that control of the police fell under the authority of the individual Länder. Adenauer then asked the Allies to authorize the creation of a federal police force that could enforce the authority of the central government. This request led British leaders to see such a force as an ideal interim solution, both for the problem of internal security and for rearmament. Robertson argued that the creation of a 25,000-man force would ensure protection from the East German forces as well as providing a quiet and unprovocative way of beginning the formation of a German army. The police force was also a good idea for bargaining reasons, because the request had come from the Germans and needed simply to be "approved" by the Allies. Although the High Commissioner was concerned about the French and Soviet reaction, he thought the police solution was the one least likely to produce political complications. In his view the best answer would "be found in a gradual process whereby German strength is progressively increased as allied, and especially French, strength develops, and that process should be so gradual that the Kremlin remains uncertain and unwilling to act until it is too late."[12]

To assist in setting up such a force, Robertson suggested that the Chancellor appoint a "security advisor." This should be the "right kind of German," someone "who could ultimately become very useful to us." He suggested former General Schwerin, who had had contacts with the British before the war and had also played a peripheral role in the July 20 plot against Hitler. Adenauer directed Schwerin to begin planning the creation of a gendarmerie with a mandate to both guard the internal security of the Federal Republic and provide defense against a possible East German attack. British involvement with Schwerin irritated American officials in Bonn, who complained that the British were "utilizing pressure for creation of a German police force as a first step toward the remilitarization of Germany." In the strained atmosphere following Britain's refusal to join the Schuman Plan, Acheson interpreted the British move as the type of unilateral action likely to "wreck" the High Commission. Though he was not opposed to the creation of a small federal police force for the Bonn area, Acheson distinguished between this issue and the question of rearmament. He said to McCloy, "If the British indeed told Schwerin that the US could 'be brought into line quickly' they are seriously misinformed." President Truman strongly supported the Secretary's protest to Bevin. Although the coalition supporting rearmament was making some progress, success seemed to lie in the distant future.[13]

Indeed the coalition of forces against German rearmament controlled both the terms of debate and the most influential leaders and groups. The Western Allies learned from the reaction to Adenauer's *Plain Dealer* interview and from public opinion polls that opposition to rearmament was particularly strong within Germany. As one HICOG report put it: "For the first time in modern German history the population has lost its military ardor and would not, without considerable difficulty, cooperate in the revival of any kind of military force." Another analyst noted that "militarism is thoroughly discredited in West Germany" and "the small groups which might welcome militarization have no power at present." State Department officials were particularly concerned because the "democratic elements we are supporting," which did not want rearmament—trade unions, churches, youth groups, and political parties—would be undermined by any reversal in Allied policy. The Social Democrats, too, sharply criticized Adenauer's position, arguing that any type of German rearmament would make reconciliation with other European countries extremely difficult. Schumacher also feared that any public discussion of "remilitarization" would embolden radical right wing and nationalist circles.[14]

The French, whose memories of three wars and the atrocities of

Nazi occupation were still fresh, remained strongly opposed to German rearmament. After reading Adenauer's *Plain Dealer* interview François-Poncet declared that "the creation of a German army in any form was absolutely out of the question." The political fragility of Fourth Republic governments made them reluctant to touch such an inflammatory issue. During the November 1949 debate on the Petersberg Protocols, speculation in the American press about a new German army cost Schuman "at least 40 votes" in the French Assembly. Although Schuman's policy of reconciliation with Germany was popular with the Allies, ordinary Frenchmen had mixed feelings about it. The presence of the powerful French Communist party, as well as France's military weakness, affected the French stance toward both the rearmament issue and the Soviet Union. Confident that they understood Russian fears of Germany much better than the Anglo-Saxon powers, and constrained by domestic politics, the French argued that German rearmament would be so provocative to the Soviets that it could lead to an attack on Western Europe. With an army of only 300,000, half of which was committed to a growing war in Indochina, French politicians attached singular importance to avoiding any such provocation and preserving the peace of Europe.[15]

Despite the efforts of their military men and High Commissioner, British political leaders also remained leery of committing themselves to a policy of German rearmament. Bevin still distrusted the Germans, telling the House of Commons in March 1950 that "the Hitler revolution did not change the German character. It expressed it." Although recognizing the value of the police solution, the Foreign Office regarded discussion of German rearmament at the London Foreign Ministers Conference in May 1950 as "premature" because of France's opposition and concern about provoking the Russians. The Foreign Office also believed that if the Germans acquired their own army too quickly, they might demand the withdrawal of Allied occupation troops. British diplomats worried that "the Americans, under such pressure, would be only too inclined to withdraw their troops from Germany," an outcome that would be disastrous. The British also believed that Germany's commitment to the West was still uncertain— that "we have no firm assurance that Germany will not throw in her lot with Russia." In the spring of 1950 the struggle over the rearmament issue was still "over the horizon and we need not and indeed should not go into it now."[16]

Washington's civilian decision makers were the most important opponents of rearmament. Dean Acheson was primarily concerned about the effect of such a decision on France. He recognized that German rearmament posed a "double problem": to build up Western strength required unity, and German rearmament would fracture that unity. The Secretary agreed with the conclusion of the London conference that although Germany was the "central point of the struggle between East and West," policymakers could not lose track of the "relations to be established between Germany and other European powers." Delighted with Schuman's coal and steel initiative, Acheson wanted to give him time to build domestic support for his reconciliation policy. A premature push for German rearmament could topple Schuman and bring to power French leaders more hostile to both Germany and the United States.[17]

American leaders also worried about "a renewed German menace." The continuing fears of another Rapallo, with a German-Soviet alignment, along with the concern that Germany might play off East against West, remained part of the Secretary's thinking about rearmament, as did the question of its effects on Germany's fragile democracy. The State Department's Bureau of German Affairs argued that despite the Soviet threat "we cannot ignore from the long-range point of view the vital importance of obtaining the right kind of Germany." Rearmament was "premature"; more time was needed "to develop democratic tendencies on the part of the German people." In opposing the creation of a gendarmerie, Acheson believed that "strong centralized German police forces" were an "inherent danger to democracy." In these views he had a strong ally in President Truman. After reading two Defense Department reports, one urging German rearmament and the other backing cooperation with Franco's Spain, Truman wrote that both were "decidedly militaristic and in my opinion not realistic with present conditions." Across the top of the page he wrote in longhand, "Both as wrong as can be." An avid reader of history, he was determined not "to make the same mistake that was made after World War I," and he was particularly conscious of parallels in regard to Germany. Though personally identified with the Berlin airlift and the reversal of American policy toward Germany, Truman distrusted the Germans. If Germany did need such a police force, he insisted that a "proper approach" be found which could insure that such a force "will maintain order locally and yet not be allowed to develop into a training ground for a military machine that can combine with Russia and ruin the rest of the world."[18]

McCloy's views were close to those of his Washington superiors. He was less worried about the abstract danger of "militarism," but he opposed German rearmament. In his Stuttgart speech in early February 1950 he stated flatly, "There will be no German army or air force." In speaking to other American diplomats in Europe he criticized "the idea of a foreign legion, or a contingent of German troops among the Allied forces" as a "defeatist idea," which would have the effect "of making the Germans believe we are dependent on them." Subjected to Adenauer's "continual pressure" for either an Allied commitment to defend West Germany or permission to build up a German "police force," McCloy argued that "our Army is the best guarantee of security we can give the Germans," and that the Russians would not attack Western Europe because they feared American nuclear retaliation. When Adenauer suggested sending twenty thousand Germans to France for military training in order to create an "international legion," McCloy discouraged the idea. In a letter to his old boss, Henry Stimson, he wrote that rearmament "would mean the abandonment of all serious efforts to nurture the German state into a liberal constructive element in Europe," for the Bonn government would almost certainly be subservient to a new military organization. Adopting an interpretation of Germany's past similar to the French view, McCloy told Stimson: "Germany always had two bosses: one the General Staff and the other the Rhine industrialists." Referring to the Schuman Plan and his own recent encounter with Ruhr industrialists, he noted, "We still have the latter only a little chastened. Let us not take on the other for a while."[19]

Nevertheless, despite McCloy's opposition to German rearmament, his position was more flexible and pragmatic than Washington's. He was sympathetic to Adenauer's argument that the Bonn government needed some way to enforce its power, especially in an emergency, and believed that a "small" police force, supported by a "forceful Western European organization and policy," would satisfy the West Germans. His own concern was that the "major element" lacking in Western Europe was any "sense of strength in the West," military or political, and he hoped that the United States, Britain, and France would increase their military forces. "Build up strength to the west of Germany, and when it is done let us see then how the land lies and the new state has progressed." In the long term McCloy continued to believe, as he did on the matter of German industry, that a politically united Europe would be the most lasting solution. Privately he told

Adenauer that within a future political union the Germans would "bear arms" and have an "equal" responsibility for security. Expecting that Germany would gradually move toward full membership in NATO, he argued that the United States must work for "a new Europe, united as never before in the face of an overwhelming danger [from the East.]" This was the only way, in his view, to "readjust" the "permanently lost European balance."[20]

McCloy's belief that the dilemmas of German rearmament could only be resolved within the larger framework of a "new" Europe was to be sorely tested after the outbreak of the Korean War. But to an impressive degree the High Commissioner and the men around him recognized that the central issue would not be the number of German troops or strategic plans under which they operated. The central question would be political: how could Germany resume its legitimate position within the European state system, maintain its security, and be a source of stability and strength rather than a danger to its neighbors?

The Korean Catalyst and the Decision to Rearm Germany

The Korean War was the Pearl Harbor of the Cold War, an event which catalyzed and transformed the American response to the Soviet Union. Unlike the Vietnam conflict the North Korean attack, a massive armored assault across the thirty-eighth parallel, left little doubt about the responsibility for the aggression. Although historians have raised questions about Stalin's "approval" of Kim-Il-Sung's attack, the presence of Russian T-34 tanks with the North Korean forces was enough evidence for American leaders. For these men the attack confirmed the view of Soviet imperialism expressed in NSC-68—an imperialism which combined traditional Russian expansionism with Marxist-Leninist revolutionary objectives. Using the proxy forces of their satellites, the Soviets seemed determined to challenge the West as Hitler and Mussolini had in the 1930s. For President Truman, who had learned the "lessons of Munich," there was only one response; military action. Not only did Truman send American forces to save South Korea, but he reversed his previous policy of restricting the defense budget. Expenditures for new planes, ships, and other weaponry more than tripled, reaching more than $50 billion by 1952.

The recommendations of NSC-68, which had seemed extreme in April, were approved by the end of September 1950.[21]

During the summer of 1950 the atmosphere in Washington changed dramatically as the country's leaders prepared to meet a challenge they equated with the Second World War. Only a fully mobilized and rearmed America could prevent the outbreak of war, or if deterrence failed, fight such a war successfully. One reporter, returning to the United States after spending the summer in Europe, observed this "change in the national psychology" and was "shocked by the war talk and the emphasis on war preparedness." The bleak news from Korea, with American and South Korean forces retreating in disarray and then being penned into the Pusan Perimeter, fed this mood of mobilization. Some even argued that America should seriously consider "preventive war" while it still held a strategic nuclear advantage over the Soviets. MacArthur's successful landing behind enemy lines at Inchon in September did little to ease the mood of crisis, and the Chinese intervention later in the year brought the world closer to war than at any time since 1945. The atmosphere of sustained crisis over these months is unique in the history of the Cold War.[22]

The Korean invasion also stimulated European fears regarding Russian intentions and led the NATO countries to request more American military assistance, an increase in U.S. forces in Europe, and an integrated NATO defense system headed by an American supreme commander. Americans and Europeans immediately saw parallels between divided Germany and divided Korea. Although the continued presence of American occupation forces in Germany made an important difference, events in Korea gave the build-up of the East German Bereitschaften a sinister twist. Further, Soviet calls for the withdrawal of occupation forces from Germany seemed designed to create a situation similar to that in South Korea before the invasion. East German leaders were anxious to use the Korean "example" to intimidate their Western counterparts. Walter Ulbricht, the General Secretary of the East German Communist party, told his compatriots, "If the Americans in their imperialist arrogance believe that the Germans have less national consciousness than the Koreans, then they have fundamentally deceived themselves." He went on to proclaim that East Germany would not build a new seaport because soon "democratic Germany" would have Hamburg and Lübeck. Such propaganda had an impact on Western estimations of Communist intentions. Though confident that the Army could resist an attack by the East Germans, the American Commander in Germany concluded that an "attack on West Sectors of Berlin by maximum Bereitschaften strength probably would succeed now; certainly would succeed by 1 March 1951 if force increases are made according to capabilities." Foreign Secretary Bevin told his Cabinet at the beginning of September: "I seriously fear that next year the Soviet Government will seek to repeat in Germany what they have done in Korea." The French were afraid the Russians might launch a preventive war within three months, before the United States had had time to mobilize; and in mid-July François-Poncet even discussed with Adenauer's assistant, Herbert Blankenhorn, how to evacuate the Bonn government in the event of an attack.[23]

The Korean War shifted opinions decisively toward rearmament. Political and psychological pressure from Bonn interacted with Congressional pressure in Washington to produce a powerful momentum for action. In this effort McCloy played a critical role, both through his interpretation of German sentiment and his attempt to shape policy in the direction of a "European" army. When fears of an East German or Soviet attack contributed to a general crisis of confidence in the young Federal Republic, McCloy relayed these concerns to Washington. Although the populace remained calm and reports of panic buying or hoarding were exaggerated, the public mood was fatalistic—a war weariness that inclined most West Germans toward neutrality and away from support for the West. Industrialists bought advertisements in Communist newspapers as a form of "insurance" against political change. The British observed cases in which the German police were reluctant to act against Communist disturbances. Although the Communists lacked popular support, West Germans tended to ask fatalistically, "What will I do when the Russians come?" The British High Commissioner concluded that "failing any evidence of our resolve there will be an increasing tendency to compound with the Russians while there is time."[24]

The political elite in Bonn reacted much more directly to events in Korea. When East German leaders threatened trials before "People's Courts" for "Adenauer, Pferdmenges, Reuter and other traitors," the American liaison, Charles Thayer, reported that Bonn's reaction "verged on the hysterical." Bundestag members "cleaned out the market [for cyanide] prepared to take their lives when the Communists come." Blankenhorn told McCloy's deputy, General Hays, that the

Germans would draw their own conclusions from America's retreat in Korea. Kurt Kiesinger, a CDU deputy who would later became Chancellor, told Thayer that the Allies should prepare a military redoubt in Brittany from which to mount a last stand against a Communist offensive. When news leaked out that McCloy was compiling a "list of important Germans" who should be helped to escape in the event of an attack, he was overwhelmed by people asking that their names be added to the list. Even Adenauer wanted to purchase firearms from the Americans to defend his office. In a meeting with the High Commissioners on July 12, 1950, he argued that unless the Allies took "steps to convince the Germans that some opportunity would be afforded them to defend their country in the event of an emergency," the situation might deteriorate further and Germans might rethink their policy toward the Soviet Union. He complained about the "real vacuum in all Western preparations" as well as his own lack of knowledge "of Allied plans in the event of an attack."[25]

In part to appease Adenauer, whom he saw as "still a little weak—mentally, morally, and physically," McCloy authorized secret talks between his own deputy, General Hays, and Adenauer's security adviser, General Schwerin. McCloy was struck by Adenauer's appeal to allow the Germans to fight with the West, and he told General Handy, the American Commander in Germany, that perhaps Germans should be allowed to enlist in the American Army. McCloy also urged Washington to advise the Germans that "we would permit them to fight shoulder to shoulder with us when the need should arise." The report of the first meeting, on July 17, between Schwerin and Hays strengthened McCloy's sense that something must be done quickly. Schwerin gave Hays a memorandum and a list of thirteen questions, including, for example, where and how quickly the Soviets might invade, what assistance the West Germans could give to hinder such an invasion, and whether Germans would be allowed to fight with the Allies. Other questions followed a worst-case scenario: how the German government could be evacuated; what should be done about the eight to ten million refugees who might flee such an invasion; what could be done about fifth-column sabotage; how foodstuffs would be provided to the population; how "the greatest possible number of young Germans" could be safeguarded and evacuated for future assignment to military units; and what should be done to protect key industries and scientific institutes.[26]

The day after receiving Schwerin's questions McCloy cabled Acheson and Byroade and reiterated his suggestion that Germans be allowed to enlist in the American Army, adding that Washington should consider whether to "permit larger groups to train and fight in the event of an emergency." He realized that this required a "radical change in our present European defense plans," but "in light of Korea" it must be considered. Finally, as Acheson recalled, McCloy put his position "most dramatically" by stating, "If no means are held out for Germans to fight in an emergency my view is that we should probably lose Germany politically as well as militarily without hope of regain. We should also lose, incidentally, a reserve of manpower which may become of great value in event of a real war and could certainly be used by the Soviets against us."[27]

A few days later McCloy reinforced this secret warning to Washington with a radio interview that was designed to put pressure on decision makers. Asked whether American troops would defend Germany "without the help of German contingents," McCloy began by saying, "There are no German military contingents in Germany and we are not establishing them." But then he expressed a view clearly influenced by Adenauer: "I suppose there would be very many Germans who would be prepared and anxious to defend Germany in the event of an attack, if given the opportunity." Denying that this meant either "rearmament" or an "offset" to the East German forces, McCloy put the issue in terms likely to appeal to an American audience: "In the event of an attack such as took place in Korea I believe it would be very difficult indeed to deny the Germans the right and the means to defend their own soil."[28]

McCloy's view rested not only on simple military arithmetic. He believed that in the long run the stature of the Bonn government with its own people would be affected by its participation in or exclusion from the system of Western security established by NATO. But more important, Congress was already raising the question of whether the United States should defend Europe when the Europeans were reluctant to make use of German resources and manpower. To American legislators "it seemed illogical to build a defense of Europe without incorporating a German component" and "unfair to all parties that U.S. equipment and manpower should protect German territory unless the Germans shared in the common enterprise." In the long run McCloy suspected that an American commitment to Western Europe's defense would become politically impossible to sustain without German participation.[29]

The pressure from Germany and from Congress forced Washington decision makers to face a question that shows the influence of McCloy's messages: as President Truman posed it to Acheson on July 25, 1950, "How can German manpower be used without establishing a German Army?" "Losing Germany," with its resources and manpower, was a nightmare for American leaders who had "lost China." Other factors also played a role in weakening the opposition to German rearmament in Washington. During July the military stepped up its own pressure for a reversal of policy, using McCloy's cables as proof of the need to act. A number of key officials, including Paul Nitze and Averell Harriman, changed their views on the issue, complaining that Byroade and the Bureau of German Affairs had taken a "business as usual attitude" and had not seen the "connection between the Korean situation and the one in Germany." The French opposition to German rearmament also appeared to be wavering. David Bruce reported from Paris that French leaders despaired of the effectiveness of purely "national" efforts to provide defense and believed "NATO should be expanded into a real collective defense effort with real central direction rather than merely a program to step up national efforts with coordinated planning." Bruce noted that the French thought one of the advantages of a really "common NATO defense" lay in the treatment of Germany. Even the question of German rearmament might be viewed differently, the French told Bruce, "if the Germans are made soldiers in an Atlantic community army or even a European army."[30]

Bruce's report on the French pointed the way to a solution which both Byroade and McCloy were already considering. Byroade, fearing that Washington was being "stampeded without thinking through the implications of a change in policy," thought that the earlier objections to German rearmament, especially the danger it posed to civilian democratic government, had not disappeared. Adopting the Schuman Plan as a model, he told Acheson that the solution rested with some type of European army. After agreeing to advocate the idea to the President, Acheson insisted that Byroade and McCloy coordinate their approaches and work out the concrete details. When he met the President at the end of the month, Acheson told him that the earlier proposal of German rearmament, which both men had opposed, was the wrong way to proceed. The question should not be "whether" to bring Germany "into the general defensive plan," but how this could be done without "disrupting" the alliance and allowing Germany to act as "the balance of power in Europe." Reviving a German General Staff or German military supply center in the Ruhr were examples of the wrong approach and "would repeat errors which had been made a number of times in the past." The President agreed, adding his own list of historical mistakes concerning Germany, "from Napoleon's time on." When Acheson told the President that the State Department was considering a "European or North Atlantic army" to integrate Germany's military and economic potential into the West, the President approved.[31]

With this mandate McCloy and Byroade produced the arguments and plans for a European army, which would be referred to during the next few months as either the European Defense Force (EDF) or the European Security Force (ESF). McCloy and his advisers, principally Robert Bowie and Colonel Al Gerhardt, concerned themselves with the political necessity of the European approach. In an August 3 cable to Byroade, McCloy argued that the "time is now ripe for a basic solution of the problem of defense of Western Europe." Accepting the Europeans' argument that they could not survive another "liberation," he asserted that Europe's defense could not "be achieved merely by strengthening national armies." France lacked the capacity, "if not the will," to bear the brunt of Western Europe's defense, making it essential that there be "real contributions of German resources and men," to defend Europe "effectively." Nevertheless, McCloy repeated his pre-Korea insistence that it would be a mistake to re-create a "German national army now or in the foreseeable future." Such a step would undermine "democratization," be opposed by the majority of Germans, and create the risk of a future "Schaukelpolitik," with Germany playing off East against West or ultimately "joining the Soviets." A "genuine European army" offered a way out of the dilemma, allowing the West "to convert our present weakness into real strength." It would give the French the hope of effective defense without the "risk of a German national army" and would appeal to the strong European sentiment among the Germans. Most important, however, it would achieve the American goal of a "dual containment," providing an effective defense against Russia while at the same time integrating Germany into Western Europe and giving the "best possible insurance against further German aggression."[32]

McCloy also sought to deal with the expected objections to such an ambitious scheme. To those who feared it "would complicate our problem" and unnecessarily delay an effective defense, he responded that with "bold action" a European army could be created within a year or eighteen months. He also contended that the Soviets might find such an approach less provocative than a German national army, but in any case Soviet disapproval was a "necessary risk." Finally he acknowledged that Germany could not be a second-class member of such an army but must become "a substantial equal" within a "very limited time." He concluded by noting that "time is essential" and urging American support for the idea at the earliest possible moment.[33]

Back in Washington Byroade seized upon McCloy's arguments, feeling that they supplied a cogent and compelling answer to those who questioned why such a concept should be adopted. His own work examined the more specific aspects of forming an army. It made unified command arrangements and procurement the "heart" of the European army, intending to use this military "integration" to further political and economic integration. Byroade believed NATO's "Supreme Commander" should direct a common procurement and supply organization. The Supreme Commander would have an integrated staff, on which German officers would serve; but there would be no separate German General Staff, and the highest German grade would be division commander. Although other countries would be able to maintain separate national forces for use in overseas possessions or internal disturbances, all German forces would be part of the European army. Recruitment would be on a national basis, with forces organized into either Regimental Combat Teams (RCT) or divisions, as the Supreme Commander decided.[34]

To assist him in refining this proposal and defending it in discussions with the Defense Department, Byroade asked McCloy to send Bowie and Gerhardt to Washington. These three advisers then proceeded to prepare a draft paper for submission to the NSC. Following Gerhardt's advice, Byroade agreed that the Supreme Commander should not be "Czar over both field forces and all economic aspects of the problem as well," and that procurement could be handled within "the framework of the NATO Military Production and Supply Board." He also worked to cut down other areas where there was any overlap with NATO structures. To Byroade's original proposal Gerhardt and Bowie added limits on the types and quantities of material and equipment which Germany would be allowed to manufacture, completely excluding heavy weapons and tanks. Although they insisted again that "no General Staff and no German military command structure" would be set up, they did allow a federal ministry for Germany which would organize the recruitment of "raw blocks of manpower not organized in combat units." These groups would be turned over to the European supreme commander for organization and training that would emphasize "the European character of these units."[35]

While his advisers hammered out the specific proposal in Washington, McCloy lobbied for the European army among the other American representatives in Europe, principally Ambassadors David Bruce and Lewis Douglas, as well as Charles Spofford, the U.S. Representative to NATO. Spofford's fellow representatives were impressed with the concept, but they stressed the need for a strong American commitment in Europe, in the form of both an American to be appointed Supreme Commander of NATO and an increased number of American combat troops. McCloy accepted their views, arguing that not only would such steps serve a psychological purpose, but they would also deter Moscow from any thought of using the East German forces alone. He also hoped the British and French would match any increase in U.S. forces. Reiterating his commitment to the European army as the "only practical means for mobilizing Europe for effective defense," he stressed the importance of a "single command and unified staff." He also believed the United States should take an immediate decision, pointing out that "the uncertainty as to time available for strengthening European defense and the great desirability of having largest possible strength by next summer make each month too precious to allow delay."[36]

The Defense Department strongly opposed the concept of a European defense force. To military leaders the State Department's EDF or ESF would not only be a hopelessly complicated political organization which would delay the establishment of an effective defense, but it would involve "a number of difficult and gravely important military problems." This approach made commitments to the Europeans without requiring promises that they would do what was necessary for their own defense, that is, quickly rearm the Germans. The Defense Department insisted upon German soldiers as a "first step" in defending Europe, not as an inevitable though gradual development. The military also argued that NATO was "the appropriate framework for promoting the integrated collective defense." The Joint Chiefs of Staff asked why the sovereignty of other countries should be reduced within a European arrangement when the simpler solution was to "raise Germany's status, and accept her, subject to controls, into NATO." To satisfy the fears about a new German military, they recommended that German divisions remain under the direct control of Allied Commanders, and that Germany should not have naval and air forces or produce heavy weapons. They agreed with the State Department that instead of a German General Staff there would be only an administrative and training staff. The difference between the two perspectives was crystallized in the military's hope to exploit for the West the very nationalism which worried McCloy and Byroade. They put little stock in "European" enthusiasm, arguing that nationalism was the key to all the defense efforts of the Western Union and NATO. As for McCloy and Byroade's view that the Germans were opposed to creating a national army, the army planners "believed that such *could not be a true indication of German opinion.*"[37]

Adenauer encouraged the American military's view that the Germans were eager to bear arms again. Concerned that Moscow might seek to employ East German forces as the North Korean forces had been used, he considered possible scenarios ranging from an all-out East German invasion to more limited actions, such as seizing the city of Hamburg or Lübeck near the zonal border. At one point in July he considered sending a direct request to President Truman for the immediate dispatch of more American soldiers to Germany. In mid-August when he returned from a vacation in Switzerland, Adenauer received pessimistic reports from his security advisers on the build-up of East German forces, one of which estimated that they would number some 150,000 by the end of 1951 and 300,000 by 1952. "Incensed and angry," he confronted the High Commission over the lack of Allied proposals for the defense of West Germany. Noting the "state of great demoralization" in West Germany, he contended that most West Germans would respond with a neutral and defeatist attitude in the event of an East German attack. Stalin wanted to gain Germany with as little damage as possible, and the Soviets could "neutralize" America's atomic advantage. Since it was hardly likely that the United States would respond with nuclear weapons to an East German attack, it was necessary for the Allies either to increase their own forces or to allow West Germany to build up a force capable of handling the East Germans. Though Adenauer still favored German participation in a "European army," he argued that the immediate need was so pressing that such an army was too distant a hope to be of much use. Instead he proposed recruiting a German "defense force" of 150,000 men, an offer he made public the same day in a *New York Times* interview.[38]

Before the September Foreign Ministers' conference Adenauer revised his offer, giving different figures and providing confusing answers on whether the men would serve as a police force or as regular soldiers. In his Security Memorandum, given to McCloy at the end of August, the Chancellor also added important political conditions, insisting on an end to Allied occupation as a condition for rearmament. But his original offer had encouraged the American military's view that the Germans were eager to get back into uniform. The "package proposal" that resulted from the bureaucratic negotiations between the Pentagon and the State Department before the New York meeting reflected some compromise between the two positions, even though the military's concerns dominated. This proposal demanded immediate steps to create German armed forces in return for the dispatch of additional American troops and the appointment of an American Supreme Commander. Reference was made to a "European defense force," but this term expressed only a "concept," not an actual organization, and it had little in common with McCloy and Byroade's original proposal. Integration of the various European forces would be minimal. Although there would be an "international command staff," the military units would be "nationally generated" so as not "to impair their morale or effectiveness." Although the Germans would provide ten to twelve divisions, their officers would not serve on the international command staff and the units would be restricted from using certain heavy weaponry. The proposal omitted any discussion of the political consequences of rearmament.[39]

Despite the difference between his own ideas and the final proposal, McCloy waged a relentless campaign to emphasize the "European" elements that remained. He told Averell Harriman that "if we are to rearm the Germans, we must make certain that Germany does not erect a national army now or in the future." The only way to avoid this would be to set up a "thoroughly integrated force with real delegation of authority and not merely a coordinated group of national armies." McCloy saw no contradiction between encouraging the European nations in the direction of integration and having America make its contribution through NATO. "The Europeans are obviously in a different situation than we are and should be urged really to merge their defense efforts into strong European institutions." To Secretary of Defense Johnson, a much less sympathetic listener than Harriman, McCloy stressed the resulting discontent in Germany "if we attempted to recreate the Wehrmacht as an independent national force." Youth, the churches, labor, and the middle class would oppose such a step. But, referring to public opinion surveys which the High Commission had conducted, he argued that these groups would favor "a German military contribution to a European Defense Force." While carefully deferring to the military's judgment about the degree of integration, McCloy pleaded that we "not lose sight of the basic concept of an integrated European Force." He even leaked to a group of reporters, including Ferdinand Kuhn of the *Washington Post,* a detailed account of the American proposal a few days before the New York conference. The wording of the story—that the United States would propose "a fully armed German force of ten divisions integrated into a West European Army"—emphasized McCloy's arguments that the Germans opposed the re-creation of "anything approaching the German Wehrmacht."[40]

More than other American leaders, McCloy recognized the political implications of Germany's participation in Western defense. In a report to President Truman he argued that "the occupation [could not] as a practical matter, continue for an indefinite period" after the Germans joined the EDF. He urged that the Allies negotiate a series of agreements with the Germans, gradually relinquishing their controls. "Thereafter, the occupation would continue only as a security against aggression." Although he wanted to achieve greater "democratization" of German society, he told the President that "certain of the things we would like to see done in Germany will not be completed." But "we are forced to accept this as unavoidable in order to attain the larger objective of binding Germany to the West." McCloy hoped that the integration of Germany into Western Europe would safeguard democracy and the liberal constitutional order that American reform programs were designed to establish.[41]

From New York to Brussels: The Search for Agreement

Secretary of State Acheson arrived in New York with the carefully constructed "package proposal" which the French would later call the "bomb at the Waldorf." Indeed, although Acheson conceded the "essential correctness" of the Pentagon's strategic objectives, he would have preferred not to force the issue, hoping that the "inevitable logic of mathematics" would make German rearmament seem a necessity to the Allies. The tightly bound "package" was a tactic he himself found "murderous," more an ultimatum than a negotiating position. Yet this approach had been necessary in order to obtain the most revolutionary aspect of the American proposal. For the first time in its peacetime history, the United States was prepared to station a large part of its army in a foreign land and to appoint a Supreme Commander to lead this force and those of its Allies. This was the real founding of NATO.[42]

The package proposal caused consternation among the Allies, further dividing the British and French. Bevin, concerned about a Korean-style attack within Germany, had planned to urge approval in New York of Adenauer's "police force" to balance the East Germans. Because Acheson had objected to Schwerin's activities earlier in the summer, Bevin mistakenly thought that he might have difficulty convincing the Americans to take even this cautious first step. The British Chiefs of Staff had wanted to create "twenty German divisions" for the defense of Western Europe, but the Cabinet had rejected their proposals in favor of Bevin's plan. Bevin even managed to secure French approval for the police force idea, though Paris insisted that the Länder, rather than Bonn, should control the police.[43]

Although Bevin was surprised by the sweeping nature of the U.S. package proposal, he was privately pleased with the offer to send additional divisions to Europe, a long-sought objective of British policy. He also recognized that the American proposal would create new difficulties, giving additional leverage to the Germans by "asking" them to form an army, intensifying political problems for the French, and risking Russian displeasure. Bevin told Acheson that the "police force" idea was preferable to the American plan: "You've got the right idea, me lad, but you're goin' about it the hard way." Yet despite his reservations Bevin supported the American proposal, mainly because Europe would receive a Supreme Commander and U.S. troops. The Cabinet was more hesitant, until it was persuaded that American financial assistance to British defense programs was dependent on German rearmament.[44]

Was the British proposal a better alternative than the American? The answer remains unclear. It was less frightening to the French. But their insistence on decentralization would have prevented the police force from "evolving" into an organized, centrally controlled army. Schuman told the British ambassador in Paris he was worried that a German general of the "old school like Seeckt" might get command of such a police force, and some French observers saw a parallel with the "Black Reichswehr" of the 1920s. As for the Germans, their response to the British plan was also divided. Despite Adenauer's willingness to raise a police force, he would probably have sought extra concessions from the Allies when the police began resembling soldiers. Schumacher and the SPD opposed the police idea outright, mainly because it gave Adenauer an independent instrument of power. And the Americans shared this mistrust. The State Department told the British that the Chancellor might use such a force "for quelling social unrest" among the refugees, unrest that was not "connected with the Communist tactics." The Americans saw the British plan as containing the dangers of an independent German army *and* a centralized police force. Though there was less overall resistance to the police idea than to a new German army, the proposal provoked strong opposition. Shortly after the New York conference the British themselves recognized this and abandoned it.[45]

The French reacted much more bitterly to the American package proposal than did the British. "Schuman took the indivisible package very hard," Acheson recalled in his memoirs. "He embraced every part of it enthusiastically except German military participation." Before New York, Schuman had convinced himself, despite clear warnings, that the question of rearmament would not arise. Like the British he viewed the principal threat in Germany as a Korean-style invasion, which an increase and redeployment of Allied occupation forces could meet. In his view a German army would only provoke the Soviets, bringing on the general war in Europe which the French most feared. At the same time the French government insisted that only a fully integrated defense effort held any promise for Western Europe. It planned to ask the United States for a degree of unity in defense planning and financing that went well beyond what was politically possible for an American government. Fearing the inflationary consequences of rearmament, the French wanted "guarantees" of massive American military assistance. They also wanted the defense of Europe to extend as far east as possible, insisting that France must be "defended" and not "liberated." Yet at the same time they would not allow French soldiers to become "the infantry of Europe." The defeat in 1940 had left the government and people with little confidence in the "purely French ability to create an effective military establishment or to withstand aggression." Only if assured of "massive mutual support from [its] allies . . . on the spot upon the outbreak of hostilities" would the French government and public support an effective defense program.[46]

Because of France's plea for massive American assistance, Washington expected its grudging acceptance of the package proposal. Americans underestimated its deep-seated, emotional distrust of Germany and German militarism. They also misunderstood Schuman's political position within the coalition government, and in particular his relationship with the French Socialists, the SFIO. Although accounting for only 20 percent of the National Assembly, the Socialists possessed a "disproportionate strength" and were essential to the Pleven government's survival. The SFIO had taken an anti-Communist line, but it shared the French left's strong anti-German sentiments. No one was more symbolic of this attitude than the Socialist leader and Defense Minister, Jules Moch, whose son had been cruelly tortured and executed by the Germans. Moch told Americans that a new "German military establishment . . . would cause alarm and probably engender grave political consequences in France." In his and his party's view, German rearmament, with the memory of "Hitler's hordes" still fresh, would not only be disgraceful but would hand the French Communists a golden opportunity to mobilize the French public against the government. Moch, who had been instrumental in getting the Communists out of the government, feared the domestic political effects of rearmament as much as its international consequences.[47]

Despite the best efforts of Acheson and Schuman, the New York talks broke down. The United States appeared heavy-handed, threatening to withdraw its assistance unless the Allies agreed to its terms. The French appeared "stubborn and vengeful," unwilling to accept reality. Paris also found itself increasingly isolated as countries like Norway, Denmark, and the Netherlands, all of which had been occupied by the Germans, swallowed hard and supported the American proposal. The British reversal of position further weakened the French stance. Under pressure from both the Americans and other Europeans, Schuman found himself making a passionate and emotional plea to the NATO Council of Deputies, warning of the dangers of German militarism, treachery, and irredentism. Although conceding that Germany would "someday" join the Western defense force, he argued that the Allies must wait until they were certain the German contribution would "enhance and not endanger security."[48]

The collapse of the talks raised temperatures on both sides. Responding to the French argument that the "delicacy" of their public opinion would not allow for German rearmament, McCloy wrote Acheson, "I think the time has come to tell these people that . . . U.S. opinion is getting damn delicate itself." If there was an attack in the next months, McCloy continued, and "U.S. troops should get pushed around without German troops to help them because of a French reluctance to face facts, I shudder to think how indelicate U.S. opinion would suddenly become." Yet McCloy's emotional outburst did not keep him from seeing the political question as far more important than the simple number of German troops. "Uppermost in my mind is the fear that Germany would drift away from the real desire of most people in West Germany to become incorporated into a Western community." McCloy feared that if Germany were left unprotected and outside of Western defense plans, it would develop a "neutrality complex," and then France would be "in a fix." Germany would eventually want an army, and if France tried to stop it, the interwar pattern, "the old dance of death" of Franco-German antagonism, would reassert itself. Acheson shared McCloy's fears. Referring to McCloy's note, he wrote the President that "we cannot accept any French position which puts us back to the position of the twenties when we were adamant in not making any concessions to the Germans who were on our side, and then yielded under pressure to the Germans who were against us."[49]

Acheson, who was not wedded to the package proposal, sought a compromise. Truman's firing of Louis Johnson and his appointment of General George Marshall as Secretary of Defense removed a barrier to cooperation between the two Departments and softened the sharp edges of the proposal. Marshall, who was much more sensitive to the political questions involved, emphasized the "problem of detailed practical arrangements" for the integrated force and the Supreme Commander, rather than insisting on German participation. Acheson, for his part, thought the French might agree to give private rather than public assurances of cooperation in German rearmament. Schuman had told him at the end of the New York talks that France was considering its own proposal on European defense, and that it should not "drag on the end of a chain" held by the United States. Ambassador Bruce in Paris suggested to Acheson that "if Schuman could relay to his Cabinet a course of conduct inspired by us but giving the French Government an opportunity to assert Continental leadership, we might possibly obtain a happy and even unexpected result." When Acheson encouraged such a proposal, he heard from the Luxembourg Foreign Minister, Joseph Bech, that Jean Monnet was already hard at work on such an idea.[50]

Monnet had recognized soon after the Korean War began that it would have serious implications for the proposed Schuman Plan. He predicted that the American request for German participation in defense arrangements would threaten the balance between France and the Federal Republic, giving the Germans increased leverage during the most important phase of the negotiations. Soon after the American proposal of German rearmament at the New York talks, Monnet perceived a "stiffening of resistance" in the German delegation's attitude at the Schuman Plan talks. The boom in steel production occasioned by the American rearmament drive—which led to an increased volume of export orders from American companies to Ruhr concerns—promised German steel manufacturers an eventual lifting of quotas and restrictions without the necessity of joining the Schuman Plan. (The Allies already exempted defense-related production from the German steel quotas.) Adenauer's appointment of Robert Lehr as Interior Minister to replace Gustav Heinemann also indicated a cooling of German interest in the Schuman Plan. Lehr, a member of the Board of Directors of August-Thyssen, criticized the Schuman Plan as France's way of safeguarding its "steel hegemony with the aid of Germany, which France could not achieve against Germany."[51]

Monnet believed that saving the Schuman Plan required a compromise between France and the United States on the issue of German rearmament. France needed a proposal both in order to regain the initiative and reenlist the sympathy and support of Americans who backed the Schuman Plan and to head off a bilateral American-German military alliance that would, from the French perspective, increase the danger of war in Europe. In Monnet's view, German rearmament needed to be delayed, at least until the Schuman Plan was in effect and Germany was more securely linked to Western Europe.[52]

In mid-October, with a proposal only partially completed, Schuman sought, as he had done with the Coal and Steel Plan, to gain "some indication . . . as to whether or not this possible solution of the German rearmament impasse would be favorably regarded by the US Government" before presenting the proposal to the French Cabinet. The "possible solution" that Schuman first put forward to the Americans, however, was nothing more than a vague promise that France would take the initiative in setting up a European Continental army "immediately" after the signing of the Schuman Plan. This army would be one of the components, along with the British and the American forces, assigned to the defense of the North Atlantic area. Germany would "enjoy a status of equality, subject, of course, to the restrictions and controls which existed" as a result of the occupation. Acheson reacted to this proposal with reserve, noting that it was "too indefinite for specific criticism." He did, however, reaffirm that the United States would welcome "some application of the Schuman Plan concept to the military field."[53]

Even without a strong American endorsement, Monnet, Pleven, and Schuman pushed on with their work, using the same team of advisers that had written the Schuman Plan. But the result, the Pleven Plan, proposed not so much a genuine European army as a French Foreign Legion for Europe. Speaking before the French Assembly on October 24, 1950, Pleven described a European army of 100,000 men, with German soldiers integrated "on the level of the smallest possible unit." To avoid anything approaching a separate German General Staff or Defense Ministry, he called for "une fusion complète" of the human and material components of a European army. (Although the unit size was left unclear, Moch later suggested integration at the level of 1,000-man battalions, a suggestion whose sheer impracticality inspired more ridicule than any other aspect of the Plan.) Pleven proposed the creation of a European Ministry of Defense that would deal with recruiting, training, and budgetary questions. Except for Germany, the states participating in the European army would have separate national forces outside of Europe, a concession designed to protect the French Empire. To delay German rearmament Pleven insisted that the creation of the European army should await both the completion of the Schuman Plan and the negotiation of the "political institutions of a united Europe." He emphasized the equivocal character of the proposal by ending his speech with a call for renewed four-power talks with the Soviet Union, talks which might avert any need for German rearmament. As a result of its compromises and deliberate vagueness the Pleven Plan received the French National Assembly's narrow approval.[54]

The Pleven Plan was not much more discriminatory toward Germany than the original American proposal for an EDF. But its proposal to postpone German rearmament until after the creation of a politically united Europe made it a transparent attempt to delay rearmament—perhaps indefinitely. Unlike the Schuman Plan, which had been greeted with enthusiasm, the Pleven Plan received mixed reviews from the start. Officially Acheson welcomed it, saying that "it represented a further approach towards the objective of bringing the common interests of the free nations of Europe more closely together within the framework of the North Atlantic Community." Privately he thought the proposal "hopeless" and urged French Ambassador Henri Bonnet to inform his government that its position should not be "rigid," but that it must allow "progress" on the German question. In a conversation with British Ambassador Oliver Franks, Acheson showed an understanding of Schuman's dilemma: "Schuman found himself in the position where he could neither accept the U.S. position nor turn it down." More important, he told Franks that many of the "problems" the British saw in the Pleven proposal were problems the Europeans would one day have to confront, "when our troops and other non-Continental troops would no longer be necessary in Europe and went home." But for the immediate future Acheson wanted to sidestep the delay inherent in the French idea.[55]

Acheson's reaction was charitable compared with the treatment Pleven's proposal received from the NATO Defense Ministers at their meeting in late October. Emmanuel Shinwell, the British Defense Minister, was "rabid" on the subject. The French proposal, he argued, "would only excite laughter and ridicule" in the Soviet Union. This reaction reflected the British perception of French duplicity, for French officials in London were telling the Foreign Office that the Pleven proposal, which was intended only "to meet a Parliamentary emergency," was "military and political nonsense." The French also knew that the division was the smallest effective military unit, and their suggestion regarding integrated battalions was only a way to stymie American plans for a German army. The British, for their part, were concerned that French tactics could backfire, preventing American participation in the creation of an effective European defense.[56]

Defense Minister Jules Moch's presentation of the Pleven proposal also contributed to its negative reception. Moch had accepted the proposal only under pressure from other members of the French Cabinet. His absolute refusal to discuss anything but the French proposal created the impression of extreme intransigence. Acheson commented that "it would be impossible to exaggerate the unfavorable character of the impression created on the other European Representatives . . . The feeling is such that we do not believe the French proposal could be accepted even if it had full U.S. support." Moch's behavior at the conference reflected his concern for French politics and his deeply held personal beliefs about the Germans. Madame Moch, dressed completely in black, sat directly behind her husband during the conference. To some she seemed "an angel of death," keeping vigil so that her husband would resist American pressure and not betray their murdered son. Acheson commented, "It is our own view that Moch has dealt the cause of French leadership in Continental Europe, which we have encouraged, a severe blow."[57]

In contrast to the negative reaction of the NATO Defense Ministers, the American diplomats in Europe showed more sympathy for the French approach. Bruce, who had consulted with Monnet on early drafts of the proposal, recorded in his diary, "Personally I am enthusiastic about the approach which would do much toward bringing about a closer association amongst the free nations of Europe." Douglas, though stationed in skeptical London, noted that, although much needed to be clarified, "the proposal may be another important means for bringing about Franco-German rapprochement, thus permitting the formation of an effective defense of Western Europe." McCloy reacted more warily. He told Acheson that "running through the whole document I see the possibility of delay and diminution of the vigor of the concept of prompt and decisive action." Yet he welcomed an invitation from Monnet to visit Paris to discuss the proposal further, telling Acheson, "I believe we must make the best of the French proposal, if *France's intentions* are sincere, for I despair of an effective European defense without France."[58]

For the French, McCloy's visit afforded an important opportunity. If they could convince the High Commissioner, who they believed had the confidence of both Acheson and Adenauer, they could begin the process of bringing the Americans and Germans behind their proposal. McCloy, whose "independence and goodwill" inspired much

respect, would lend substance to their case. At a meeting attended by
McCloy, Bowie, Schuman, Pleven, and Monnet, the French officials
stressed the major issues. First they emphasized the "defensive" aspects
of the Pleven Plan, in implicit contrast to the overly aggressive American package proposal. The relatively small size of the army, and its
control by Europeans, would avoid provoking the Russians to take
preemptive action. It would also avoid giving the Germans an opportunity to wage war to regain their lost territories. Second, the French
insisted that only if the Americans gave their support to the plan
would the Germans agree to participate. The French leaders knew—
and they had seen this in connection with the Schuman Plan—that if
the Germans perceived a choice between a French and an American
idea, they would choose the American. Third, the French promised
that any discrimination would exist only in the transitional phase of
the proposal, assuring McCloy that the "Foreign Legion" provisions
would disappear when the organization become permanent. They also
assured him that they would act as quickly as possible to finish the
Schuman Plan negotiations and to set up machinery for the army plan.
Finally, they argued that German recruiting should only start under a
European authority, and that the first German soldier should wear a
European uniform.[59]

McCloy, who came away from the meeting convinced of the "sincerity" of the French, told Washington that France's "impelling fear
was . . . that a new German national army and General Staff would
immediately begin to plan in terms of war of revenge for the return
of the eastern provinces." The French had assured him they were "not
seeking to follow a dilatory course in regard to this problem." When
he returned to Germany, he called Blankenhorn and defended the
basic principle of the Plan, emphasizing that the French would eventually accept Germany's equality within the European army. The
American interest in the Plan helped soften the Chancellor's reaction.
Before talking to McCloy, Adenauer had told his advisers that the
Pleven Plan was discriminatory toward the Germans. He also disliked
its linkage with the Schuman Plan, which he viewed, quite correctly,
as a form of French pressure on the Germans. Adenauer was further
dismayed by the lack of any provision for American "leadership and
participation" in working out the details of the European army.
McCloy, after admitting that he himself could not endorse the Plan
in its existing form because he doubted its practicality, urged the

Chancellor to emphasize in general terms the importance of reaching an agreement with the French. These assurances led Adenauer to take a more favorable public position, calling the Pleven Plan an "important contribution to European integration, ever one of the main objectives of German policy," and agreeing to assist in "consultations" on the Plan.[60]

McCloy's intercession with Adenauer stemmed in large part from his concern over the deteriorating political situation in Germany. Indeed the controversy between the French and the Americans had temporarily obscured the growing unrest in the Federal Republic, where the Allied interest in rearmament had provoked increasing opposition. Adenauer's offers to recruit 150,000 men had given a false impression of the ease with which the Germans would return to uniform. In fact he was far out in front of German public opinion, which, despite the events in Korea, remained strongly opposed to anything smacking of militarism or a new national army. Moreover, the Allied disagreement only encouraged those who advocated a policy of neutrality in the Cold War. It also led German leaders to increase their political and military demands for concessions, and to insist that any German defense contribution must be given on terms of equality.

The opposition to rearmament in Germany never became a cohesive and united movement; it consisted, rather, of a diffuse set of viewpoints and perspectives, ranging from absolute pacifism at one extreme to a neo-Nazi refusal to fight for the despised republic at the other. The widespread sentiment captured in the expression "ohne mich," or "leave me out," reflected a desire to escape from the Cold War and the conflict between the United States and the Soviet Union. McCloy thought the "average German . . . is torn between the realization of the need for an adequate defense and the fear of the possible consequences of German participation in the defense system." Situated on the front line of the Cold War, with vivid memories of the ruthlessness of Russian policies in Eastern Germany, many Germans believed, as a shrewd British diplomat noted, that "it might even be better to let the Russians occupy Western Germany, than to fight for the Americans and risk getting taken prisoner by the Russians."[61]

The Social Democratic party gave some unity and strength to those opposing rearmament. Schumacher reversed the party's longstanding opposition to rearmament, arguing that the SPD would now accept rearmament, but only under certain conditions. Politically he de-

manded the abolition of the Occupation Statute and the satisfaction
of German demands concerning the Ruhr Authority and the Saar.
Militarily he insisted that the Allies station a massive force along the
Elbe to "shield" the Germans while they were rearming, and he also
wanted Allied strategy to change from defensive to offensive. In the
event of a Soviet attack, the overwhelming strength of the Allied-
German forces would insure that the decisive battles would be fought
beyond the eastern borders of Germany, between the Vistula and
Niemen rivers in Poland. Germany would not serve as a buffer zone
for France, and Germans would not provide "cannon-fodder" to protect an Allied retreat. Rather Schumacher wanted the Allies to accept
a reunified Germany with its 1937 borders as one of their strategic
objectives and war aims.[62]

Schumacher's call for an even greater Allied build-up and his adoption of an "offensive strategy" struck some observers, especially the
French, as an "irredentism of the Left," an attempt to gain political
support from refugees from the "lost territories." But despite the
nationalist and even aggressive overtones of Schumacher's position,
the SPD also campaigned as the party of peace, and its posters proclaimed that a vote for the Christian Democrats would be a vote for
"remilitarization." The fact was that Schumacher saw the rearmament
question as his best opportunity to force new elections and oust the
Adenauer government. His rigid insistence on Allied preconditions
appealed to those Germans, including the "ohne mich" voters, who
wanted to postpone the fateful decision as long as possible. Initial
returns on the SPD's position were quite impressive. In November
1950 the party scored impressive gains in state elections in Hesse and
Würtemberg-Baden and for the first time in its history achieved a
plurality in Bavaria. In public opinion polls the SPD was the most
popular single party, with a strength approaching 40 percent. Adenauer's popularity tumbled to a low point of 24 percent in late 1950.[63]

SPD opposition weakened Adenauer, but he was also hurt by opposition from his own supporters. One of the most important laymen
in the Evangelical Church, Interior Minister Gustav Heinemann, represented the Protestant wing of the CDU, and he saw his position in
the Cabinet as an attempt to preserve the delicate confessional balance
within the Christian Democrats. Heinemann was a strong opponent
of rearmament, casting his opposition in moral and religious terms:
"God has twice dashed the weapons from our hands. We must not

take them up a third time." (Adenauer's rejoinder to this was that "God has given us our heads to think with and our arms and hands to act with.") Heinemann also feared the effect of rearmament on the possibility of reunification, and he objected to Adenauer's military assurances to the Western countries without the Cabinet's approval. He sought to resign after Adenauer had given his Security Memorandum to the High Commission at the end of August, but the Chancellor persuaded him to stay on. Heinemann, however, was a close associate of Pastor Martin Niemöller, a strong opponent of rearmament and advocate of neutrality and reunification. When Niemöller attacked the Chancellor for making "secret" agreements with the Allies to rearm Germany, and vowed that the Protestant Church would oppose "remilitarization," Adenauer demanded that Heinemann disassociate himself from the Pastor. When Heinemann refused, Adenauer finally accepted his resignation.[64]

The Heinemann resignation, which hurt Adenauer politically, forced him to recognize the difficulties he would face in dealing with the rearmament question. The day after the resignation he declared in a national radio broadcast that the Federal Republic was under no obligation to rearm, and that any decision would have to be approved by the Bundestag. He told McCloy privately that "the initiative for German armed contribution [must] come from the allies." McCloy also learned, as a result of the Heinemann resignation, that the opposition to rearmament would constrain Adenauer's options and make it difficult for him to accept measures he might have adopted only a few months earlier. When Washington expressed a brief interest in reviving the British idea of using "mobile police formations" as an intermediary step toward rearmament, McCloy argued that such "halfway measures" played "directly into the hands of those in Germany who are striving to avoid any definite action aligning Germany with the West." He added, "This group is very large—Heinemann, Noack, Niemöller, are not isolated figures by any means." This domestic opposition made it crucial for the Allies to avoid any Diktats to the Chancellor.[65]

Following on the heels of Heinemann's resignation was another embarrassment, the firing of former General Schwerin. The immediate cause for this was an off-the-record interview Schwerin had given to a number of Bonn reporters, in which he had sought to clarify his activities. Adenauer, who had forbidden Schwerin to talk to the press, used the incident as an excuse to dismiss him. The Chancellor's action headed off protests within his own party, both over his usurpation of parliamentary authority in appointing a "defense adviser" and his employment of a former general in such a politically sensitive position. As Schwerin's replacement, Adenauer selected Theodor Blank, a prominent Catholic trade unionist and CDU Bundestag member. He charged Blank with handling "all questions arising out of the reinforcement of Allied troops" in the Federal Republic. In reality, Blank was to set up an embryonic Defense Ministry and plan for the creation of German forces.[66]

In the midst of Adenauer's political troubles came another offer from the East for reunification and the settlement of the German question. On October 20 at a meeting in Prague the Soviet Union and its East European allies called for a four-power agreement to prevent "the remilitarization of Western Germany" and the "threat of new aggression" in Europe. The Soviets proposed the creation of an All-German Constitutional Council composed of an equal number of representatives from East and West Germany. Even though the proposed equality was hardly representative of the West's greater population, the Soviet offer triggered interest among the European Allies and in West Germany. Both French and British leaders thought that an understanding on Germany might defuse tensions and appeal to their constituencies. In Germany the discussion of rearmament had already triggered demands for a renewed attempt to overcome the country's division. The theologian Karl Barth joined with Heinemann and Niemöller in criticizing rearmament for driving a permanent wedge between the two Germanies and creating the preconditions for civil war.[67]

Adenauer, who was feeling both international and domestic pressure, began to seek more extensive concessions from the Allies. Without consulting his Cabinet he took a new memorandum to the High Commissioners' meeting on November 16. Although he assured them it was not a list of "demands," the memorandum detailed the changes needed to alter the "defeatist" attitude of the Germans. It referred to the lack of action taken on his earlier Security Memorandum and concluded, "I no longer consider . . . a revision of the Occupation Statute as sufficient." Along with "contractual agreements" to end the occupation, Adenauer insisted on a variety of "generous acts"—economic, legal, and financial—in the Allies' relationship with Germany.

Among them would be a halt to all remaining dismantling, a relaxation of all the limits on German industry, removal of the restrictions on scientific research, and official participation by the Federal Republic in all questions of decartelization and deconcentration. Adenauer asked for "independent neutral experts" to determine how much his country could afford to pay in occupation costs and as a defense contribution. Quoting President Truman, he stressed the connection between "strength in dealing with the outside world and social security at home." If Germany's special burdens were not understood, its "will to defense" would be "lowered."[68]

The rest of the memorandum requested concessions to nationalist sentiment. Adenauer asked for an end to war crimes trials, as well as the commutation of the remaining death sentences. He demanded the "complete restoration of German sovereignty in the administration of justice," as well as an end to the extradition of Germans to foreign countries. In conclusion he told the High Commissioners that the "state of public opinion is not healthy," and that they must act to reverse this situation. "Otherwise it will be very difficult, if not impossible, to win over the minds of the German people to a voluntary cooperation in the defense of Europe." All the High Commissioners agreed to transmit Adenauer's "requests" to their governments. McCloy, although he hoped that the demands would not be seen as "a sort of trade for a German contribution," concluded his own report by agreeing with Adenauer that the situation "is not good and may be serious," and that "Adenauer's outright championship of the West has to be supported. We can see no one else who has taken a similar stand."[69]

Although McCloy urged support for Adenauer, he was exasperated by the Germans' attempt to link every issue to their defense contribution. For example, one prominent German clergyman, who wrote to McCloy asking for $400,000 to rebuild a church, tied receipt of the money to Germany's willingness to rearm. Erhard tried the same tactic when the Ruhr Authority enforced a coal export quota on Germany. The Bundestag also refused to accept one of the Allied decisions made in New York, which asked the Federal Republic to take responsibility for prewar Germany's international debts. Members of the Bundestag charged that the Allies wanted a "blank check," and that any acknowledgment must take into account Germany's changed circumstances. The German refusal to ratify this step angered all the

High Commissioners and stalled progress on modifying the Occupation Statute.[70]

The increasing demands of the Germans, along with the pressure of outside events, led the Western Allies, who realized that Germany would continue to raise the stakes until the West could present a united front, to seek a compromise on the issue of German rearmament. For all its failings the Pleven Plan did indicate some movement on the part of the French, in that it recognized the necessity of German participation in defense. Having concluded that "time is working for us in France but increasingly against us in Germany," the Americans sought a "provisional or transitional agreement" with the French. Chinese intervention in Korea late in November, followed by a disastrous American retreat, produced the worst war scare since the eve of Munich in 1938 and made the need for Western unity seem even more imperative.[71]

The proposed compromise bore the name of Charles Spofford, the American who was serving as chairman of the NATO Council of Deputies. The Spofford Plan rested on the conclusion that the "dilemma now confronting us is fundamentally political rather than military in nature." One of the key compromises it proposed concerned the size of German military units. The Americans would agree to accept the regimental combat team of between 5,000 and 6,000 men as the initial size of the German units, even while insisting that the division—between 12,000 and 15,000 men—was the smallest practicable fighting unit. (The Joint Chiefs of Staff opposed this compromise strenuously.) In return for this concession the French would scrap the requirement that German contingents could join the European force only after it was in operation. France also received assurances that German forces would never exceed more than 20 percent of the European army. The Americans would then agree to send to Europe a Supreme Commander—the World War II hero, General Dwight David Eisenhower—to take command of NATO forces.[72]

The convoluted attempts to find a compromise on German rearmament even inspired some humor. In the midst of the holiday season American journalists in Frankfurt sang, to the tune of "Hark! The Herald Angels Sing":

> Hark! The High Commissioners Sing
> German Army in the spring

Just in case the übermensch
Want to go and fight the French
We will keep divisions small
Give them no tanks at all.[73]

The French hesitated before agreeing to the Spofford Plan. They still wanted a more direct linkage between the raising of German forces and the creation of a European army and European political institutions. They also wanted more American support for their approach to German rearmament through the Pleven Plan. With the talks deadlocked in late November, and with American forces retreating in Korea, Acheson penned a personal appeal to Schuman, urging him to agree to Spofford's compromise. He emphasized the "dangerous drift of German opinion" that was occurring in the "absence of a concrete proposal" from the Allies and offered a restrained statement of support for the French approach to German rearmament: "If your government, in close consultation with the Germans and other European Governments, could evolve the main outlines of a plan for binding the free nations of Europe more closely together in the spirit so well represented by the Schuman Plan, we could reasonably hope for a long-term solution of our many problems, be they political, military, or economic." Acheson closed his letter with a renewed assurance of America's commitment to Europe, stating his conviction that "the broad framework of the Atlantic Community is an essential part of the free world structure, whether it be from the point of view of global security or of permanently ending the threat of *German* domination."[74]

Acheson's pointed reminder that the Americans had not forgotten about the German danger helped Schuman persuade his Cabinet that the letter represented the "final decision of the American government." In Paris Bruce negotiated the final French agreement to the Spofford Plan in return for the publication of a version of Acheson's letter. Despite vigorous opposition from the American military, which feared that the United States could end up "sharing the responsibility for this project, and by so doing, indirectly urging the smaller European countries to join the attempt," Acheson strengthened his lukewarm endorsement of the French approach. He agreed to send American observers to a European army conference and "to assist in bringing its deliberations to a successful conclusion." Although Acheson's letter broke the impasse, he would later regret even this limited promise to support the French proposal.[75]

Agreement on the Spofford Plan allowed the Allies to deal with the Germans from a position of strength. Acheson described this as an effort to "bring the German issue once more into proper perspective by stressing that the problem is a defense organization *for Western Europe,* in which the Germans would have the opportunity to participate." "Without appearing to do so," the new strategy was designed to put the "German matter on ice for a little while." More bluntly Acheson told the Cabinet that "it is important to let [the Germans] stew for a time." Both Adenauer and Schumacher had made sharp attacks on the Spofford Plan that had offended Acheson. Schumacher had called it a "betrayal" of the American promise to insure "equality" for the Germans, while Adenauer had rejected it because he believed it treated the Germans as "cannon fodder." Acheson was particularly angry over the strident opposition of the SPD, noting that "it is a curious contradiction . . . that the strongest clamor for German 'equality' comes from traditional anti-militarists who, at the same time, oppose the re-establishment of a German national army, and who might logically be expected to cooperate in devising structural safeguards." To defuse this opposition, and to make the Germans less certain of their own importance, Acheson believed it was necessary for the Allies to play hard to get.[76]

The Brussels conference in mid-December 1950 took place in an atmosphere "tinged with fear," with Soviet threats against German rearmament leading to speculation that war was imminent. Under intense criticism in the United States for his "softness" toward communism, Acheson nevertheless was able to find support from France and Britain for his policy of letting the Germans "stew for a time." The French still wanted a conference with the Soviets, and the crisis in Korea only intensified their concerns. Pleven made it clear that although the French would agree to the Spofford compromise, they would insist that NATO "not proceed with the actual rearmament of Germany until another opportunity has been made to try to reach a negotiated settlement with the USSR." Unlike the Americans they were determined to keep German rearmament an open question and one that could be reversed. "If a new political situation should result from these [four-power] conversations," they argued, a "fresh examination" of the Spofford formula could still take place. The British shared this view. They considered prospective negotiations with the Russians as one way to put the Germans back in line and curb their appetite for concessions. The Chinese intervention also had an immediate impact, causing the Foreign Office to argue that Russian warnings must be taken seriously, and that the Allies must opt "for a measure of realistic caution," even at the expense of American disapproval. The only reservation which Bevin himself had was the effect on German morale, but he agreed that "we should find [in Germany] a measure of relief in all political camps that this issue has been postponed."[77]

With these shared sentiments the three countries agreed at Brussels to proceed with an overall plan for Western defense, including the appointment of General Eisenhower as NATO's Supreme Commander. On German rearmament they authorized two sets of negotiations: one at Bonn conducted by the High Commissioners and under NATO auspices; and the other in Paris, dealing with the French suggestion of a European army. They agreed as well to explore the prospect of four-power talks with the Soviet Union, a concession which Acheson grudgingly made. He had objected vociferously to Schuman's view that the Four-Power Agreements on Germany were still in effect and that the West risked "provoking" the Soviets through German rearmament. Acheson insisted that to "concede that we were so bound by our four power agreement on Germany that we could not make any move even though that move was in our interest, would be a fatal concession to the USSR." To Acheson, the Yalta and Potsdam accords were "outmoded and dead," but he recognized that public opinion in Britain and France would constrain further action unless there was an attempt to reach an agreement with the Soviet Union.[78]

Washington's determination to put the German issue aside temporarily solved the problem of burgeoning German demands. When Adenauer detected the shifting mood of the Americans, he assured McCloy that despite his public rhetoric his requests to the Allies would remain modest. He said that the "pillars" of his foreign policy were "rapprochement with France, good relations with the UK, and a strong attachment to the U.S." Adenauer's protestations notwithstanding, McCloy and his advisers recognized the political difficulties that would attend German rearmament. While Acheson was securing French approval of the Spofford Plan, the American High Commission was formulating its own plan of action to deal with the rearmament issue. McCloy himself worked out a "package program" designed to provide a "constructive solution to the German problem" that would not need to wait for action from the individual governments. He told Acheson that the disturbed state of German public opinion, along with Schumacher's agitation for equality, had convinced him that "German participation in defense will have to be accompanied by a definite program for change from occupation to contractual status within a specified period." Putting these two proposals together would make it more difficult for the SPD to argue the issue of equality. More important, McCloy continued, the only way of reconciling French and German views on rearmament was "within the framework of a European defense structure." This approach would appease French concerns for security, allow eventual German equality, and "be much more acceptable . . . to the strong sentiment in Germany for European integration." To bring this about, he believed that the "U.S. must take a strong, positive stand in support of the working out promptly of a structure for a European Army under European political control." Otherwise either British objections or the distrust between the French and the Germans would defeat such a European program. McCloy closed his argument with the appeal for a "bold and definitive conception for Europe, offering the basis for long-range stability and strength."[79]

McCloy's analysis set forth the threefold policy he advocated and sought to follow during his remaining eighteen months in Germany. His first priority was the Schuman Plan, for only when that was signed and sealed would the French discuss rearmament seriously. The second step was to turn the Pleven Plan into a militarily practicable program while at the same time preserving the momentum it would give to European integration. McCloy urged involving the NATO Supreme Commander in the negotiations, using his military expertise to force the French to accept technical changes. From public opinion polls taken in Germany McCloy knew that although opposition to a new German army remained strong, support for German participation in a "West European Army" had reached almost 60 percent. He was certain that a European approach to rearmament would provide "a popular appeal to the German spirit of self-defense and loyalty to Western European unity powerful enough to drown out Schumacher's drum-beating and appeal even to his party followers." The third part of McCloy's plan was to end the occupation through a series of contractual agreements which would gradually restore Germany to equal status in Europe. In order to meet the often conflicting demands of the Germans for equality and of the French for security, the contractual negotiations would take place simultaneously with the rearmament talks. This would make it clear that Allied willingness to permit Germany's return to sovereignty was linked to its contribution to the defense of Western Europe. At the heart of McCloy's approach was vigorous and purposeful American leadership. As he told Acheson, "our government must have a clear policy and must be willing to exercise leadership and pressure in order to achieve that policy." The "genuine advance toward European union" would be the "*surest means to elicit Germany* for a collective security system adequate to cope with the Soviet challenge."[80]

Washington gave McCloy tentative approval to move ahead with his plan, telling him to inform Adenauer that the "development of our proposals will be greatly influenced by success or failure of Schuman Plan and coming Paris talks and that anything he can do that will contribute to agreement will be helpful." In essence McCloy's plan was an attempt to solve the problems at the heart of the "dual containment" policy, a policy which sought to contain and integrate Germany into the West while at the same time resisting Soviet expansionism. The "European" solution was the way through which the Federal Republic of Germany could become a "free" and "equal" partner in the Western alliance, without the possibility of using its new freedom to leave that alliance and bargain with both East and West. McCloy recognized the need to balance the political sensitivities of the Germans with the French demand for security against both a Soviet threat and a future German threat. All this could be accomplished only through strong and consistent American leadership, for only such leadership could provide the necessary pressure and incentives to overcome the ancient hatreds, let alone the more modern institutional and bureaucratic barriers, that divided Western Europe.[81]

6

Dealing with the Past: Moral Integration

In their strategy of "dual containment" McCloy and the High Commission approached the "integration" of the Federal Republic largely in terms of economic, political, and military institutions and arrangements. But there was another plane on which West Germany would need to reenter the community of nations. "Moral integration" could begin only when Germans came to terms with the horrors of the Nazi era, both by prosecuting the perpetrators of the crimes and making amends to the victims. This "reckoning with the past" (Vergangenheitsbewältigung) was an essential aspect of bringing the Federal Republic into the West and reconciling Western nations to its presence. In this realm, however, McCloy achieved only mixed results, sometimes even setting back the process of dealing with the German past.

As in other aspects of integration, the United States could exercise an important influence on the process. On a personal level McCloy played two significant roles. The first had to do with his decisions of January 1951 regarding the fate of almost a hundred convicted war criminals held at the Landsberg prison in Bavaria. The second concerned the provision of restitution to Germany's victims, and more specifically the negotiation of the Federal Republic's treaty with the state of Israel. Although McCloy's authority and involvement differed in these two affairs, the situations were connected. World opinion considered the treatment of war criminals and their victims as an indication of the extent to which the new Germany had broken with its Nazi past.

The Landsberg Cases

It was ironic that McCloy, who had played a crucial role in devising the concept of the Nuremberg trials, would as High Commissioner review their results. At the first and most famous of the trials, the four-power tribunal decided the fate of such Nazi notables as Hermann Göring, Rudolf Hess, and Albert Speer, who were incarcerated in the Spandau prison in Berlin. After this trial ended in October 1946, each of the major powers carried out proceedings in its own zone of occupation, with its own nationals as judges. The American proceedings were the most extensive. Between October 1946 and April 1949 twelve United States tribunals indicted some 185 relatively high-ranking Germans, grouped by either the type of crime committed—medical experimentation, the shooting of hostages—or the organization to which they belonged—branches of the SS, the German armed forces, major industries, or government ministries. Those convicted, numbering about a hundred, fell directly under McCloy's jurisdiction as High Commissioner. (The American Army also tried some 1700 defendants, including the perpetrators of the infamous Malmedy massacre. These "Dachau cases" remained under the Army's jurisdiction and were not reviewed by the High Commissioner.)[1]

Controversy dogged the trials from the very beginning and helped create the conditions underlying McCloy's review. Although the trials resulted in an impressive record of Nazi crimes, some critics characterized them as "victor's justice," while others, including Senator Robert Taft, called them an example of "political justice" closer in practice to Soviet behavior than to American tradition. George Kennan believed the presence of Stalin's judges at the original trial had made a "mockery" of the purpose of the procedure, which was to repudiate "mass crimes of every sort." Even though later trials were held without the Russians, the Cold War transformed the atmosphere in which they were held, directing American hatred away from Germany toward the Soviet Union. As time went on, the sentences meted out to convicted war criminals became lighter than those of the earliest trials. Although General Clay reviewed almost all the sentences before leaving Germany in May 1949, convicted defendants from the early trials, and their numerous and often influential supporters, called for another review of their cases which would take into consideration the "prejudices" of the immediate postwar period. Indeed because of complaints of brutality and torture, a Congressional committee investigated the handling of the war crimes cases, specifically the Malmedy case. (Senator Joseph McCarthy played a major role in pushing this inquiry.) Although the committee found the complaints exaggerated, its investigation furthered the impression that the trials had been held in a prejudicial atmosphere and that the results should be subjected to a new inquiry.[2]

The growing awareness that there had been a German resistance to Hitler also softened attitudes toward the former enemy. Books such as Allen W. Dulles's *Germany's Underground* emphasized the heroism of the July 20 plot to assassinate Hitler as something which might "inspire" Germans to build a new democratic nation. That there had been Germans in leadership circles who had not shared Hitler's criminal aims and had even actively resisted him undermined the wartime view—upon which the trials were initially based—that all high German officials, in both the public and private sectors, had been engaged in a wide-ranging conspiracy to conduct a war of aggression and conquest. General Clay acknowledged that although "no particular policy or directive of the occupation forces [could] be traced to the fact of the resistance, the growing awareness of its character and extent among the officials of the Military Government tended to create a greater respect toward the German people and therefore a greater disposition to accelerate a revival of German governmental controls." When survivors of the resistance—the "other Germany," as it came to be known—also pleaded for mercy for convicted war criminals, this added to the pressure on the Allies to respond with greater leniency.[3]

By 1949 Clay was aware of the changing climate of opinion regarding Germany and the trials. He expressed this in what he himself realized might seem a "ghoulish" request. Twice in March 1949, as it became clear that he would soon be replaced, he urged that the stay of execution for those defendants convicted of capital crimes be lifted. "I would not like to have a mass execution and yet I do want to free my successor from this thankless task to give him a clearer and more constructive task." He added that this was "one of my inheritances I do not want to pass on." Clay believed that his position as Military Governor during the "punitive" phase of the occupation would make it easier for him to sign the additional death warrants. He knew that his successor, sent to cultivate German opinion in the new "constructive" phase of the occupation, would face extraordinary pressures—primarily in Germany but also from the United States—to commute the sentences. The Landsberg defendants were able, however, to delay the execution of their sentences through further appeals to the United States Supreme Court. Having been unable to carry out the executions, Clay handed over the fifteen unresolved capital cases to McCloy with an apology.[4]

Clay's understanding of the situation in Germany was extraordinarily prescient. The new West German government continuously appealed for the defendants and provided German public opinion with a strong means to pressure the Western allies. By 1949, as Marion Dönhoff, the liberal publisher of *Die Zeit,* commented, Germans had turned strongly against the trials of industrialists, ministers, and generals, people whom "public opinion never identified with the worst aspects of the [Nazi] system." Many Germans came to believe "the Allies were misusing the tribunals to get rid of groups and individuals whom, for some reason or other, they found troublesome." The unresolved capital cases also drew particular attention. The abolition of the death penalty in the Basic Law, which led Germans to regard further executions on German soil as an affront to German sovereignty, created another reason for leniency. (The three Western powers had already executed more than four hundred war criminals.) Finally many Germans were hoping to draw a line over the past once and for all—a Schlusstrich. They argued that with their nation on the road to recovery from the Nazi period, the United States should direct its attention toward Germany's future, not toward its past.[5]

Before going to Germany McCloy had defended the Nuremberg trials and had been "annoyed by the ignorance" of skeptical New York lawyers, who worried that "Goering, Kaltenbrunner, and Company are being unfairly treated." Upon his arrival there he encountered the pressure which Clay had predicted. One of the first appeals came from Chancellor Adenauer, who cited both the delay in the execution of the sentences and the abolition of the death penalty as reasons to commute the death sentences. Important private citizens, including the banker Eric Warburg and Professor Kurt Geiler of the University of Heidelberg, asked McCloy to review the cases for possible "miscarriages of justice." Protestant and Catholic leaders also appealed for a new review. Cardinal Frings of Cologne pleaded for commutation of the death sentences because many of the defendants' actions did "not stem from a criminal disposition." Two bishops, Hans Meiser of Munich and Theophil Wurm of Stuttgart, led the campaign against the war crimes trials for the Protestant Church. And requests were received for a consideration of parole for medical and other reasons, or for a consideration of "new" evidence not available at the time of the trial.[6]

McCloy responded to these petitions with both firmness and conciliation. He defended the Nuremberg trials to Adenauer, telling him that the "defendants were guilty of deliberately torturing and killing hundreds and in certain cases thousands of helpless human beings." He rejected any notion of an amnesty, noting that such a move, which "would . . . be taken as an abandonment of the principles established in the trials," might convey the idea that "those crimes have . . . been sufficiently atoned for [and] that the German people should now be allowed to forget them." Behind the scenes, however, he sought to determine the range of his authority. He first commissioned a legal opinion from his General Counsel, which affirmed that the High Commissioner had the right only to *reduce* sentences, "taking into consideration that the judgment of the tribunal as to the guilt or the innocence of any defendant is final and not subject to review." He then established a system of time off for good behavior, giving prisoners credit for five days each month from the beginning of their sentence. McCloy justified this system by noting that it was used throughout the United States and Europe and that it served the interests of prison discipline because a prisoner could lose the credited time as a punishment for offenses. He also appealed, typically, to expertise: "it is a practice which has been . . . accepted as being sound in all modern penology—among all modern penology experts." (Whether war criminals should have been treated in the same way as ordinary criminals was a question that McCloy did not address.) He insisted that it was "in no sense an indication of any attitude of unwarranted leniency on my part towards war criminals." This new system, however, did serve to speed up the release of a number of war criminals, including the industrialist Friedrich Flick, who was freed in August 1950 after having served five years of his seven-year sentence.[7]

With the good-conduct system in place, McCloy asked Secretary of State Acheson in February 1950 for permission to establish a "War Crimes Clemency Board." In November 1949 the Army had created the War Crimes Modification Board to handle the hundreds of Dachau cases that required review, and McCloy wanted to deal with the Nuremberg cases in a similar fashion. Responding both to the clamor within Germany and to his own sense that discrepancies existed between the individual sentences, McCloy wanted to provide for a comprehensive review of all the cases under his jurisdiction, and especially the capital cases. He emphasized that "whether clemency is warranted in a particular case must be decided after thorough and dispassionate review of all relevant factors." What he needed in order to make such a judgment was "a board of qualified individuals who are recognized for objectivity and independence of judgment." After remarking that an extensive review would be too much for his own staff to handle, he noted that the "mere addition of staff assistants would not achieve review by [a] body capable of expressing independent opinion." Pointedly reminding Acheson of the "strong and conflicting views expressed here, in England and in the United States concerning proper disposition [of] war crimes sentences," McCloy emphasized that to win public acceptance his actions must be based "upon thorough and dispassionate review and advice." He concluded by adding that "my own conscience is involved and though I am prepared to make ultimate decision and accept ultimate responsibility I require the help of such a group." Acheson quickly replied that "inasmuch as you feel so strongly necessity for forming special group to review death sentences [I] am prepared to proceed if special precautions are taken on handling publicity."[8]

The High Commissioner hoped that an expert, independent panel might help to dampen the political controversy surrounding any review of the war crimes cases. Despite the passions involved, he believed that if "persons of high standing such as judges, lawyers and penologists" could be persuaded to work on such a review, "their recommendations will carry weight with public opinion in the United States and elsewhere." Both McCloy and Acheson feared adverse publicity, especially if it gave the impression that the Allies were questioning the jurisdiction of their Nuremberg courts or reviewing the decisions made by these courts. They also feared that "individual groups" might give the decision a "mistaken interpretation"—a veiled reference to their concern that Jewish organizations would criticize any further review. To counter such attacks McCloy emphasized that the panel was not to "review the decisions of such Tribunals on questions of law or fact," though it could consider "newly discovered evidence not available at the time of trial." Acting as an "Advisory Board on Clemency for War Criminals," it would only consider questions related to the issue of clemency. He told one critic that "every civilized legal system affords convicted prisoners the opportunity to file petitions for clemency," thus repeating an argument he had used in introducing the concept of time off for good behavior.[9]

Yet McCloy's approach to staffing the panel reveals that he himself was not sure whether he was establishing an appellate court or a clemency board. Searching for men with reputations of "integrity and objectivity," he wanted a three-man board with at "least one member, or former member of the judiciary and . . . preferably a parole board man." He demanded that those selected should have had "no previous association with the war crimes trials and should not have publicly expressed themselves concerning the trials," hoping that their "recommendations should be free of any charge of partiality or prejudice." When the Chief Justice of the Supreme Court, Fred Vinson, refused a request to allow sitting or retired federal judges to sit on the panel, McCloy and Acheson were forced to look to the state courts for candidates. Drawing upon his past associations and contacts, McCloy persuaded Judge David W. Peck, the Presiding Justice of the Appellate Division, First Department, of the New York Supreme Court, to assume chairmanship of the panel. Peck was held in high regard by his colleagues, but he could go to Germany only during the summer, when he was free of his judicial responsibilities. To assist him McCloy found another New Yorker, Frederick A. Moran, the chairman of the New York State Board of Parole and the governor's chief adviser on matters relating to parole and clemency. Moran played a particularly important role in the panel's deliberations, going to Germany well before the other panel members to meet with the Landsberg prisoners and conduct an investigation into the personal history, background, and character of each. The final member of the "Peck Panel" (or Advisory Board) was Conrad E. Snow, an Assistant Legal Adviser to the Department of State, whom McCloy admired for "his conscientious thoroughgoing work in Washington during the war."[10]

McCloy wanted a speedy review, primarily to dispose of the political problems caused by the cases. The Panel began its work in April 1950, when Moran went to Germany for his preliminary visit. He stayed for ten days and then returned to the United States with the judgments in the various cases. All three Board members convened in Washington to consider these judgments before going to Munich, where hearings began on July 11, 1950. During the next six weeks they considered all the petitions for clemency filed on behalf of the defendants, reviewing the 3000 pages of judgments and considering written and oral presentations from some fifty defense counsel representing 90 of the original 104 defendants. The Panel had neither the time nor the interest to review the more than 330,000 pages of evidence used in the trials. On August 28, 1950, the members of the panel met with McCloy in Frankfurt and submitted their report. They recommended reductions in the sentences of 77 of the 93 defendants, including the commutation of seven of the fifteen death sentences. For the other 14 defendants the commission ended up making no recommendation, since McCloy's liberalized good-behavior rules meant that their sentences had expired or were due to expire shortly. Two of the industrial cases, I.G. Farben and Flick, were in this group.[11]

The Peck Panel sought to appease all sides by combining a strong defense of the Nuremberg principles with a wide-ranging leniency. It supported the Nuremberg picture of a Nazi conspiracy to conduct aggressive warfare, emphasizing that the organizations considered— the SS, the Wehrmacht, the concentration camps, the courts, the government, and the major industries—were parts "all integrated in a massive design which despite its madness was thoroughly worked out to incorporate every endeavor." It rejected the defense of superior orders, noting that "no one man can make an entire nation goosestep to his will"; "there had to be willing cooperation." The Panel insisted that if "there is to be a world of law and justice, individuals in positions of some authority at least must be answerable for their acts." It also rejected the charge that Nuremberg represented ex post facto law, arguing that "rudimentary laws of humanity, including elemental laws of war such as those relating to the treatment of prisoners, reprisals and hostages, were old and international law long before the Nazi war machine was set in motion, and were as much a part of German military and civil law as they were of international law." It concluded with the stark statement: "Murder, pillage and enslavement are against law everywhere and have been for at least the twentieth century."[12]

Although the Panel reaffirmed the general principles of Nuremberg, when it came to specific individual punishments it declared that "each defendant is being judged solely upon the basis of his individual action." On that basis it found that many of the defendants occupied "such subordinate positions" that they were "little more than common members of a criminal organization." In reaching this judgment the Panel decided to consider all the individual cases together as a group, taking into account the "differences in authority and action among the defendants" and placing them "in proper relation to each other and the programs in which they participated." This approach, which followed logically, though not automatically, from the Nuremberg concept of a coordinated and planned Nazi conspiracy, had important implications for many of the lesser defendants. When compared with men like Otto Ohlendorf or Paul Blobel, who supervised and directed thousands of murders, the bureaucrats and industrialists seemed far less criminal and deserving of punishment. The Panel, which tended to excuse such "white-collar" war criminals as men caught up in forces beyond their control, admitted that "if we have erred, we have erred on the side of leniency." By considering the cases as a group it strengthened this inclination toward leniency.[13]

The Panel's report also showed that it had moved beyond its official mandate by considering the quality of some of the judgments which the original tribunals had made. Although it had "worked under a directive that it was not to review the judgments on the law or the facts," it had concluded that its authority to review the sentences "required a differentiation between specific facts found and established in the evidence and conclusions that may have been drawn therefrom. We have considered ourselves bound by the former but not by the latter." This was a distinction without a difference. The Panel was claiming to accept the facts found by the Nuremberg tribunals—for example, that a particular defendant was a member of the board of directors of Krupp or an official in the Ministry of Justice, and that the evidence demonstrated crimes committed by that industrial organization or ministry—but it did not accept the conclusion that a particular defendant had direct responsibility for the crime unless the evidence so demonstrated. The problem was that the Panel did not review all the evidence because the vast bulk of it was not contained in the judgments. Nor did it hear from the prosecution, which proved to be a serious omission when it began to question the quality of the judgments or even to consider supposedly "new" evidence. Both of these procedural flaws—the failure to consider all the evidence and to hear from the prosecution—led McCloy's own General Counsel, Robert Bowie, to criticize the Panel's report for its "excessive" leniency and to urge McCloy to reject some of its recommendations.[14]

Bowie's call for tougher sentences reached McCloy during the tumultuous last months of 1950. In September 1950 McCloy told Truman that because of rearmament and the need to bring Germany into the West "certain of the things we would like to see done in Germany will not be completed." While actively engaged in the rearmament debate during the second half of 1950, McCloy was also considering the Peck Panel's recommendations. Later he grew defensive about this connection, telling one critic, "I received the Board's conclusion . . . many months before there was any question of German rearmament." This was not true. Although he had set up the Panel before the rearmament issue surfaced, he received its final report on August 28, 1950, two weeks before the New York conference.[15]

The rearmament decision provided additional ammunition for the continuing, and intensified, efforts of German leaders to urge full clemency and pardon for the Landsberg defendants. A group of Bundestag deputies from all the major parties told McCloy that they felt it "their duty to call for modification of the death sentences," especially in view of "political and psychological factors at a time when Western Germany was being called upon to make a military contribution to Western defense." In a meeting with the High Commissioners on November 16, 1950, Adenauer renewed his request for an end to all war crimes trials, as well as the "commutation of all death sentences not yet executed to sentences of confinement, since capital punishment has been abolished by Article 102 of the basic law." He also urged the "widest possible clemency for persons sentenced to confinement." One deputy, the young Bavarian Franz-Josef Strauss, thought the effect of any additional executions on American-German relations would be "devastating." Even the victims of Nazi brutality joined in the chorus calling for clemency. The SPD leader, Kurt Schumacher, insisted that executions would violate German sovereignty. He was joined by such figures as Inge Scholl, whose sister and brother, leaders of the White Rose resistance movement, had been killed by the Nazis. Bishop Neuhäusler of Munich told McCloy that now that the "German Federal Republic has been called upon to form, together with Western powers, a strong defensive bloc against the Bolshevism of the East," the United States should show mercy toward the Landsberg prisoners. The two ex-Generals, Adolf Heusinger and Hans Speidel, who were Adenauer's chief advisers on rearmament, told the High Commission's Bonn liaison that "if the prisoners at Landsberg were hanged, Germany as an armed ally against the east was an illusion."

Some Germans even threatened McCloy's life and the safety of his family, so that bodyguards had to be assigned to protect his children. Observing this intense and emotional campaign for clemency, the new British High Commissioner, Ivone Kirkpatrick, told his superiors in London that "it is a regrettable fact that even moderate Germans such as the Protestant bishops and sensible SPD men who have suffered from Nazi persecution resent the war crimes trials . . . the question does poison feeling toward the West."[16]

The German agitation had little effect on Washington, which left matters in McCloy's hands. In November 1950 his Assistant General Counsel, John Bross, informed Acheson that McCloy planned to approve at least nine death sentences and commute the others. In reply Acheson cabled McCloy that although he was aware "that there are individuals and organizations both in Germany and the US which believe all death sentences in these cases should be commuted, I am impressed by the fact that these cases were carefully considered by the trial tribunals, by Gen. Clay, by your advisory board and by yourself, and in each case where you propose execution I understand the opinion has been that no clemency or mitigation of sentence was warranted." Acheson concluded, "Accordingly I concur in your proposed course of action, and leave to your discretion the time when [the executions] take place." President Truman showed the same support for McCloy. When he was urged by a Missouri friend, a member of his Masonic lodge, to grant clemency, Truman curtly replied by sending him a copy of McCloy's decisions, saying, "I have to accept this as the situation because there is no way for me to interfere with things inside Germany." Although Truman's statement was not technically correct—he could have insisted that McCloy commute the sentences— it does show that the final decision in the Landsberg cases rested with McCloy.[17]

McCloy considered the "formulation of intelligent, objective and equitable decisions" in the Landsberg cases "one of the most important problems facing me in connection with the occupation of Germany." He told the delegations of Germans who visited him with petitions that "of all the problems that he had confronted in Germany this was the most difficult and the one on which he had spent the most time." Adding that it was also a duty which he "intensely disliked," he said that it was "most distressing to have to decide this problem." Despite many years as a lawyer, McCloy had had little experience with criminal law, and he had "never before been subjected to the ordeal of having to determine whom I should deprive of liberty or life." Consequently he followed a rather unorthodox procedure. He was willing to speak to almost anyone about the cases, accept new petitions and evidence, and hear new witnesses. He even traveled to Landsberg to meet with a number of the defendants. His friends observed that McCloy agonized over the decisions, especially the capital cases. At one point he "locked himself in his home, reading and rereading the testimony." One staff member, who recalled seeing McCloy poring over the records of one of the SS cases late into the night, was impressed with his "deep concern and scrupulous sense of obligation for the rights and privileges of a single individual."[18]

Although he had reached some preliminary decisions in November, McCloy delayed announcing them, in part to avoid the spectacle of executions during the Christmas holidays. The delay also gave him more time to try to convince German leaders of the justice of his actions. He told them that their contention that the death sentences had been delayed too long seemed to imply that the reviews and legal procedures were somehow cruel and inhumane, and he pointed out that without those reviews some men who would otherwise have been executed would not be. Moreover, the Basic Law did not apply to the Nuremberg trials, which had been conducted by international courts at a time when there was no German government. Many of the crimes had been committed against non-Germans. When one Bundestag member suggested that the excesses of the Nazis "should be cancelled out by a great gesture of clemency," McCloy was amazed that such an argument could be offered seriously. He reminded the Germans that these were "crimes of historical proportion," a "spasm of criminality which had aroused world-wide indignation." He was also disturbed by the German "tendency to put things under the carpet and refuse to acknowledge what actually happened." The German people, he emphasized, must "understand the enormity of what had been done." He told them that at times they seemed to have almost no conception of how the rest of the world perceived Germany and the horrors of Nazism.[19]

Yet McCloy also made it clear that he had tried to find reasons for clemency. Despite the nature of the crimes he had "strained to find some grounds for clemency and had persuaded himself that he was justified in commuting certain of the sentences." He added that "when

I go through these cases, I do so without hatred and I try to temper justice with mercy." In some cases, however, he could find no justification for mercy; he "could hardly believe that the men who perpetrated these crimes were human." While repeatedly telling the Germans that he was not "executing anybody for political reasons," he also reminded them that he "had to view things from an international as well as a bilateral perspective." Reacting to expressions of concern about the effect of the cases on U.S.-German relations, McCloy commented that "if our relations depend on these individual cases, then our friendship hangs on a thin thread indeed." Although it was his intention to grant clemency in as many cases as possible, he remained "deeply disturbed" about the effect this might have outside Germany, fearing a "worldwide reaction of cynicism and disillusion."[20]

McCloy's final decisions did create the impressions he had hoped to avoid. On January 31, 1951, he extended commutations, paroles, and reductions of sentences to 79 of the 89 war criminals still imprisoned at Landsberg who came under his jurisdiction. He affirmed only five death sentences, sparing four condemned prisoners on the basis of "a little new evidence" he received at the last minute. He commuted the sentences of these four to life imprisonment, and the other six capital cases to terms ranging from ten to twenty-five years in prison. In the great majority of cases McCloy followed the recommendations of his Advisory Board, although he was more severe than it had been toward several of the German lawyers and doctors who had been convicted. Perhaps with the rearmament controversy in mind, McCloy took pains *not* to exercise any special leniency toward the military cases he reviewed. He denied clemency to Field Marshall Wilhelm List and General Walter Kuntze because of their responsibility for the murder of hostages in the Balkans, but he did leave open the possibility of a medical parole for both elderly men. He denied clemency to three other generals—Hermann Reinecke, Hans Reinhardt, and Hermann Hoth—because of their role in the killing of prisoners and partisans. Later he told critics that he had "sought to distinguish between those who I felt acted on grounds of military security in partisan warfare and those who I felt were merely carrying on Nazi political and racial policies." McCloy's refusal to pardon these five military men angered many former German soldiers, some of whom suggested that any decision on rearmament be delayed until all "so-called" war criminals had been released.[21]

The foreign coverage of McCloy's decision focused on the release of thirty-two prisoners on the basis of time served. Most of these had received term sentences of ten years or less at their original trial, and McCloy's sentence reductions, coupled with time off for good behavior, allowed them to walk free. Among them was the armaments manufacturer Alfried Krupp, who left the Landsberg prison to celebrate a champagne brunch with his supporters. Not only did McCloy free Krupp, but he restored his property, which had been ordered confiscated at his original trial. At the stroke of McCloy's pen Krupp was transformed from a convicted war criminal to one of Europe's richest men.[22]

On the Krupp case McCloy followed the recommendation of the Peck Panel, which had concluded that Krupp's sentence and the confiscation of his property were excessive penalties when compared with those of Flick and Farben. In revoking the confiscation order the Panel quoted Justice Jackson's statement to the London Conference on the establishment of the Nuremberg courts: "We have no such penalty, and for historical reasons, that would be extremely unacceptable to the American people." McCloy thought Alfried Krupp "an inconsequential figure in the steel company," who "in a very real sense inherited his father's place in the dock." In his view it was Gustav Krupp, Alfried's father, who had helped finance Hitler and the Nazis, and he would have been tried if he had been well enough. McCloy did not believe that Alfried Krupp deserved a longer sentence than either the other Krupp directors or those tried in the Flick and Farben cases.[23]

The sharp contrast between the reaction to McCloy's decisions within Germany and outside the country illustrates the political dilemma McCloy faced in his need to balance the concerns of the Western nations with the attitudes of the former enemy they wished to gain as an ally. In Germany attention was focused almost entirely on the condemned prisoners, and increasingly passionate appeals were made for the commutation of the remaining death sentences until the executions took place in early June. The German press generally commended McCloy's thoroughness and impartiality but criticized the confirmation of the death sentences, again citing the Basic Law's abolition of capital punishment. Surveys made by the High Commission found strong support for the clemency actions McCloy had taken, including the Krupp decision. The thousands of letters the Commission received "were virtually unanimous in favor of clemency," coming from writers in the "upper income brackets or of an intellectual and conservative background." The Commission's liaison in Bonn also reported that the "reaction of politically-conscious Germans on whom after all the future of German policy largely depends has been considerably more satisfactory than one could have justifiably expected considering all the circumstances." This reading of German sentiment proved to be more accurate than other, more pessimistic assessments. Despite fears to the contrary, the agitation over the Landsberg cases faded away quickly after the executions had been performed.[24]

Partly because McCloy had paid much less attention to preparing foreign opinion for his decisions, the angry reaction to the release of Alfried Krupp was predictable. One English newspaper ran a cartoon of Hitler and Göring sitting in Valhalla, reading a newspaper with the headline "Krupp freed." In the caption Hitler was asking Göring, "Should we have hung on a little longer?" The London *Times* refrained from editorial comment, but the *Manchester Guardian* ran a letter noting that "there is a mercy which is weakness and even treason against the common good" and pointing out that the "happenings in Germany over the war criminals" reflected the truth of this statement. The Labour party was "particularly incensed" by the release of Krupp, whom it regarded as the preeminent symbol of "capitalism and the arms industry." As one editorial put it, Alfried Krupp was a man "who has his hands stained with the blood of British soldiers, Russians, Americans, and Frenchmen, Poles, Belgians, Dutchmen, in short, the blood of millions." The European reaction also connected McCloy's action with American interest in German rearmament, arguing that it was designed to "curry favor with" and "appease" the Germans. The French newspapers saw Krupp's release as an indication of America's failure to understand the roots of German militarism. *Le Figaro* commented that "Mr. McCloy and his countrymen have not had such close relations with Krupp as we had by means of the famous Bertha gun, which was named after his mother. Maybe that can explain their mildness." In both Britain and France the Krupp pardon symbolized America's excessive haste to rehabilitate and rearm Germany. The leftist *Franc-Tireur* called Krupp's release "the worst thing about the war crimes trials," while the conservative *Paris Presse* said it had "practically destroyed Franco-American understanding."[25]

In the United States public opinion was mixed. The *New York Times* generally approved McCloy's action, commenting, "If there have been errors in the present decisions, they have been errors on the side of mercy." If the Germans condemned these crimes, "there is some hope for the German future." The *Washington Post* was more skeptical. It could not understand the release of Alfried Krupp, who "bears a share of responsibility for Hitler's assumption of power and the implementation of his plans." An editorial cartoon in the same paper pictured the smiling jailer, McCloy, opening Krupp's cell while in the distance Stalin snapped a picture for his propaganda album. In the more liberal *Nation* Telford Taylor, the former Nuremberg prosecutor, blasted McCloy's decisions as the "embodiment of political expediency, distorted by a thoroughly unsound approach to the law and the facts, to say nothing of the realities of contemporary world politics." Taylor worried that the release of Krupp would make an excellent weapon for Communist propaganda. He concluded that McCloy's decisions "dealt a blow to the principles of international law and concepts of humanity for which we fought the war."[26]

After the executions McCloy wrote to Justice Frankfurter, "It was a most unpleasant ordeal, but in connection with it I think I experienced some human reactions that had never come my way before." In part McCloy was recording his reaction to the morally wrenching task of signing death warrants. He was also expressing the exasperation of a man at the center of a system of contradictory political pressures who must craft a decision which will satisfy the sense of justice of many nations with very different cultures and different experiences in World War II. Although McCloy insisted that "he was not executing anybody for political reasons" and that "at no moment did I consider any political or extraneous matter," his Landsberg decisions were fundamentally political, expressive of his search for a compromise between the concerns of the different Western nations and the Federal Republic. McCloy was in a position not unlike that of the state governor who attempts to weigh his community's concern for justice with individual appeals for mercy.[27]

McCloy was well prepared to deal with the German reaction; despite the popular uproar he held to his decisions and carried out the executions. This reaction convinced him that the Germans still did not understand the criminality of Nazism. He angrily told Cardinal Frings of his disappointment that "many of the leaders of German thought to whom I felt I had the right to look for support and understanding in these decisions, [instead] manifested a tendency to put my words and those of my officials under a microscope for the purposes of detecting flaws which . . . have nothing to do with the main issues involved in these cases." They did not understand that "we face a situation where the sympathy should be not so much for the perpetrators of the deeds as for their victims." McCloy's Landsberg experience may well have reinforced his preference for a cautious approach to the release of Germany from her obligations to the West. Both the resurgence of the neo-Nazi Sozialistische Reichspartei (SRP), which scored its first electoral success in May 1951, and the agitation over the Landsberg cases demonstrated the need to bind Germany thoroughly within the West and strengthened McCloy's resolve to oppose any solution which would give it the freedom to revert to its old nationalism and authoritarianism.[28]

McCloy was not well prepared to meet criticism from outside Germany, and he responded to it with a prickly defensiveness and weak rationalizations. For example, he explained his establishment of the review board as giving the accused the right to appellate review and wrote to Eleanor Roosevelt that the additional review was justified because "unlike criminal cases in the U.S. and England there was no provision for further court review of these cases for possible errors of law or fact after the court of first instance passed on them." This statement, which contradicted McCloy's original injunction to the Peck Panel to confine itself to clemency issues, led critics to note that the Peck Panel's review was so hasty and one-sided as to constitute a "sham" appellate review. As another example, McCloy repeated his opinion that Krupp "took his place in the dock largely because his father was on his death bed at the time," ignoring the fact that the Allied prosecutors had always intended to try Alfried, who had become the official head of Krupp in 1943, for the war crimes of his business enterprise. Realizing that his father, Gustav, was a much more important figure, they had expected him to stand trial in the first international proceedings. When Gustav was judged too ill to be included, the prosecution substituted Alfried at the last minute, to have a representative from one of Germany's leading armament manufacturers. Alfried was subsequently tried for crimes which occurred when he alone was responsible for Krupp's activities, including plundering and slave labor.[29]

McCloy's defensiveness about Krupp led him to minimize Krupp's responsibility for the crimes of the company. He described Krupp as merely a "consenting participant" in the employment of slave labor, adding that "slave labor was disposed of by government agencies and it was controlled, housed, and fed by such agencies—not by Krupp." Telford Taylor responded that Krupp "undertook the construction of a plant near the Auschwitz concentration camp, with the avowed expectation of using the inmates as a labor supply." "Krupp," Taylor noted, "cooperated with the Nazi government's slave labor policies not reluctantly or under duress, but willingly." Both men exaggerated, though Taylor had the better argument. Few German firms "wanted" to employ slave labor, but almost all acquiesced in its use. As the historian Peter Hayes has recently shown in his study of I.G. Farben, the Nazis manipulated the labor supply in such a way as to make it difficult for Farben's managers, given their training and mentality, to refuse to use slave labor. But it would not have been impossible to refuse such labor or to treat it more humanely, and some German businessmen did act in this courageous fashion. McCloy's statements minimized the individual responsibility of the industrialists for Nazi crimes, thereby undermining one of the central principles of Nuremberg.[30]

It is true that McCloy was not the only one to minimize the industrialists' wrongdoing. In 1947 and 1948 the American judges had been relatively lenient toward the convicted industrialists and their managers: Friedrich Flick, a member of Himmler's "Circle of Friends," was sentenced to only seven years' imprisonment, and the Farben directors received even lighter sentences. But there is no question that the German industrialists regarded McCloy's action as a vindication of their innocence. One wrote McCloy that "the liberation of Alfried Krupp has rejoiced our economic leaders." Further, McCloy's action gained him a certain prestige among Germany's industrial elite, which would be tested during the Schuman Plan negotiations. Their "vindication" did not, however, dispose the industrialists to show a generous attitude toward their former slave laborers, for most of them refused to make any financial restitution to these workers. (Later in the 1950s McCloy would play a key role in convincing Krupp to provide restitution for some of its wartime slave laborers.)[31]

McCloy's Landsberg decisions set in motion a process that would lead to the release by 1958 of all the war criminals remaining in American custody. German leaders, including Chancellor Adenauer, continued to press for freedom for these criminals, often stressing their need for medical parole or the positive effect a release would have on "German public opinion." In the Cold War atmosphere of the 1950s, Adenauer's continuing pressure yielded results. Acheson considered the "war crimes sentences" an "irrelevant obstacle" to progress in Germany's integration into the West. As part of the negotiations for their contractual agreements with Germany in 1952, the Allies created the Interim Mixed Parole and Clemency Board, which became the Mixed Parole and Clemency Board when Germany finally regained its sovereignty in 1955. These Boards, as indicated by their names, consisted of representatives from both the Western powers and the Federal Republic. They operated under regulations similar to those given to McCloy's original Advisory Board, and they continuously reviewed the various cases, generously granting petitions for parole. The Americans wanted to free prisoners as "quietly and discreetly" as possible, so as not to stir up protests in the United States. During the period 1953–1958 the two Boards released all of the remaining war criminals from Landsberg, freeing the last four in May 1958. The French and British followed the same pattern, releasing the remaining war criminals they held in Germany by 1958.[32]

The freeing of war criminals was one result of McCloy's Landsberg decisions. The other important result was the return to power of Alfried Krupp, who was to become one of the creators as well as beneficiaries of Germany's economic miracle in the 1950s. After his release and under Allied pressure Krupp agreed to sell his holdings in the coal, iron, and steel industry, and in return the Allies agreed to lift restrictions on his other industrial enterprises. Over the next few years, under the adroit leadership of Krupp and his talented deputy, Bertoldt Beitz, the Krupp firm made a dramatic reemergence into world markets, participating in industrial projects in Asia, Europe, and South America. Whether it was building a heavy machinery plant in San Paulo or supplying American-designed rolling mills to India and Pakistan, Krupp played a major role in Germany's export boom. In 1959 Alfried Krupp argued that his pledge to divest himself of his coal and steel holdings had been "given under compulsion." He won a series of extensions of the Allied order, based on the tenuous argument that no buyer had been found to purchase his coal and steel assets "at an acceptable price." Indeed Alfried was able to escape the Allied order entirely, but financial problems in the late 1960s ultimately led to the dissolution of the firm in 1968, a year after his death.[33]

Both the quiet release of the remaining war criminals and the resurgence of Krupp and other industrialists were the legacies of Allied policies whose larger goal, the "integration" of Germany into the West, allowed the Federal Republic to slip into amnesia about its past. Without McCloy's intending it, his Landsberg decisions contributed to the German Schlusstrich mentality about war criminals. When U.S. involvement in the punishment of these criminals ended, the German government showed little desire to act on its own. After 1955, in fact, Bonn claimed that the Allies had restricted Germany's jurisdiction in such cases, because no one tried by the Allies could be tried again for the same crime. This attitude on the part of the government reflected popular sentiment. Surveys showed a deep cynicism toward the Nuremberg judgments, as well as majority support for the proposition that "we should cease trying people now for crimes they committed many years ago." In the late 1950s neither German political leaders nor the majority of their constituents were interested in grappling with the questions of the past, and the Western powers did not press the point upon them.[34]

There is no doubt that McCloy's Landsberg decisions contributed to the refusal of Germans to face the past and allowed some war criminals to escape justice. But, to his credit, McCloy resisted popular pressures to commute all the death sentences, and he never failed to defend the Nuremberg principles, even when his actions seemed to contradict them. As mistaken as American leniency toward Nazi war criminals was, it is important to remember, as John Mendelsohn noted in his study, that "if our goal included removal from public life of war criminals . . . the program succeeded to a remarkable degree in Germany and only partly so in Japan."[35]

McCloy and Wiedergutmachung

McCloy's decision to follow a lenient path toward the Nazi war criminals undoubtedly led him to press the Germans even harder for a generous policy of Wiedergutmachung, or restitution, toward the Jews and the state of Israel. His support for restitution was based on both moral convictions and political necessity. Seeing the Holocaust as one of "the darkest, blackest pages of human history," he believed the Federal Republic had to confront the "terrible legacy of the Hitler persecutions" with a generous program of restitution. Nevertheless he was not blind to the political benefits of Germany's restitution program. Among the most important opponents of America's rapid rapprochement with Germany were liberal and Jewish organizations, which echoed the sentiments of Israel's Foreign Minister, Moshe Sharett, when he told the United Nations in September 1950, "The people of Israel and Jews throughout the world view with consternation and distress the progressive readmission of Germany by the family of nations, with her revolting record intact, her guilt unexpiated, and her heart unchanged." Despite the Cold War atmosphere of Washington, such groups had an important voice in the Democratic party and with President Truman, who was himself inclined to believe that Nazism was an inherent part of the German character. To convince this important segment of American public (and elite) opinion that the Federal Republic was a *new* Germany, with the desire to make amends for the crimes of Hitler, a generous restitution policy was essential.[36]

McCloy's role in the restitution issue was less direct than his involvement with the war criminals, leading some recent German literature to express skepticism about his actual influence. McCloy's influence was important, but he used it in a more careful and more subtle way than he did on some other issues where the American interest was more immediately apparent. He wanted to avoid the charge that the United States was either "forcing" the Germans to provide restitution or that it was "indifferent" to such a gesture. Either impression would only have increased the unpopularity of Wiedergutmachung among the Germans, as well as having a negative effect on public opinion in other countries. The German public, although expressing agreement with the general principle of restitution, placed little priority on assisting the Jews, and a majority actually opposed the treaty with Israel. McCloy also needed to balance his concern for the restitution issue with the other priorities of American policy, such as securing a German defense contribution and promoting Germany's economic recovery. But within these constraints he played a decisive role in moving the Adenauer government to follow its better instincts, overcome its domestic opposition, and take a small first step toward reconciliation with the Jews.[37]

From the very beginning of his tenure in office McCloy placed a high priority on Germany's attitude toward its own Jewish community. In July 1949 he told a conference of German Jewish delegates in Heidelberg that "the world will carefully watch the new Western German state, and one of the tests by which it will be judged will be its attitude towards the Jews and how it treats them." He also emphasized "that the moment that Germany has forgotten the Buchenwalds and the Auschwitzes, that was the point at which everyone could begin to despair of any progress in Germany." One of his first actions while still Military Governor was to reverse a previous decision of General Clay's and approve a General Claims Law for indemnification of the victims of Nazism. McCloy's words and actions made it clear to German leaders that the United States would favor initiatives toward restitution, just as he made clear to them the interest of the United States in Franco-German rapprochement.[38]

To strengthen this message further, McCloy played a direct role in assisting the Jewish Restitution Successor Organization (JRSO) in its activities in Germany. The JRSO, established by American decree, was declared the legal successor to all heirless Jewish property in the American-occupied zone. It was empowered to dispose of this property and use the proceeds for general Jewish purposes. Under the leadership of Benjamin Ferencz, a former Nuremberg prosecutor, the JRSO worked with the individual Länder in the American zone in an attempt to obtain restitution. Ferencz later recalled that he went to McCloy "dozens of times with problems," and he could not recall "a single time when I went away other than being completely satisfied with the way [McCloy] handled it." The High Commissioner often assisted the JRSO in pushing the German Länder into action. In April 1950 he told a meeting of the Minister-Presidents that they should work with the JRSO to arrange "some sort of global settlement" which would provide a speedy solution to many of the claims. He pointed out that this "would make an excellent impression abroad where a certain amount of bad feeling and criticism has been created by the long delays." After these negotiations for global settlements began, the High Commission continued to serve as mediator between the Länder and the JRSO, especially when it became clear that "the Germans do not have enthusiasm for the bulk settlement." As one American official noted, "The Germans profess the view that numerous JRSO claims will turn out to be against innocent third parties or against buyers from former Jewish owners who have not claimed restitution because they received full value and do not feel themselves in any way wronged or aggrieved." During the next two years the various Länder reached agreements on bulk settlements with the JRSO, but not without considerable "prodding" by McCloy. Informed of Bremen's settlement with the JRSO, McCloy wrote Minister-President Wilhelm Kaisen that "I know you share my view of the importance of [restitution] in the development of Germany's future international relations." McCloy also made sure that the JRSO's administrative expenses were included in the mandatory occupation costs and did not require repayment to the German government.[39]

Of even greater significance for the restitution question was the negotiation of the Luxembourg Treaty of 1952 between the Federal Republic and Israel. The difficult path to this treaty has been described in detail elsewhere. Despite the importance of Adenauer's desire for reconciliation, as well as the persistence of the negotiating teams from both nations, foreign influence did play a decisive role in securing the treaty. Without foreign pressure, opposition to the treaty, consisting of powerful forces in both countries, might have produced a stalemate. Political leaders in both Germany and Israel drew strength from the perception that negotiations resulting in a treaty would find support in "world opinion," by which they meant the United States.

Israeli leaders were very critical of the American-sponsored rehabilitation of the Federal Republic. It took serious economic difficulties within Israel to overcome their aversion to negotiating directly with the Germans. In January and March 1951 Israel submitted notes to the four occupying powers, demanding the payment of reparations in the amount of $1.5 billion. The Soviet Union did not respond, but the Western powers replied that they could not force Germany to make such a payment and advised Israel to deal directly with Germany. Although various informal and highly secretive contacts had occurred between Germans and Israelis in 1949 and 1950, the first meeting between Adenauer and David Horowitz, governor of the Bank of Israel, took place in Paris during the final negotiation of the Schuman Plan in April 1951. American diplomats helped arrange this secret meeting, acknowledging the implicit connection between Germany's acceptance by the West and its need to make a gesture toward Israel. In September 1951, only a few days after the Allies had agreed to begin the final phase of negotiating the contractual agreements and the end of occupation, Adenauer spoke movingly in the Bundestag, expressing a willingness to make amends to the Jewish people for the "unspeakable crimes" committed in "the name of the German people."[40]

Adenauer's support for restitution stemmed from his religious and moral convictions, a strong appreciation of the contributions of German Jews to German life, and his deep distaste for the vulgarity of anti-Semitism. But although Adenauer's underlying motives were moral, he never lost sight of the political aspects of the question. The timing of his September speech was clearly designed to improve the general atmosphere for his talks with the Allies, and most important, to strengthen his standing with American leaders and public opinion. (Schumacher and the SPD also strongly supported Adenauer's position on this issue.) The Chancellor had heard from McCloy that the major U.S. concerns about Germany had to do with the persistence of Nazi beliefs and the question of whether Germany had really embraced democracy. Adenauer also believed that American Jews had a powerful influence on American policy toward Germany, and he hoped to reduce their opposition through a program of reparations. Indeed the positive response of American and world opinion to his speech must have confirmed his estimation. The *Washington Post* called it "the best thing that [has come] from Germany since before 1933," the *New York Times* termed it "a phase of moral regeneration," and other newspapers around the United States and in Europe echoed these sentiments.[41]

In December 1951 on a trip to London Adenauer met secretly with Nahum Goldmann, the president of the World Jewish Congress, and agreed to set $1 billion (DM 4.3 billion) as a basis for negotiations. Although he had not secured Cabinet approval, Adenauer's unilateral declaration helped secure an Israeli willingness to negotiate despite intense popular opposition. In Israel thousands demonstrated outside Parliament on January 9, 1952, as it approved negotiations by a vote of 61 to 52. In Germany opposition was more muted but just as significant. The Finance Minister, Fritz Schäffer, vigorously protested Adenauer's commitment, arguing that Germany could not afford to specify any amount until its defense contribution and the question of its external debts were resolved. With talks set to begin in London on the settlement of Germany's outstanding debt, Schäffer hoped to delay any German commitment to Israel. He found an ally in Hermann Abs, the prominent banker and leader of Germany's delegation to the London talks. Their opposition led Adenauer to back away from his commitment to Goldmann by instructing his negotiators to bide for time and try to ascertain what the Israelis "really wanted."[42]

Negotiations between the German government and the Israelis began in March 1952 at the Hague. The United States, though not a direct participant, informed the Israelis that it would "await with sympathetic interest the outcome of the [Hague] negotiations." The Americans wanted Adenauer to pursue the talks, but at the same time they feared any German attempt to shift the responsibility and financial burdens of Wiedergutmachung to American shoulders. Yet when Abs asked the United States to suggest postponing the negotiations with Israel, the State Department rejected the notion, fearing the political effects in Israel. McCloy assured Nahum Goldmann, "While I told the Chancellor that I could sympathize with those who had responsibility over the extent of commitments covering the military contribution, the debt settlement, and payments to Israel, I thought it would be unwise to postpone commencement of the discussions." When Adenauer told his Cabinet of America's continuing interest in negotiations, one of the Cabinet members noted "the influence of McCloy."[43]

Despite American encouragement the Hague talks still faced enormous difficulties. The Israeli government had set its initial demand at $1 billion, but the Jewish Claims Conference, representing Jews outside the Federal Republic and Israel, asked for an additional $500 million. The Germans, however, stressed their "limited ability to pay" because of incomplete economic recovery and the unresolved matter of foreign debts. They insisted that the London and Hague negotiations were connected, and Abs argued that Germany could not take on additional obligations without the approval of its foreign creditors. To the Israelis this argument seemed to betray Adenauer's original position that Germany's commitment was fundamentally moral and not simply another financial obligation with an even lower priority than Germany's earlier debts. Soon it appeared that the talks would collapse.[44]

In this tense situation the Israeli Ambassador in Washington appealed to Acheson to intervene with the Germans. He stressed the difficult political situation in Israel which would result if the Germans attempted to "dovetail Hague and London Conferences." Acheson responded cautiously, stressing that it was reasonable for the Germans to consider their other commitments, and that the United States did not want to "press Germans into commitments which might increase German dependence on US aid." Yet he also made it clear (and emphasized this to McCloy) that the "Germans should recognize unfortunate repercussions which would ensure [sic] if they now appear to have been insincere on their offer to negotiate." He added that the United States could not tell the Germans how large an offer to make. McCloy, for his part, requested a memorandum from Ferencz on whether there was "anything in U.S. policy directives to mitigate against" intervention in favor of obtaining an agreement in the Hague negotiations. Ferencz assured him that "if a breakdown of negotiation between Israel and Germany were threatened U.S. policy would favor taking steps to avert such a breakdown, providing no other U.S. interest was seriously threatened."[45]

McCloy wanted the Germans to reach an agreement with the Israelis, and he warned them of the consequences if talks failed. At the same time, with rearmament, the debt question, and the health of the German economy at stake, he could not afford to put too much pressure on the Germans, thereby taking the risk that they would say, as Adenauer had at a Cabinet meeting, "If the USA has such a strong interest in the completion of a treaty between the Federal Republic and Israel, they should help us, so that we really can afford it." McCloy also feared that the Germans would try to make it appear that American policy concerning the London conference was interfering with a settlement with Israel. These suspicions were well placed. The Germans did attempt to persuade the Americans to assist them, with Abs asking McCloy for "U.S. assistance in form of returning assets or other method of financing Israeli payments." McCloy rejected this suggestion and "immediately advised Chancellor that the object of the exercise was a gesture of fair treatment by the Federal Republic not by the United States." McCloy did initially share Abs's view that it might be unwise for the Federal Republic to name a concrete sum in its offer to Israel. But the arguments of the German negotiators, Franz Böhm and Otto Küster, convinced him that such a definite figure was politically essential to the Israelis.[46]

Although Böhm and Küster were permitted to mention the figure of DM 3 billion as a new basis for negotiations, Adenauer and the Cabinet would not allow them to give the Israelis any commitment as to the amount, timing, or form of payment until after the London conference. The Israelis reacted by suspending negotiations and refusing to return until they had received, at least unofficially, "a satisfactory proposal from the German government as to the amount it was prepared to offer." As the final phases of the contractual negotiations were occupying both the Chancellor and the High Commission, and the opposition of Schäffer and Abs remained strong, the danger of a complete collapse in the Hague talks increased. Early in May Schäffer called in Böhm and Küster to berate them for having expressed sympathy for the Israeli claims at a press conference. Küster decided to resign, while Böhm stated that he was prepared to do so unless the German government changed its attitude. At a Cabinet meeting on May 14, 1952, however, Schäffer's continuing opposition prevented any change of policy, leading one of the Chancellor's advisers to lament that a breakdown in the talks would lead to a "general deterioration in public opinion in all the Western countries, with effects on European integration and the inclusion of Germany in the Atlantic community that can not yet be foreseen." As a result of this continued intransigence, Böhm also decided to tender his resignation.[47]

On May 19 Hermann Abs approached the Israeli representatives with an unofficial offer of "initial annual deliveries of goods amounting to the sum of one hundred million D. marks—a sum that might possibly be doubled on the strength of certain anticipated American measures of assistance to Germany." Abs gave no indication of the total sum Germany would be prepared to pay. The Germans, who had been informed by the Americans of the serious political and economic conditions in Israel, apparently thought the "Israelis so broke that they would khapp [grab] and accept anything." This crude calculation was mistaken. The Israeli negotiators rejected Abs's offer "instantaneously." Goldmann wrote directly to the Chancellor, calling the offer an "insult" to the Jewish world, and hoping that it did not "represent in any way your own ideas." He sent a copy of his letter to McCloy, asking that it be forwarded to Acheson and commenting, "I know that you will continue to do your best, as you have done in the past, and you are surely aware how deeply grateful all of us are to you."[48]

Goldmann's appeal for American intervention did not go unheeded, though that intervention took place very quietly. Only a few days before the Abs offer was made, McCloy had assured the State Department: "Chancellor fully aware of U.S. interest in facilitating early agreement and may wish to use conversation with Secretary [Acheson] as pressure on Finance Minister." When Adenauer realized that the Abs offer had failed, he disavowed knowledge of it and asked Böhm not to resign but to meet with Goldmann in Paris to ascertain what would be an acceptable offer. Adenauer informed McCloy of these steps, and McCloy told Goldmann that he would "hear some important news within the next few hours." The new German offer which Böhm took to Paris was DM 3 billion over a period covering between eight and twelve years. Although Goldmann had certain reservations about the offer, he accepted it as a basis for renewing negotiations. The Israelis still insisted on a formal and firm proposal, but they recognized that Adenauer's offer would be acceptable and constituted a breakthrough.[49]

During the next two weeks Adenauer received additional indications that the United States and the other Allies would welcome a German agreement with Israel. At the signing of the contractual agreements between the Allies and Germany both Acheson and British Foreign Secretary Eden told Adenauer that they wanted the negotiations with Israel to end successfully. Acheson stressed "the importance US attaches to having a settlement of the matter reached which is satisfactory to both sides." He emphasized that it was "primarily a moral issue" and that the United States was disappointed "at reports that Germans seemed to be hoping for US aid to assist them in settling claims." This was "evading moral responsibility," and the United States would provide no aid for such a purpose.[50]

Acheson's message had its impact. The crucial talks took place in Bonn on June 10, and the Germans agreed to pay DM 3.5 billion, with annual payments starting at a rate of DM 200 million. Adenauer reported to McCloy, who was in Washington testifying on behalf of the contractual agreements, that he believed "a settlement is in sight." At a Cabinet meeting a few days later Schäffer contended that restitution benefited only Jews and asked what should be done about the other "non-Aryans." His descent into Nazi terminology caused an eruption from Adenauer, who rejected his arguments and emphasized the importance of the treaty "for the relationship with the USA." A month later, when reports indicated that the Cabinet might reject the part of the treaty which guaranteed DM 450 million for the Jewish Claims Conference, McCloy cabled Adenauer that such an action "could not only endanger the entire work of the Hague Conference, but also could have serious consequences above all else with regard to the reconciliation of Germany with the Jewish people, which for Germany's future and international position is so significant." The Cabinet approved the money for the Claims Conference, and the treaty was signed in Luxembourg in September 1952.[51]

The Federal Republic fulfilled its commitments under the Luxembourg Treaty, and its deliveries to Israel came to an end in 1965. Though it was not apparent at the time, the direct reparations to Israel would constitute only a small part of the DM 90 billion which Germany has paid out in restitution for the crimes of the Nazi era. Mere restitution could not bring about Germany's reconciliation with the Jewish people, but it was an essential first step. A "decisive motive" for the completion of the treaty was the concern, felt by the Bonn government and Chancellor Adenauer, that without such an action Germany's integration into the West would be either endangered or made impossible. McCloy played a crucial role in conveying that message to the German leaders.[52]

McCloy entered government service in 1940 as Assistant Secretary of War under Henry Stimson.

McCloy at the Kasserine Pass in Tunisia, March 1943. As Assistant Secretary of War, he made frequent trips to the front lines.

Andrei Gromyko, Henry Stimson, and McCloy at Potsdam, 1945. McCloy considered the Soviet negotiators "sharp thinkers and firm."

Cologne at the end of the war. "No one of Germany's enemies could wish for a more complete sight of destruction."

Berlin: the Brandenburg Gate, May 8, 1945. "The misery of [Berlin] and the conflict between East and West hangs over you all the time."

Averell Harriman, McCloy, and David Bruce. Both the ECA and the Paris Embassy welcomed McCloy's appointment as High Commissioner.

The three Allied High Commissioners, Brian Robertson of the United Kingdom, André François-Poncet of France, and McCloy, signing the Occupation Statute, September 21, 1949. The commissioners differed sharply on how to deal with the new Germany.

Konrad Adenauer asserting his Teppichpolitik (carpet policy) before the signing of the Occupation Statute. (Also in the picture, from left to right, Fritz Schäfer, Thomas Dehler, Jakob Kaiser, and Franz Blücher.)

"Reconstruction in Berlin with Marshall Plan assistance." The Marshall Plan symbolized the American commitment to Germany's economic recovery.

McCloy touring Germany's first important penicillin plant at Farbwerke-Hoechst, built with the aid of Marshall Plan counterpart funds.

Rebuilding the Volkswagen plant in Wolfsburg. The speed of Germany's economic revival unsettled its neighbors.

Kurt Schumacher addressing a rally in Berlin in opposition to German rearmament, December 1950. McCloy's relationship with the fiery Socialist leader deteriorated during the crisis over rearmament.

Harry S Truman, McCloy, and Dean Acheson discussing German policy, January 1950.

Jean Monnet, the French internationalist. He played a crucial role in devising the Schuman and Pleven plans, and he worked with McCloy to secure American support for a united Europe.

General Thomas Handy, General Dwight D. Eisenhower, and McCloy during Eisenhower's trip to Germany, April 1951. McCloy helped convince Eisenhower to support the European Defense Community.

"Hold It, Please"

"Hold It, Please." This political cartoon by Herblock suggests that McCloy's decision to release convicted war criminal Alfried Krupp will provide grist for Stalin's propaganda campaign against the United States.

Anthony Eden, Konrad Adenauer, Dean Acheson, and Robert Schuman at the signing of the contractual agreements, May 1952. The EDC and contractual agreements were the unofficial peace treaties ending World War II.

McCloy and Dean Acheson at a press conference following the signing of the contractual agreements.

John and Ellen McCloy leaving Germany, July 1952. McCloy would continue to be an important friend of the new Federal Republic.

John Foster Dulles and Konrad Adenauer. Dulles, like McCloy, developed great respect for the German Chancellor.

Frankfurt before and after its rebuilding. Germany's peaceful reconstruction was one of the United States' most lasting contributions to postwar Europe.

McCloy, Gerald Ford, and Walter Scheel in June 1975 after the announcement of the John J. McCloy Fund for German-American Exchanges.

7

Ties That Bind: Economic Integration

The Brussels Conference agreements papered over the crisis caused by German rearmament, but they did not prevent serious debate in America and Germany over the wisdom of alliance policy. In the United States such figures as former President Herbert Hoover, Senator Robert Taft, and former Ambassador Joseph Kennedy attacked Truman's decision to dispatch American forces to Europe, questioning its strategic wisdom, its commitment of American resources, and its constitutionality. The "Great Debate" of early 1951 had an immediate impact on West Germany, where it stirred Adenauer's fears of American neo-isolationism and the possibility of a four-power agreement at Germany's expense. Seeking to reassure McCloy of his country's fidelity to the West, the Chancellor went so far as to "renounce for a time the thought of a reunited Germany" if that meant an "unarmed neutralized Germany rather [than] one thoroughly integrated with the West and capable of being defended against Eastern encroachments." A neutral disarmed Germany would be drawn to the East as certainly as "a filing" would be drawn to "a giant magnet." In contrast, Schumacher told McCloy that the "unification of Germany was the all-important issue," even at the risk of "temporary neutralization."[1]

The growing polarization between CDU and SPD, evident in the debates on both rearmament and reunification, also served to limit American choices in Germany. Only a few months earlier McCloy had recommended to Truman that the United States "consider the possibility of encouraging a coalition German government" in order to "consolidate opinion and action" on the rearmament issue. The furor over rearmament, however, separated the parties even further. Although McCloy still hoped the European approach would bring the Socialists to support rearmament, he was drawn more and more into supporting the aged Chancellor, considering him the most steadfast supporter of American policies in Germany. Henceforth McCloy sought to speed the process of bringing the Federal Republic of Germany into a "new Europe," integrated and "united as never before" in its economic, military, and political institutions. His first step was to revive the Schuman Plan, using the waning but still formidable power of the American High Commission.[2]

The Schuman Plan in Trouble

In December 1950 during the Brussels Conference McCloy had told Secretary of State Acheson that if the United States did not act within the next few weeks, the Schuman Plan would be a "dead duck." Not only had German resistance to the Schuman Plan increased in the wake of the Korean War, but Allied plans to restructure Germany's heavy industry, embodied in Law 27, were meeting fierce German opposition. Moreover, the French government was making the implementation of Law 27 the sine qua non for its acceptance of the Schuman Plan. Monnet had found that French industrialists, especially the "maîtres de forges" (ironmasters) of Lorraine, preferred their private arrangements, including the old European steel cartel, to any that might be made by a new public agency. David Bruce, describing Monnet's concerns, noted that it was "very doubtful that the French government can break power of its steel cartel and convince its public that equal treatment is being granted if German steel industry is permitted to maintain what in French mind is an overwhelming advantage."[3]

By the beginning of 1951 the Schuman Plan was in great danger of succumbing to the transnational coalition of French and German industrial interests, which was seeking to modify the plan so as to make it politically unacceptable to both countries. To some extent the United States was responsible for this state of affairs because its push for rearmament had changed the balance of power between the French and German negotiators. At this point, with progress on rearmament held hostage to the fate of the Schuman Plan and with the prospect of four-power talks looming, Acheson authorized McCloy to use his influence to bring about a settlement. American intervention was politically risky, for it increased the danger that the Schuman Plan would be seen as an "American" attempt to reshape Europe, rather than a European product. Nevertheless, the possibility that the plan would fail, with the resulting blow to American prestige on the eve of negotiations with the Russians, triggered vigorous American intervention.[4]

The United States was not a direct participant in the Schuman Plan talks, but during the final consideration of Law 27 McCloy took control of negotiations with the Germans, insisting that he was serving as an "honest broker" between them and the British and French High Commissions. Of the four areas of disagreement still remaining, two were relatively easy to resolve. The Allies and Germans did not differ greatly on the number of successor "unit" companies, with the Allies proposing 29 and the Germans 23. Nor was there fundamental opposition to the German argument that, with the Schuman Plan firmly in place, production limits should be abolished and the Germans themselves should determine the issue of ownership. The French grumbled over this, but they could not escape the logical implication of equality that the Schuman Plan provided.

But on the issues of the Ruhr's *Verbundwirtschaft* ("combined economy") and the future of the German coal sales agency, disagreement was intense. The term "combined economy" described the vertical integration of steel and coal production in the Ruhr. Historically the Ruhr had been characterized by a high degree of vertical integration, and the steel industry owned more than half of Germany's coal production. With a passion bordering on religious zeal, German steelmakers argued that their efficiency was rooted in this "economic structure which, in its ability to withstand crises, has aroused envy and admiration the world over." The Adenauer government strongly defended it and told the High Commissioners that its break-up would lead the Bundestag to reject the Schuman Plan.[5]

Although American lawyers in the High Commission, such as Robert Bowie, labeled the German view of the combined economy a "myth," the strongest opposition came from the European allies. The British wanted separate organizations for the coal industry and the steel industry, similar to those for the nationalized industries in their own country. They would support vertical integration only where it was necessary for "purely technical reasons." The French, with a steel industry dependent on German coking coal, feared German control of the price and supply of coal, especially in times of shortage. If German steel firms owned their supplies of coking coke, they would be "fully independent of coal shortages which may, in times of full production, hamper their competitors in other countries."[6]

Indeed the European coal shortage of late 1950 and early 1951 confirmed French fears. In October 1950 the Ruhr Authority forced the Germans to maintain the level of their coal exports to other Western European countries, even though the Korean War boom had produced a coal shortage in Germany. The bitter protests of the Germans at this forced export reinforced the French conviction that more German coal had to come onto the open market, rather than being produced in captive mines. Both the French and the Americans saw this as a way to avoid a repetition of "the unbalanced development of the post World War I period," which would be "at odds with the purpose of the Schuman Plan to create an equal basis for competition." In practice the United States had to help the French steel industry at the expense of the Ruhr, in the hope of creating a more equal "economic" balance of power between France and Germany.[7]

Similar concerns fueled the dispute over the future of the Deutscher Kohlen-Verkauf (DKV), the centralized sales agency for the Ruhr's coal. From 1893 onward a single organization had handled all the sales of Ruhr coal. After World War II the British, the occupying power in the Ruhr, reestablished the DKV, not only to regulate sales but, in times of oversupply, to help allocate orders and insure the survival of marginal mines and prevent unemployment, and in times of high demand to allocate orders among customers and spread the benefits of increased production among the collieries. The DKV also served technical functions that had commercial consequences. The mines produced quite different varieties and types of coal, and the DKV pooled these supplies to make "it easier for buyers to place orders for just what they wanted and for the Ruhr to dispose of its poorer grades." In pursuing its function of centralizing sales and stabilizing employment, the DKV enjoyed strong support in Germany, especially among the trade unions. The Germans strongly believed that "national existence [depends] upon careful, planned, scientific exploitation of both the coal deposits and the coal consumers."[8]

The British favored the continuance of the DKV, seeing it as a "wedge for nationalization." They were also impressed by the support it received from the German trade unions and the SPD. Monnet, however, opposed the DKV for the same reason he opposed the Ruhr's combined economy: his fear of its monopoly control over coal. He believed that two articles forbidding cartels should be placed in the Schuman Plan treaty, even though he faced significant opposition on this point from French Cabinet ministers who were influenced by the steel industry. At the same time Monnet's opposition to the DKV strengthened his standing with the Americans, whose support would be decisive in the final negotiations. The Americans, for their part, conceded the need for a "period of transition" to give the German coal companies time to set up their own sales agencies and the German government time to set up machinery to deal with allocation in times of shortage. But they considered the DKV a cartel pure and simple, "completely inconsistent with both Law 27 and the Schuman Plan"— an organization that could "exercise coordinated control over the marketplace" and thus restrict competition and create a monopoly. They realized, too, that its continued existence would both reduce support for the Schuman Plan in the United States and encourage French steel companies to maintain their own single buying agency.[9]

The Negotiations

American intervention in the Law 27 negotiations aimed at resolving these two major issues. McCloy and Bowie adopted a "good cop, bad cop" negotiating style, with Bowie threatening the Germans and McCloy voicing moderation. Bowie repeatedly warned Erhard, the German Economics Minister, that unless his country presented serious proposals "the High Commission would have no option but to use its reserve powers in the fullest degree in order to ensure the Allied aims under Law 27." Unless the Bonn government came up with "concrete proposals" that reflected a "willingness to compromise," further negotiations were impossible. McCloy assured the Germans that he did not want a "dictated" solution (a term associated with the Treaty of Versailles), but he urged them to recognize Allied concerns and to propose their own program within these guidelines.[10]

To reach a compromise, Bowie urged Erhard to engage in old-fashioned "horse trading." When it became clear that the Germans and Americans differed on the appropriate size of four of the future "unit" steel companies, Bowie proposed that the Germans select two over which they wished to bargain. He followed the same procedure with the issue of vertical integration by suggesting a formula allowing a steel company to own between 55 and 80 percent of its coal requirements. Bowie was firmly against DKV, but he agreed that some time would be needed to phase it out. Initially Erhard was reluctant to accept any of the proposed compromises. Though known to oppose cartels and to be relatively unsympathetic to heavy industry, he was not yet the powerful figure he would become after Germany's "economic miracle" had been secured. His position within the Adenauer government was shaky, and he was battling with Finance Minister Schäffer and Vice Chancellor Blücher for the control of economic policy. Ultimately, however, Erhard's refusal to make a commitment to Bowie reflected the unwillingness of the Adenauer government to act without the approval of the Ruhr industrialists.[11]

Two weeks later the Germans returned with a proposal which reflected their unwillingness to bargain. Instead of offering to compromise on the size of two of the unit companies, they added two more companies to the disputed list, one of which was the firm that had been spared by the Petersberg Protocols, the August-Thyssen steel works. Arguing that this firm was not a viable unit company on its own, they proposed to merge it with Rheinische Röhrenwerke, an important steel finishing plant. Further, to provide for the needs of expanded steel production goals, Erhard called for the steel industry to own more than 100 percent of its estimated need for coking coal. He also rejected the abolition of the DKV, noting the strong support it enjoyed among the German trade unions, whose support in turn would be critical to the Bundestag's approval of the Schuman Plan.[12]

Bowie rejected the German response, telling Erhard that the DKV must be abolished. He also announced that individual steel producers would not be permitted to own more than 75 percent of their coal supply. This figure represented a compromise designed to obtain agreement from all three Western powers. It also provided a built-in incentive to increase coal production (which the Americans favored), because firms would be free to increase their production from these "captive mines." In addition, that 75 percent figure applied only to individual steel producers and not to the aggregate or "global" needs of the industry, and therefore the percentage of coal production controlled by the steel industry would shrink from more than 50 percent to 16 percent.[13]

The uncompromising German proposal which Bowie rejected reflected the concerns of the Ruhr industrialists. Led by Hans-Günther Sohl of Vereinigte Stahlwerke and Günther Henle of Klöckner, they pressed their government to "bombard" the Americans with objections to Law 27. In a series of letters to McCloy and personal meetings with him they argued that the American proposals were "one-sided" and "dictatorial" and that Germany should be free to restructure its industry as it wished. Henle complained that Bowie's suggestion of "contracts" as a substitute for ownership of coal supplies was not a sufficient guarantee. He insisted that other countries need not worry about Germany's control of coking coal, since these countries, particularly France, controlled most of the iron ore needed for steel production. In his view, the Ruhr's combined economy was essential for Germany to compete equally in the Schuman Plan, though he assured McCloy, somewhat disingenuously, that he did not mean to "barter [European] integration and joining the Schuman Plan against each other." Wilhelm Zangen of Mannesmann had already made it clear to Erhard that "cooperation with the Schuman Plan on the part of the German steel industry has prospects for success only to the extent that the limits [on the combined economy] specified by the government's proposal are safeguarded. Failing this, it is preferable to break off the negotiations."[14]

The strength of resistance from the industrialists triggered the Americans' long-standing suspicions about the "Ruhr magnates," about their authoritarian political leanings, their interest in trade and possibly political ties with the East, and their "feudalistic" attitudes toward their workers. McCloy took Henle to task for expressing "the view that failure to adopt the German proposals in all cases is arbitrary and unfair." He also pointed out that the very argument the industrialists were using—"that ownership of such coal by steel companies is necessary to assure their supply in times of high steel production and coal scarcity"—confirmed the fears of other countries that the Germans would have an "undue advantage" during such periods. McCloy noted that Germany was not as dependent on French iron ore as the French were on Ruhr coal—a reference to the availability of Swedish supplies. Refusing to let the Germans turn the issue into a matter of "fundamental principle," he suggested shifting the discussion "from the plane of abstract principle to the plane of practical adjustment," where compromise would be possible. He then arranged a meeting in Frankfurt with Pferdmenges, Sohl, Henle, and representatives from Krupp and Mannesmann. McCloy told these industrialists that the British and French would take a far tougher line than the Americans on the issue of the combined economy. (Whether they could have prevailed on such a hard line without American support, he did not say.) Then for more than five hours he listened to the Germans' technical objections to both the restructuring of the industries and the division of the mines, showing them that he took their objections seriously and was moved by their presentation.[15]

But the steelmakers confused McCloy's willingness to listen with his political judgment on the merits of the German demands. On February 12 he gave Adenauer the final text of the agreement worked out by Bowie, Erhard, and the two German negotiators at the Schuman Plan conference, Walter Hallstein and Walter Bauer. The Americans had arranged that two articles of the Schuman Plan treaty would contain provisions against cartels and "excessive" concentrations, thus appeasing German concerns about "equality" with other nations in the coal and steel union, as well as American concerns that the Schuman Plan might be perceived in the United States as a giant cartel. The agreement also contained some additional concessions to the Germans, including the rejection of a French proposal that limits should be placed on the steel production of individual plants. The Americans allowed three new combinations among the unit companies, though they refused the merger of Rheinische Röhrenwerke with August-Thyssen. On the combined economy McCloy held to the 75 percent formula. Telling Adenauer that the agreement represented "the absolute limit which has any prospect of acceptance," McCloy echoed Bowie's threat that further demands could "result in the loss of these concessions." McCloy reiterated that the DKV was a monopoly and could not be allowed to continue, but he agreed to a "substantial period of transition before the dissolution of the monopoly."[16]

McCloy urged Adenauer to recognize that the proposal was a "generous" concession to German views. The Chancellor, however, was in a politically vulnerable position, weaker than he had been a year earlier. Some observers believed that only the Basic Law's restrictions on a no-confidence vote were keeping him in power. The rearmament issue had precipitated his drop in popularity, while inflation and the suspension of trade liberalization in late February had further damaged his prestige. In addition, he faced special problems with the Ruhr industrialists stemming from the Mitbestimmung controversy. At the end of January the German trade unions had threatened to strike in defense of their right to Mitbestimmung, or parity codetermination, in the coal and steel industry. (Under codetermination labor possessed an equal voice in management of the heavy industries.) As the deadline for the strike approached, Adenauer had intervened personally, putting pressure on his industrialist friends to accept codetermination as a permanent reform. After the successful settlement the industrialists expected Adenauer to return the favor by supporting their views on Law 27. The Free Democrats, Adenauer's coalition partners, were not only unhappy with codetermination but also opposed the Allied position on Law 27. Because of the significance of Law 27 and the Schuman Plan, and the "unrest" stirred up among both industrialists and trade unionists over the Allied proposal, Adenauer told McCloy he would take a direct role in the negotiations.[17]

The two men met on February 18 to discuss the contrasting proposals. McCloy emphasized the degree to which the Allies had made concessions on all the major issues, and the degree to which he had pressed the French to accept these compromises. Adenauer, who had not kept up with the negotiations, confined himself to a discussion of the combined economy, and all his arguments seemed to McCloy to have been "supplied by [the Ruhr industrialists]." When Adenauer argued that anything less than full coverage of the industry's needs would cause "economic and social chaos," McCloy perceived an attempt by the industrialists to "attain [an] artificially preferred position for German steel." The next day he called Jean Monnet in Paris to tell him that the German proposals were not only unacceptable but were "animated by a spirit of domination." Yet he hesitated to act, especially in view of the German claim that French resistance was softening. Monnet, after assuring McCloy that the French government had not changed its position, urged his friend to give Adenauer an ultimatum: accept the February 12 proposals or the High Commission would dictate a solution.[18]

Adenauer continued to dispute the issue of coal production, challenging the figures which the Americans were using to compute the 75 percent arrangement. He pointed out that the figures used to calculate the needs of German steel producers were based on actual steel production figures from 1938 to 1943, while the figures for coal production were based on estimated goals for 1953; and he demanded that calculations for both should be made on the same basis. Because

Germany's steel producers were planning a significant expansion in capacity, such a recalculation would have given the Germans control of 5.2 million additional tons of coking coal. Adenauer minimized this increase to McCloy, juxtaposing a few million tons of coal against the "greatness of the problem that, in respect to the Schuman Plan and European policy, now stands before us." Finally, arguing that the Schuman Plan's High Authority could handle the dangers presented by vertical integration or by a monopoly like the DKV, he asked that the High Authority be allowed to decide these matters after the treaty had been signed.[19]

McCloy was not unsympathetic to the Chancellor's position, but he emphasized to Adenauer the "profound significance of Schuman Plan for Europe and the West especially in light of impending Four-Power Conference." He also made it clear that the American proposal was the best compromise possible. He refused to give way on the production figures which the Americans were using, even though he conceded that there was a legitimate argument for using the same base figures for all the calculations. The American objective, however, was to expand coal production and reduce the amount of coal controlled in captive mines, and to use the projected figures for German steel production would have placed too much coal under the control of the Ruhr industrialists and given Germany an undue advantage.[20]

Adenauer's arguments were not the only ones McCloy had to deal with as the negotiations neared their climax. The Ruhr industrialists recruited the former Secretary of War, Robert Patterson, to intervene with McCloy and plead their case. Patterson's actual client was the Arbeitsgemeinschaft der Schutzvereinigung für Wertpapierbesitz, an association of shareholders in the various companies affected by Law 27. Led by Carl Christian Schmid, a man "who worshipped power and yet never managed to get enough of it for himself," the association worked closely with the major steel industries in their campaign against Law 27. Schmid came up with the idea of hiring Patterson, an old friend of McCloy, and when his association could not afford the $10,000 fee, the industrialists picked up the tab. They were convinced that a man of Patterson's prestige would sway the High Commission. Some even thought that he could convince McCloy that a "German defense contribution" could best be made from the steel production of the very firms the High Commission wanted to break up.[21]

Patterson's legal brief, entitled "Restoration of the Rule of Law," did not disappoint them. It was a wide-ranging attack on the High Commission, referring to its antitrust policies as "executed without regard for those basic principles of justice which in the U.S. have uniformly restrained courts from arbitrary and oppressive actions." Patterson maintained that because there were no precedents for such a policy as Law 27, the High Commission had to administer the statute according to American procedures. (He ignored the Allied aspect of the occupation.) By American criteria "the provisions of Law 27 plainly transgress the requirements of due process of law." He compared it to a "bill of attainder," without safeguards against arbitrary action and with inadequate and overly narrow provisions for appeal. The implications of Patterson's brief were clear: the United States would have to end its decartelization policy if it wished to meet its own legal standards.

The offer of an additional $15,000 convinced Patterson to go to Germany to plead his case personally with McCloy. On landing in Frankfurt he conferred immediately with McCloy and Bowie, who had also worked closely with him in the War Department. McCloy was angry about Patterson's efforts and believed them highly improper, but he also recognized that Patterson could help make it clear to his "clients" that no further compromise was possible. After several conferences McCloy convinced Patterson that with the Schuman Plan on the line, he should help prevent a serious crisis in U.S.–European relations. Subsequently Patterson went back to his clients with the advice that "after review of the situation" they should "adopt [the] American solution of maximum of 75 percent of coal requirements for any steel plant . . ." (Patterson later wrote apologetically to McCloy, well aware, as he put it, of "the sense or irritation that men on distant outposts cannot help feeling when those back home who are not charged with particular responsibility bob up and offer their opinions.") Because of the build-up of the Patterson visit by the Germans, his reversal of position put additional pressure on the Adenauer government to accept McCloy's compromise.[22]

After the Patterson visit Adenauer and McCloy met again on March 2 for a final review of their differences. Following a long discussion of the figures the Americans had used in their calculations, Adenauer indicated his willingness to accept the American-prescribed compromises. This willingness strengthened McCloy's conviction "as to [Adenauer's] own sincere belief in [the] European idea and in practical integration with the West." In return for his acceptance, Adenauer asked McCloy to meet with both the trade unions and the Ruhr industrialists, to convince them of the necessity for compromise. (He knew that some industrialists, particularly Sohl of Vereinigte Stahlwerke, did not want the government to agree to this American "Diktat.") Both of these powerful groups needed to realize the constraints on his position as well as the reasons for the Americans' insistence on their compromise proposal.[23]

The next day McCloy conferred with the trade unionists for more than four hours. He again stressed the necessity of reaching agreement "prior to the beginning of the conferences of the Big Four." Admitting his own feelings of pessimism during the course of the negotiations, he emphasized that failure of the Schuman Plan would produce a "very reserved attitude towards Germany" in the United States. Having issued this warning, McCloy offered an incentive, saying that he attached "great importance to the fact that the Americans would like to lift all restrictions imposed on the German economy in order to free it from all fetters so that the development of the German economy might lead to increasing wealth." After this introduction McCloy went on to explain the American views on the combined economy and the DKV. In reply, the unions expressed a willingness to be conciliatory, even acknowledging their own distrust of "certain industrial persons and governmental circles." Although they defended the combined economy, the union leaders directed most of their attention to the dissolution of the DKV, arguing that it offered the only way to secure the proper distribution of coal "according to quality and the balance of costs for unprofitable mines, as well as for steady employment." McCloy suggested the compromise of a three-year transitional period: the DKV would be liquidated, but the High Authority of the Schuman Plan would find a solution for maintaining the advantages which the DKV offered, without re-creating the same type of monopoly. This compromise seemed to satisfy the union leaders, and the next day McCloy went to Paris and secured Monnet's agreement.[24]

Next McCloy held two meetings with separate groups of industrialists, one lasting five hours and the other seven. These meetings were not like the earlier negotiating sessions. It was clear that McCloy was no longer prepared to bargain. In each session he laid out the larger reasons for reaching agreement, emphasizing the importance of the

Schuman Plan to the United States and the necessity for presenting a "unified front against the East." He assured the industrialists that if the Schuman Plan was signed, he would work for an end to the Ruhr Authority and Germany's steel quota. He also emphasized that there was simply no further room to compromise because he had extracted all he could from Paris and London. Although he would be flexible in some individual cases and allow linkages of coal and steel ownership which were a few percentage points above the 75 percent limit, that limit was the best that could be achieved. At this point the Germans raised numerous specific objections, but they soon realized they had been presented with a fait accompli. When McCloy had been called from the meeting to take a telephone call from Acheson, he returned to inform the group that the Secretary urged swift completion of the talks. Sohl spoke privately to McCloy after the meeting, saying that he was deeply disappointed in the final agreement, especially because of the amount of coal allowed to the Thyssen works. The High Commissioner listened sympathetically but replied, with a corresponding gesture, "My hands are tied."[25]

McCloy's personal diplomacy led one of his intermediaries to report that "you have won the battle" and that the Ruhr "will not do anything which might endanger the conclusion of the Schuman Plan." On March 8, in an executive session of the High Commission, McCloy told his British and French colleagues that the American government "felt strongly that everything possible should be done to get the Schuman Plan signed without delay," emphasizing that it must be completed before the French would move toward revising the Prohibited Industries Agreement and discussing a German defense contribution. McCloy concluded by telling the High Commissioners that he expected Adenauer would soon put forward the American compromise as the German plan for Law 27. On March 14 Adenauer's letter arrived, clearing the way for the treaty. It was initialed five days later, and it was signed at a formal ceremony in Paris the following month.[26]

The Aftermath of the Agreement

The signing of the Schuman Plan was one of the first major steps toward greater European economic and political unity. Like the Marshall Plan, it raised enormous expectations which far outstripped its reality. Yet what is interesting about the Law 27 controversy and the Schuman Plan is the extent to which they succeeded despite the failure of Law 27 to change the structure and practices of Germany's heavy industry in any significant manner.

On one level the success of Law 27 and the Schuman Plan was one of McCloy's most important achievements as American High Commissioner. Jean Monnet admitted that the treaty "would never have been signed but for Mr. McCloy's support." McCloy's efforts went a long way toward mending the tear in the fabric of American-French relations created by the rearmament controversy. French opinion recognized that "without the United States, the French theses on decartelization and deconcentration in the Ruhr would have continued to be rebuffed by the Federal Republic." The State Department believed that "the French and Germans would not have stuck together in an effort to find an agreed solution without some catalyst pulling them together." Failure of the negotiations would have been "a major set back to United States policy in Europe." Indeed the Schuman Plan provided a key foreign policy success at a critical time, strengthening those American leaders who argued that the Europeans were deserving of a sustained U.S. commitment. It further strengthened the Western position at the Paris Four-Power talks, which ultimately would break down in June without agreement on an agenda. And it confirmed McCloy's role as one of the most powerful and influential figures guiding American policy toward Europe.[27]

For his part McCloy promoted the Schuman Plan at every opportunity. He assured the Germans that it was a measure of their reliability as partners with the West. After a trip to the United States in June 1951, he told Adenauer that people regarded the plan as a "glorious affair," even though "nobody knew what it really meant." There was a growing conviction that "Germany could be trusted again." Publicly he insisted that the ratification of the plan was "a sort of test of whether the European countries are yet prepared to work together in creating a progressive European community which will advance the interests of all and overcome the cleavages of the conflicts of the past." Such statements made it clear to the French and Germans that American leaders regarded the Schuman Plan as far more than a scheme for dealing with the problems of heavy industry; they saw it as a "great and constructive step toward European peace and union."[28]

The unqualified American support for the Schuman Plan also

strengthened Adenauer's position. Despite the American pressure to accept Law 27, Adenauer benefited from the public perception of an important foreign policy success. By a roughly two-to-one margin Germans approved of the plan, and Adenauer's symbolic trip to Paris in April to sign the agreement contributed to his stature with the German public. FDP leaders, who had opposed Adenauer's position on both codetermination and Law 27, were reluctant to seek the Chancellor's ouster precisely because of these foreign policy successes.[29]

The SPD, however, took a strong stand against the Schuman Plan, with Schumacher calling it "an agreement between Poncet and McCloy to tie German industry to France." In an echo of his "Chancellor of the Allies" statement after the Petersberg Agreements, Schumacher declared that the Schuman Plan, rather than a treaty, was "the execution of the will of the victorious powers . . . which had to be accepted by the Chancellor." Acceptance of the plan, Schumacher remarked, meant "occupation for the next fifty years." His bitterness grew when the DGB, the trade-union organization, announced tentative support for the plan. Schumacher went so far as to tell the American liaison in Bonn that "had not the SPD sponsored opposition the radical right would have assumed leadership and transformed the opposition into a neo-Nazi nationalism," which would have had "millions" of supporters. The very stridency of these attacks may have served Adenauer's interests rather than the SPD's. Industrialists, reluctant to join forces with the Socialist leader and fearing that his nationalist opposition would limit their ability "to focus public opinion on the central economic questions" of the plan, found it more difficult to oppose the plan openly. Some even came around to the viewpoint of Günther Henle, who wrote to a sympathetic American, "We have to make the best of it." More important, the SPD leader's assault on Adenauer further cemented the tacit McCloy-Adenauer alliance. Privately McCloy told Adenauer how much he deplored the "bitterness" which Schumacher brought to his opposition. That opposition confirmed McCloy's realization that there was no practical alternative to Adenauer's leadership if American policy in Germany was to succeed.[30]

The celebration of the Schuman Plan did not include the British, who remained deeply skeptical toward Monnet's policy of treating "Germany as an equal within a supranational organization, while deny-

ing her equality as a national unit and even trying to prevent her from
becoming one." This policy, as the new Foreign Secretary, Herbert
Morrison, commented, "rested on a very dangerous illusion," for West
Germany already constituted a national unit and such treatment
could drive the Germans "into alliance with the East." The British
also objected strongly to both the 75 percent agreement and the
phasing out of the DKV. They resented the fact that although McCloy
had used their views to threaten the Germans, he had excluded the
British from his direct mediation efforts. Nevertheless those in the
Foreign Office, despite their skepticism about the Schuman Plan and
French schemes for European integration, had for a long time "wished
to place no obstacle in the way of a settlement and must be particularly
careful to do nothing which might lead to an accusation that we were
trying to do so." When American newspaper reports indicated that
the British might hold up the signing of the Schuman Plan, the
Foreign Office suspected a "propaganda campaign" designed to compel their acquiescence. But despite resentment at being compelled to
rubber-stamp McCloy's proposals, London authorized Kirkpatrick to
agree, noting that abstention would be "misrepresented as an expression of impotent anger against the Schuman Plan."[31]

The British also abandoned their diminishing hopes of seeing the
nationalization of German heavy industry. From the British perspective, the determination of the Americans to restore private ownership
was so overwhelming that resistance could only damage Anglo-American cooperation in other more important areas. The Americans believed that Schuman Plan would eliminate French resistance to turning
the Ruhr industries back to their German owners. Private ownership
could be safely restored, because the "barons of the Ruhr" would
conduct their business under the watchful eye of the new European
agency. The United States saw in the plan a substitute for its own
largely unsuccessful attempts to achieve more fundamental reforms of
German industrial organization and practices. By creating a supranational structure to control and supervise European heavy industry, a
structure like the Washington regulatory agencies of the New Deal,
America could speed the end of the occupation without abandoning
its commitment to control Germany's resurgence.[32]

It is ironic that the McCloy compromise on Law 27, which was so
critical to achieving final agreement on the Schuman Plan, had relatively few long-term consequences. Adenauer, in his original letter of

March 14 accepting Law 27, had proceeded "from the assumption that one of the principles behind Law 27 is the creation of economically viable structures." The twenty-four unit companies were created, but not all remained separate for long. During the 1950s the Schuman Plan's High Authority permitted a series of "reconcentrations," six involving coal and steel ownership and eight involving steel and steel processing plants. In some cases this was the result of "the economic advantages of concentration" reasserting themselves "very quickly over the more political considerations which had prevailed in the decartelization programme." As for the combined economy, the reconcentration simply demonstrated "the weight of tradition," with industrialists arguing into the mid-1950s that "coal and steel must again be united with one another." Klöckner, Mannesmann, Hoesch, and even August-Thyssen reacquired mining companies within only a few years of the proclamation of Law 27. As one study concluded, "by 1958 . . . all traces of Law 27 had been obliterated."[33]

A more prolonged struggle took place over the future of the DKV. The trade unions submitted a plan to replace the agency with another "central selling agency for Ruhr coal," leading McCloy to demand of Adenauer that "the German representatives be instructed to act in conformity with your letter of March 14." But the resistance remained powerful. The need for trade-union support for the ratification of the Schuman Plan, along with the decreasing desire of the High Commission to intervene actively while the end of the occupation was being negotiated, led McCloy to compromise further. The dissolution of the DKV was postponed until April 1953, almost two years later than originally planned, and then it was replaced by six sales organizations, coordinated by the Gemeinschaftsorganisation Ruhrkohle (GEORG). This proved to be merely a cosmetic change, for the six organizations "remained associated by numerous personal and business links, the common device of interlocking directorates which normally thwarts political interference."[34]

With both the combined economy and the DKV reasserting themselves, how was a crisis in Franco-German and, implicitly, German-American relations avoided? Larger changes in the postwar European economy, particularly in the situation of coal and steel, provide one answer. One of the most important changes was a decline in coal consumption by industry, along with increasing competition from newly opened mines overseas. The strong demand for coal after the war and during the Korean boom came to an end in 1953, and the French fear that the Germans would use their "coal weapon" to attain an unfair advantage over other Europeans disappeared as large supplies of American coal flooded the European market. In addition, coal was progressively replaced by cheaper sources of energy, such as oil and hydroelectricity. In 1957 oil provided 11 percent of the energy needs of the Federal Republic; by 1963 this share had grown to 32 percent. When, by the second half of the 1950s, the increasing supplies of coal led Ruhr industrialists "slowly and apparently with wet eyes" to conclude that "the age of the *Verbundwirtschaft* was over," they began to sell off their mines and buy their coal on the open world market.[35]

An opposite development occurred with regard to steel. French policy during the Law 27 negotiations had been designed to reduce what the French perceived as Germany's advantages in steel production. They had assumed that the market for steel products, particularly the more expensive output of the new continuous wide-strip rolling mills, would remain limited. (This was one reason why the Military Security Board, which vetoed Thyssen's bid to purchase such a wide-strip rolling mill in 1951, did not relent until 1953.) But, contrary to expectations, the demand for steel remained strong until the end of the 1950s, and the expansion of the German automobile industry actually benefited the French steel industry by helping to keep the new mills built under the Monnet Plan in constant production. The overall economic expansion of West Germany through the 1950s and early 1960s also served to reduce the relative importance of the Ruhr. Heavy industry gradually lost its dominance within West Germany as electrical engineering, chemicals, and car manufacturing helped bring to an end steel's economic leadership in the Federal Republic.[36]

These developments make it appear as though the struggles over Law 27 were irrelevant, as though they were battles over problems that were soon to become historical. One could say that coal and steel, critical elements in the first two world wars and an important part of the symbolism of the Schuman Plan, were irrelevant in the age of nuclear weaponry and guided missiles. Yet such a conclusion lacks an appreciation for the real achievement of McCloy, Monnet, and the other sponsors of the Schuman Plan. Politically the plan had great significance in postwar European history: it was one of the critical steps that broke away from the tragic pattern of the interwar era. The renewed expansion of Germany's heavy industry was a major symbolic barrier to the cultivation of Franco-German rapprochement, which in turn was central to both the future stability of Western Europe and the success of America's "dual containment" policy. The creation of the Coal and Steel Community removed this set of economic issues from the political arena and placed them under a "permanent international governmental organization, with some public appearance of neutrality, to regulate them." The "institutionalization" of cooperation helped dampen the fears of other Europeans, particularly the French, while at the same time affording the Germans an "equality" which made their integration into the West politically acceptable. All of this occurred because of American willingness to use its power to act as a European "pacifier," to compel cooperation between the former enemies and break the cycle of European civil war.[37]

The Payments Crisis

The successful completion of the Schuman Plan was part of the three-pronged strategy McCloy and his advisers had devised to end the Allied occupation and tie the Federal Republic to Western Europe and the United States. The future of the Ruhr had been a central stumbling block to a unified Western approach to Germany, whose removal augured well for progress in the other two areas, rearmament and the contractual negotiations. Yet the question of heavy industry was not the only economic issue which aroused concern. The crisis in Germany's foreign trade balance early in 1951 threatened to reverse the trend toward economic liberalization and the reduction of trade barriers, which Americans hoped would further European economic integration. This crisis cast McCloy in a role similar to that which he had played in connection with the Schuman Plan. In this case he used his power over Marshall Plan assistance to influence the Adenauer government in the direction of more cooperative policies, to ease the fears of other Europeans and keep Germany securely bound within the expanding Western economy.

The crisis in Germany's foreign trade was actually a reassertion of pre-1945 trading patterns. Since 1945 the Allied Military Government had controlled Germany's trade and made deals through bilateral arrangements. Reversing the pattern which had held since the late nineteenth century, most of occupied Germany's exports consisted of raw materials, particularly coal. The Adenauer government and par-

ticularly Economics Minister Erhard were determined both to expand
Germany's trade and to reestablish its position as a leading exporter of
finished goods. This would require a rapid increase in the size and
variety of imports, to give German manufacturers the raw materials
they needed to resume industrial production. In mid-1950 the Allies
provided Erhard with the means to expand Germany's imports. The
European Payments Union (EPU), established in July, was a multilateral clearing house designed to facilitate intra-European trade. Under the EPU the various claims and obligations arising from intra-
European trade were settled periodically through a common pool.
Germany received an initial quota of $320 million within the EPU.
After the outbreak of the Korean War German industrial production
rose rapidly, creating a heavy demand for imported raw materials and
foodstuffs. With the overall price of such commodities rising, German
importers, strongly encouraged by Erhard's ministry, went on a buying
spree. These German purchases, made primarily from the overseas
colonies of EPU countries, rapidly exhausted the $320 million quota,
and by October 1950 there was nothing left. Some action was necessary to keep Germany from leaving the EPU, which would have
constituted a major setback to trade liberalization and the recovery of
the German economy.[38]

Americans had put their hopes in the EPU, seeing it as another step
on the road toward European unity. It is true that it took an approach
to integration very different from that of the Schuman Plan and that
it embraced a larger group of countries, but it formed a vital part of
the overall strategy of "enmeshing" Germany in the West. Erhard
gambled correctly that the United States would not let the EPU
collapse, especially in the midst of the rearmament crisis. Acheson,
preferring to keep a low profile in the resolution of the crisis, urged
Milton Katz, the Marshall Plan's Special Representative in Europe, to
push the "EPU managers" into "taking appropriate action," with the
assurance that "the U.S. will back them up."[39]

The Western European countries, acting through the Organization
for European Economic Cooperation (OEEC), tried to get the situation under control. "The problem was," as the historian Michael
Hogan has put it, "how to force a program of self-help on West
Germany that would not have debilitating economic and political
repercussions in that country and across Western Europe." While some
countries, such as Norway and France, wanted tough action against

the Germans, others, especially Holland and Denmark, did not want any restrictions placed on their access to the German market. The British, one of the chief beneficiaries of the German purchases, sympathized with the more lenient view, worrying that a severe policy might slow Germany's production and actually worsen its balance of payments difficulties. The Managing Board of the EPU appointed two advisers, Per Jacobssen and Sir Alec Cairncross, to review West Germany's import policy and make suggestions for changes. They concluded that the problem was temporary in nature, and that Germany's initial quota was too low. Other recommendations included "measures to curb credit, raise taxes, avoid deficit spending, restrict long-term investment, and keep import licenses within the minimum permitted by the trade-liberalization program." The German government accepted this advice, and in December it received an additional $120 million credit from the EPU.[40]

The Americans were not completely satisfied with the Jacobssen-Cairncross report, but they were reluctant to block the European program and weaken the authority of the EPU. Therefore, although they formally supported the report, they withheld the additional aid that the Germans and the OEEC requested. At the same time they continued to press Erhard to adopt more wide-ranging regulations over the German economy, such as controls on raw materials, consumer rationing, and wage and price controls. Erhard, who saw himself as the champion of American capitalism in West Germany, resisted imposing controls that would threaten his liberal economic policies. When a European coal shortage developed late in 1950, he also resisted demands for rationing and attacked the Ruhr Authority for imposing export quotas on German coal. Further, he argued against any sharp credit contraction or deflation to deal with the balance of payments crisis, which he thought would have serious social and economic effects and would hinder the increase in production needed to overcome the deficit. He also emphasized the Jacobssen-Cairncross view that the problem was temporary.

In February 1951 the Chinese intervention in Korea, which sent prices of raw materials skyrocketing, combined with the loosening of German import controls to create another balance-of-payments crisis. By February 22 the Germans had exhausted their second EPU credit and were forced to suspend trade liberalization. This time American officials were angry. Milton Katz urged that all Marshall Plan assistance to Germany be immediately suspended. He regarded German reluctance to adopt any controls as an indication that the Federal Republic was "taking advantage" of ECA aid to stockpile raw materials. Consequently he insisted that assistance to Germany should be "related solely to those actions Germany is in a position to take which would support [the] defense effort of U.S. and other defense partners." Privately he threatened the expulsion of the Federal Republic from the EPU, if that seemed the only alternative to a repetition of "the Schachtian policies of the thirties." By "Schachtian policies" Katz meant that the Germans were "deliberately incurring a payments deficit" and then forcing other countries to adjust "by exchanging access to the German market for tariff concessions from their creditors and additional aid from the EPU."[42]

In thus identifying Erhard's EPU tactics with the Third Reich's trading policies, Katz revealed the deep mistrust toward Germany which was still felt by American and West European leaders. Yet Germany's balance-of-payments problems arose more from its weak government's inability to make difficult economic choices than from a calculated plan. Already engaged in the rearmament crisis, Adenauer was reluctant to choose among various nostrums offered by his ministers. But at this point he was warned that Germany faced a major disaster. The President of the Central Bank, Wilhelm Vocke, who had close contacts with the Americans, told him that "expulsion from the EPU would be the death blow to the European idea, the Schuman Plan, and above all the German economy." Vice Chancellor Blücher echoed the warning that the Americans were losing patience, and that Germany's Marshall Plan assistance was in jeopardy. The leaders of the government coalition in the Bundestag also advised "urgent measures" to halt the deterioration in Germany's economic position. Finally on March 6, 1951, in the midst of the Schuman Plan negotiations, McCloy himself sent a letter to the Chancellor threatening the suspension of aid if the "necessary adjustments" were not made in the Federal Republic's economic policy. These adjustments were to be made primarily "in the fields of import priorities, internal allocation and priorities of materials in short supply, export priorities to essential NATO users, and effective priority for logistical support of our occupation forces."[43]

McCloy's bargaining position with Adenauer was particularly strong in March 1951. Not only was the payments question a problem, but a grain shortage was developing in the Federal Republic that might lead to the reimposition of bread rationing if the United States suspended its Marshall Plan assistance. Adenauer had resisted pressures to raise grain prices, just as he had been reluctant to adopt the economic controls the Americans requested. It is no wonder that his first reported reaction to McCloy's letter was the exclamation, "Donnerwetter!"[44]

Nevertheless, McCloy's letter helped Adenauer develop a policy to resolve the economic crisis. With the letter in hand he could break through the opposition of Erhard, and others in the Cabinet and ruling coalition, to the government's taking a more active role in the economy. In his reply to McCloy, Adenauer stressed his willingness to establish the necessary joint committee with the Americans to set up a priorities and allocation system. He promised to strengthen the Law for the Safeguarding of the Economy, giving the government the power to "establish an absolutely safe priority system for exports, especially in the case of raw materials supply." He also set up an Inter-Ministerial Coordinating Committee under Vice Chancellor Blücher's chairmanship, to coordinate the government's approach to economic policy. When Erhard complained about the selection of his rival, Adenauer shot off a sharply critical letter listing the various failures of the Economics Ministry. Erhard then offered to resign, but Adenauer refused to let him.[45]

At the same time that McCloy was pressuring the Germans to put their house in order, he was defending Adenauer to his superiors and urging Washington to consider the question of ECA aid to Germany "in relation to [the] broadest U.S. foreign policy objectives rather than in connection with [the] new and considerably narrowed criteria" which Katz had suggested. He denied that the Germans had used ECA aid for "indiscriminate commodity stockpiling" and "luxury consumption." Pointing to Germany's defense contribution, its participation in the Schuman Plan, and its loyalty to the West, McCloy concluded that a suspension of aid would "seriously jeopardize" the American objective of a "stable democratic order in Germany, with rising living standards and the will to defend itself."[46]

Having gone out on a limb for the Germans, McCloy was justifiably delighted with Adenauer's positive response and promised Adenauer to release immediately a $23.5 million allotment for the purchase of grain. The Chancellor, who had come to recognize that American intervention had certain advantages for him, suggested that McCloy address another letter to him "on the urgency of carrying through the legislative program on taxes so that he could make use of the letter for speeding the legislative process." The Germans also agreed to cooperate with a series of measures which the OEEC established, to help share the burden created by the suspension of trade liberalization. On the domestic front, in early April Erhard announced a "new economic program" which would increase coal prices, direct more investment to heavy industry and housing, and provide special treatment for exporters. McCloy told Washington that the Adenauer government was "beginning to extricate itself from economic quicksand, and hence related political dangers." He believed that "the anti-control philosophy as such is now rapidly losing ground and . . . work on practical questions of method, machinery, timing, and range of economic controls can now proceed."[47]

Despite McCloy's interest in "practical" adjustments to insure Germany's political and economic stability, one result of the American intervention, as the historian Werner Abelshauser has noted, was the return to traditional corporatist methods in the making of German economic policy. To comply with the American request Adenauer relied on the Federation of German Industry and cooperation with the private sector rather than on direct state regulation. The industrialists gave the Americans what they wanted in terms of factor allocation and investment planning. This new policy also led to the investment aid law, which steered more investment into Germany's coal and steel industries. When the Ruhr industrialists administered a scheme of import and export controls, they cooperated in a way that Law 27 had been designed to prevent. Consequently the American action, which was intended for only an "emergency" period, actually increased the influence of industrial associations and trade unions on economic planning.[48]

Ironically, no sooner had McCloy intervened than the necessity for strict controls began to fade. A downturn in prices on the world commodity markets helped increase supplies of raw materials, and Germany's "slowly maturing exports of industrial goods" allowed her to begin running surpluses with other European countries. By May 1951 the Federal Republic had repaid its EPU credit, and in January 1952 it was able to reintroduce trade liberalization. In the same year it achieved one of the first in a long series of trade surpluses.[49]

Although McCloy's direct role in the payments crisis was not so significant as in the Schuman Plan negotiations, his intervention did help the EPU weather its first difficult year. And the EPU, for its part, played an important part in Germany's economic recovery. In an evaluation of the crisis a year later McCloy noted that it had filled the central role in Germany's trade expansion. Its absence "would have meant [a] low level of exports to almost all countries in EPU outside of Sterling and French franc areas since they [were] either unable [to] export high volume to Germany, or Germany [was] unable to import high volume from them." The growth in Germany's foreign trade, which amounted to 25 percent of its GNP, was a spur to overall trade liberalization as well as a key to Germany's own economic recovery. The EPU, McCloy concluded, helped channel exports to the West and decreased German interest in trade with the Soviet bloc. This contributed to the political result of further "enmeshing" Germany in the multilateral trading order created and guided by the United States.[50]

Both the Schuman Plan and the EPU served the Western strategy of furthering the economic integration of the Federal Republic into Western Europe. American officials used their economic weight to strengthen those forces in Germany which favored integrationist policies despite the short-term risk to German interests. In his sponsorship of Law 27, as well as during the balance-of-payments crisis, McCloy insisted that the Federal Republic play a cooperative role within the European economy. In addition, his insistence on the necessity of Germany's economic rehabilitation made it clear to other European countries that the German problem could not wait until a slower, more "balanced" recovery became possible. Western Europeans came to realize that they would have to adapt to renewed German strength if they wanted continued American involvement. The same lesson would soon become clear in the military field, as McCloy and his advisers pursued the next step in their plan to secure German allegiance to the West.

8

The Skeleton Key: Military Integration

In mid-1951 American leaders made one of the most fateful diplomatic decisions of the early 1950s. Washington threw its full support behind the French proposal to create a European Defense Community (EDC), a military arrangement which would "merge" the armies of France, Germany, Italy, and the Benelux nations into a supranational organization similar to the one set up by the Schuman Plan. The EDC was to consist of armies wearing a common uniform, receiving identical pay and training, and having an integrated command. A political commissariat would serve as Europe's defense ministry with authority to raise, train, and equip these armies, as well as to determine in part, a common budget.[1]

American support made the EDC one of the central issues of international politics. Those critics who have asked why the United States chose to back such a cumbersome approach to German rearmament have dismissed the EDC as a French effort to delay German rearmament, a diplomatic trap into which the Americans fell. But such evaluations fail to take into account the constellation of forces and personalities that made the EDC appear not only the ideal solution to the dilemma of German rearmament but also the most practical way to proceed.[2]

The Negotiations at Petersberg and Paris

The Brussels compromise of December 1950 could not conceal the continuing divisions among the Western Allies on German rearmament. Despite the U.S. commitment to rearmament, Britain and

France were determined to slow the process in the hope that four-power talks might produce a compromise. In early February Prime Minister Attlee attached four conditions to a German defense contribution: prior Allied rearmament, safeguards to prevent the reemergence of a German military threat, the strengthening of Allied forces in Germany before the creation of German units, and agreement with the West Germans on the level of their contribution. Prime Minister Pleven visited Washington toward the end of January 1951, and after appealing for more aid for the war in Indochina he reminded Truman and Acheson that the French people feared the outbreak of war in Europe above all else, and that they sympathized with the Russians' fear of German rearmament, which was completely "understandable."[3]

Within six weeks of the Brussels conference two sets of negotiations began, one at AHC headquarters on the Petersberg in Bonn and the other at the Quai d'Orsay in Paris. The two sets of negotiators followed two different paths to German rearmament. Those at the Petersberg took the NATO track, devising methods for bringing Germany and German soldiers directly into NATO. Those in Paris would seek to develop the Pleven Plan's European Army, including Germany within a joint European force presumably—though not necessarily—subordinate to NATO.

The Petersberg talks, which began on January 9, 1951, were conducted by the three Deputy High Commissioners—General George Hays for the United States, John Ward for Britain, and Armand Bérard for France. The U.S. military wanted these discussions to produce a plan for a speedy German rearmament, but because the Deputy Commissioners had no program, they were obliged to solicit from the Germans proposals for their own rearmament. Unable even to say how many soldiers the Allies ultimately expected from Germany, the Commissioners could only provide a figure of 100,000 for the "immediate transitional period." (The U.S. Joint Chiefs envisioned a 500,000-man army, while the French insisted on no more than 100,000 men.)[4]

Allied passivity allowed the German negotiating team to seize the initiative. Led by Theodor Blank, a man selected more for his political acceptability than his military expertise, the Germans insisted on Gleichberechtigung (equality), even in the smallest details. Blank demanded that the parking space for his automobile be next to those of the other delegation heads. On the first day of the talks, when an

English sergeant told the Germans they would have to use the rear door, Blank refused and did not enter the building until the Allies relented. These details symbolized the Adenauer government's need for Allied acceptance of its political equality in order to confirm its own legitimacy and win domestic approval for a German military contribution to Western defense.[5]

Although the Germans reminded the Allies that the demilitarization policies had left "no basis in Germany for the organization and equipment of German troops," and that under Allied laws it was "illegal" even to discuss military activities, the Germans had already begun planning for the re-creation of their army. In October 1950, with Adenauer's approval, a group of former generals, meeting secretly at a secluded monastery, had produced the Himmeroder Memorandum, which outlined a force of twelve divisions, or approximately 250,000 men, whose principal mission would be to provide a "forward defense" between the Rhine and Elbe rivers and prevent the capture of a significant amount of German territory. Rejecting the notion that German forces would serve primarily as Europe's infantry, or as cover for an Allied retreat, the Himmeroder Memorandum called for heavily armored and mobile divisions, supported by tactical aircraft and coastal defense forces. At the Petersberg talks the German military experts— former Generals Hans Speidel and Adolf Heusinger—felt justified in lecturing their negotiating partners on military strategy and tactics because of their unique experience as "the only country to have fought the Russians." They showed particular contempt for the French-sponsored Pleven Plan, which was militarily impractical—a "flimsy European coat over a German foreign legion." Speidel quoted from the *United States Field Manual* to demonstrate that the smallest unit designed for independent use in combat was the division. The smallest division, he said, numbered at least 10,000 men, twice the size of the combat teams endorsed by the Spofford Plan and much larger than the regiments of the Pleven Plan. Emphasizing the importance of homogeneous armored divisions for "proper coordination" in the field, Speidel also ridiculed the Pleven Plan's mixed divisions, in which "Bavarians would want saeurkraut and beer, French troops white bread and wine, and Italians spaghetti and Chianti." Privately he and other German military men feared that the Americans were insufficiently suspicious of French motives and might try to force Bonn to accommodate the "discriminatory" proposals.[6]

Nevertheless, the Germans enthusiastically agreed that their new armed forces should be incorporated into the integrated NATO force under the Supreme Commander. Their understanding of the degree of integration and their willingness to accept specific and discriminatory restrictions, however, were at odds with the Western Allies' Spofford Plan. The Germans insisted that any controls or prohibitions which NATO applied to their forces would have to be applied to other countries as well. They also proposed the creation of a German Ministry of Defense, under control of the Bundestag, with a civilian defense minister at its head and an "Inspectorate General" subordinate to him. The Inspectorate General, a military officer with the rank of General, would be the Supreme Commander of all the German soldiers. The Spofford Plan had avoided the creation of a separate German defense ministry, proposing only an administrative agency to handle matters of recruitment and personnel, while leaving planning, intelligence, and operational staffing with NATO. The office of Inspectorate General smacked of a German General Staff, which all the Western countries had opposed. Simply put, the German proposals allowed for the possibility of independent military action, a possibility that threatened Allied unity and risked provoking the Soviets.[7]

After twelve meetings the Petersberg talks culminated in a "factual" report, dated June 6, 1951, which virtually reproduced the German plans. When it was submitted to the individual governments, it attracted support in the United States and the FRG. The U.S. Army, despite some reservations about the political demands of the Germans, was generally pleased with their proposals. The direct entry of the Federal Republic into NATO appeared the simplest and most expeditious way to obtain a German defense contribution. Chancellor Adenauer, along with his military advisers, naturally favored the Petersberg approach, although he was concerned about the delay in obtaining political concessions and greater military security from the Allies. German demands for a larger voice in Allied decisions had not been satisfied by the first major revision of the occupation statute, proclaimed at the beginning of March 1951 and allowing for the creation of a German foreign ministry. In April Adenauer had complained to the High Commissioners that despite the security guarantee of the September New York conference, the Allies had done nothing to increase their forces. He believed this failure had led to "considerable mental instability" among the German people, the growth of extremist movements on the left and right, and an increase in the appeal of neutralism. The Chancellor blamed the French and British for the delays, fearing that their interest in a four-power agreement with the Soviet Union would lead them to abandon the Federal Republic. In a direct message to McCloy sent shortly after the completion of the Petersberg talks, Adenauer detailed his grievances against the French, ranging from their treatment of German war criminals to their prohibition of a pro-German political party in the disputed Saar. Although the Chancellor assured McCloy that he remained committed to Franco-German reconciliation as the "essential precondition for a good European policy," he urged Washington to press the French to act in a more conciliatory manner.[8]

In fact the thrust of Adenauer's message to McCloy was that America should look to Germany as its most reliable ally in Europe. Commenting on Europe's history since 1918—in particular the decline of European power and the concurrent rise of the Soviet Union—Adenauer stated that the Soviet leadership was pursuing an expansionist foreign policy to divert its people's attention from internal problems. He added, "We in Germany experienced the same thing under Hitler." The presence of American soldiers in Europe was still restraining the Soviets, but it was doubtful whether America would commit its troops to Europe over the long run. Adenauer wanted American policy to help Europe and Germany become strong enough to constitute a "dam against the pressure of Soviet expansion." Only the German people, stoutly anti-Communist and anti-Russian, could erect an effective protective barrier against Soviet expansion.

Adenauer's history lesson, written for McCloy and an American audience, revealed his belief that the American commitment to Europe was vital not only to his own political future but also to the creation of a united Europe. While giving lip service to Franco-German reconciliation, Adenauer really wanted a stronger American-German relationship that would pay less heed to French sensitivities. His own commitment to Europe did not take precedence over Germany's security and political equality. Thus, although he did not explicitly endorse the Bonn report, he would have been content to rearm Germany along those lines, *provided* Germany's position under NATO included concessions that would lead to political equality and end the Allied occupation.[9]

The French government held the key to such political concessions, and it sponsored its own talks on German rearmament. In mid-February, almost six weeks after the opening of the Petersberg discussions, the European Army talks began in Paris among the representatives of France, the Federal Republic, Belgium, Italy, and Luxembourg. (The Dutch joined the talks later in the year.) The Germans sent a low-ranking delegation which had been instructed to propose plans similar to those being presented at the Petersberg talks, but to avoid allowing the blame for a possible breakdown in the discussions to be placed on Germany. Quickly the Germans "locked horns" with the French over the size of the basic unit in the proposed European army. The French wanted mixed divisions of between 16,000 and 17,000 men, each consisting of two or three regimental combat teams from different nations. The Germans were willing to discuss mixed corps as the basic unit, but insisted that these should be made up of homogeneous national divisions consisting of between 10,000 and 12,000 men. Although the haggling centered on numbers, the real issue was the possible rebirth of an independent German military, which the French feared would follow the creation of German "divisions." They told the Germans that such large units might eventually fight a "war for liberation for the east German territories." Because the preliminary four-power discussions were already under way and general elections in France were set for June, the French government was unwilling to make any concessions on the "size of the basic unit and level and integration of the proposed army." Fearful of "Communist propagandist exploitation of the division concept," the Quai d'Orsay pursued a policy of "minimum publicity and was content to give the public the impression that the conference was deadlocked or quiescent."[10]

The Paris talks made little progress, and both Bonn and Washington grew skeptical about the possibility of their success. Adenauer told McCloy that the initial French proposals were so "deficient" that he had taken special precautions to prevent leaks which would outrage the German public. General Speidel dismissed the French approach as designed to "torpedo" the American plans for rearmament. Acheson complained that the "permanent institutions" (such as the Council of Ministers and European Defense Commissioner) in the European Army had taken precedence over practical plans for a German defense contribution. He refused Ambassador Bruce's request to press other European nations to accept the French proposals. Increasingly he saw the Paris talks as unlikely to yield results in the near future.[11]

Yet debates over the size of divisions and a future united Europe could not hide the central dilemma facing the Western nations. How could German military strength be restored without either posing a danger to the West or provoking war with the East? It was a dilemma which seemed insoluble.

The Decision to Support the EDC

In late June 1951, with the Petersberg talks completed and the Paris talks deadlocked, Washington was inclined to support German rearmament under the direct auspices of NATO. Acheson told Bruce, "We believe it unwise [to] deviate materially from [the NATO approach] as it would, if accepted, produce German units at earliest possible date." Although aware that this approach was likely to provoke French opposition, Acheson was nevertheless confident that he could win over the French by expressing support for the European army as a "long range" American objective. Yet almost immediately—that is, less than two months later—despite resistance from the State Department, the Pentagon, and German leaders, the U.S. government committed itself to support a version of Pleven's European Army, the EDC. This change of direction resulted from the combination of a unique set of circumstances and a unique group of American leaders. Foremost among them were McCloy, Bruce, and Eisenhower, American "Europeanists" who were convinced that America should forego the short-term advantage of German soldiers for the potential long-term advantage of greater European unity and consolidation.[12]

In his efforts to rally Washington behind the European Army idea McCloy was reacting to events in Europe during the first half of 1951, and particularly to disturbing developments in Germany. In May 1951 the radical right-wing Sozialistische Reichspartei (SRP) had drawn 11 percent of the vote in Landtag elections in Lower Saxony. This neo-Nazi party, led by ex-General Otto Remer, one of the men who had put down the July 20 plot against Hitler, favored a neutral Germany, and its success coincided with the agitation over the Landsberg executions. It opposed Adenauer's rearmament policy as betraying Germany's interests, especially reunification, and it regarded collaboration with the Soviet Union as a legitimate way of restoring Germany's power and unity. Although only 13 percent of all Germans polled wanted the SRP to have a role in national politics, only another 20 percent said they would do "everything in their power" to stop such a party from coming to power. In American and West European eyes, this apathy among the Germans and their lack of resistance to a Nazi reincarnation demonstrated the shallow roots of the young democracy.[13]

In January Acheson had assured Pleven that the United States would not "let Germany be a neutral bloc in the center of Europe, which would try to play the East off against the West." Nevertheless, German sentiments, as measured by the High Commission's polls, showed an almost equal split between support for Adenauer's policy of Western integration and the opposition policy of neutralism. The Chancellor's own approval rating was below 30 percent, and support for German participation in an "Atlantic pact army" had declined by almost 20 percent from October 1950 to June 1951. These indicators of public sentiment affected McCloy's perception of the problem at hand, leading him to search for a dramatic way to check the erosion of German support for the West.[14]

McCloy believed that Allied policy needed to move in two directions. First the Allies should offer the Germans substantial "equality" within the Western alliance. Public opinion polls suggested that if the Germans were assured of equal status almost half of the opponents of rearmament would change their minds. In addition, by conceding equality the Allies could undermine the Social Democratic opposition to Adenauer, which had adopted "equality" as their political slogan. McCloy argued that only Western proposals "sufficiently definite so that the Germans will know what they are being offered"—proposals which allowed "the exercise of the attributes of sovereignty"—could win the "sizable majority" needed in the Bundestag to approve a defense contribution.[15]

Second, McCloy wanted a European framework for German rearmament. The polls indicated that more Germans would support rearmament if the question were framed in terms of German participation in an Atlantic or European Army rather than as a simple re-creation of the Wehrmacht. Enthusiasm for a united Europe was strong, particularly among better educated, more affluent, and younger Germans. This enthusiasm, which was a reaction against the shrill nationalism of the Nazi period, reflected the spirit of German idealism and its historical mission. It was also based on the pragmatic assessment that without unification Western Europe would find it difficult to resist Soviet expansion. And for some Germans "Europe" became a covert way to assert German national interests in a world which no longer cared to hear of them. A perceptive British diplomat, Con O'Neill, observed the mixture of these various impulses and commented that "the Germans regard part of their historical mission as having been for many centuries the defense of European civilization against Asiatic barbarism." Hitler had exploited such sentiments in his propaganda about a "New Order" within Europe and his "crusade" against Bolshevism. O'Neill added wryly that it was "irrelevant" to the Germans "that the other nations of Western Europe look very dubiously on the German claim to have been a persistent and loyal defender of their civilization."[16]

McCloy recognized that although German conditions demanded action, French politics and public opinion imposed restraints on American policy. The Petersberg approach faced stubborn opposition from the French, who would not accept full German equality outside of the constraints of a European army. At first French diplomats had tried to convince McCloy that Washington should avoid "haste or pressure" and allow Paris a "further opportunity to play a major role in working out a satisfactory situation with the Germans." Later, after the Petersberg discussisons had ended, they told him that they wanted the Petersberg and Paris reports to be "synchronized," which would "give an opportunity to reconcile differences before transmittal to the entire NATO group." They feared that if NATO received the reports separately it would favor the Petersberg approach, once again isolating Paris. Hervé Alphand, the French negotiator at the Paris conference, told McCloy that "the importance of the European army concept [was] especially to make clear to the French and Russian people the determination not to permit the revival of a separate German military establishment which might have the power to go off on an Eastern campaign, perhaps dragging the West with it." This French position led McCloy to think that "the answer to these difficulties may lie in the European Army concept which may provide a better means to reconcile French and German views than revision of the NATO directive."[17]

The European Army also appealed to McCloy because he believed America would eventually withdraw from Europe. Although the Great Debate of 1951 had affirmed Truman's right to dispatch troops to Europe, few U.S. leaders expected the troops to remain there. McCloy told a British critic of American policy that "in the long [run] United

States opinion and [the] United States economy will not long support" an American presence in Europe. Bruce assumed that one of the dangers of the Petersberg approach was that "after US commander and US troops are withdrawn, [national] components of NATO will surely revert to separate [national] armies unelss there is permanent European political structure." The beginning of truce talks on Korea in early July was a further reminder that any lessening of East-West tensions would renew calls for the withdrawal of American forces.[18]

This belief in an eventual American withdrawal was shared by General Dwight D. Eisenhower. After his appointment as Supreme Commander of NATO in December 1950, Eisenhower had made a tour of the NATO countries, to raise their morale and secure commitments for increased defense expenditures. By encouraging Europe to believe in its capacity for its own defense, Eisenhower hoped to counter American isolationists who criticized European weakness and inaction. The General spoke movingly of his "unshakable" faith in Europe, "the land of our ancestors," and of the "underlying courage of its people . . . their willingness to live and sacrifice for a secure peace and the continuance and the progress of civilization." Preaching the gospel of Europe to both discouraged Europeans and skeptical Congressmen, Eisenhower's infectious optimism helped bring about an increase in Congressional appropriations for military assistance. But Eisenhower continually stressed that the American role in Europe was temporary, necessary only until the European countries had restored their ravaged economies and regained political self-confidence and military strength. He told one friend, "If in ten years all American troops stationed in Europe for national defense purposes have not been returned to the United States, then this whole project will have failed."[19]

Both McCloy and Bruce recognized that Eisenhower could play the critical role in convincing Washington of the virtues of a European approach to rearmament. The General's enormous prestige as well as his political savvy and military expertise would make his position on German rearmament decisive. In attempting to sway Eisenhower, McCloy enjoyed the advantage of his wartime work and friendship with the General. When McCloy had resigned from the War Department in 1945, he had told Ike that he had "difficulty placing anyone on a level with you and General Marshall." Eisenhower had responded warmly, telling McCloy that "there is no one whose judgment I value more highly." The two men were strikingly similar in temperament and politics. Both were self-made, proud of their rise from humble origins, and pleased with their access to the world of wealth and privilege. Both were internationalist Republicans, accepting many of the social innovations of the New Deal yet distrustful of its "leveling" tendencies. They both believed in the power of inspirational leadership and prided themselves on their ability to resolve differences among reasonable men.[20]

McCloy had already sought Eisenhower's assistance on German issues. When the General was planning to leave Germany out of his January 1951 itinerary, McCloy pleaded with him to change his mind, saying that Eisenhower's presence would strengthen morale and show "a resolve to defend areas West of the Rhine." McCloy also told Eisenhower about stories circulating in Germany to the effect that the General did not want German help. Some former German generals remembered his denunciation of the German officer corps and his refusal to shake hands at the signing of the surrender agreement. Other German soldiers, including Adenauer's military advisers, Speidel and Heusinger, were insisting that the Allies issue a declaration that the ordinary Germay soldier, who had served in the Wehrmacht rather than the Waffen-SS or other Nazi organizations, had served "honorably." Eisenhower decided to go to Bonn and make a special effort to defuse the tension. When Speidel and Heusinger were pointed out to him at a reception at McCloy's house, Ike approached them, saying, "Ah, the generals," and shook their hands. Speidel later said that this small gesture had brought a "certain reconciliation" almost immediately. Eisenhower also affirmed publicly that he had "come to know that there is a real difference between the regular German soldier and officer and Hitler and his criminal group." "For my part," he continued, "I do not believe that the German soldier as such had lost his honor." That certain individuals had committed "despicable acts" did not reflect on the "great majority of German soldiers and officers." Eisenhower frankly told the Germans that despite his hatred of Germany during the last war he was prepared to say, "Let bygones be bygones." He also assured German leaders that he "would not tolerate second class membership" in any army which he led, and that the German contribution would have to be made "on a free will basis without any pressure from outside."[21]

McCloy believed that the Eisenhower trip had made a "very fortunate impression" on the Germans and would "further cement their instinct for siding with the West." If they were convinced of Western strength and of their acceptance as equals, he told Eisenhower, they would line up with the Western Allies. McCloy added, "Whatever may be the diversities in Europe, and there are many, there is a growing sense of the necessity for unity, and your visit was a very concrete representation of it." During the next few months McCloy repeated this message to Eisenhower, seeking to draw him into the German rearmament question. In mid-March he sent General Hays and Colonel Gerhardt to brief Eisenhower on the Petersberg talks and obtain his views "on the essentiality [*sic*] and urgency of the German contribution for an adequate defense of Western Europe." Eisenhower reaffirmed his interest in German soldiers but emphasized that "a political base must be established for the German nation, which would enable the German people to wholeheartedly support a German con- tribution." He expressed sympathy for the European Army talks in Paris, which were "a forward step in the further political integration of Europe." If some progress could be made in that direction, "some sacrifice in 'costs' (presumably rapidity and effectiveness of military units) could be made." Eisenhower did not feel that the size of the military unit in the proposed European Army was an insuperable barrier, as he himself favored smaller divisions. But he understood the French concern for security, pointing out that "if his son had been tortured by the Germans [as Jules Moch's had been], he would not be very sympathetic towards the Germans."[22]

Not only was Eisenhower sensitive to the political issues, but he was willing to have the international staff of the Supreme Headquar- ters of Allied Powers in Europe (SHAPE) "arrive at an objective military study, which would take into account and satisfy the political factors," and which "he could recommend . . . to the respective governments." Such a proposed solution "must provide for a big enough concession by the French so that the Germans could win popular support for the proposal in Germany, and similarly that the French should be able to take home a sufficient concession from the Germans to satisfy their popular opinion." Ike even thought that if he "converted the national elements of his staff to a proposal," they would become advocates of that proposal to their own government. In reporting Eisenhower's views to Washington, McCloy acknowl- edged that the General was not committed to "any action on this problem," but he hoped that it might present the possibility of "future lines of action."[23]

Eisenhower proceeded with characteristic caution. With the Truman-MacArthur controversy going on in the United States, he was reluctant to take any position which could be construed as military "interference" in a political question. Nor had he abandoned all his original skepticism about the European Army idea. Early in March he told *New York Times* reporter Cyrus Sulzberger that the European army idea was like "putting the cart before the horse" because "it would represent a political unity that does not yet exist." He considered the technical difficulties involved in command and organization to be enormous. He also feared that the European Army would be "more divisive than unifying in its effect"; and later he said—with deliberate exaggeration—that he believed it as "cockeyed an idea as a dope fiend could have figured out." Nevertheless, Eisenhower's frustration with the slow progress of European rearmament, his sense of the political and economic weaknesses within Europe, and the difficulties he experienced in dealing with twelve separate countries made him think that NATO needed "some spectacular accomplishment" to break through these barriers of inertia. He was annoyed when Europeans told him that they were waiting for American deliveries and aid before undertaking their own efforts: "Merely because some American promise may have been a little bit too enthusiastically made does not excuse the European country from doing its best to meet its own security problems." Eisenhower feared that the Europeans expected to lean indefinitely on American support, and the General wanted to find a way to break down this psychological and political dependency.[24]

Eisenhower found the solution to his problems in the dream of a politically united Europe. He wrote in his diary early in June, "I am coming to believe that Europe's security problem is never going to be solved satisfactorily until there exists a U.S. of Europe . . . I think that the real and bitter problems of today would instantly come within the limits of capabilities in solving them if we had this single government." He added, "I believe *inspired* leaders could put it across. But everyone is too cautious, too fearful, too lazy and too ambitious (personally)." A United Europe would allow America to reduce its aid "both in amount and duration," and it would be a "tragedy to the whole human race" if such a union did not come about. "With this one problem solved—all lesser ones would soon disappear."[25]

Eisenhower's enthusiasm for the creation of a united Europe reflected the atmosphere of Paris during the spring of 1951. Talk of a possible European federation was rife in both American and French leadership circles. The European states seemed too small and fragmented to cope with the challenges of the new bipolar world. The pressure of a unified Sino-Soviet bloc, on the one hand, and a powerful United States, on the other, pointed toward unity as the only way for Europe to regain an independent voice in world affairs. To many Europeans the political convulsions surrounding General MacArthur's firing demonstrated the volatility of American public opinion and underlined the importance of European action before the United States turned away from Europe.[26]

With Eisenhower already leaning toward a European solution, McCloy made another attempt to involve him in the negotiations on German rearmament. At the conclusion of the Petersberg talks he sent the General a copy of the report along with a handwritten personal note. Telling Eisenhower that he was "anxious to achieve results," McCloy added, "I would be glad to support [the European Army] but only on that condition *and* only on the condition that the scheme was an effective one from a military point of view." He then suggested that Eisenhower meet with Jean Monnet, a man who "thinks on broad terms and . . . can put the case for the European Army as well as any." Monnet had already been advised that he would have to convince the Americans both that the plan was not simply "a device to avoid and to delay a German contribution" and that it made sense from a military point of view—which would mean dropping the idea of units smaller than divisions. McCloy told Eisenhower he had informed Monnet that "in the last analysis you [Eisenhower] were the one to decide the matter and that you were quite as well equipped to deal with the political nuances." Rather disingenuously McCloy closed the letter by noting he had "not finally made up [his] mind on the matter."[27]

At the luncheon meeting between Monnet and Eisenhower, Monnet said that "Europe would become responsible and strong only if it were united." Otherwise every nation would seek power for itself, and this would be disastrous in the case of Germany, which would seek strength "in agreement with the East." A short-term Allied plan which sought to "rush into raising a few German divisions on a national basis, at the cost of reviving enmity between peoples, would be catastrophic for the very security of Europe that such a step would be intended to ensure." The long-term solution would be a European army, which would "give France, Germany, and then their neighbors common resources to exploit and defend," thus helping Europe to "recover the will to resist." Eisenhower was intrigued by this explanation, which corresponded with his own beliefs about the necessity of restoring Europe's self-confidence and independence. He told Monnet that "what you're proposing is that the French and the Germans should wear the same uniform. That's more a human problem than a military one." Sensing Eisenhower's increasing interest, Monnet replied, "What we have to do first of all is make people aware that they're facing the future together." When General Gruenther, one of Eisenhower's chief aides, interrupted to ask about the size of the integrated divisions, Eisenhower cut him off, dismissing his concerns as those of a "typical technician" who could "only see the part you're interested in—you don't look at the problem as a whole." To Eisenhower the "real problem" with Europe was not "the strength of the divisions" but the "human" problem of how to "organize relations between people," and he was "all for" taking the steps Monnet proposed.[28]

For Eisenhower, as for McCloy and Bruce, a United Europe, somewhat resembling the United States, had become the "skeleton key" to unlocking the solutions to Europe's problems, from ending Franco-German enmity to containing the Soviet "threat from the East." Ike said to a Congressional committee, "I tell you that joining Europe together is the key to the whole question." On July 3, 1951, in an address at the English Speaking Union in London he stated that "with unity achieved, Europe could build adequate security and . . . continue the march of human betterment that has characterized western civilization . . . " One of the major advantages would be an "early independence of aid from America and other Atlantic countries." In the meantime the effort to achieve a "workable European federation would go far to create confidence among people everywhere that Europe was doing its full and vital share in giving this cooperation." Although Eisenhower did not mention the European Army by name, contemporary observers interpreted his speech as providing support for the French ideas, especially Monnet's concept of Europe.[29]

The Pentagon's resistance was still a formidable obstacle. In June 1951 McCloy returned to Washington hoping to find a way to reconcile the Petersberg report with French plans. After briefing the President and Acheson he conferred with the Secretary of the Army, Frank Pace, and General J. Lawton Collins, the Army's Chief of Staff.

In discussing the Petersberg report McCloy noted Germany's conditions for participation, especially political equality. If the European Army concept could be made effective, he believed the French would ultimately permit German divisions and a German Ministry of Defense. At another meeting he told a more senior group of Defense officials, including his old friend Robert Lovett, then Assistant Secretary of Defense, and General Omar Bradley, the Chairman of the Joint Chiefs, that the Army's practical objections could be addressed only if the United States supported the general concept behind the French plan. He agreed to warn the French "that any European Army must create no interference in command from above or below General Eisenhower; it must permit no delay in putting German troops into the field; it must have an objective of creating a permanent arrangement remaining long after the need for NATO or United States' participation in Europe."[30]

Despite McCloy's efforts the military leaders remained skeptical. They doubted the morale of a force which would lack a "national spirit" and worried about the practical problems of language and differences in equipment. Moreover, the delays involved in creating such an army seemed interminable, while the need for soldiers in the field was immediate. General Bradley wondered why a European army was needed if the French had agreed to allow German divisions. McCloy replied that such an army was designed to prevent independent action by individual nations, especially Germany. General Collins stressed the complicated problems a European army would pose in terms of chain of command and strategy. He also raised questions about the deployment of its forces, and the effects this might have on American and British units. Would the Supreme Commander have the same authority to deploy the troops of a European army as he had over his other forces, or would another commander create political problems in the chain of command? Collins insisted that "the method by which forces would be fought [sic] and handled with regard to terrain was the most important factor." McCloy partially disarmed the General's criticism by accepting it and admitting that "it was this type of practical approach that the French needed."[31]

By the end of June 1951 the time seemed ripe for a new American initiative. The four-power "exploratory" talks, under way at the Palais Rose in Paris since the beginning of March, had adjourned on June 21 after failing to reach an agreement on an agenda for a Council of

Foreign Ministers meeting. The French elections on June 17 had cleared another roadblock. Although foreign policy concerns were not absent from the campaign—one Gaullist slogan proclaimed, "We want the other Western powers to be our allies, not our masters"—the election turned largely on the issues of electoral reform, economic policy, and aid to church schools. General de Gaulle's party did not "sweep the country" as many had expected, but its seats in the 627-member assembly did increase from 23 to 117. The Communists, on the other hand, lost almost half their seats, dropping from 179 to 101. The other big loser was Schuman and Bidault's centrist party, which dropped from 145 seats to 88. The election shifted France's "political center of gravity a good way towards the Right," and the initial result was a six-week period of negotiations, followed by the ouster of the Socialists, led by Jules Moch, from the governing coalition. In early August René Pleven, who was sympathetic to Monnet's ideas, became Prime Minister for the second time.[32]

The State Department's desire to regain the initiative challenged the American Europeanists. In a cable sent to Bruce at the end of June, Acheson paid lip service to the European Army as a "long term approach to the problem of European defense," but he stressed the advantages of the Petersberg formula and the necessity of forming German military units "without further delay." In the long term, he said, the United States would probably withdraw its forces from Europe and would "regret to see" the restoration of "national forces solely under national control," especially in the case of Germany. He emphasized, however, that the "concept of a European force can never be realized until there is an organized force in the field and that once this process is in motion it will automatically ease solution of many problems now appearing difficult." His concept of a European army was simple—essentially a matter of nomenclature. First the nations participating in the Paris conference would place their military units under the command of General Juin, NATO's Central Sector commander. Then, "from the point of view of the forces on the ground, the heart of the European Army would be already in existence." In due time "a political protocol or treaty of simple form" would be signed, which would commit the European nations to place their forces under supranational control. The negotiators, Acheson emphasized, "must proceed along simple lines."[33]

Acheson's cable caused consternation in Paris. From the French perspective, a simple treaty or protocol was no substitute for careful negotiations and precise agreements. If Germany was admitted directly into NATO, France would have little or no possibility of convincing the Germans that they had to sacrifice a limited part of their sovereignty to join a new European army. Bruce could see that the French National Assembly would never approve the immediate admission of Germany into NATO, and that an American demand to that effect would produce another serious alliance crisis.[34]

There was, however, a loophole in Acheson's cable which the Europeanists exploited. Though it insisted that the formation of German units should proceed without further delay, it said that if there could be "a conciliation of Bonn and Paris approaches to military side of problem at early date, we would be prepared to lend our utmost efforts to French in supporting, or even helping devise, if they so desire, methods for completing a workable civilian super structure for European Army." Acheson wanted the Europeans to participate in the alliance's defense planning as they had in the Marshall Plan organization. Bruce seized upon this point, as well as on Acheson's general support for a European army, in his lengthy but elegant response. His "long telegram" not only argued for the European Army as a long-term objective but also contended that it offered the "best method of achieving our short-range objective of rapidly building European defense, including German contribution." One reason for the delay in the Paris conference was "uncertainty about real United States' attitude toward European Army." With strong American support and assistance from Eisenhower's headquarters, the European Army treaty could be finished along with the contractual agreements granting Germany's political sovereignty, a condition which the Germans regarded as essential. Bruce promised that the French would accept German divisions and forego discriminatory safeguards if the European Army approach was followed. He agreed that the Petersberg and Paris approaches should be merged, but suggested that SHAPE undertake the work because the "prestige of Eisenhower will make it easier for French and others to accept decisions and to work out compromises." Bruce knew that Eisenhower himself would favor a European approach.[35]

McCloy, too, continued to push for a merger of the Petersberg and Paris solutions. Calling Germany the "key battleground in the Cold War," he told a national radio audience in the United States that it was a "fundamental principle of all proposals made to date that whatever German contribution to defense is made may only take the form of a force which is an integral part of a larger international organization." He made it clear that the United States remained opposed to anything resembling a German General Staff or a German national army, adding, "There is no real solution of the German problem inside Germany alone. There is a solution inside the European-Atlantic-World Community." When he returned to Germany, McCloy adopted a bolder stance. As in earlier controversies he made a number of public statements which gave the misleading impression that Washington had already approved the solution so that only the details remained to be worked out. For example, he told an airport news conference that the United States would not move to implement the Petersberg proposals, but that it would give the Paris conference more time. The reason for this was that "we always have contemplated tying together the two plans." When the story appeared in the papers the next day, McCloy cabled Washington to deny he had made a "press statement," but he conceded that the "fact that I referred to Paris talks at all seems to have disappointed many who hoped we would repudiate them outright and declare at once for German sovereignty."[36]

Among those who were disappointed were the German military negotiators, Blank, Speidel, and Heusinger. Attending a July 4 reception at McCloy's house the next day, they were told by their host that the Petersberg solution was not workable, but that a European army could be. This so angered Blank that he informed McCloy in a "decisive tone" that the Pleven Plan was "completely unacceptable," and then broke off the conversation. The SPD leader, Kurt Schumacher, was even more opposed. He ridiculed the suggestion that the Petersberg and Paris approaches could be successfully reconciled. After being briefed by McCloy on the Washington talks, Schumacher responded that he remained committed to his concept of defending Germany by carrying the war into Eastern Europe. He insisted that the Allies create sufficiently strong forces to "insure *Germany would not become the battlefield* of the next war" and dismissed any attempt to make the Pleven Plan a workable military proposal.[37]

Despite such opposition, the critical figure in Germany was Adenauer. McCloy told him that the United States was "sincerely and objectively" prepared to support the concept of a European army and that the Petersberg talks had provided a "basis for hope that further compromises were possible." The European Army had three advantages: it removed French objections to German rearmament; it was in harmony with long-range U.S. objectives favoring a closer European association; and it provided the necessary economic resources for an adequate defense, a task that no single country could afford. Adenauer reacted cautiously, emphasizing that the Allies could only defeat the Russian determination to neutralize and demilitarize Germany by rearming Germany swiftly. But ever sensitive to the shifting winds from Washington, he expressed his support for the European Army concept as a "long-range" solution and offered to send Blank and the two generals to Paris to work on an agreement. At the same time he made it clear that his own thinking was closer to the Pentagon's than to McCloy's. "Whereas a European Army is necessary," he told McCloy, "Germany's contribution should not be made dependent upon the result of the Paris meetings if they do not reach an early settlement."[38]

The German negotiators' arrival in Paris accelerated the talks. On July 10, 1951, Blank presented the Petersberg report as the German position, arguing that the Paris conference should continue its "long and arduous" work of creating a supranatural army only as a long-term solution. "La Bombe Blank," as the French called the German proposals, forced Paris to deal with the Petersberg proposals. Progress was made on one of the stickiest issues, the status of French soldiers not assigned to the European Army. A tentative compromise specified that all forces in Europe would be part of the European Army, while forces in the overseas possessions or assigned to internal security duties would remain national.[39]

The final burst of inspiration for the European Army plan came from Eisenhower. A few days after returning to Germany McCloy told Averell Harriman that he wanted "to get over to Paris myself as quickly as possible as it is going to take a lot of coordination in my judgement before this thing really begins to roll." McCloy saw "no prospect of success unless Eisenhower takes a more active part and interest in German participation." As it happened, Ike had already decided that "we ought to be showing Germany how definitely her national interests will be served by sticking and working with us." When McCloy arrived in Paris on July 17, he told Eisenhower of his meetings at the Pentagon and his own conviction that "if he, Eisenhower, would directly interest himself in the situation and more or less act as an arbiter on the question of military practicality . . . one very large element of delay might be removed." He further assured Eisenhower that the Germans and French were likely to follow whatever military guidance he provided. "Somewhat to my surprise," McCloy remembered, Eisenhower agreed completely and said that the "French proposal would have to be taken seriously." The next day Ike dispatched a cable to Secretary of Defense George Marshall announcing his position: "I am convinced that time has come when we must all press for the earliest possible implementation of the European Army concept." Eisenhower added that he was prepared "to do whatever I can to break the present impasse and thereafter to assist as best I can to obtain European army units, including a German contribution at the earliest possible time."[40]

Eisenhower's well-timed intervention had a dramatic effect on the discussions in Paris. One of his first steps was to appoint an observer from SHAPE to attend the conference and offer advice and guidance on military questions. The General himself suggested that the term "European Army" be dropped in favor of "European Defense Forces," because the proposed organization was not a "military field organization" but rather "an agency which includes primarily a directing organization concerning itself initially with the problems of training, equipping, and administering forces later to be assigned to NATO command." (The term "EDF" had been developed by Byroade and McCloy in July 1950.) Eventually the name "European Defense Community" (EDC) came into use along with the EDF, to parallel the European Coal and Steel Community of the Schuman Plan.[41]

After Eisenhower's intervention critics could no longer scoff at the military "impracticality" of the French proposal. During the next few months he and his advisers transformed the military characteristics of the Pleven Plan's European Army. They jettisoned the Spofford Plan's concept of "combat teams" and insisted on the division as the smallest practicable unit for military organization. But they proposed divisions smaller than the average American division—12,000 to 13,000 men as opposed to 15,000 to 18,000—and the French designated each of these units a "groupement," a euphemism more acceptable to public opinion. The French also agreed that during the initial build-up, problems of logistics, equipment, and costs would be examined and determined in close liaison with SHAPE. Finally, General Eisenhower "would have full power to organize and deploy European units as required by any military situation," a concession designed to meet objections such as those of General Collins.[42]

With both Eisenhower and Washington pressing for quick results, the Paris conference produced a fifty-page interim report on July 24, 1951, sketching in broad outlines the creation of the EDC, whose "final aim is the fusion, under joint supranational institutions, of the armed forces of the participating countries with a view to assuring the defense of Europe on a permanent basis and to guarantee the peace against all threats, whether present or future." The Defense Community, an "essential step on the road towards European unification," would involve "no discrimination whatever among the member states." The Forces created would have a "common supply system" and a "common armament program," both designed to make the costs of defense "less burdensome" than the costs of a purely national effort. Although a transitional period would be necessary, the EDC, by "pooling the interests of peoples," would constitute "a guarantee for all that nationalistic considerations with all their dangers will disappear and give way to the collective will of the European Community."[43]

McCloy and Bruce, the orchestrators of the Europeanist strategy, sent a joint telegram to Washington urging that the basic treaty for the EDF be completed in the "shortest possible time." Because of German demands for political equality and French concerns for security, there was "no tentative or interim solution which will result in recruitment of a German soldier because it could not meet these essential conditions." The United States should stop trying to push the Petersberg proposals or any other interim plan and should "use every influence and all appropriate pressures to get French-German agreement promptly on suitable treaty, creating European institutions and agencies with adequate powers to solve detailed problems and fixing basic principles to guide their solution." To deal with Congressional critics who favored a speedier process, McCloy and Bruce argued that the EDF would be the best safeguard against German militarism, the most efficient and effective way of mobilizing European resources and using American aid, and a spur to the political integration that was needed to overcome Europe's weakness and political confusion.[44]

Nevertheless, Acheson remained skeptical, telling an aide that "we could not tie ourselves absolutely to the European Defense Force concept." He recognized that the issues involved in the creation of the European Army, especially "finance, production, and the ultimate control," cut deeply into the sensitive realm of national sovereignty. The United States must not be "trapped into a position where we would have accepted the European Army as a step which must precede any other action." Despite this prophetic warning, the momentum behind the EDF, led by the unanimous chorus of advisers in Europe, convinced Acheson to support the decision to "go all out" for it. NSC-115, a "Definition of United States Policy on Problems of the Defense of Europe and the German Contribution," which was approved by President Truman on July 30, 1951, committed the United States to full support of the EDF as the preferred method of German rearmament. American approval, however, was made contingent upon three conditions: the EDF would serve under NATO command, progress on a political arrangement "restoring substantial German sovereignty" would continue, and a "specific plan for raising German contingents at the earliest possible date" would be developed. Washington also cautioned against delaying the formation of German contingents until all the EDF agencies were in operation, suggesting that because German units were needed "at the earliest possible date," existing national agencies might be delegated to begin recruitment.[45]

Despite the conditions contained in NSC-115 McCloy and Bruce regarded it as the unqualified endorsement of the French approach which they had sought. Both were determined to push the EDF as "the most practical and swiftest road to our objective," rejecting the possibility of "tentative or interim solutions." The Germans tested McCloy's resolution at the end of August 1951, when Adenauer sent McCloy a proposal for a "provisional solution" to the problem of German rearmament. Arguing that "time is short" and there were still a "great number of political, military, legal and other questions" to clarify before the EDC agreement was made final, he suggested a provisional agreement, starting "with the legal and military measures necessary for the creation of European armed forces without delay." In Adenauer's plan a provisional European Defense Council, composed of the defense ministers of all the European countries and the United States, would constitute "the trusteeship organ for the future European Defense Community." Acting as a coordinating body of the respective nations, it would fix the precise extent of the German defense contribution. A German Defense Ministry and a superior German Military Authority would carry out the Council's directives within the Federal Republic.[46]

Adenauer's plan was in some measure a revival of the Petersberg proposals, though it employed "European" titles for its new creations. McCloy rejected it outright, telling the Chancellor that "efforts to find short-cuts outside the Treaty . . . will only divert energy from the main job, create doubts and suspicions, and delay the accomplishment of the final objectives." McCloy objected particularly to the creation of a German national force before the EDC came into operation. Such a move would strengthen "nationalist sentiment" against the European concept, as well as reduce support for it among German military men. Nor would it achieve the economic advantages of integration that the EDC was presumed to possess. He also thought that the necessary safeguards on such a German force would be "less acceptable to Germany from both a military and political standpoint than European integration." Finally, he urged Adenauer to turn his attention back to the EDC talks, rather than searching for a quicker method of rearmament.[47]

McCloy's rejection of Adenauer's provisional approach shows his commitment not only to the goal of federation but to the French government. Monnet, to win over his French colleagues, had assured them that the Americans were "prepared to lend their full support to the creation of a European Defense Community." Any indication that the United States would allow Germany to reconstitute a national army, even as a temporary measure, would have weakened the position of such pro-American, European-oriented leaders as Pleven and Schuman, who had already swallowed the unappetizing prospect of German divisions and the disappearance of a French national army in Europe. The EDC itself, originally a French idea, was fast becoming a target of growing anti-American sentiment in France. On the right, General de Gaulle condemned it as a "stateless melting pot" and criticized the idea of merging the chief symbol of the French state, the Army, into a European force. From the left, Jules Moch denounced the American-sponsored changes in the Pleven Plan for having completely distorted the original proposal.[48]

Nevertheless, American diplomats remained determined to push ahead with the EDC. Shortly before the Foreign Ministers' meeting in September 1951, McCloy visited Paris for a meeting with the new French Cabinet. He reminded them that despite the doubts of Pentagon officials, the United States was supporting the French position on German rearmament, and that "it was really up to the French to exhibit some vigor, enthusiasm and ingenuity in getting ahead with the German contribution." After warning them that a Germany "joined with the East or with the threat of going to the East . . . could exhibit tremendous pressures on France," he said that this "was no time for France to equivocate or draw back in respect to Germany." The United States, having supported the Schuman Plan, the decartelization of Ruhr industries, and the European Army, had a right to expect "that France would now take bold steps . . . thus expediting the time within which Germany could take the most eloquent form of contribution to the West, namely [become] a participant in the common defense of the West."[49]

The American support for the EDC was a bold attempt to restructure Western Europe. McCloy, having won American backing for a European solution to rearmament, next directed his attention to the political problems which remained. Recognizing early that political and military equality would have to proceed together, he faced the challenge of negotiating the "contractual agreements," the long and complicated substitute for a peace treaty that would end World War II.

9

How Free Should
the Germans Be?
Political Integration

At a meeting of the High Commissioners and Chancellor Adenauer in December 1950, François-Poncet informed the German leader that "the occupying powers take the view that the essential principle which provides their presence in Germany with a legal basis cannot be modified for the time being." The "essential principle" was Germany's "unconditional surrender" and the Allied assumption of "supreme authority," embodied in the declaration of June 5, 1945. Adenauer reacted skeptically, asking why the Allies could not place their rights in Berlin and Germany on a "contractual basis." McCloy responded that "a contract or treaty can always be invalidated by either side giving notice." The United States, he continued, considered its position "in the middle of Europe . . . an extremely important one," and "we're not going to play with that until we're sure where we stand." This statement angered Adenauer, who interpreted it as showing the Allies' desire to prolong the occupation indefinitely. "Unconditional surrender of a country does not give the power to which it is made the right to keep such a country occupied for an indefinite period," the Chancellor exclaimed defiantly, his outrage expressing the sensitivities of a people entering their sixth year of a relatively benign, but still oppressive, military occupation.[1]

The argument between McCloy and Adenauer reflected one of the major problems of the contractual negotiations. To differing degrees, the Western Allies wanted to end the occupation and yet "hedge their bets" on what the future might bring in Germany. Could they trust this new political elite of elderly Weimar veterans and returned exiles to guide Germany toward democracy, or would they be faced with a revival of German authoritarianism and nationalism? The Allies also feared jeopardizing their legal standing in Germany and Berlin, which was critical in dealing with the Soviet Union. The German leaders, for their part, worried that the Allies would not deal with them in the spirit of equality that alone could make the policy of Western integration acceptable to their people. An even darker fear was that they were fundamentally expendable to the West, cannon fodder on the battlefield, a buffer territory of retreat in the event of war, or a pawn in a four-power deal with the Soviets.

These suspicions and fears underlay the negotiations, which were extraordinarily complex. The complete collapse of the Nazi government, the extent of the claims against it, the wide scope of the occupation reform measures, the continuing division of Germany, and the unique position of Berlin—all these factors burdened the talks with considerations and technicalities beyond those of earlier peace settlements. The Allied and German representatives confronted a bewildering array of issues, from the profound question of "supreme authority" to more mundane matters such as the hunting and fishing privileges of American soldiers. Added to these problems were the difficulties of reaching intergovernmental agreement among the Allies and intragovernmental agreement in both Washington and Bonn. To complicate matters further, the Soviet Union offered the possibility of German reunification as a reason for delaying agreement. To succeed, Western diplomats would need to construct a transnational coalition of political leaders which, although fragile in its shared interests, was still stronger than the contradictory forces opposing it. McCloy and Adenauer were at the center of these negotiations. Both were determined to create the basis for a new relationship going "beyond the scope of a traditional alliance" between the United States, Western Europe, and the Federal Republic of Germany.[2]

A Right to Intervene?

Despite their commitment at Brussels, the Western Allies did not initially assign a high priority to the contractual negotiations. During the early months of 1951 their attention focused upon the Schuman Plan and the rearmament question, with the prospect of four-power talks and the French elections giving additional reasons for delay. The Allies, however, also worried that the Germans were pushing for political equality before committing themselves to contribute to Western defense. Typically the French, fearing that these German efforts cloaked a resurgent nationalism, argued that if the Allies did not retain "supreme authority," they would be "just where [they] were in 1919." The British speculated that the "Germans would enter into series of contractual arrangements and then declare that they were not disposed to go through with defense contribution." McCloy put it even more bluntly when he told Adenauer that the Allies "would not abandon [their] powers only to find the Federal Republic taking a neutral position." He saw rearmament, the return of political sovereignty, and the Federal Republic's orientation toward the West as inextricably linked.[3]

For the Germans, however, the Allied concept of the contractual arrangements (or "contractuals") left much to be desired. Although they acknowledged that Allied authority over the questions of German unity and the status of Berlin "coincided" with the Federal Republic's interests, German diplomats argued that contractuals could also regulate the right of the Allies to station soldiers in Germany and provide for their protection. The constant Allied insistence on "supreme authority" was "hardly compatible" with the transformation of the relationship from occupation to alliance. Recognizing that the Allies did not intend to continue exercising their occupation powers, the Germans saw their own task as twofold: to insist on a joint declaration with the Allies on the "basic principle" of equality in the "new relationship" that the contractuals would create, and to attempt to limit "the practical application of supreme authority short of an emergency, thus giving [the] German people a sense of greater autonomy."[4]

The Allies preferred a piecemeal approach to the negotiations, refusing to issue any declarations or concede any overriding principle. At the end of February 1951 they gave the Germans a list of "39 points" as the basis for contractual negotiations. The points fell into six categories: security questions in relation to Germany's military and economic contribution to defense, the support and security of Allied forces in Germany, the internal reforms the occupying powers had carried out, the status of Germany's international agreements, the special situation of Berlin, and the protection of foreign interests in the Federal Republic. The Allies took pains to specify that the list was for informal discussion only, "to indicate to you the extent of the problems which call for study in this connection." They added the further caveat that the list was not "exhaustive" and that "not all of the points included in the list are susceptible of regulation by contractual arrangement at the present stage"; some would "only be resolved in the peace treaty."[5]

When the negotiations actually began—between the High Commission's political advisers and a team of young lawyers from the newly restored Auswärtiges Amt, the German foreign office—the Germans saw immediately that the concept of "supreme authority" ran like a "red flag" through the Allied position papers. The Allied negotiators tried to reassure their German counterparts informally that their insistence on "supreme authority" was primarily intended to guarantee their legal rights in Berlin. Disputing a German argument that standing on legal claims was a "worthless fiction" in dealing with the Russians, they insisted that the Russians often "came around" and dropped objections when the Allies could refer to specific agreements and precise treaty rights. This argument convinced Wilhelm Grewe, the young lawyer who headed the German delegation, and he argued within the Auswärtiges Amt that Germany's relations with the Allies could not be placed on a strictly legal and traditional alliance basis. Grewe's contacts with American diplomats, particularly the Bonn political liaison, Charles Thayer, predated the war, and his perspective on this issue was far more pragmatic than that of the German foreign office. Yet even Grewe objected to the extension of supreme authority to other aspects of the post-occupation status, especially the presence of Allied forces and the unrestricted right to declare a state of emergency. On these matters, as well as on the Allied desire to retain influence over many other issues ranging from industrial controls to the German police, the German negotiating team agreed with the British diplomat who wrote that the early Allied drafts were "little more than a reincarnation of the Occupation Statute under the guise of a treaty."[6]

The Allied restrictions, especially those concerned with the treatment of their forces, reflected the strong influence of the American military, which was particularly eager to retain its right of "direct action" in the event of a breakdown of order in the Federal Republic. But the restrictions also reflected the deep divisions among the Allies themselves, ranging from the severity of the French to the liberality of the British, with the American High Commission falling somewhere between. To overcome the divisions, as well as to elicit German cooperation and ideas, both the American and British negotiators informally encouraged the Germans not to wait for an Allied position on every issue, but to come forward with their own proposals. Especially on such thorny questions as the rights and privileges of Allied forces and the declaration of a state of emergency, the Allies needed to know from the Germans what was politically and publicly acceptable. They recognized that even the most carefully crafted agreements would collapse if the Germans did not cooperate in their execution. In addition the Americans and British could use the German position as a wedge in compelling the most reluctant ally, usually the French, to accept a compromise. Some of the negotiations even took place on a strictly bilateral basis between McCloy and the Germans, completely excluding the British and French High Commissioners and the American military, partly in order to pressure those groups to make concessions.[7]

Encouraged by the Allies, and seeing the U.S.-Japanese Peace Treaty as an encouraging model, the Germans devised their own draft security treaty in the summer of 1951. At his vacation residence in Bürgenstock, Switzerland, Adenauer and his advisers put together a treaty which, while avoiding the term "supreme authority," conceded to the Allies reserve rights over Berlin and German unity. It also accepted, though not so explicitly as the Allies wanted, the connection between the change in Germany's political status and its military contribution to Western defense. In other respects, however, the treaty sought equal rights for the Germans and iron-clad guarantees from the Allies. It demanded that relations between the Federal Republic and the Western Allies "be governed exclusively by treaties concluded between them and by general rules of international law" and insisted upon a right of consultation before the Allies exercised emergency authority. The treaty reaffirmed the Allied security guarantee of September 1950, strengthening it with the proviso—clearly influenced by Schumacher's criticisms—that the Allies station enough forces in the Federal Republic "to make any attack a heavy military risk for aggressor." Adenauer also wanted an "economic security" guarantee from the Allies, specifically, their commitment "to continue their economic assistance" with the "view to excluding economic chaos and unemployment as well as danger of development of totalitarian system resulting therefrom." Referring to Adenauer's most basic fear, that of a "sell-out" by the Allies, the treaty stated that the parties would "consult one another with respect to all questions concerning their relations to states of Eastern bloc."[8]

McCloy understood Adenauer's desire for tight guarantees, but he doubted that the American Congress would ever approve them. He himself engaged in a running debate with Washington officials during the summer of 1951 over whether the United States should promise to protect the "liberal-democratic order" in Germany against totalitarian extremism. McCloy believed that the "tender plant of German democracy, whose roots were not yet deeply set," would "wither and die" if the Allies withdrew their support. After sounding out German leaders, he concluded that an Allied guarantee would strengthen those in Germany who might lack the "civic courage" to resist extremists. Americans, he said, had a "tremendous investment in our victory and occupation in Germany, and our future could be instantly and directly affected by any defection in Germany." The State Department's Bureau of German Affairs opposed McCloy's untraditional approach and repeated the usual arguments about respecting Germany's political independence. Henry Byroade, who referred to McCloy's view as a "serious infringement on German sovereignty" and a future target for German nationalists, argued that the Germans would not become "enthusiastic members of our club if we retain a 'safety first' attitude which would be a form of control over their domestic development." He went so far as to suggest in a note to Acheson that "the whole success or failure" of American policy in Germany "may rest on your decision on this one fundamental point."[9]

Byroade exaggerated the significance of the point, but his desire to make the Germans "enthusiastic members of our club" captured the spirit of American policy. As the Foreign Ministers assembled in Washington in September 1951, they faced this issue along with a host of others in their attempt to bring an end to the occupation.

The Washington Conference and the General Agreement of November 1951

The Washington Foreign Ministers meeting, followed by the NATO conference in Ottawa in September 1951, covered the full range of issues which concerned the Western Allies, from the Korean peace negotiations to the admission of Greece and Turkey into NATO. But the decisions on Germany and the pace and nature of Western rearmament dominated the talks. The Washington conference confirmed the Allied commitment to the European Defense Community as the best method of German rearmament. Acheson told the British and French that "the U.S. . . . gave vigorous enthusiastic and full support to the plan. There would be no turning back and no doubts." Although the British had been largely excluded from the U.S.-French dealings over the EDC, they endorsed the arrangement as well. Skeptical toward the "American tendency to give uncritical encouragement to any scheme of European integration," they nevertheless adjusted their thinking to this American enthusiasm. London was impressed with Eisenhower's willingness to make the Pleven Plan both "militarily effective" and, more important, "subordinate to SHAPE." As a result, the British saw no alternative to the EDC for the immediate future.[10]

The Allies coupled their endorsement of the EDC with an attempt to scale back the increasingly onerous financial demands of rearmament. Acheson had been concerned for some time that "we were trying to move our allies and ourselves faster toward the rearmament for defense than economic realities would permit." By mid-1951 the United States was devoting some 14 percent of its GNP to defense, far more than most of the NATO allies. But the difference between the levels of prosperity in the United States and Europe made these percentages a deceptive indicator. General Marshall noted that "a cut of five percent in the European standard of living meant the difference between white bread or black on the table," while for Americans it might mean the difference between "buying a radio or television." The British, who had taken the lead in NATO with a £4.7 billion rearmament program, were particularly anxious to reduce their costs. Prime Minister Attlee believed that "the need to sustain morale and to maintain a reasonable standard of living amongst the peoples of the West is just as important as the need to increase defences." The French experienced similar problems, exacerbated by their war in Indochina. At the Ottawa meeting the NATO allies established the Temporary Council Committee (TCC), which was "intended to determine exactly the economic resources of each [NATO] member and to recommend how they might be used for the common welfare." The Executive Committee of the TCC—Averell Harriman for the United States, Sir Edmund Plowden for Britain, and Jean Monnet for France (later called the "Wise Men")—faced the task of establishing criteria for defense contributions which took into consideration the substantial differences within the alliance. As one of the first exercises in "burden-sharing," the TCC established the principle of the supranational coordination of defense expenditures in peacetime.[11]

The Foreign Ministers also reached decisions on some of the more difficult issues involved in obtaining a "General Agreement" with the Germans that would undergird the new relationship and the subsidiary agreements. On the question of intervening to protect German democracy, Acheson proposed a compromise formulation. Both the British and the French supported a right to intervene, and Acheson accepted McCloy's argument that it "was necessary to meet quickly and vigorously any disruption of the public or constitutional order." But he suggested that rather than explicitly reserving a right of intervention, the maintenance of the "liberal democratic basic order" should be one of the premises of the entire arrangement with Germany, permitting the Allies to declare a state of emergency in the event of any threat to the democratic system. Worried that the Allies might want to intervene too often, Acheson insisted that "there really must be a grave threat" before any action was undertaken. "If Remer [the leader of the neo-Nazi SRP] picked up five or six additional seats," he added, "that would not constitute a threat."[12]

Although Acheson showed an awareness of German sensitivities on this issue, the overall approach of the Foreign Ministers was restrictive. They did review Adenauer's draft treaty, but they rejected it as a basis for negotiations. Even while calling their own approach "a complete transformation of the nature of the relationship" with the Federal Republic, they stressed that Allied rights rested upon "the supreme authority assumed by the Allies in respect of Germany by virtue of the Declaration of 5 June 1945." The proposed Allied treaty, which contained no additional security or economic guarantees for the Federal Republic, included an unrestricted right of the Allies to declare a state of emergency, an inspection agency to police security restrictions, and a Council of Ambassadors which would coordinate Western policies. The Allies granted no special rights of consultation to the Federal Republic, either in dealings with the East or in calling for a state of emergency, and they insisted that the FRG complete the Allied-mandated programs of decartelization, restitution, and reparations. Within some of the subsidiary treaties, such as the one dealing with the protection of the military forces, there were a number of discriminatory clauses, some providing for the unrestricted exemption of Allied soldiers from certain German laws and the subjection of some German civilians to Allied military justice.[13]

As a symbolic gesture the Foreign Ministers instructed the High Commissioners to abandon the Petersberg mansion and conduct all subsequent negotiations with the Germans at their respective residences. But this gesture did little to remove the sting of the Allied proposals. Adenauer reacted with genuine indignation, telling the High Commission, "No German Federal Government could ever affix its signature to such an agreement." To the Chancellor the Council of Ambassadors was a continuation of the High Commission with a different name, while the lack of a security guarantee in the treaty meant that the Allies could withdraw their unilateral declaration at will. The special security restrictions on German military production and research violated the principle of equality upon which the EDC was based. As the Washington meeting was breaking up, Adenauer told Kirkpatrick "that he could see no prospect of a successful outcome to our negotiations." He reminded the High Commissioners of the "provisions of our Basic Law concerning the vote of no confidence against the Federal Chancellor and new elections." Were he to sign such an agreement, he added, the Bundestag would probably oust his government.[14]

Adenauer's anger and his threats reflected both sincere outrage and calculated political maneuvering. In McCloy's view, Adenauer wanted "a security contract embodying the mutuality of old type European military alliances rather than . . . Atlantic security concept . . ." The Chancellor himself considered the Allied restrictions to be excessive—a sign of continuing mistrust. The Allies had underestimated the general German weariness with the occupation and the desire for greater autonomy. To Adenauer they seemed to have little concern for his difficult domestic political situation: they had "pulled the rug out from under him" in his struggle with Schumacher and the SPD. Although the Chancellor's use of the SPD leader as a bogeyman was a fairly routine ploy, it was not without justification. The SPD had increased its vote by an average of 10 percent in the state elections since August 1949, and more than half of the West German public felt the Western Allies exercised too much influence over the Bonn government. Adenauer was further irritated when Schumacher acquired a copy of the Allied proposals and took the opportunity to criticize them for relegating Germany to the position of a "second-rank power for an indefinite period." At the same time Adenauer's own coalition was fraying at the edges. The Free Democrats were taking an increasingly independent, more nationalistic policy line, even associating themselves with some of the more militant veterans' organizations. Adenauer may have been exaggerating his political difficulties to the High Commissioners, but his concerns were real.[15]

A new Soviet and East German initiative on reunification further complicated the Chancellor's political situation. On September 15, 1951, the East German leader, Otto Grotewohl, issued a call for free, equal, and secret elections to establish a German National Assembly. Grotewohl's speech contained two major concessions. It withdrew an earlier demand that the two Germanies have equal representation in any all-German assembly; and it called for the holding of "free elections," a proposal not emphasized in earlier East German appeals. Despite this second concession, however, both the Soviets and East Germans opposed any suggestion that elections be placed under international supervision.[16]

The Grotewohl offer reawakened interest among many West Germans, including such pro-American figures as Ernst Reuter, the Mayor of Berlin, in the possibility that the Soviet Union might favor reunification. Schumacher, too, urged that the negotiations on Western integration be slowed so that every avenue to reunification could be explored. Although Adenauer saw little reason to change his policies, he did use Grotewohl's note as a weapon against the Allies, telling them that their contractual proposals were the "best support Grotewohl could obtain." But with Allied encouragement he responded to the East German offer by proposing a variety of initiatives centered on free elections. His proposal for United Nations supervision stymied the Soviet campaign and temporarily defused the SPD's opposition. The issue faded temporarily, but American officials were certain that it would reappear before the treaties were signed.[17]

Despite Adenauer's political problems and the East German initiative, McCloy was determined to maintain a tough posture toward the Germans during the contractual negotiations. He told the Chancellor that the Grotewohl offer would not lead the United States to raise its "bid" for the Germans, and he told Washington that "our line [should] be that we do not intend to abandon our principles whether Germany contributes or not." A veteran in the art of negotiation, McCloy wanted to keep the Germans concerned about the "vast imponderable of US support," warning them that if they did not act constructively the United States might pull back from Europe. "All cards are not in their hands," he believed, and to give the Germans the "contrary impression [would] prejudice both a sound political and a sound military solution of the German problem." As the debate over the "liberal-democratic" clause indicated, McCloy was also worried about Germany's political development during the rest of 1951. He feared that if "the steadying influence of Adenauer were withdrawn and economic conditions took a turn for the worse over the next few years, it is not inconceivable that we would see in Germany a strong nationalist development." For these reasons McCloy was willing to accept some delay in negotiating the contractuals, to sit out Adenauer's indignation and allow "German opinion to resettle before we can put it confidently to a real test."[18]

The members of the State Department's Bureau of German Affairs (BGA) were indignant with McCloy and with HICOG's approach. They blasted McCloy for "smothering our policy in the mantle of self-imputed righteousness" and for failing to recognize that German participation in Western defense was the overriding U.S. priority. For this reason they wanted to accept German positions on such issues as deconcentration and restitution, which they saw as subordinate to the defense question. The BGA's political advisers were certain that HICOG was "failing to assess properly the strength, determination, and ingenuity of the forces opposing settlement with the Western powers which find their focus in the SPD." McCloy's deteriorating relationship with Schumacher, along with his strange suggestion that Washington was leaking details of the contractuals to Schumacher's camp, convinced the BGA that HICOG was inhibiting constructive negotiations. They believed McCloy was deceiving himself in thinking that "the Western Powers can gain their objectives merely by remaining firm all along the line." Adenauer, despite his political weakness, was negotiating from a "position of strength."[19]

Despite his annoyance with HICOG, Colonel Byroade was aware that on these issues "we seem to stand alone against the British, French, HICOG and the rest of Washington." He even acknowledged to McCloy that "it appears to your staff that we are trying to fight the German battle for them in advance." Byroade's position was indeed somewhat unusual, for he believed that "the final result with the Germans will be much nearer our position on many, many matters than that which is being agreed tripartitely for presentation to the Germans." In the long run his prediction turned out to be accurate, because when the agreements went into effect in 1955 many of the restrictions had been removed. But in October 1951 the BGA staff found themselves with a "rather frustrated feeling" as McCloy and HICOG conducted the contractual negotiations in their own style and with their own priorities.[20]

Two issues dominated the negotiation of the General Agreement: the nature of "supreme authority" and the "state of emergency" question. The retention of the term "supreme authority" violated Adenauer's conception of political sovereignty. It symbolized his "Potsdam nightmare," with Germany a powerless entity still at the mercy of the victorious Allies. Although he was prepared to concede the Allies "special rights with respect to Berlin and the unification of Germany," he insisted that these should be derived from agreement and not from a declaration of surrender. Nor did he believe that a reserve right was needed to protect Allied troops, since this could also be based upon a treaty. He saw the issue of supreme authority as intimately connected with the Allied insistence on retaining a Council of Ambassadors and a special inspection authority on security issues. It demonstrated that the Allies were unwilling to trust the Federal Republic, an unwillingness that could become a self-fulfilling prophecy by undermining his authority and encouraging forces hostile to Western integration.[21]

For the Allies, their rights in Germany and Berlin were "based squarely on supreme authority and not on other sources." To weaken or divest themselves of that authority would, as McCloy saw it, "jeopardize our rights in connection with [the stationing of our] troops or with Berlin," and these rights, which were essential in dealing with the Soviet Union, were as much in Germany's interest as they were essential to the Allies. McCloy even stressed to Adenauer that the "retention of supreme authority . . . did not mean that we were endeavoring to restore our entire authority as regards Germany since we were prepared to grant it full practical sovereignty in domestic and foreign affairs . . . " Especially on such questions as the protection of American soldiers, however, the "unprecedented character" of the American commitment made it essential to American public opinion and the Congress that "our rights were unequivocable."[22]

The determined Allied stance on supreme authority finally led Adenauer to borrow McCloy's word and appeal to the Allies "to tackle the question on a practical basis." He told the Allies that "he was prepared to give us everything we wanted in a treaty, but could not accept that we should reserve it by supreme authority." Adenauer frankly acknowledged the validity of Allied concerns about future political developments in Germany, and the fear that events could spin out of control. After admitting that this was "a reasonable apprehension," he stated that "he had just as great an interest as we in seeing that democracy in Germany was not swept away." But could not such a protection be arranged through mutual agreement? Why did the Allies insist on reserving this right through supreme authority, "90 percent" of which they were willing to abandon without concern in regard to the Russians?[23]

Adenauer's willingness to concede the substance of the supreme authority issue weakened Allied insistence on the exact words. As McCloy noted, the Chancellor was "sincerely desirous of giving us rights we need if we can find an appropriate formula re sovereignty." Starting from this common ground, the negotiatiors reached a delicate compromise. They shortened Article I of the treaty to affirm simply that the "Federal Republic shall have full authority over its domestic and external affairs, except as provided in this Convention." They also agreed to rephrase those elements of the treaty that referred to the declaration of June 1945, and not to mention it or use the term "supreme authority." Instead they would simply reaffirm "the rights, heretofore exercised or held by them," relating to the stationing and security of their troops, Berlin, and "Germany as a whole, including the unification of Germany and a peace settlement." For its part the Federal Republic would agree not to take actions "prejudicial" to these rights and to "facilitate their exercise."[24]

These compromise formulations still amounted to a German recognition of Allied authority. They also replicated in Germany a form of divided sovereignty not unlike the American political system of federal-state relations. With hundreds of thousands of Allied soldiers providing its security, the Federal Republic could not enjoy "political sovereignty" in the classic and traditional sense. The new formula called for "practical sovereignty," allowing the German government to take over most functions of everyday administration while leaving the question of final authority obscure enough to keep both the German and American public satisfied with the arrangement.

The Germans still hoped to constrain Allied authority, defining the conditions under which it would be exercised and insisting on consultation. These issues arose immediately, during consideration of the "state of emergency" clause—that power which allowed the Allies to assume full authority in the event of an emergency. The initial Allied position gave the Council of Ambassadors the right to declare a state of emergency, "after consultation with the Federal Government, in order to meet situations which will be clearly set forth in our agreements." To the Allies, such situations included an armed attack on the Federal Republic, a "grave disruption of public or constitutional order or the grave threat of such disruption," or a request from the Germans themselves. They stressed that "under no circumstances" would they allow their right to protect their own troops to be affected by the treaties. McCloy was particularly sensitive to the possibility of political problems with Congress if the Army should argue that the treaty kept its commanders from protecting American GIs.[25]

For their part the Germans recognized that the Allies would not station thousands of troops on German soil without adequate guarantees for their safety. Adenauer himself wanted the matter handled as "generously" as possible, well aware of its political implications in the United States. But the Germans saw a need to distinguish these Allied soldiers, if only symbolically, from the occupation armies under which they had lived. They insisted on an additional clause, Article IV, which stated that the "mission of the armed forces stationed" in Germany "will be the defense of the free world, of which the Federal Republic and Berlin form part." They also restricted the right of the Allies to bring in forces from other countries without the approval of the German government. They were unsuccessful, however, in making the various NATO treaties between the United States and its other European allies the model for the stationing of troops in Germany. Although the Germans won some important concessions, McCloy advised them that the stationing of so many American soldiers in the FRG created a "special situation" which made impossible the use of the standard NATO treaty.[26]

Adenauer's most important objection related to the Allies' unrestricted right to declare a state of emergency. Adenauer argued that "no Bundestag would accept such a proposal without safeguard against abuse." He wanted some forum to which his government could appeal if it believed that the state of emergency was not justified. Such a proposal, he noted, would be "in line with constitutional practices."

The High Commissioners declared that they could not make the security of their troops "dependent upon judgment of an outside body," but Kirkpatrick suggested that the Germans could appeal to the NATO Council of Ministers to review the question. The Allies were also willing to forego any reference to a Council of Ambassadors, allowing that the right to declare a state of emergency would belong to the governments themselves. Adenauer accepted both concessions, recognizing that a right to appeal to the NATO Council would eventually create a case for Germany's admission to that organization.[27]

By the time Adenauer met with the Western Foreign Ministers in Paris in November, most of the preliminary issues had been settled with the High Commissioners. The Chancellor created a brief flurry by announcing that he considered the Allied assurances of support for a reunified Germany to include Germany's "lost" territories beyond the Oder-Neisse line. This move, designed to strengthen his position with the refugee groups in the Federal Republic, created a potentially "explosive issue" for the Allies, but he did not press it after receiving an assurance that any solution of Germany's eastern boundary would "await a peace settlement." Adenauer's primary concern at this meeting (his first with Acheson since November 1949) was his "Potsdam nightmare," and he asked whether the "occupying powers [would] use Germany as a pawn in attempting to reach a settlement with the Russians." He noted that public opinion in England and France appeared so deeply hostile to Germany that it would probably accept a peace with the Soviet Union at Germany's expense. Then what would the Americans do? And would their position change after the next election?[28]

Acheson's answer was straightforward, and it reinforced what McCloy had been telling the Chancellor during the preceding months. He said that the Chancellor "could be sure that neither the present U.S. Government nor any now discernible successor from either party . . . would countenance the sacrifice of one of our allies in an attempt to appease the Communist powers—an effort as futile as it was immoral." Acheson added, however, that the American commitment also depended on German conduct. As long as Germany acted as a "good European neighbor," America would treat it as an "equal partner with an equal voice in policies and decisions." This reassurance, McCloy later reported to Acheson, had strengthened Adenauer's own resolve to push ahead with the remaining negotiations.[29]

The conclusion of the General Agreement at the Paris conference was only the first step toward a final contractual agreement. Acheson himself complained how little progress had been made on such thorny issues as Germany's financial contribution to defense and on future security controls. Yet he also recognized that the Western "club" was growing bigger: he told President Truman that "the fact that the four of us met on a basis of equality is of greater importance in Europe than any of the specific agreements reached at the meeting." Acheson was convinced that "our security against Germany for the future lies more along the lines of tieing [*sic*] Germany in every possible way to the west through such mechanisms as the Schuman Plan, European defense force, and eventually NATO." It would no longer be possible, he added, "to accomplish two contradictory programs, i.e. that of bringing Germany wholeheartedly into the west on a basis of equality, and that of retaining a distrustful attitude resulting in obvious inequality." The Secretary exaggerated somewhat, for at the heart of the negotiations during the remaining months of 1951 was the reformulation and redefinition of "equality" and "sovereignty" to fit the realistic need to contain both Germany and the Soviet Union within a divided Europe.[30]

Winter of Crises and Decisions: The London and Lisbon Conferences

The winter of 1951–52 was a trying time for American policymakers. Following the hesitant progress of the November meeting in Paris, it appeared that the entire structure of agreements—the Schuman Plan, the EDC, and the contractuals—might collapse under the weight of Franco-German mistrust and suspicion. The French Deputy High Commissioner, Armand Bérard, referred to the "revival of disagreements" among the Allies, and even the usually optimistic McCloy became downcast. Washington had granted him "a degree of flexibility" to work out solutions "which will fit the political situation in Germany and be consistent with developments in the EDF conference in Paris," but he found himself continuously stymied by the French and the Germans. While recovering from a skiing accident in late January, he admitted to his old teacher, Justice Frankfurter, that "things are at sixes and sevens again and I am *almost* depressed."[31]

The stalemate of early 1952 exposed the erosion of the political forces that had allowed America's "European strategy" to make rapid progress. Western Europe's sense of an external threat had dissipated, and as the need for unity in Europe seemed to fade, old anxieties and fears resurfaced. Nowhere was this more evident than in France, where the political creativity which had given birth to the Schuman Plan and the Pleven Plan succumbed to an attitude of "catastrophism." Burdened by continuing inflation, drained by the war in Indochina, and concerned about the rapid resurgence of Germany's economic power, the French directed much of their resentment toward Americans and American policy, while many referred derisively to their country as a "satellite" of the United States. The sense of decline from great-power status accentuated the bitter internal divisions within the country as Frenchmen battled over economic policy, the role of the state, educational reform, and agricultural subsidies. These divisions on domestic issues often made it impossible to assemble a governing coalition or reach coherent decisions on foreign policy. After the elections of June 1951, which weakened the moderate center, the assembly had become polarized, with the Communists on the left and the Gaullists on the right. The first three months of 1952 witnessed three different French governments attempting to cope with the major issues of France's European policy.[32]

American diplomats saw clearly enough the divisions within French foreign policy, especially toward Germany. Acheson referred to France as having "two minds" about Germany, a desire to integrate it into Europe, on the one hand, and a desire to control it by means of a four-power arrangement with the Soviets, on the other. These two tendencies in French policies obscured a more fundamental aim, which Americans misunderstood or too easily dismissed. French leaders, from the right to the non-Communist left, wanted to maintain their country's status as one of the three major Western powers. Bidault's concept of an "Atlantic High Council for Peace" and Pleven's hope for a "three-power consultative body . . . to coordinate policy on a worldwide basis" reflected this basic French concern. Even Monnet's European ideas derived much of their political support from being seen as another way of maintaining France's "Big Three" status. As Georges Bidault later put it, "While France wishes to build Europe, it does not wish to be engulfed by it . . . The creation of the European Defense Community could not separate France and the other territories and countries who were marching with her along the road to progress from the association of the Big Three."[33]

During much of 1950–51 the French government experienced no

contradiction between its European-oriented policies and its desire for a special status within the West. But as the treaties came closer to completion, and as the relentless logic of equality within the EDC was recognized, the French began to distance themselves from their progeny. The changes adopted in the original Pleven Plan, designed to make it militarily viable, also limited the control which the French could exercise over the German forces. The Germans, in their own desire to achieve equality, saw the EDC as the perfect way to deal with a host of politically sensitive issues, from the question of controls on German industry to armaments manufacturing and the cost of maintaining allied troops. Adenauer became one of the EDC's most eloquent defenders, even arguing for extending the duration of the treaty. "It is necessary that our children be bound, at least for a period of fifty years, which will permit them to profit from the experience we have gained." The German negotiators, McCloy noted, "have so completely accepted the concept of the European Army that they have rather frightened the French of the consequences."[34]

French concerns about the EDC were also manifested in their increasing resentment toward the British for refusing to join it. The French, who feared that in the EDC they would be "trapped" and left alone with Germany, doubted their ability to remain equal with their Teutonic neighbor without the presence of the British. They also perceived the position of Britain as a special favor accorded by its Anglo-Saxon partner, the United States. The parliamentary leader, Paul Reynaud, predicted in October 1951 that unless Britain changed its position the French Assembly would never approve the EDC. The French also feared that their presence in the EDC might eventually deprive them of their position in NATO's Standing Group, slowly reducing France to a status similar to Italy's. The subordination of the EDC to NATO's Supreme Commander, although a military necessity, underlined to many Frenchmen the inferior position France would be accepting in the EDC.[35]

The war in Indochina also weighed heavily on the French, increasingly affecting their attitudes toward the EDC. French forces under the dynamic leadership of General Jean de Lattre de Tassigny had repulsed a major Vietminh offensive early in 1951; but by the end of the year the French had suffered very serious setbacks, and de Lattre died of cancer in January 1952. Many Frenchmen were convinced that France could not mount a serious defensive effort in Europe, equal to that of the Germans, while the war continued. The one possible solution was increased American assistance. Even though the United States was already bearing about one-third of the cost of the war, Pleven and Monnet appealed to the Americans: "The reason for French hesitations [on the EDC] can only be removed when the United States Government is prepared to engage itself to provide dollar assistance and earnings to France adequate to give France the opportunity to have a level of economic activity consistent with supporting operations in Indochina and a defense force in Europe equal to that of Germany." The British saw the same problem for France: Churchill told the Americans in January 1952 that "the French were [not] doing their full part towards this European army but that this was due to the fact that they had to fight 'like tigers' to protect their empire in Indochina." This "constant drain" made them "more apprehensive about the arming of the Germans."[36]

French apprehensions were revealed in a message sent to Acheson by Foreign Minister Schuman at the end of January. Earlier in the month the EDC negotiations in Paris had "resulted in agreement on most of the institutional problems and the narrowing down of disagreement on most of the remaining problems." The six nations had reached compromises on the establishment of a Board of Commissioners, the principle of unanimity in the Council of Ministers, and the determination of the common budget. Yet the increasing progress of the EDC, with its commitment to equality and "non-discrimination," created a problem for the French. Schuman told Acheson that the EDC treaty could not contain "the precautions and barriers which the allies, at Brussels and then at Washington, have considered to be indispensable to guard against the latent danger which would result from a Germany freed from every restriction." It was necessary, therefore, to incorporate special restrictions into the contractual agreements, including prohibitions on the manufacture of German armaments such as artillery and gunpowder, a restatement of the prohibition of Germany's membership in NATO, and the reimposition of the Spofford Plan's restriction of German forces to "one-fifth of the forces of the Atlantic Army." Schuman also asked for an American and British "guarantee" of the EDC against "the long term problem of a possible secession of the Federal Republic."[37]

The Schuman letter warned Acheson of trouble ahead. He interpreted it as reflecting Schuman's "diminished authority with Cabinet

and Assembly and a hesitance to move from authorized positions."
(The French Assembly would vote on February 19, by the fairly
narrow margin of 327 to 287, to endorse Schuman's position on the
EDC, including the proposed guarantee.) To further complicate the
issue, the French launched a new initiative on the Saar. On January
25 they appointed an Ambassador to the disputed territory, a move
which, as Schuman told Acheson, was designed "to maintain . . . the
economic union of France and the Saar [which is] an essential element
of the economic balance inside the European community." This initiative came from the Quai d'Orsay, which was already cool to Schuman's European plans and expected a negative German reaction that
would slow the progress of the EDC and the contractual negotiations.
As McCloy later put it, the French move "almost upset the apple cart."
On January 29 Walter Hallstein, one of Adenauer's pro-European
advisers, called the French move "a violation of previous Franco-
German agreements on the Saar." Bundestag leaders, whom Adenauer
had not consulted in connection with the contractual negotiations,
seized upon the Saar issue to attack his conduct of foreign policy. In
a resolution passed on February 8, the Bundestag called on the government "to do all in its power in order that the population of the
Saar may at last recover their political liberties." It also appealed for
German membership in NATO. Under pressure from the deputies,
Adenauer pleaded with McCloy for American mediation of the dispute
and for American insistence that the French concede the right to free
elections for the Saar.[38]

McCloy sought to defuse the Saar issue, pressing Adenauer to
propose a "European" solution for the disputed territory. McCloy,
who viewed the Saar as an insignificant but potentially dangerous
issue, an "open wound on the body of Europe," supported its "Europeanization," with the capital of the territory, Saarbrucken, becoming the site of the Schuman Plan authority and the Saar itself enjoying
political autonomy under a superstructure erected by the European
Council. Above all he steered the Germans toward moderation, urging
Adenauer to tone down his public statements so as not to give anti-
German officials in the Quai d'Orsay more ammunition. Acheson, too,
insisted that Schuman and Adenauer meet privately to reach an understanding. The American pressure succeeded in shelving the Saar
question until after the EDC and contractual agreements were signed
(as they would be in May); McCloy believed that a final solution

would require "pressure from the outside upon both France and Germany."[39]

The other disputes between France and Germany were not postponed. When King George VI died on February 6, 1952, his state funeral afforded an opportunity for the Foreign Ministers to meet in London. Acheson was determined to tackle the major issues standing in the way of the contractual negotiations: security controls on German military production, the treatment of war criminals in Allied custody, Germany's membership in NATO, and the amount of Germany's defense contribution. The most difficult and contentious issue was the security question. As Schuman's letter had indicated, the French wanted explicit prohibitions on German weapons production to be included in the contractuals. They demanded a ban not only on German production of "atomic, biological, and chemical weapons, long-range and guided missiles, military aircraft, and naval vessels other than minor defensive craft"—which the United States and Britain supported—but also on civil aircraft, which only Britain supported, and on all "heavy military equipment," including gun barrels and propellants, which neither Anglo-Saxon power supported. Although the Germans were not especially eager to resume arms production, Adenauer argued that a sweeping restriction against it would constitute discrimination against Germany and make Bundestag passage of the EDC agreement impossible. He believed the EDC's central budget and procurement structure was protection enough against a self-sufficient and nationalistic German army. Nevertheless, recognizing the need to reach agreement, the Chancellor was willing to consider other solutions. Before the London conference McCloy had urged him to weigh a "special German undertaking" by which Germany "in the light of existing conditions would voluntarily agree to prohibit by German law the production of [specific] categories of armaments." Adenauer showed interest in the idea, but he continued to emphasize the political importance of avoiding the acceptance "of any system which implied discrimination against Germany."[40]

German willingness to adopt self-restraint in arms production proved to be the key to the solution. Adenauer not only agreed to issue a declaration that Germany would not produce certain listed war materials—to be defined in talks with the High Commissioners—but he also agreed that the EDC could restrict armament production in "strategically 'forward' areas," such as Germany, and that this would not be discriminatory. The Americans supported Adenauer in excluding gun barrels and propellants from the listed materials, in part because they believed that the "short supply of ground armament and powder" meant that "German resources should be utilized." Schuman, however, resisted this concession, stressing the psychological effect which the names of German arms producers, especially Krupp, would have on other Europeans. And despite Adenauer's willingness to provide a written assurance that Germany would purchase, and not manufacture, civil aircraft, Schuman feared that a simple German declaration could be "repealed." Adenauer, after responding with an exasperated "Have confidence!" urged Schuman to accept his undertakings. (The specific list remained undecided at the London meeting, but later—at Lisbon—Schuman would show himself more flexible, in part because of American promises to give France substantial economic assistance.)[41]

Adenauer's conciliatory posture also expedited the solution of two other issues. To deal with the war criminals, he agreed to the establishment of an advisory board composed of an equal number of Allied and German representatives. This board would handle all matters of administration and clemency for the prisoners. In addition he agreed not to press the issue of German membership in NATO. Schuman in return did not insist on a "negative" decision that would specifically prohibit the Federal Republic from joining the alliance.[42]

The agreements with the Germans helped the progress of the contractual negotiations, but they did not strike at the root of the French insecurity about the EDC. The question of providing guarantees continued to pose difficult problems for both British and American policymakers. Acheson argued that the entire EDC-contractual arrangement was premised "upon Germany's joining in and loyally adhering to the EDC"; should Germany secede, "it would be a matter of greatest concern to the US." Nevertheless, because of the political situation in the United States, where the Truman administration was in its final months, he was reluctant to ask Congress for additional treaty obligations. He believed that existing Congressional resolutions, which "approved the maintenance of our forces in Europe as long as those might be necessary for the security of the West," were sufficient guarantees of the EDC.[43]

To the British the problem appeared in a different light. When Churchill and the Conservatives returned to power in October 1951, some hoped that British policy toward Europe and European integration would change, and that Britain would consider membership in the EDC. Churchill, after all, had been one of the earliest advocates of a European army. But Churchill had two foreign policy priorities: to reestablish Britain's special relationship with the United States, which he believed had suffered under Labour's leadership; and to solidify ties within the Commonwealth. Although he supported the EDC, he stated often, "We do not propose to merge in [it]." He disliked the federational aspects of the force and told Acheson that what he had "hoped to see were spirited and strong national armies marching together to the defense of freedom singing their national anthems. No one could get up enthusiasm singing, 'March, NATO, march on!'" There was no possibility that Britain under Churchill would join the EDC, for as he put it, "I love France and Belgium, but we cannot be reduced to that level."[44]

Churchill's disdain did not keep his Foreign Secretary, Anthony Eden, from attempting to find ways to bolster the EDC. Although the Foreign Office was much more skeptical than the American State Department about the EDC's chances for success—to the point of considering alternative schemes for German rearmament in December 1951—it also recognized that the United States was committed to the EDC, and that the successful negotiation of the project might be critical to keeping the Americans interested in the forward defense of Europe. London was also willing to support French efforts at European integration because integration would serve to control German power. Reacting to Schuman's letter to Acheson, a British official commented that "we see no better alternative policy than that on which we are now engaged to rivet Germany to the West while preventing her from again dominating Western Europe."[45]

The British were also aware that American leaders, despite official denials, wanted them to either join or accept a closer association with the EDC. In December 1951 Acheson had answered a question about Britain's reluctance to join by saying that "everybody had hoped that another decision might be reached and that we still hoped that if the scheme went forward the British might find ways of participating in some way and perhaps eventually of joining it." When challenged by Eden, Acheson had toned down his statement, but Congressional actions and newspaper comment reflected American disappointment in British policy. To counteract U.S. opinion, Eden was prepared to give Schuman a much stronger guarantee of British support for the

EDC in the event of German secession than Acheson was able to provide. But because the French Assembly continued to demand full British participation, the French government changed its position at the London meeting and asked the British not to issue a unilateral guarantee. (Such a guarantee would, paradoxically, have indicated that the British would not participate in the EDC.) Britain, therefore, did not issue a guarantee until the end of March 1952, in response to a request to join the EDC received from the six nations participating in the negotiations.

The Federal Republic's financial contribution to Western defense was the only issue left unresolved at the London talks of mid-February 1952. Although the outlines of the German economic miracle were becoming apparent, German leaders still worried that economic problems might undermine their democracy and its Western orientation. Adenauer and his Finance Minister, Fritz Schäffer, feared the possible inflationary consequences of a heavy defense burden. Early in January Adenauer had appealed to the Allies on grounds of "equality" to allow the "Wise Men" (the Executive Committee of the NATO's TCC) rather than the Allied High Commission to examine Germany's economic situation and reach a conclusion on its defense contribution. The Germans claimed that their many social costs, especially those concerned with refugees and support for the city of Berlin, should be counted as defense expenditures. They also asked the Allies to reduce the occupation costs for their armies, which encompassed luxuries such as personal maid service and free train travel. To avoid the appearance of continuing to pay occupation costs, the Adenauer government wanted to make its entire defense contribution, including support for Allied forces, through the EDC.[47]

The Allies had agreed to the German request to allow the TCC to review the question, and in London they presented Adenauer with the findings of the Wise Men, who had concluded that an annual contribution of DM 11.25 billion ($2.6 billion) was appropriate. They had accepted some, though not all, of the special German social costs, but had left for negotiation the division of the contribution between support for Allied forces and the build-up of German units. Adenauer would not agree to accept this amount without first returning to Bonn to consult his Cabinet. Acheson and Eden urged him to do so immediately. Both hoped that he could obtain final Cabinet agreement before the end of the NATO conference at Lisbon, which was to follow the London talks. To help the Chancellor politically they suggested a further 10 percent cut in occupation costs over the next twelve months, and they allowed the German contribution to be made to the EDC directly, with the support costs for American and British forces to be automatically returned to the United States and Britain. As Acheson noted, this was "purely a matter of procedure but will allow the Germans politically to fuzz up the issue of continued 'occupation costs' which would otherwise cause Adenauer considerable domestic difficulty."[48]

Despite the Foreign Ministers' assistance, Adenauer faced important domestic obstacles. After the Rome NATO conference in November 1951, in which a German defense contribution of DM 13 billion ($3 billion), had been proposed, Adenauer had stated that Germany could afford only DM 8 billion. By the time the Germans made their submission to the Wise Men, they had raised their total contribution to DM 10.6 billion, which Schäffer termed "the absolute limit," but which included a number of expenses that were only peripherally related to defense. Schäffer, the leader of the Bavarian offshoot of the Christian Democrats, maintained that any increase "would result in open and rapid inflation," and that "any new inflationary threat . . . would destroy the economic and social order, and, therefore, result in a major victory for the Soviets in the cold war." Even though he exaggerated the danger, he had enough political strength in Adenauer's fragile coalition to keep the Chancellor from acting quickly on the Allied request. McCloy, who found Schäffer impossible to negotiate with—"he objects to everything and talks forever"—urged Adenauer to overrule his Finance Minister, reminding him how important it was for Acheson to obtain an agreement at the Lisbon conference in late February. But it took a personal appeal from Acheson in the waning moments of that conference to convince the Chancellor to accept the Allied figure. Then Adenauer told Acheson that he was "deeply moved" by his appeal and the "fairness" with which he viewed the German situation. Adenauer also recognized that a success was crucial for Acheson's dealings with Congress, and he did not want to stand in the way of that success. McCloy told one former assistant, "It was [the Chancellor's] attitude at London and the acceptance of the financial contribution which made the conferences a success more than anything else."[49]

Acheson celebrated the NATO conference at Lisbon as a "grand slam" for American diplomacy. There he obtained Adenauer's agreement on Germany's contribution, Schuman's final agreement on security controls for Germany, the formal admission of Greece and Turkey to NATO, and the approval of the TCC report. This report set NATO's force goals at some fifty divisions by the end of the year, including twelve German divisions. This promise of a European military build-up helped assure Congressional passage of military assistance funds as well. Indeed in large measure the success of the entire project came from American willingness to undertake the lion's share of the financing. To help secure French agreement at Lisbon, the United States promised France $600 million in economic aid for its rearmament effort in Europe and its war in Indochina. (A few months later the United States would need to provide an additional $150 million for the French war effort.)[50]

American hopes arising from the Lisbon conference were soon disappointed, however. The French government was forced to resign over its request for a 15 percent tax increase to meet its obligations under the Lisbon program, and the British also began cutting back on their ambitious promises of rearmament. But NATO itself had moved from the loose treaty of alliance which it had been in 1949 to a military organization, with headquarters in Paris, "controlling a defense line of 4000 miles, from the North Cape to the Caucasus." In this transformation Germany was becoming the most important element, and its Chancellor an increasingly central figure in American plans for Europe. Acheson's admiration for Adenauer had become equal to if not greater than McCloy's. The Chancellor's willingness to make concessions at decisive moments earned him important political capital with the Americans. Acheson remarked, "Often I found myself agreeing with [Adenauer] contrary to the views of the other two [foreign ministers]." Having entered office concerned primarily with Schuman and French politics, Acheson was beginning to readjust his map of Europe. This would become increasingly clear as the EDC-contractual negotiations entered their final phase, where they were to be severely tested by a bold proposal from the Soviet Union.[51]

The Stalin Note of March 10, 1952

The success of the London and Lisbon talks seemed to clear the way for the rapid conclusion of the EDC-contractual negotiations, but the

Allies and the Germans were forced to grapple with a number of other important matters before an agreement could be signed. Among these were major issues, such as the clarification of Allied emergency rights and the continuing French demand for a "guarantee" of the EDC, and more minor but particularly troublesome matters, such as the specific division of German expenditures between the support of Allied forces and the build-up of German units, the privileges of Allied forces in Germany, and even the wording of Germany's endorsement of the Universal Declaration of Human Rights. Because of the multitude of concerns and interests affected by the EDC and the contractuals, the potential for delay was enormous. McCloy noted that there "is a tendency to embrace each point of difference, no matter how minor, as a further means of postponing the ultimate conclusion."[52]

To Acheson and McCloy, delaying the agreements could prove their undoing. Acheson, who believed that "the same forces which led to the necessity for winding up the occupation in Japan are also operating in Germany," feared that even if the EDC agreement was not ready, the Germans would demand to "go through with the regime provided for in the contractuals." He thought this could "produce all sorts of problems with France and may end us in a first-class mess." Acheson also feared that if the agreements were not finished quickly, the Senate would not be able to approve them before recessing at the end of June; then "consideration would be postponed until January 1953, with all the delay and uncertainty that that involves." His worries were not unfounded. The political authority of the Truman Administration was already waning, and its ability to act decisively would disappear when the election campaign began. Although a Republican victory appeared likely, its consequences were uncertain. The Republican presidential campaign of Senator Robert Taft, who had opposed the NATO treaty, opened the possibility that the next administration would take a far more skeptical view of the agreements. Even though General Eisenhower was certain to give Taft strong opposition, it was not clear in the spring of 1952 that he would prevail in the nominating struggle. Furthermore, if the treaties were continually delayed, it would tarnish Eisenhower's achievement as Supreme Commander, weakening his position against the isolationist wing of the party. This political uncertainty, coupled with worry about resurgent isolationism, led Acheson to press for the speedy signing of the agreements.[53]

In March 1952 the American approach to Germany and Europe

faced a renewed Soviet challenge. Since 1945, as Churchill had already told the American Congress, the Soviet Union's behavior had, ironically, served to strengthen Western unity and to build "a different and a far better world structure than what [the Soviets] had planned." But on March 10 the Soviet Union came forward with a bold new approach to the German question. Drawing the Western Allies' attention to the fact that "although seven years have passed since the end of the war in Europe a peace treaty with Germany is not yet concluded," the Stalin Note proposed four-power negotiations to establish an all-German government and conclude such a treaty. The nonpolemical tone of the Note, along with its new concessions, seemed to indicate a genuine Soviet desire for accommodation. The most dramatic reversal from previous policy was its stipulation that "Germany will be permitted to have its own national armed forces (land, air, and sea) which are necessary to the defense of the country." In addition, Germany would be permitted to have its own armament industry. There should be no limits to German trade or economic development, and a reunited Germany should become a full member of the United Nations. The Note called for the restoration of all civil and political rights to "all former members of the German army, including officers and generals, [and] all former Nazis, excluding those who are serving court sentences for the commission of crimes." The one remaining demand was that such a reunited Germany could not join "any kind of coalition or military alliance directed against any power which took part with its armed forces in the war against Germany."[54]

The Note was vague on certain questions, including how to guarantee Germany's nonaligned status, elect an all-German government, and determine the territorial boundaries of a reunited Germany. Yet the Soviets' remarkable volte-face on the rearmament issue posed a dramatic challenge to the Western powers. Stalin's Note appealed to a wide range of groups within Germany, from conservative businessmen and industrialists interested in expanding their markets to neutralists, ex-soldiers, and former Nazis. Even Dean Acheson, who was strongly opposed to negotiating with the Soviets, conceded that the note "in both tone and substance marked [a] considerable advance upon previous proposals."[55]

What was the significance of the Stalin Note? Was it a genuine offer of German reunification, a "missed opportunity" to defuse the Cold War that was ignored by the Western powers because of their desire for a rearmed West Germany lodged securely within the NATO alliance? Or was it a clever propaganda move, designed by Stalin to prevent the signing of the EDC-contractual agreements, disrupt the unity of the West, and justify the increasing "Sovietization" of East Germany? It contained elements of both, and it had both strategic and tactical importance; but it is impossible to give a final answer to the question until the Soviet records are made available for study.[56]

Although the public nature of the Soviet proposal lends itself to the propaganda interpretation, both the timing and content of the Note indicate a serious Soviet initiative. Soviet commentary in early 1952 emphasized less the threat posed by a rearmed Germany than the danger of a Germany "integrated within a western military alliance, with the resources of both Europe and America at its disposal." The Soviets argued that "plans for the creation of 'European Army' are, in truth, plans for resurrecting the fascist Wehrmacht under American control," and that the "Bonn militarists" were counting on "being able to achieve their irredentist goals within the framework of the aggressive Atlantic bloc." Just as the Americans did not believe they could defend Western Europe without Germany, so the Soviets believed that, without Germany, NATO did not pose a real danger to the Eastern bloc. But after the Lisbon conference the Soviet Union found itself confronting the rapid development of a West German state in an anti-Soviet military alliance.[57]

Faced with this change in the "correlation of forces," Stalin's policy toward Germany shifted focus. In his book *Economic Problems of Socialism in the U.S.S.R.* the Soviet leader implied that a reunited Germany might "break out of American bondage" and pose more of a threat to the West than to the Soviet Union. Soviet and East German commentators rediscovered the Rapallo treaty of 1922; they celebrated its thirtieth anniversary in early 1952 and advocated following the "path which reflects 'the spirit of Rapallo,' a path toward creation of a united, strong, non-aligned, and peace-loving Germany." As a model for relations between such a "peace-loving" Germany and the Soviet Union, East German commentators suggested the Soviet peace treaty with Finland, which obligated that country "to refrain from participation in any coalition directed against the USSR." As one student of the Stalin Note has concluded, there was "at least the *possibility* that Stalin was toying in early 1952 with the idea of a non-aligned Germany in a final drastic attempt to prevent a West German adherence to the EDC."[58]

Whether or not the Soviet move reflected a sober calculation of the shifting "correlation of forces," it appealed strongly to the German public. As one opinion survey noted, although strong anti-Communist sentiment existed within the Federal Republic, "it is unwise to go any further and attempt to conclude that there is positive German liking for the Western course of action." The "preponderance of West Germans" preferred "to remain neutral and stay completely out of the East-West struggle." By some measures of German sentiment, reunification was preferred to Adenauer's "Westintegration" policies by a nearly two-to-one margin. Many undoubtedly recognized that neutrality was an illusory goal. Still the net result of these feelings was *not* a rallying behind Adenauer's policies, but a paralysis of the political will to act, a fear of doing anything that might jeopardize future reunification. American insistence on speeding up the contractual negotiations was resented for just this reason. Stalin's initiative appealed to those Germans who, as McCloy put it, "feel that they are being pressured into action which they genuinely dislike, and believe they are being used for the accomplishment of American policies which they consider alien to their interest and contrary to their preference." These ambivalent feelings were registered in the political weakness of the Adenauer government as it approached its election year of 1953. Late in April 1952 the Adenauer coalition lost control of the Bundesrat, the upper house of the German Parliament. The Stalin Note held the potential for further weakening the Chancellor's position. As McCloy put it, the "Kremlin may be expected to press vigorously to split Adenauer off from the rest of Germany, Germany from West Europe and West Europe from US."[59]

Clearly the Soviet proposal struck at a point of acute vulnerability for the Western allies. While recognizing that Stalin's proposals were effective as propaganda, they saw the potential danger to their larger goals in Europe. According to Anthony Eden, the Soviets "are sincere in these proposals because, though there is danger in them, they would on balance, suit them well." The Quai d'Orsay also believed that the proposal "was a serious but very dangerous attempt to settle the German question." The Americans were even more skeptical. The State Department's Policy Planning Staff (PPS) believed there was only "one chance in ten" that the Russians were prepared "to pay, if necessary, the price of free elections in order to block West Germany's entrance into EDC." Although it recommended probing Soviet intentions, the PPS argued that "whatever [the Soviet] motives, the bargaining position of the Western Powers would be improved by prompt signature of the EDC Treaty."[60]

This strategy of prolonging the exchange of notes with the Soviet Union until the EDC and contractual agreements could be signed became the Western approach to the "battle of the notes." For a variety of reasons, including Acheson's preoccupations in Washington and with the Korean situation, the British seized the initiative for the West. In the Allied reply of March 25, 1952, they went beyond the American concern over the question of free elections and sought to clarify other aspects of the Soviet offer, raising the ticklish issue of a reunited Germany's territorial boundaries as well as the right of such a Germany to join the EDC. Eden was particularly eager to avoid a simple return to the four-power control of Germany similar to the situation in Austria, where the result had been political stalemate. He also wanted to prevent the re-creation of a united Germany, which could eventuate in the election of an SPD leader like Schumacher, who "would probably reverse Adenauer's policy of integration with the West and go for a policy of neutrality and maneuvering between East and West." The French, who wanted to avoid anything that might permit Germany to return to its seesaw policy between East and West, would not allow German unification without the reimposition of severe restrictions. Schuman assured the West German leaders that acceptance of the Soviet offer would lead to new four-power controls—a liberating change for the East Germans but a considerable step backward for West Germany.[61]

Although the Allies took the lead in orchestrating the response to the Soviets, McCloy's views had an important influence on the Chancellor and within Germany. McCloy was not surprised by the Soviet move, having warned Acheson earlier to expect a new approach on the reunification issue. He told Bowie a few days after the Stalin Note was received, "It is one I have been expecting a long time." McCloy interpreted the Note as he had the Grotewohl message of September 1951—as an indication that growing Western strength and pressure were forcing Soviet concessions: "The Soviets are playing their heaviest cards as one expected they would do to deflect our policy of European integration." McCloy's message to the Germans was simple: "If the Germans were now to delay, the American reaction might be to wash our hands of the entire project and let the Germans fend for themselves." He added that the "Germans must now give evidence of what side they were on." McCloy did not believe that a country as large, dynamic, and economically powerful as Germany could remain neutral, and he thought that the Soviets would inevitably pressure a neutral Germany into their bloc. Thus Germany's fate would resemble Czechoslovakia's, not Finland's. Yet, although he did not believe the Soviets would allow genuinely free elections in their zone, he recognized the political importance of responding constructively to their proposal. In his speeches he called on the Russians to make a number of simple "goodwill" gestures to demonstrate their sincerity. Among these he listed some which had strong West German support, such as the release of German POWs in the Soviet Union, the release of political prisoners in East Germany, and the free circulation of West German publications in East Germany.[62]

McCloy's rejection of the Soviet offer, and his conviction that it should not delay the EDC-contractual negotiations, reinforced the Chancellor's position. Adenauer's tough stance on the Stalin Note, along with his continued insistence on both free elections under United Nations supervision and the right of a united Germany to join the EDC, in turn affected the American perspective on possible talks. Acheson considered consultation with Adenauer on the Western replies as "essential," partly because of the political leverage the Chancellor had gained through his concessions at London and Lisbon. This became clear during discussions concerning the Allied reply to the second Soviet note, dated April 9, 1952, which suggested four-power supervision of elections. The Americans proposed including in the reply an "offer to meet with the Russians through the High Commissioners in Germany to discuss plans for having the United Nations Commission or some neutral body investigate conditions throughout Germany to see whether free elections were possible in all parts of it." Even McCloy thought that it was "important prior to ratification [of the EDC-contractual agreements that] quadripartite conversations will have taken place which can clearly demonstrate the insincerity of the Soviet offer." Had it not been for the strong opposition of Adenauer, the Americans might have prevailed on the British and French to include this proposal for talks in the reply. But Adenauer told McCloy that after serious consideration for one day and "through half the night" he had definitely decided that the U.S. proposal for a meeting in Berlin "would be a mistake at this time." He feared that a meeting would strengthen those in his own Cabinet who wanted to delay signing the contractuals, as well as providing support for the Social Democratic opposition. Therefore the Allied reply of May 13, 1952, merely repeated its proposal for a United Nations commission to determine conditions for elections.[63]

Adenauer believed that the Soviet offer posed a danger to Germany's security by giving encouragement to those in Britain and France who were willing to arrange a settlement with the Soviet Union at the expense of Germany. In his view a freely elected German government should take part in any four-power talks from the very beginning. He was also worried that if Germany showed itself too eager to jump at the Soviet offer, it would forfeit the trust which he had forged between it and the Western powers, especially the United States. McCloy's emphasis on the need for Germany to decide in favor of the West had a strong influence on the Chancellor, as did Acheson's insistence that the West must achieve "situations of strength" before negotiating with the Russians. In Adenauer's view, the Federal Republic also had to be firmly anchored within a strong and rearmed Western alliance system before it could undertake negotiations with the Soviets. He argued, in effect, that only his "policy of strength" could bring about reunification under conditions acceptable to the West German electorate. He himself had doubts about the political reliability of the German people and believed that the nationalism and extremism of the past might reappear if Germany was not securely linked to the West.[64]

Adenauer's critics argued that the Chancellor had no real interest in reunification. His quick dismissal of the Stalin Note and his statement that "it would make no difference whatever to his Government's policy" led Jakob Kaiser, the minister for all-German affairs, to accuse him of acting "more American than the Americans." Political opponents, and not a few supporters, thought Adenauer feared that in elections in a united Germany the Social Democrats would become the majority party. For this reason, they believed he was deliberately misleading Germans with his "policy of strength," because he knew full well that his policy of Westintegration would preclude reunification. The Social Democrats bitterly attacked Adenauer, arguing that "the unity of Germany was too important to be decided by hunches and that, therefore, every last effort must be made to determine beyond a shadow of a doubt whether the Russians really mean business."[65]

The SPD was unsuccessful in its attempt to force the Allies to open negotiations with the Soviets. Encouraged by Adenauer, the Allied strategy of delay resulted in the completion and signing of the EDC and contractual agreements by the end of May 1952. On May 24 a Soviet note had arrived that differed markedly from earlier notes in its threatening tone and polemical denunciation of the West's policy in Germany: "The real meaning of the agreement of the North Atlantic bloc with the government of Adenauer can comprise only the further strengthening of the aggressive character of the North Atlantic group of powers presently striving for the direct union with the German revanchists who represent the most aggressive circles in Europe." Two days later the East German government issued new border regulations, beginning a process of sealing off the Soviet zone from the West and creating a five-kilometer "No-Man's Land" along the zonal border. It seemed, as one American diplomat put it, that the Soviets had decided to "harden East Germany into a thoroughgoing satellite." These actions strengthened the Western position in Germany, leading Eden to tell Acheson and Schuman with some satisfaction that the West had won the "battle of the notes." Because of this victory both the British and the French felt that the Western Allies could consider beginning four-power talks. Eden believed such a meeting would "improve prospects of ratification, especially in France and Germany." The French thought, "Our main concern should be to discover what the Russians really want in Europe." Schuman suspected that the Soviets feared not Germany alone, but Germany "acting as an instrument of the United States." He may have hoped to convince them that the EDC had been designed by the French to prevent just that eventuality. But even though the Allies wanted negotiations after the signing of the EDC and contractual agreements, the Soviet Union displayed little interest.[66]

The Stalin Note of March 10, 1952, has acquired almost legendary importance in the Federal Republic as signaling the point at which the chance for immediate German unity was lost. This view far overstates the significance of the Soviet move, for the opportunity to negotiate remained until Germany joined NATO in 1955. It is clear, however, that the Western powers, principally the United States, insisted that German leaders make a choice between pressing for negotiations for reunification and following the path of European integration and tight association with the United States. Adenauer made that choice. In view of the contrast between the troubled history of Bismarck's Germany and the development of the stable, democratic society of Adenauer's Federal Republic, it is up to the Chancellor's critics to prove that a different choice would have been preferable. They are correct, however, in pointing out that the Chancellor was reluctant, largely for political reasons, to force his people to confront the choice as starkly as he himself saw it or his opponents presented it.[67]

The Bonn-Paris Treaties

Even without the Stalin Note, the last weeks of the contractual negotiations would have proved exhausting for the participating diplomats. The pressure to finish the agreements in time to obtain Congressional approval produced marathon negotiating sessions and all-night meetings. McCloy and Adenauer had been the key figures in setting up this schedule. Early in April McCloy had demanded, and Adenauer had eventually accepted, that the High Commission and the Germans "adopt a conference procedure whereby all would work continuously at the job until completed and that particularly we must not let the Easter holidays interfere." Between May 6 and May 22, 1952, eleven all-day meetings were held with the Chancellor, and these all-day sessions stretched far into the night. The session of May 15, for example, began at 10:00 A.M. and continued until 5:30 A.M. the next day, resuming again at 10:00 A.M. Kirkpatrick later recalled that he had never gone through so "punishing an ordeal." But the "ordeal" had important consequences. At all levels of the negotiations, among the High Commissioners, their advisers, and their German counterparts, the sheer intensity of the effort created a strong sense of common purpose and genuine friendship. The German negotiating team noted the change from the "icy" atmosphere at the beginning of the talks to a real sense of partnership and good humor by the end of the discussions, which gave the Germans the "equality" and "membership in the club" feeling they had sought. Even Finance Minister Schäffer, who caused the Allies the most trouble in negotiating financial arrangements, could say, "We are sitting in the same boat and want to get the defense treaty passed." The Americans felt the same way. Acheson noted that this "was a period not only of settling differences but of growth of understanding." Allied concessions, as McCloy noted, came from the "recognition that in the new relationship the Federal Republic was justified in demanding full equality."[68]

One consequence of the American deadline was, however, a weakening of the Allied position. The Allies kept careful track of their concessions to the Germans, and in early May they turned over to Bonn a list of the 116 concessions they had made. A few days later at a negotiating session McCloy commented with exasperation, "All right, then. This is now the 122nd concession the Allies have made to the Germans." The Allies abandoned some of their reform programs, including the idea of changing the civil-service and freedom-of-trade laws, and allowed others, such as decartelization and deconcentration, to be drastically scaled back. Although the total number of concessions seems excessive, the original Allied position had left room for compromise. More than a quarter of the concessions came in the "transitional arrangements," where they increased the speed with which the Germans would regain authority, rather than changing the direction of policy. Twenty-seven concessions were made in the status-of-forces treaty, where the original draft had allowed the Allies to continue treating much of the Federal Republic as a simple military security area. The Allies also "traded" concessions in one part of the agreement for German agreement to another part. McCloy traded away an Allied exemption from the special German "equalization of burdens" tax in return for securing certain rights to restitution for victims of Nazism.[69]

The financial issue was the most difficult. Although Adenauer had agreed to the overall total of the German defense contribution at Lisbon, the uncertainty as to when the treaties would be ratified led the Allies to set the German contribution at DM 850 million per month. But as if to confirm the old adage that "the devil is in the details," the Foreign Ministers had left it to the High Commissioners to define exactly what this amount included as well as its distribution between the support of Allied forces and the build-up of German units. In addition, Finance Minister Schäffer, who was taking a direct part in the contractual talks, was determined to limit Allied occupation costs, insure an "equal" distribution between Allied forces and the new German units, and secure additional revenues from the Allied forces. McCloy complained angrily that Schäffer acted like "a Bavarian cow trader over the taxes he would like to collect from Allied personnel." Schäffer was equally "obsessed" with the claims issue, hoping to charge the financial claims of German citizens against the Allied forces to the monthly defense contribution.[70]

Schäffer's rigid position would have been less difficult for McCloy if his own flexibility had not been restricted. He faced two formidable obstacles within the Allied "team": the U.S. Defense Department and the British High Commission. The Defense Department wanted to insure that none of the "occupation costs" the U.S. Army had incurred in Germany were "disallowed" by the ceiling on Germany's monthly contribution to Western defense. Secretary of Defense Lovett told Acheson that "it would be undesirable to have the Congress gain the impression that our dollar burden will be increased now or in the future, either directly or indirectly by reason of the failure of the Federal Republic to retire obligations incurred during the occupation period." In order to prevent such a possibility, the Allied military commands increased their occupation costs to DM 1.4 billion for March 1952 and DM 900 million for April, substantially above the DM 600 million per month that the Foreign Ministers had agreed on in London. Adenauer complained bitterly about the unanticipated costs, sharing Schäffer's view that they endangered the Federal Republic's financial position. Schäffer even predicted "an orgy of spending" by the Allied forces in the last months before the contracts came into force. Although McCloy did not share their sense of danger, he did acknowledge that these "additional burdens" had not been considered by the TCC in its evaluation of Germany's capacity to pay, and that therefore the Allies should include some of the new costs in Germany's defense contribution.[71]

At the same time McCloy pressed for economies in the military's expenditures in Germany. He knew that the Army's European Command (EUCOM) was reluctant to part with the special privileges it had come to enjoy in Germany, including domestic servants, free train travel, the requisitioning of private homes and hotels and recreation facilities for the exclusive use of soldiers, and unrestricted hunting and fishing rights. These privileges were sore spots to ordinary Germans, and in many respects they carried the same political weight as the abstract issue of supreme authority. (Schäffer made them a part of his standard political speech, insisting that the Germans could no longer "afford" such Allied "waste and extravagance.") For its part the Army argued that cutbacks in its privileges would damage the morale of its forces, and that "elimination of luxury items by the United States might remove a lever from our hands to be used to force the French and British to give them up." To battle the Army's reluctance, McCloy brought over to Germany his longtime friend and law partner, Chauncey Parker, who had helped him organize the High Commission in 1949. After months of frustrating negotiations with EUCOM, and with McCloy's approval, Parker went public in his campaign, denouncing the Army's insistence on its "luxuries" and noting that in the last instance it was "the American taxpayer holding the bag." The strategy worked, and Lovett ordered EUCOM to accept the end of the privileges without waiting for the French and British.[72]

Armed with these reductions, McCloy took on the more formidable task of convincing the British High Commission. Ever since the Washington conference of September 1951 the British had expressed concern about what Prime Minister Attlee had called "the far reaching economic and financial problems which will arise from any German defence effort." Strapped by its increasing defense and social welfare costs and suffering from another balance-of-payments crisis, Britain could not afford a rapid reduction in the German support payments, which would have necessitated increasing British defense spending by an unacceptable 7 percent over three years. As one Foreign Office official noted, "The financial consequences of German rearmament, not clearly foreseen when the original decisions were taken, are now looming up with increasing menace." Throughout the contractual talks and especially during their final weeks, the British position was that "we must get the full costs of our forces in Germany met for as long as possible." British leaders, who recognized that as soon as German rearmament was authorized, the Federal Republic would want to spend its money on building up its own forces, hoped they could delay this authorization until at least mid-1953. Despite their commitments to the French and within NATO, the British were prepared to threaten the United States with the withdrawal of their forces from Germany in order to assure continued German support. The threat was dramatic, but it was more effective in getting Acheson's attention than in giving London a real alternative.[73]

McCloy was able to use the unilateral American reductions in occupation costs to persuade the British and French military forces to accept a 10 percent reduction in their own expenses. (The British complained that the Americans had an "obsession with the question of maids.") But on the crucial question of the division of German expenditures during the first year the British negotiators were under "rigid instructions" to demand "at least DM 600 million per month prior [to] ratification and at least DM 510 million per month from date [of] ratification to 30 June 1953." The British were also reluctant, as McCloy noted, to accept a plan whereby the Allies would receive more of the DM 850 million over the first six months than over the last. They feared that any reduction in their request for support would be considered a tacit "admission that the Allies can get along on this low rate and thus prejudice our case in second year." With the Germans demanding an equal division of the DM 850 million between Allied and German uses, the possibility for compromise appeared slim.[74]

McCloy told the Germans an equal division of their defense contribution would not make sense for the first months of the build-up, for they would not be able to find enough manpower or military equipment to spend the money on. He got Schäffer to agree reluctantly to a type of "sliding scale" for the first year of the agreements, which would provide the Allies with the majority of the funds—DM 511 million—during the first six months and DM 319 million for the following three months, with the final three months subject to negotiation. The State Department pressed the British to allow their negotiators more flexibility and the result, after a series of marathon meetings in mid-May, was the acceptance of this sliding scale of payment. The British insisted, however, that Germany could not begin to build up its forces until the contracts were ratified, thus providing an "answer to those who think that the Germans are going to be armed before the French." Both the British and French recognized that the sooner German contingents were formed, the greater would be the competition for the limited amount of military equipment available from the United States. The Americans' willingness to go along with their view represented still another concession to the European perspective that, despite Lisbon, the speed of German rearmament and of European rearmament in general should slow to a politically acceptable pace.[75]

Other controversial issues also threatened delays. McCloy needed to use his considerable influence with the Defense Department to prevent EUCOM from insisting that the right of its commanders to take "preemergency action to provide for the security of their forces" should be "in the form of a reserved right and not subject to arbitration." McCloy recognized that the Germans would view such an unqualified right as the "continuation of the occupation statute." He believed that the emergency clause itself was sufficient, and that to restate the right would be "politically difficult to achieve, and conceivably unwise, as in certain circumstances it might be useful to have recourse to arbitration ourselves in [the] event [that] failure to cooperate in non-emergency periods did occur." The Defense Department conceded the issue, but this was a matter of form rather than substance. The Germans had already recognized in Article 5, Section 7, of the treaty that "any military commander" could "take such action [as] appropriate" in the event of a threat to his forces.[76]

In the final days the problems of German politics intruded into the negotiations. As a result of elections in the newly created "Southwestern State" of Baden-Württemberg, Adenauer's governing coalition lost its majority in the Bundesrat. Arguing that this development endangered passage of the EDC and the contractuals, Adenauer proposed to rewrite the treaties, dividing them into two sections. He wanted to place all the provisions that affected the rights and privileges of the Länder in one section that would have to be passed by the Bundesrat. The other part would require approval from the Bundestag alone, where Adenauer's coalition retained a majority. He also proposed removing certain points, especially those having to do with finances, from the treaties altogether, on the ground that they deserved more consideration and should be included in a separate treaty in the future. But McCloy, in a special meeting with Adenauer, maintained that although some flexibility was permissible in the formulation of specific provisions, the Allies would never agree to such important changes simply to avoid the Bundesrat. McCloy added that "US Congress would never ratify in this session two independent treaties, leaving open possibility that later German Parliament might accept first treaty favorable to it and reject second."[77]

Adenauer's last-minute attempt to change the treaties reflected his shaky political condition in May 1952. His coalition came close to open revolt when he finally began to inform Bundestag deputies of the provisions of the treaties. The most vocal opposition came from the smaller right-wing parties, the Free Democrats (FDP) and the German Party, which maintained that "no responsible German politician could support contracts which 'resembled Versailles Treaty.'" One FDP leader even proclaimed that he would "rather see the Russians march in than assist voluntarily in reducing Federal Republic to status of puppet." (McCloy noted generously, "Undoubtedly he did not really mean this but it does reflect atmosphere now existing in entire coalition.") These politicians objected to such features as the emergency clause, the "humiliating" imposition of an obligation to aid Berlin, the German agreement to administer war crimes sentences, and the continuation of certain occupation laws. McCloy recognized that although the parliamentary leaders had genuine concerns, some of their anger was directed against the Chancellor for his lack of consultation and was derived from a desire to posture in public as more patriotic than the government. Intervening again, McCloy told a group of Bundestag deputies that he would consider their objections, but he "made it very clear at same time that I [could] make no commitment of any kind to them because of delicate balance of interests necessary for ratification of treaties as contribution to long-term international objectives and as proof of permanence of US interests in Europe." His meeting with them, McCloy believed, had "considerably diminished" their opposition to the treaties.[78]

The deputies were successful, however, in opposing Article VII, paragraph 2, the so-called Binding Clause, which stated that a "unified Germany shall be bound by the obligations of the Federal Republic" under the treaties and "shall likewise be entitled to the rights of the Federal Republic" under the treaties. Originally Adenauer had wanted this clause added, hoping to "emphasize . . . that the unification of Germany should not bring with it any reduction in the liberties granted to the Federal Republic" by the contractuals. He wished to prevent any reimposition of four-power control that would negate the rights he had won from the Allies and deny Germany a voice in its own fate. The Allies, although willing to accept the clause, added the provision that if a reunited Germany was to have the FRG's rights it would also have to assume the FRG's obligations. The Bundestag deputies objected that this would be a "huge political blunder," for the Soviet Union could "make similar treaties with east zone government and thus perpetuate division of Germany." State Department officials, notably Philip Jessup, recognized the same problem once the exchange of notes with the Soviet Union began. When Acheson arrived to meet with the Foreign Ministers for the final EDC-contractual negotiations in late May, the issue remained troublesome. He proposed that the West German government "agree that it would not join in creating and transferring its power to any new government that did not agree to assume and abide by the international obligations of the Federal Republic." When Adenauer objected that the Western powers did not seem to accept a reciprocal obligation not to enter into an agreement which impaired the rights of the Federal Republic, Acheson assured him that although the Allies possessed a reserve power to deal with questions of German unity, they "did not interpret this reserve power as permitting them to derogate from their undertakings to the Federal Republic." Adding a letter to this effect to the treaty satisfied the remaining German objections.[79]

The final issue facing the Foreign Ministers was the French desire for a guarantee of the EDC against the possibility of German secession. Though Schuman had raised this matter in London and the British had provided a guarantee in March, he told Acheson that the "principal objection" of the French Cabinet "was unsatisfactory nature US-UK guarantees in tripartite declaration." Acheson knew that he could not go to Congress to obtain the type of assurance the French wanted. The best he could offer was a declaration, made jointly with the British, that "if any action from whatever quarter threatens the integrity or unity of the [EDC], the two Governments will regard this as a threat to their own security." At first this did not satisfy the French Cabinet; the Foreign Ministers debated the entire night before the French conceded. On May 26 and 27, 1952, the contractuals and the EDC treaties were signed in Bonn and Paris respectively. As McCloy cabled Bowie, "It was a close squeak."[80]

Though Acheson took the occasion to "welcome the Federal Republic on its return to the community of nations," the Germans received the treaties with resigned acceptance and even hostility. Shortly before the signing, polls had shown that almost half the populace had not even heard of the contractual agreements. After they were signed, this awareness increased, but still only 33 percent knew enough about the treaties to support them, while 19 percent were opposed. Opposition from the Bundestag, especially from the Social Democrats, prevented Adenauer's plans for a holiday and celebration. The biggest gatherings were held to protest the treaties. At a rally in Munich that attracted several thousand demonstrators a sign appeared depicting a cross with an American army helmet and bearing the words, "U.S and Adenauer—For them should we fight and die?" From his sick-bed, Schumacher argued that the "Peace Contract" would not bring peace because it blocked the reunification of Germany. In an echo of his "Chancellor of the Allies" attack, he condemned the

"McCloy-Adenauer coalition" and proclaimed that "whoever approves the General Treaty ceases to be a German."[81]

Only in the United States did the treaties find enthusiastic support. As if to belie Acheson's fears, the Senate listened respectfully to his and McCloy's appeals for quick action, and with only a handful of dissenting votes it passed the contractual agreements. Though the United States was not a signatory of the EDC treaty, many senators praised the idea, hoping it would lead to a United States of Europe. When one senator challenged McCloy about the possibility that Schumacher might repudiate the treaties, the High Commissioner praised the SPD leader as a "very patriotic and pro-Western" leader, who might seek revision but would respect the agreements. Schumacher attacked McCloy for this statement, saying he would not be bound by the treaties. The SPD leader was failing rapidly, however, and he died in August 1952.[82]

The Senate's ratification of the Bonn accords was the crowning achievement of the Truman Administration's German policy. McCloy called the agreements "solid proof of our desire for a peaceful alliance" with the Federal Republic. The treaties were an "act of faith—faith in a free Europe and a free world." He confidently predicted that the reunification of Germany would come "when you combine the resources and the strengths of the entire free world and . . . the utter 'unsinn' [nonsense] of the Iron Curtain becomes apparent." Adenauer appealed to McCloy to extend his stay in Germany through the middle of July, asking that he talk "with Bundestag members" as the "authoritative American representative." McCloy's role in the negotiations and his popularity in Germany made him the decisive spokesman for American policy. Despite their relative apathy toward the negotiations he had led, more than two-thirds of all West Germans who recognized McCloy's name believed his administration had been to the advantage of the Federal Republic. The CDU's press service, perhaps predictably, concluded that "[McCloy's] name will forever remain a part of German postwar history as the name of a good friend." The *Frankfurter Neue Presse* editorialized that "McCloy has done more [for Germany] than even the most hopeful among us could have believed." An SPD representative, one of a group wishing McCloy farewell, took the High Commissioner aside and told him, "You don't have to worry about us, Herr Mac." McCloy also enjoyed praise from the United

States, where the *New York Times* called his policy in Germany a "shining success" and *Time* reported that "McCloy himself, the Germans recognized, had done more than any other man to transform the Bonn Republic from the status of defeated enemy to the role of needed friend."[83]

10

The New Look: Eisenhower and Dulles, 1953–1955

In his memoirs Secretary of State Acheson commented, "It would have been better all around if the constitutional calendar had called for an election a year later rather than at that peculiarly critical moment." Acheson believed that in another year the Truman Administration would have had "a good chance" not only to help Schuman get the EDC through the French Assembly but to settle the Korean War. But America's influence on European developments diminished as the election campaign got into full swing and a transition period loomed ahead. Both the United States and Britain ratified the EDC and contractual treaties quickly; in France and Germany, however, they were bogged down in political and constitutional controversy. In December 1952 State Department Counselor Charles Bohlen noted that there had been "a steady loss of momentum" in the ratification process, "highlighted by the postponement by the German Government of ratification until the early part of January, at the earliest, and the growing indication of great difficulty with the French Assembly." Although the State Department studied some alternatives to the EDC, Acheson remained committed to it, and he suggested that a statement from President-elect Eisenhower would "be most important in reversing [the] current unfavorable trend with respect [to] EDC ratification in both Germany and France." McCloy, who had returned to private life as the head of the Chase Bank in New York, also appealed directly to Eisenhower, relaying the suggestion he had received from Adenauer that the new Administration appoint an "American personality of high prestige and importance" who would "devote his time to the great question of integration and of economic and military cooperation in

Europe." Some State Department officials, including the Policy Planning Staff head, Paul Nitze, objected to tying American policy to the fate of the EDC, but in early January Eisenhower, in a public message to Adenauer, stressed the "importance of a growing European unity and the establishment of a European Defense Community." The General added that "such a development would contribute much to promote peace and the security of the free world."[1]

Eisenhower's statement was no surprise, in view of the critical role he had played in making the EDC a prominent part of American policy. But after the 1952 election campaign, in which Republicans had attacked the Truman Administration's "cowardly" policy of containment and talked of "rolling back" Soviet gains in Eastern Europe, the continuity in American policy toward Germany was (and remains) impressive. Despite the talk of a "New Look" in American foreign policy, Eisenhower and his Secretary of State, John Foster Dulles, followed the basic initiatives, methods, and goals which Acheson and McCloy had established—the necessity of Germany's integration into Western Europe, its rearmament within the EDC, the importance of Franco-German rapprochement, and the need to use American power to achieve these ends. Indeed, as John Lewis Gaddis has pointed out, Dulles was even more committed to this approach than Acheson. He told the Joint Chiefs of Staff (JCS) at one of their first meetings in January 1953 that "from the political standpoint" the EDC was "much to be preferred," because it would "combine Germany and France in a manner more trustworthy than a treaty relationship." Echoing McCloy's sentiments, Dulles told the JCS that "the problem in Europe has been the recurrent conflicts between France and Germany leading to recurrent wars." To Dulles, "EDC was the symbol that France and Germany had buried the hatchet." It was an important factor in keeping the American people interested in the fate of Europe and preventing a return to isolationism.[2]

Though the dour and religious Dulles was very different in temperament from McCloy, the new Secretary of State not only listened to the former High Commissioner's advice but used him in the first years of the Administration to convey messages to Adenauer and other European leaders. He also followed McCloy's advice by choosing James Conant, the President of Harvard University, as High Commissioner, rather than Robert Murphy, Ambassador to Belgium. Both McCloy and Acheson had warned Dulles that Murphy would not be acceptable to the French, particularly because of his personal hostility toward Jean Monnet. Dulles also shared McCloy's enthusiasm for European unity. He too was a former Wall Street lawyer, but his diplomatic experience had begun with the negotiations for the Versailles Treaty. He, too, counted Jean Monnet as a close friend and was determined to use American power to encourage the movement toward European unity. Following Adenauer's suggestion again, Dulles appointed David Bruce as U.S. Representative to the Coal and Steel Community and as American Observer at the EDC talks. He also named Robert Bowie to head the Policy Planning Staff. Both appointments demonstrated the continuity of America's European policy and the new Secretary's commitment to the "integrationist strategy" for dealing with the German problem.[3]

The President's commitment to this strategy was equally strong. Eisenhower continued to see the EDC as the best way to contain both Soviet expansionism and German nationalism. He reassured reluctant French leaders that this strategy would "integrate [the Germans] in a federation from which they could not break loose." He also believed the EDC would allow the United States to reduce its forces in Europe and its military assistance to the NATO allies. In one of the most distinctive features of the New Look strategy, Eisenhower was determined to reduce the defense budget; he was convinced that excessive military spending would undermine the economy and the private enterprise system and could ultimately lead to a "garrison state." Believing that "economic stability and military strength were inseparable," he hoped that by restraining defense spending he could lower taxes and restore a balanced budget.[4]

The EDC was the solution to so many problems and appealed so strongly to America's self-image as a model for Europe—Senator Fulbright termed it "an effort to unify in the same or similar way that we did in 1787"—that it was difficult for American leaders to adjust to the changing international conditions that robbed it of some of its appeal. The death of Stalin in March 1953, which removed one of the strongest motivations for European unity, brought with it a relaxation of tensions. When Stalin's successors declared that "there is no litigious or unsolved question which could not be settled by peaceful means on the basis of mutual agreement with the countries concerned . . . including the United States," a break in the East-West deadlock seemed to be near. The possibility of a four-power settlement as an alternative to the division of Germany resulted, as it had during the contractual negotiations, in delay and second thoughts, especially in Britain and France.[5]

Prime Minister Churchill thought the time was ripe for new four-power discussions, and he attempted to convince both his own Foreign Office and the Americans that this was the case. Churchill had grown increasingly sympathetic toward the idea of a unified, neutral Germany as the solution to the German question. When the Foreign Office, convinced that Russia's aim was "the future control of Germany," resisted Churchill, he declared that a reunited Germany would never become an ally of the Soviet Union. This conclusion was based on his perception of the German national character, which "rises superior to the servile conditions of the Communist world." The continuing "hatred of Bolshevism," which "Hitler focused upon," as well as the example provided by the Eastern zone under Communist rule, would also make Germany immune to Communist subversion. After a series of messages to Moscow, with replies which he interpreted as showing a willingness for talks, the Prime Minister sought to convince the new American President of the need for negotiations with the Soviets.[6]

Neither Eisenhower nor Dulles was attracted by the Churchill proposal for talks. Eisenhower thought it could be misinterpreted "as weakness or overeagerness on our part [that] would militate against success in negotiation." He also believed such a meeting would disconcert the allies, particularly the Germans, as well as have an "unpredictable" effect on Congress, which was still considering the defense program. There must be "some evidence, in deeds, of a changed Soviet attitude"—such deeds as a Korean armistice, an Austrian peace treaty, and a new Russian policy toward Eastern Europe that would allow "the free choice of their own forms of government." Beyond the Korean armistice, which was reached in July 1953, the Soviets found it difficult to comply with the American conditions. When the new Soviet leadership encouraged the Stalinist East German regime to pursue "a less harsh path toward socialism," the result was the uprising of thousands of East German workers on June 17, 1953. Some 275 Soviet tanks and thousands of soldiers were sent in to crush the rebellion.[7]

This fierce reaction demonstrated the Russians' determination to maintain their presence in Central Europe. It may also have dispelled any illusions which the Kremlin had about the sympathies of East German workers. Subsequent Soviet offers of reunification would never express the same generosity toward the Germans as the Stalin Note had, and the Soviet fear of a reunified Germany continued to increase. The Eisenhower Administration, however, saw the East German uprising as confirming the wisdom of its policy of strength and even as opening the possibility of reunification. American officials concluded that the Soviet use of force had demonstrated "the failure of Russian policy insofar as making converts of the working people" and alleviating the severe economic problems of East Germany were concerned. West Germany did, indeed, seem to exercise a "magnetic" effect on the East. Rejecting the notion that membership in the EDC would preclude German reunification, Eisenhower told Adenauer that it was his "conviction that the strengthening of the Federal Republic, through adoption of the EDC, the contractual agreements and further progress in the integration of Western Europe, can only enhance the prospects for the peaceful unification of Germany." Privately he noted that events in East Germany might develop to a point where it might even "become impossible for the Communists to hold the place by force." What the Soviets might then do, Eisenhower did not suggest, although his Administration was prepared to negotiate a demilitarized zone arrangement and other security controls if that would result in a Soviet pullback from East Germany.[8]

Eisenhower and Dulles's growing confidence that reunification was a realistic possibility did not signal a change in their policy toward the EDC. In August 1953 the Eisenhower Administration, in policy paper NSC 160/1, reaffirmed its support for the integration strategy toward Germany, linking it strongly to the reunification of Germany. European integration was the key to stability in Europe and "the best means of solving Europe's economic, political, and defense problems." Although a united Europe would constitute "a counterpoise, not a menace, to the Soviet Union," it would at the same time exercise "a strong and increasing attraction on Eastern Europe, thus weakening the Soviet position there and accelerating Soviet withdrawal from that area." German reunification would also have this dual impact on the Cold War. Reunification was "essential for an enduring settlement," but it "must not be bought regardless of price." The only acceptable solution was "a unified democratic Germany allied to the free world," which would "represent a major step in rolling back the iron curtain."

Because the Soviets seemed "unlikely to accept unity on these terms at this time," however, they might try to appeal to the desire of many Germans for a "neutralized" and reunited Germany. But such a Germany would "entail sacrifices and risks to the West incommensurate with any possible gains." Among these would be the loss of German strength, both economically and militarily, along with the serious strategic and military problems that a withdrawal of American forces from Germany would entail. Nevertheless, if the Soviets were to concede free elections *and* the right of a reunited Germany to affiliate itself with the West, the United States would have to accept the minor risk that the Germans might choose neutrality over Western alignment.[9]

One reason this risk appeared to be minor was the stunning success of Adenauer in the German elections of September 1953. In the year after he had signed the contractual agreements, Adenauer's popularity rose strikingly, from roughly 33 percent of the electorate in favor of his policies to some 55 percent. In April 1953 he made a celebrated trip to the United States, meeting the President and laying a wreath at Arlington National Cemetery. His warm reception by American dignitaries was recorded in his campaign film, and he welcomed the strong public endorsement from Dulles, who proclaimed that the Chancellor's "defeat would be disastrous for Germany and freedom." In what his former Interior Minister, Gustav Heinemann, termed the "Dulles elections," Adenauer's Christian Democrats took some 45 percent of the vote, with the other coalition parties doing well enough to provide the government with a comfortable majority. (Within a few months the Bundestag ratified the EDC-contractual treaties.) The Social Democrats, under the leadership of the colorless Erich Ollenhauer, held on to their 30 percent of the electorate, but they were unable to exploit popular concern about rearmament and integration with the West. Germany's continued economic boom, marked by average annual growth rates of 10 percent, declining unemployment, and substantial increases in average income, further contributed to Adenauer's victory. To American observers, his victory and Germany's resurgence made the pursuit of European integration all the more pressing, for it seemed necessary to tie Germany to the West while the indispensable but elderly Adenauer was still guiding German policy. As the Assistant Secretary of State, Livingston Merchant, put it, "Adenauer's success in leading Germany back along [the] road of sanity and to integration in Western Europe is an historic opportunity to resolve the German question."[10]

For this reason American patience with French reluctance to approve the treaties began to wane. In the discussions of NSC 160/1, Eisenhower and Dulles resisted an effort by the Defense Department to set a deadline of January 1, 1954, as the cutoff date for support of the EDC, after which the United States would seek alternative methods of German rearmament. Both leaders remained convinced that "the advantages to the United States of [EDC's] adoption appear to justify the risks [of further delay]." Later in the year, when Eisenhower expressed his fear that the delay in adopting the EDC might lead the Russians "to take a long chance and make a really attractive offer to the Germans," Dulles responded that the Russians could not afford to make such an offer because "the situation was so unsettled in East Germany, Czechoslovakia, and Poland that the Russians could anticipate a general reaction if they allowed Germany to be unified." Although Dulles was confident about the Russians, he still sought to place more pressure on the French to take action. At a December press conference he predicted that the failure of the EDC would not only create "grave doubt whether continental Europe could be made a place of safety" but would also "compel an agonizing reappraisal of basic United States policy." Dulles repeated the phrase "agonizing reappraisal" in subsequent statements, publicly threatening that if the French Assembly rejected the EDC the United States might not remain committed to the defense of Europe.[11]

American diplomats of Dulles and McCloy's generation sincerely feared a resurgence of American isolationism. In 1953 they could point to a Congressional amendment to military assistance legislation which threatened to cut off aid if the EDC was not approved. The possibility of American isolationism, however, had lost some of its power to sway the Europeans, particularly the French. Eisenhower's victory, followed by the death of Senator Taft, meant that both major political parties shared a commitment to NATO. At the same time that Dulles was speaking of an "agonizing reappraisal" he was reassuring Adenauer that the United States recognized the importance of its forces in Europe and would maintain them "so long as it serves a really useful purpose." Eisenhower, who had reservations about Dulles's blunt public approach to the issue, thought that because of France's weakness and its concern about providing an adequate defense of Europe, "any threat by the United States to remove its forces from Europe would have absolutely no effect in securing ratification of EDC." He insisted that "we must never allow ourselves to forget that in stationing U.S. forces abroad we are defending ourselves and not merely the French. Our front line now runs east of the Rhine; our commitment in Europe boils down to doing whatever our national security interests dictate." Although Eisenhower speculated that "we could not keep United States ground forces indefinitely stationed all over the world," he had no intention of withdrawing any forces from Europe for the next two years, for "the European nations are not yet ready to take up the slack."[12]

Advances in military strategy and technology also diminished the American threat of a return to isolationism. When the decision to rearm Germany had been made, German soldiers had appeared to be the only solution to the insufficiency of American and allied forces in Western Europe. But by late 1953 the rapid development of comparatively cheap tactical nuclear weapons, along with President Eisenhower's determination to reduce defense expenditures and European resistance to the expense of the Lisbon conventional force goals, had led the Administration to adopt the policy that in case of war "the United States would consider nuclear weapons to be as available for use as other munitions." In October 1953 the Administration argued in NSC 162/2 that "the major deterrent to aggression against Western Europe is the manifest determination of the United States to use its atomic capability and massive retaliatory striking power if the area is attacked." In April 1954 Dulles told the Allies, "Without the availability for use of atomic weapons, the security of all NATO forces in Europe would be in grave jeopardy in the event of a surprise Soviet attack." Dulles added that "such weapons must now be treated as in fact having become 'conventional.'" Although the Administration did not acknowledge it, this American shift to a strategy of "massive retaliation" and a reliance on nuclear weapons served to devalue the military importance of German conventional forces. German participation in Western defense had become primarily a political issue, a way of binding Germany to the West and justifying the American presence in Europe to the American people.[13]

Although neither Eisenhower nor Dulles wanted talks with the Soviets until after the EDC treaty had been ratified, the French would not give the treaty serious consideration until the Western powers had met with the Russians again. The Berlin conference of January and February 1954 provided such an opportunity, but it only served to demonstrate the preeminent American commitment to the strategy of integrating Germany into the West. The Western Allies put forward the Eden Plan for German reunification, which called for free elections, the formation of an all-German government, and the negotiation of a peace treaty including a system of security guarantees to allay Soviet fears. Although willing to provide such guarantees, the Western powers insisted that the reunited German government should still have the right "to conclude . . . international agreements as it may wish." Dulles defended the plan as an alternative to the failed approach of the Versailles conference. Arguing that "history . . . teaches us that a stable peace cannot be achieved by some countries imposing upon other countries discriminatory restrictions," he contended that the only way to insure that a united Germany would be a peaceful Germany was to treat the German people as "equals in the family of nations." The best way to achieve this end was through the EDC, which would create a "common army so interlocked . . . that no single member of the community could in practice commit aggression." The EDC and the other plans for European integration would provide an outlet for "the great energy and vitality of the German people," a vitality which, "whether we like it or not . . . cannot be forcibly repressed for long." Dulles held that because the EDC was purely defensive it was actually in the interest of the Soviet Union. He urged the Soviets to recognize that "where a military establishment cannot act without the combined will of many countries, then only a clear defensive need can bring about the necessary concurrence of national wills." By contrast, Dulles insisted, the Soviet plan to reconstitute national forces in Germany was dangerous, for "if Germany had national forces strong enough to defend itself from external attack, it would be so strong that it would threaten all of Western Europe." (Why the Soviets would be particularly concerned about a possible German threat to Western Europe Dulles did not make clear.)[14]

Dulles's defense of German participation in the EDC on grounds of "equality" and his insistence on the "defensive" character of the EDC were not arguments likely to sway the Soviets. Indeed the Soviets exploited French uneasiness about the EDC by pointing out that a reunited Germany might elect not to remain in it, which would leave Germany without controls. Molotov, the Soviet Foreign Minister, offered the West little by way of compromise. He insisted that Germany could be reunited only within the terms of a general European security pact which would put an end to NATO and the EDC and lead to the withdrawal of American forces from Europe. (The Americans broke into laughter at this proposal.) He also took a tough line on one of the issues closest to Western hearts when he challenged the concept of "free elections." Treating the topic much more cautiously than the early Stalin notes had done, he reminded his Western adversaries of the way the Soviets had conducted elections in Eastern Europe. He denounced "fascistic" and "militaristic" organizations and insisted that "fascist degenerates" should not be allowed "to take power, even by parliamentary means, in a new all-German government." Because the Eden Plan did not insure against these forces, the Soviet Union could not accept it. The "Nazis came to power through parliamentary processes," and at that moment West Germany, whose elections the West held up as a model, was "riddled with Nazis, neo-Nazis, Revanchists and Hitler's ex-Generals."[15]

The Soviet proposals put forward by Molotov, while expressing an understandable distrust toward the Germans, reflected what one historian has called the "increasingly pallid and formulaic versions of the proposal for a unified, neutralized Germany" which the Soviets continued to offer until 1955. These proposals were the product of a large Soviet bureaucracy "that once [it has] started to do something . . . is apt to continue doing it until something makes it stop." Their growing rigidity may also indicate the Soviet preference for a divided Germany over a reunited Germany that could become part of the Western alliance. In January 1954 a Soviet diplomat told his British counterpart that if the West rejected Molotov's proposals the Soviets would prefer the division of Germany, "even if it meant West Germany in the EDC," to "a reunited Germany in the Atlantic *bloc*." As Khrushchev was to say to the French leader Guy Mollet a few years later, "I prefer 20 million Germans on my side rather than 70 million against us. Even if Germany were neutral, that would not be enough."[16]

The Western powers came out of the Berlin conference confident that there was no hope for settlement with the Russians. (Dulles was even convinced that the Soviet grip on Eastern Europe was weakening.) The Allies hoped to use what Eden called the "extreme rigidity of the Soviet attitude" to show that there was no alternative to Western action on the EDC-contractual treaties. Despite his "irritation" with the French, Eisenhower was willing to repeat America's "past assurances to France" to help "timid men overcome their own doubts." The United States also reassured those French leaders who supported the EDC, as well as the leaders of the other European countries, all of which (except Italy) had ratified the treaty, that the "US has not wavered in support of EDC and that they should not be misled by press reports that we are considering alternatives." In April 1954 the British strengthened their own guarantee to the EDC, including a pledge to place an armored division in the organization.[17]

The added guarantees still could not move the French government to act on the EDC agreement. Successive French governments had continued to postpone action and to seek additional guarantees, four-power talks, or new treaty provisions. At the heart of much of the French hesitation was a "deep pessimism," the often "unspoken . . . belief that in any community including France and Germany the latter would inevitably gain the upper hand because the Germans are more capable soldiers, organizers, business men and politicians." The increasing power of the Gaullists in the Assembly had led to the ouster of Robert Schuman from the Foreign Ministry early in 1953. With his departure the EDC had lost one of its major, if increasingly ineffective, supporters. The government of René Mayer had demanded new protocols in the treaty that would provide more freedom for French national forces within the Empire, as well as the freezing of voting rights in the EDC at a number equal to Germany's. The other five countries had gone along with most of the demands, but the French still had taken no action. Through most of 1953 they had also demanded four-power discussions before the treaties were submitted to the Assembly. And they had insisted, with American support, that the question of the Saar be settled before the treaty could be enacted.[18]

The issue that finally precipitated French rejection of the EDC was the war in Indochina. By early 1954 the United States had increased its assistance to the French in Indochina by almost $400 million, thereby funding almost 80 percent of the war effort. Despite American aid, the military situation continued to deteriorate. The fall of the military fortress at Dienbienphu in early May effectively ended the French campaign and brought to power in Paris the government of Pierre Mendès-France, which was committed to ending the war. The debacle in Indochina only heightened sensitivities in France about its status as a great power and increased the strong resentment already felt toward the United States. With the acceptance of partition in Vietnam in July 1954, Mendès-France turned his attention to obtaining some final action on the EDC. To obtain the approval of the more conservative deputies, he proposed a series of changes that effectively stripped it of its supranational features and removed most of the restrictions on French sovereignty. The United States vigorously opposed the "confused, chauvinistic, and destructive nature" of these French proposals and urged the other EDC countries to "stand firm against unrealistic concessions or destructive compromises." When the other five nations rejected the proposals, Mendès-France put the EDC before the Assembly, where it was defeated by a vote of 319 to 264, with 12 abstentions.[19]

Shortly before Mendès-France put the issue before the Assembly, Dulles had sought to convince him of the value of the EDC as against still another attempt to talk to the Soviet Union. Despite his own earlier emphasis on the role of nuclear weapons, Dulles claimed that the alternative of a "neutralized Germany" would "completely destroy NATO defense plans." Europe could not be defended without Germany, and such a proposal would "sacrifice the basis of Western security for German unity." In addition, he stressed that a neutral Germany was "illusory" and would "seriously menace European stability and security." It would also "destroy Adenauer," a result that the French could not possibly desire. These arguments, which did not sway Mendès-France, indicate how completely the policy of the United States was committed to the political goal of integrating the Federal Republic into the West, and how reluctant it was to give up that policy for any type of German reunification or neutrality, or even for an overall European settlement.[20]

The defeat of the EDC was a blow to America's European policy, but as the State Department put it in a postmortem, "We have lost a battle, not a war . . . " Indeed the demise of the EDC, rather than occasioning an "agonizing reappraisal," opened the way to settlement of the basic issues of the earlier treaty negotiations. Recognizing that the EDC had failed in part because it was seen as a "*US* project to force *premature* federation along *military* lines," Dulles wanted to avoid any idea that a new settlement would be "made in the USA." Stepping into the vacuum created by the U.S.-French impasse, British Foreign Secretary Anthony Eden proposed the expansion of the Brussels Pact treaty to include both Germany and Italy. At a conference held in London in late September 1954, the European powers accepted this substitute plan for German rearmament, with the British providing another guarantee that their forces would remain on the Continent for fifty years. Although the supranational aspects of the Brussels arrangement were minimal compared with those of the EDC, the organization could set the level of German forces and provide for some restrictions on armaments production. Chancellor Adenauer eased the way on the armaments problem by making the same voluntary declaration he had made during the EDC negotiations: that Germany would not manufacture atomic, biological, or chemical weapons, or produce long-range missiles, guided missiles, or warships of more than three thousand tons. The conference also recommended the direct admission of the Federal Republic to NATO, and the assignment of all German forces to NATO's integrated command. In return the Federal Republic agreed to renounce the use of force to obtain any territorial changes. The French, who had strongly resisted such a solution in 1951, were willing to concede the inevitable; Mendès-France, having defeated an idea that had originated in Paris, found himself isolated and too weak to oppose the strong sentiment of the other European states.[21]

The London conference also agreed to make substantial changes in the contractual arrangements with Germany. The United States pushed for a "sweeping and generous" revision of the agreements, primarily "for its psychological impact on the Germans." One analyst put it, "'Membership in the club' must be established without quibbling reservations." To assist Adenauer, who told the Western leaders that he needed a "concrete achievement" to take home from London, the three Western powers agreed to a "Declaration of Intent which instructed their High Commissioners to cease exercising certain powers" and to transfer them de facto to the German government. Within the contractuals themselves, the Allies agreed to important changes. Although retaining their reserved rights to questions relating to Berlin and the unification of Germany, they removed their right to station forces from the category of a reserved right to that of an agreed treaty right, and they strengthened the Federal Republic's right to consultation in the arrangements. The three Western powers also agreed to substantial revision of the "state of emergency" clause in Article V. Because of the significance, in both the Weimar and Nazi periods, of the state of emergency issue—one Nazi jurist had noted that "sovereignty lies in the power to declare an emergency"—the Germans had become increasingly anxious to restrict Allied powers. To accommodate these concerns the Allies first eliminated the specific listing of conditions which would lead to such a declaration and then agreed that their own rights in regard to the protection of their forces "shall lapse when the appropriate German authorities have obtained similar powers under German legislation enabling them to take effective action to protect the security of those forces, including the ability to deal with a serious disturbance of public security and order." (Ironically the German government would not be eager to enact its own state of emergency legislation, and when it did so in the late 1960s many Germans protested that it was a step in the direction of fascism and repression.) The Allies also eliminated the Binding Clause, which the Germans had come to see as an unnecessary limit "on the Federal Republic's treaty making powers." As for the remainder of the treaty, the Allies went through it "paragraph by paragraph," as Dulles said, eliminating what had become "obsolete and unacceptable" to the Germans.[22]

In general the revised treaties reflected the substantial growth of confidence in the stability of the Federal Republic that had occurred between 1952 and 1954 as a result of Adenauer's leadership and his determination to tie his nation to the West. As Dulles told the U.S. Cabinet in October 1954, "the greatest single contribution in terms of statesmanship" at the London conference was made by Chancellor Adenauer, who as a "true European . . . made real sacrifices to European principles." But there were still limits to the American faith in Germany. Dulles viewed the London conference as having salvaged "much of the value of EDC," and General Gruenther affirmed that Germany's integration into NATO would in fact "make it impossible for any single member nation to use its armed forces in Europe for nationalistic adventures." NATO's control effectively abolished the danger "of a revived German General Staff going off on its own." Despite the revision of the emergency clause, the thousands of Allied soldiers stationed in the Federal Republic constituted a de facto limit on German sovereignty—a freely chosen limit, but one that German leaders could not forget.[23]

Dulles predicted that "the Soviets would do all they could to destroy the London program, bringing pressure to bear both on Germany and on France." And indeed, after a NATO meeting in Paris had confirmed the London agreements, the Soviets proposed a four-power conference to consider the "question of creating a system of collective security in Europe." At the Moscow conference in December they warned that the NATO allies' ratification of the agreements "will be an act aimed against the maintenance of peace, and aimed at the preparation of a new war in Europe." The Soviets then expressed a willingness to negotiate German reunification on the basis of the Eden Plan, but only if German rearmament was excluded. In January 1955 they ended their state of war with Germany, stressing in the declaration that the policy of "remilitarizing . . . Western Germany and integrating her into aggressive military alignments . . . made it impossible to reach the necessary agreement on restoring the unity of Germany along peaceful and democratic lines and to conclude a peace treaty with Germany." Finally they held out to the Germans the promise of neutrality and reunification, strengthening that appeal by showing a willingness to consider such a status for Austria.[24]

The Soviet initiatives worried the Americans, who saw how eager the French and Adenauer's German opposition were to delay the ratification of the agreements. The State Department feared that "if the urgency of the Western defense policy is placed in doubt, Adenauer may lose a critical race for time to obtain German rearmament and consolidate the Federal Republic's relations with the West before a loosening of the European situation sets in." If these agreements failed, the Germans might revert to their seesaw policy and attempt to play off the Soviet Union against the West. The worst danger was the possibility of another Rapallo, for any German-Soviet combination could tip the balance of power decisively against the West. When the French Assembly voted against one section of the agreements, Eisenhower's response was immediate: "Those damn French! What do they think they're trying to do? This could really upset the apple cart in Europe." While avoiding an explicit threat to rearm the Germans unilaterally, Eisenhower and Dulles made it clear that they regarded the French action with the "utmost seriousness" and that they did not believe this represented "the final French decision in this matter." The strong American stand, coupled with an even stronger British threat to rearm the Germans without France, led the French Assembly to reverse itself and approve the agreements.[25]

Despite the Soviet offers the Western powers held firm, and the Federal Republic regained its sovereignty and joined NATO on May

8, 1955, ten years after its unconditional surrender at the end of World War II. German entry into NATO did not end discussion of the German problem, which figured prominently at the Geneva conference later that summer. But the admission of Germany into NATO did symbolize the success of the integration strategy, which Americans believed offered the best hope for reaching a stable peace in Europe. This new "organization of Europe" held the promise of avoiding the mistakes of the 1920s by anchoring most of Germany in the West and encouraging a pro-Western and democratic spirit among German political leaders and other elites. Only in this way could German nationalism be controlled and channeled into constructive outlets. When the Soviets responded to the German entry into NATO by agreeing to Austrian neutrality, Dulles's reaction captured the mixed motives of the Allies in making Germany a "member of the club." After reminding people of the great difference between the small Austria of seven million people and a Germany of seventy million, Dulles pointed out that Austria's neutrality was an armed neutrality with no limit on the size of its army. He added, "I do not think that the German people or the Soviet people or the Western European people want to see applied to Germany the concept of it being an independent state with an unlimited army." Germany was in the club largely because it would have been too dangerous for it to be outside.[26]

Conclusions:
European Unity,
Dual Containment,
and the American "Empire"

The Federal Republic's entry into NATO in May 1955 ended the initial period of consolidation and organization of the Western alliance. Although the preceding six years had seen many problems, false starts, and failed initiatives, the American government had followed a remarkably consistent policy in its attempt to avoid the "mistakes" of the interwar era and ensure a stable, democratic, and prosperous Germany. By pursuing the strategy of "integrating" the Federal Republic into the West, the United States had excluded a possible—though not likely—settlement with the Soviet Union, but it had succeeded in redressing the balance of power on the European Continent.

During this phase of the Cold War the problem of Germany was the central issue. Although the Korean War had a decisive impact on policy by accelerating the pace of developments and "militarizing" the competition with the Soviet Union, American decision makers kept their focus on the heart of Europe. Nowhere did American and Soviet interests clash more directly than in Germany, which was, as McCloy once termed it, the "cockpit" of American policy. Allied leaders took note of the failures of the interwar era to learn how not to proceed. For them, 1945 did not mark a great caesura. For the Allied High Commissioners, and for the Chancellor who sat facing them, the interwar era was still a searing personal experience filled with tragic lost opportunities. In their thinking, words such as Rapallo, Gleichberechtigung, Schaukelpolitik, and Diktat were powerfully associated with the failure to preserve the peace after World War I. Their sense of urgency came from the fear that soon a revival of German nationalism would preclude the cooperative solutions and international arrangements essential to a constructive and stable peace.

In trying to avoid the mistakes of the past, both Allied and German leaders thought in terms of the "Weimar analogy," which taught a different lesson from its more famous Munich counterpart. If the lesson of Munich was that the West could not appease aggressive totalitarian states, the lesson of Weimar was that the West must reward peaceful democracies. According to this view of the 1920s and 1930s, the Western powers had first imposed an unrealistically harsh peace on Germany, with heavy reparations and loss of territory, and had then denied concessions to the faltering governments of Weimar. Later they had watched as Hitler and the Nazis extorted similar concessions and enjoyed the prestige gained at home by these foreign policy successes. To avoid repeating this tragedy, the Allies, especially the Americans, decided to use whatever concessions they could grant to Germany to strengthen its pro-Western elites, building up their prestige in the eyes of their own people and helping them obtain a political legitimacy which the Weimar government had lacked. One of the first steps in that policy was the Petersberg Agreement, which ended the policy of dismantling. But the two dangers of such an "appeasement" policy were clear—resistance from France and other European powers which feared German strength, and a nationalist backlash in Germany, best captured by Schumacher's denunciation of Adenauer as the "Chancellor of the Allies." Yet the Americans, led by McCloy, argued confidently that if German democracy experienced "success,"—by which they meant "a rising standard of living, coupled with a reasonable degree of economic security . . . a respected voice in international affairs," and "military security"—Germany would become a reliable part of the West.[1]

Confidence in the importance of economic growth and the universal applicability of democratic government, which was deeply rooted in American political culture, strongly affected American perspectives on European developments. Even during the 1920s Americans believed that "a prosperous Germany would be a peaceful and republican Germany," and the experience of the New Deal and Second World War only reinforced the conviction that the "politics of productivity" offered one solution to the problem of aggressive German nationalism. With the Cold War forcing a mobilization of energy against the Soviet Union, restrictions against Germany made even less sense. In contrast to the interwar era, when only private American institutions had helped Weimar, American leaders hoped that their government would provide Bonn with the strength to sustain itself against the anti-democratic forces that had undermined Weimar.[2]

In many respects, however, this comparison between Bonn and Weimar was misleading, for the Western powers were in a stronger position than they realized. Germany's defeat in 1918 had not been so total or overwhelming as it was in 1945. In 1918 the German government had continued to exist, Allied troops had occupied only the left bank of the Rhine, the country was not divided, and the territorial losses were not so extensive. World War I had not been fought on German soil, but World War II with its aerial bombing had directly affected German civilians. In addition the suffering of the war and occupation did much to still the passions of nationalism and militarism. The severing of the agricultural lands in the East, and the Soviet control of Eastern Germany destroyed the Junker class, whose authoritarian political and social power had weakened the Weimar Republic. The Federal Republic was a far more homogeneous national entity than Weimar had been, and the chances for a stable democratic government to emerge were significantly greater.[3]

Another problem that arose from comparing Bonn with Weimar was that it left unresolved the question of how the United States could reconcile the strengthening of Germany with other American goals, such as Franco-German reconciliation and the containment of the Soviet Union. The answer, or "grand objective," was European integration and unity, a "gradual process that had to begin with limited but realizable plans for a functional integration of economic and defense systems." McCloy made it clear to Europeans that American support would be decisively affected by "whether or not Europe is going to be able to establish a community here in which interests are pooled, in which common approaches to the European problems are attempted, and in short . . . whether a vigorous European community as such is . . . established."[4]

Through the Marshall Plan the United States hoped to encourage this process, pushing for an integrated Western European economy similar to the large internal market of the United States. As historian Michael Hogan has noted, such an integrated market "promised the benefits that inhered in economies of scale, with the ultimate result being a prosperous and stable European community secure against the dangers of Communist subversion and able to join the United States in a multilateral system of world trade." By 1950, however, it was obvious that abolishing tariffs and freeing up European trade would not overcome the deeply rooted Franco-German enmity. Consequently such American leaders as Acheson and McCloy made it clear that they looked to the French to take the initiative while there was still time. The genius of both Jean Monnet and Robert Schuman lay in recognizing this opportunity and abandoning the bankrupt policy of restricting Germany's recovery in favor of the "European" initiatives of the Coal and Steel Community and the European Army. Though the two initiatives had different results, these French statesmen—with the help of their strategically placed American counterparts—succeeded for a crucial period in channeling American diplomatic power in directions that were more congenial to French interests, and also, in retrospect, to long-term American interests. The revival of Germany's economic strength and of its military power took place within constraints that prevented the fragmentation of the West and encouraged the slow process of Franco-German reconciliation. If one task of diplomacy is to make room—or buy time—for peaceful historical change, the American embrace of the goal of a united Europe fulfilled that function.[5]

American interest in a more united Europe also illuminates the growing importance of Konrad Adenauer. The major reason for his success was his skillful political leadership, which challenged his countrymen's assumption that leaders could be taken seriously only when they wore uniforms. It is often overlooked that Adenauer's government got off to a very shaky start. During his first year in office his "narrow" partisanship and "uninspiring" leadership led Americans such as McCloy to consider the alternative of a "grand coalition" between the CDU and the SPD. Because McCloy did not initially consider Adenauer a leader of vision or stature, the Chancellor's ability to win McCloy's support is significant. He used the hope for European unity to become, in American eyes, the indispensable political leader of Germany. He was able to distinguish between those issues on which he would have to make concessions, such as the Schuman Plan and the contractual negotiations, and those, such as civil service reform, where the Americans would give way. He himself believed in such goals as Franco-German reconciliation, European unity, and Wiedergutmachung, but the American commitment to them reinforced his

convictions and strengthened him against powerful domestic opponents on the left and right. By the end of McCloy's term as High
Commissioner, critics joked that "Adenauer is the real McCloy." (This
was at least a more desirable description than "Chancellor of the
Allies.") In this case McCloy's self-effacement was a virtue, strengthening both the concept of democratic government and Adenauer's
stature with his own people.

European integration was not the only American approach to the
German problem. American leaders knew that the "old Germany" that
had enthusiastically supported the Nazis had not disappeared in 1945.
The powerful resistance of the Ruhr industrialists to the Schuman
Plan illustrated the problems a German government would have faced
in the absence of American power. McCloy's proposal to guarantee
Germany's "liberal democratic order," as well as the numerous restrictions contained in the contractual agreements, reflect this continuing
Allied distrust. The United States pursued a "dual containment" policy
in Europe, designed to keep both the Soviet Union and Germany
from dominating the Continent. Containing Germany was not simply
a task added to the job of containing the Soviet Union. The two
policies, which were inextricably linked, were always in a delicate
balance; the United States could not contain the Soviet Union in
Europe without German strength, and it could not maintain its hold
over the Federal Republic without the Soviet threat. When the balance
between these policies was dramatically upset, as in the rush toward
rearmament after the outbreak of the Korean War, there was an alliance
crisis. The adoption of the EDC, which temporarily restored this
balance, shows how strongly the concerns about German power influenced American leaders.[6]

Although they chafed under some aspects of the occupation, the
majority of the German people did not want the Americans to leave,
seeing their presence as the central guarantee against Russian occupation. The political elite, while desiring more autonomy, also insisted
upon this strong American presence. They saw it as the sine qua non
of the Federal Republic's existence, providing protection against both
the Soviet threat and a resurgence of extremism at home. (Although
Adenauer expressed his mistrust of his own people more openly than
other German politicians, his sentiments were widely shared.) As Geir
Lundestad has suggested in the phrase "Empire by Invitation" and
Charles Maier in the term "consensual American hegemony," the

American expansion in postwar Europe met with approval from both European elites and the European public, and probably nowhere more strongly than in Germany. (Indeed "invitation" is far too weak a word to describe the German demand for an American presence and the fears created by whispers of its possible withdrawal.)[7]

Support for European integration and a continuing mistrust of the Germans also help explain the attitude of the United States toward the prospect of German reunification. Recent accounts, written largely by younger German historians, have exaggerated the degree to which the Western nations opposed German reunification and prevented negotiations that might have produced a neutral, reunited Germany. American leaders believed that in the long run they could not stand against German unity if the Germans wanted it, and they feared that the Soviet Union would make a genuine offer encompassing both free elections and a security guarantee. But the United States did see a genuine threat to European peace in allowing the re-creation of a neutral Germany able to maneuver between East and West. Immediately after World War II, when the German population looked back with longing to the power and economic success of the Nazi regime, it would have been the height of irresponsibility for an American leader to trust such an "independent" Germany.[8]

American diplomats such as McCloy were under no illusions that Adenauer's choice of Westintegration was popular; they also realized that German leaders were reluctant to make a choice in favor of the West that would expose them to nationalist demagoguery. The Americans, however, made it clear that the Germans did not have an unlimited amount of time to choose, if they wanted the United States to commit itself to the defense of the Federal Republic. Adenauer could conceal this point by arguing that the West must negotiate from a position of strength, but he recognized the commitment to the West that he was making. And although most Germans lacked enthusiasm for Adenauer's Western policy, the Soviet Union's harsh rule over Eastern Europe offered little attraction. They might have approved the contents of the Stalin Note, but they distrusted its author.

Germany's fear of the Soviet Union, joined with its dependence on the United States for security, laid the foundation for the "special relationship" between America and the Federal Republic. In recent years Chancellor Helmut Kohl has spoken of the "existential" importance of this relationship, and it is impossible to conceive of the Federal

Republic's development, or even existence, without the firm U.S. commitment. Besides promoting the idea of a united Europe, Americans cultivated direct bilateral ties with West Germany. Whether in discussions during the contractual negotiations or in the use of the Marshall Plan, this bilateral relationship was as important as the dealings among all four Western countries. The High Commissioner promoted educational exchanges with the United States and supported liberal newspapers and youth groups as well as the construction of new universities in Germany. American power and wealth, along with its pervasive popular culture, had a profound impact on West Germany, making it the most "Americanized" country in Western Europe. German leaders reaped great advantages in encouraging this special relationship and playing the role of "most loyal ally." The Chancellor's political instincts did not fail him when he featured his trip to America in his campaign for reelection.[9]

The Americans' drive for European integration, accompanied by their cultivation of a special relationship with Bonn, created not only tension but a paradox. Progress on European integration came because of American willingness to "encourage" the Germans to accept French proposals. The United States served as Western Europe's "pacifier," enabling it to develop cooperative relationships secure from either Russian or German domination. Paradoxically, while McCloy, Eisenhower, and other American leaders hoped that a united Europe would lighten U.S. commitments and burdens—and pushed such proposals as the EDC for this reason—the Europeans, and especially the French, resented America's domination. Although it is misleading to argue, as one recent study does, that Washington's push for the EDC "destroyed the European federation movement," American leaders walked a tightrope between their hope for European unity, with a consequent reduction in U.S. involvement, and the continuing divisions and national ambitions which drew America ever more deeply into the politics of Western Europe.[10]

American leaders sought, as John Gaddis has pointed out, to "reconstitute an *independent* center of power on the continent" and to lessen their commitment to Europe, but they still derived satisfaction from their own nation's leadership of the Western alliance. The successful organization of Europe during this period made the need to preserve that alliance one of the unifying convictions of all the Cold War elites. This generation of American diplomats, the Wise Men, possessed extraordinary opportunities for leadership. In an American government of divided powers, which was itself in a period of transition, they helped give foreign policy a degree of continuity and coherence it had rarely obtained. They worked together in surprising harmony, sharing similar social values, ideologies, historical experiences, and most important, the same perspective on the role of America in the world and the need to use American power to create a more stable international order. As McCloy jotted in his diary in 1945, the United States could "influence [the world] in a way no other [nation] can . . . if we have the vigor and farsightedness to see our place in the world."[11]

John Jay McCloy, whose name evokes the Founding Father who negotiated a landmark treaty of the early American Republic, is one of the best representatives of the American foreign policy elite of this period. He had, as historian Alan Brinkley noted, "a firm, unwavering confidence in the righteousness and importance of his own and his country's mission." As a self-made man he radiated optimism about the opportunities America offered for advancement. As a consensus-builder he expressed the most widely shared beliefs of this elite, without the intellectual subtlety of Kennan, the ponderous moralism of Dulles, or the withering logic of Acheson. Pragmatic and primarily interested in results, McCloy could act with expediency; he was willing to employ dubious means to achieve virtuous goals. The survival of the American state and its "national security" was the touchstone of his actions, to which the Constitution and civil liberties could be subordinated. His belief in a "foreign policy tradition," his awareness of the "direct current running from Root through Stimson to me," gave him a long-term perspective on the American people's understanding of foreign policy and the dimensions of the German problem. During the rearmament crisis he recognized that Americans would never support a commitment of men and resources to Germany unless Germany itself participated in European defense. At the same time he held tenaciously to the view that the central question was not military—the number of German divisions—but political—the firm linkage of Germany to the Western alliance.[12]

Although McCloy was a representative member of the American foreign policy elite, he was also typical of what Charles Maier calls "a new transnational political elite," which had developed in the new world of air transport and instant communications and was nurtured by America's rise to global preeminence. To a large extent the trans-national character of this elite had its origins in the economic ties established between the United States and Europe during the interwar period. World War II produced a generation of leaders whose relationships and perspectives cut across national lines. Assuming that Hitler's success owed as much to the weakness and disunity of the democratic states as to any special German military prowess, they fought the natural tendency of their countries to slip back into nationalist, protectionist, and parochial ways of thinking and acting. The Second World War had convinced them, as McCloy expressed it, that isolation—political, military, or even spiritual—was not possible in the second half of the twentieth century.[13]

This "international political class" should not be confused with the controlling capitalists of vintage Marxism or the sinister conspirators of the Birch Society. It was hardly all-powerful—witness the failure of the EDC—but its existence and activities help explain some of the choices American leaders made during this period. The McCloy-Monnet relationship is a prime example of a transnational leadership coalition that was influential in creating the Schuman Plan and the EDC. McCloy's network of associations and friendships paid little heed to nationality, entrenched bureaucracies, or proper governmental channels. Members of his and Ambassador David Bruce's staff, men like Robert Bowie and William Tomlinson, worked as closely with Monnet and their French counterparts as they did with other Americans. Monnet operated in a similar manner outside the traditional channels of the French government. Influenced by the American example, he strove to create powerful transnational organizations, such as the Coal and Steel Community and NATO, which would "institutionalize" the lessons of cooperation. The Western "club," as American and British leaders often referred to it, drew into its fold both important business and labor representatives and moderate conservative and moderate socialist politicians. Disdaining ideology and believing that "economic growth made all distributional conflicts obsolete," this new transnational political elite worked to overcome the divisions of the interwar era and lay the foundation for a lasting and stable peace.[14]

Exclusive of the Soviet threat, the greatest challenge faced by the Western club was, as Acheson put it in May 1950, the "re-introduction of Germany into community life." He believed that "no harder task" had ever been undertaken by a group of nations, but that the Germans were, "for better or worse," a part of the West. British diplomats expressed the same ambivalence when they spoke of the problem of seeing Germany, as "a full member of the club," "smoking a large cigar in front of the fire in the smoking room." While admiring Germany's extraordinary organizational and technical achievements, the Western nations feared its political unpredictability, racism, and nationalist extremism. Yet the Soviet threat—and any hope for a lasting peace—compelled Germany's acceptance by the West, the "pre-eminent Western diplomatic task" of the time.[15]

Frequently underestimating the degree of fear and revulsion they inspired, West German leaders themselves sought to join the Western club. In a revealing memorandum of January 1950 which analyzed Germany's relations with the United States, an aide urged Chancellor Adenauer to follow policies that would gain the support of "the militant interventionist elements" that had been Germany's sworn enemies, and to pull away from the isolationist elements that had formerly been its allies. Indeed the Chancellor's policies, from his plea for reconciliation with France to his offer of reparations to Israel, were consciously designed to make Germany a more acceptable member of the Western club, especially in the eyes of the country which set the rules for membership, the United States. Adenauer encouraged German leaders to cultivate American leaders, even after some of them, including McCloy, had returned to private life.[16]

For reasons that went well beyond Adenauer's calculated efforts, Germany became both a member of the club and an extraordinary symbol to American diplomats. Acheson's comment that "we could do more with the Germans" captured the sentiment that the Federal Republic was America's "ward" or "protegé" within the Western alliance. McCloy himself, who often referred jokingly to "his" Federal Republic, remained active in U.S.-German relations, playing an important role in the diplomacy between the two countries. He was a frequent unofficial emissary to Bonn, and he conducted the "Offset negotiations" of the 1960s which readjusted the costs of the American presence in the Federal Republic. McCloy also helped found such private organizations as the American Council on Germany, and his name became synonymous with close American-German ties. Till the end of his life he remained a fervent believer in the alliance he had shaped; the German tributes at his memorial service reflected the Federal Republic's appreciation of his important role. McCloy was a part of what Fritz Stern described as the "liberal Establishment," which "took a strong, almost proprietary, interest in the Alliance and most especially, German-American friendship."[17]

Whatever its characteristics elsewhere in the world—and it varied extraordinarily from region to region—the American "Empire" in Germany was less imperial than federal in character, an extension of the American political system rather than the rule of a conquered province. The Federal Republic in its early years of existence was effectively a part of the American political, economic, and military system, more like a state such as California or Illinois than an independent sovereign nation or a colony or protectorate. American soldiers guarded Germany's borders, Marshall Plan funds bolstered its economy, and a treaty guaranteed its democratic form of government. Though he may have enjoyed the allusion to ancient Rome, McCloy saw himself less as a "proconsul" than as an "American representative abroad." Acting rather like a state governor seeking reelection, he immersed himself in the debates and discussions of German life, talked constantly to German opinion leaders, and paid close attention to German public opinion. He later commented "that an evening with farmer or labor groups in Germany, with editors and publishers, with university men and women, with heads of women's or youth organizations was far more useful and interesting than attendance at any diplomatic reception."[18]

To American leaders of the Cold War generation the "economic miracle" and the success of democratic government in Germany vindicated their policies many times over. The divided city of Berlin, with its open window on the ideological chasm between the two blocs, symbolized the Cold War. The gratitude of Berliners for American assistance and their show of support for the West gave American leaders moral reinforcement and psychological reassurance in their struggle with the Soviet Union. As McCloy put it, in Berlin one could "feel" the "threat from the East," but "our common struggle for freedom" made the city "a light in the darkness." Kennedy's "Ich bin ein Berliner" speech captured this intense identification which American leaders had with the new Germany, whose liberal democracy was one of the crucial pillars of the postwar international order.[19]

There were dangers in placing Germany at the center of American policy. The view that the Federal Republic was attached to the United States was, as Ernest May has recently noted, an American perspective;

German leaders "continued to look upon the United States as a separate foreign power [which] acted on its own conception of its own distinguishable national interests." This difference in view contributed to disappointments and disillusionment, especially on such issues as reunification and the recognition of the East German regime. The building of the Berlin Wall and the American pursuit of détente after the Cuban missile crisis led to a reassessment of the relationship and a loosening of ties. German pursuit of Ostpolitik worried American leaders such as Henry Kissinger, who continued to distrust German nationalism. The Vietnam war disillusioned a generation of Germans; and to American leaders, increasing German independence threatened the alliance's foundations.[20]

Nevertheless, if one considers the fears expressed in 1949—George Kennan believed that the United States had "engendered German nationalism" and made "every mistake of Versailles," and Walter Lippmann was afraid that "everything seems to be developing in Germany, as one might have feared in one's more pessimistic moments"—the American achievement remains impressive. Although it was not the only factor in the equation, American policy gave Europe and Germany a period of peace, prosperity, and political stability. Under the American security umbrella the Federal Republic became a reliable part of the Western alliance. Although a politically united Western Europe has not yet been achieved, the Monnet dream of a single mass market is to be realized in 1992. Recent events in Eastern Europe—the crumbling of Soviet control and the formation of new democracies—seem to have confirmed Monnet's view that a united Europe would exercise a powerful, and peaceful, influence on the East. Economic prosperity has not only pacified German nationalism, but it has allowed the Federal Republic to integrate its millions of refugees from the "lost" territories and pay reparations to Israel. A postwar generation of Germans, who have grown up with democratic government in an open society, cannot imagine returning to dictatorship. The Federal Republic's political development, led by Adenauer, Willy Brandt, and Helmut Schmidt, is a remarkable success story. Even after the crumbling of the Berlin Wall and the drive toward reunification (and in mid-1990 reunification seems inevitable), Franco-German reconciliation, the dream of Adenauer and Schuman, remains a fundamental reality of Western Europe. McCloy was rightly proud to note, "We made unthinkable another European civil war. We ended one of history's longest threats to peace." This achievement was one that many ordinary Americans could cherish. After the war a reporter for *Yank* magazine discovered this inscription on the wall of the fortress of Verdun:

Austin White—Chicago, Ill.—1918
Austin White—Chicago, Ill.—1945
This is the last time I want to write my name here.[21]

A price had to be paid for these achievements. It was paid mainly by East Europeans and East Germans. Alliance consolidation within the West brought with it a deepening of the division of Germany and Europe. Although with Stalin and his immediate successors the chances for a four-power settlement were always slim, Western policy toward the Soviet Union grew increasingly rigid as the problems of cementing the Western alliance made American leaders reluctant to negotiate. The focus on Germany sometimes blinded American leaders to legitimate Soviet security concerns, as when Dulles argued that the Soviets should prefer the EDC to a separate German national army. Increasingly strident American rhetoric, proclaiming a liberation of Eastern Europe and a "roll back" of Soviet influence, raised both tensions and hopes in Europe, but had tragic consequences in East Germany in 1953 and Hungary in 1956.[22]

Within the alliance American support for Germany's rehabilitation and the EDC contributed to the deterioration in Franco-American relations which began during these years and would culminate in de Gaulle's departure from NATO in the 1960s. Ironically the development of NATO into a genuine military alliance strong enough to contain the Germans helped make French acceptance of the EDC unnecessary. Nevertheless, the priority that Americans attached to the EDC made them increasingly willing to placate French demands for assistance in Indochina. Although the United States would probably have become involved in Indochina in any event, its role in Vietnam grew substantially as it attempted to reassure the French in Europe.[23]

The Vietnam tragedy also underscores the dark side of the Wise Men's achievement. In the mid-1950s C. Wright Mills, the Columbia University sociologist, referred to the "power elite" as "crackpot realists" who had "constructed a paranoid reality all their own." The success of postwar American foreign policy bred an arrogance about America's capacity to lead other nations. This "Eurocentric" orientation and fixation on the Communist threat frequently distorted Americans' understanding of the changes and conflicts sweeping non-Western parts of the world. One sign of this arrogance was Lyndon Johnson's desire to make McCloy Ambassador to South Vietnam because he was America's "greatest proconsul" and the United States should be able to handle South Vietnam as it had Germany and Japan. Although Mills had little understanding of the problems of foreign policy, his attack on the equating of national security with global interventionism was prescient.[24]

Most significantly the intensification of the Cold War during this period, and the belief that Germany's allegiance had to be secured quickly, led to a deplorable series of compromises with the legacies of Nazism. Confrontation with the Soviet Union would inevitably have brought some compromise, since it appeared to justify Hitler's anti-Communist foreign policy. Expediency guided American leaders immediately after the war, as shown by their willingness to exploit German rocket scientists and intelligence organizations, but these actions were then outweighed by the Nuremberg trials and the prosecution of major war criminals. By 1951, however, the Americans had abandoned their search for justice against the Nazis. McCloy's leniency in the Landsberg cases, whatever the specific circumstances of the defendants, led Germans to believe, as one industrialist put it, that "now that they have Korea on their hands, the Americans are a lot more friendly." Eisenhower's statement "Let bygones be bygones" further underlined the extent to which anti-Soviet fervor distorted American judgment about dealing with Germany's past. Although the United States could not force the Germans to come to a "reckoning with the past," American actions did contribute to Germany's national amnesia about Nazi war crimes and criminals. For the United Sates, these compromises with the legacies of Nazism tarnished the moral purpose and ideals of World War II.[25]

Notwithstanding its mistakes, failures, and costs, American policy toward Germany during these years still represents one of the most successful endeavors in the history of U.S. diplomacy. Despite a wide variety of compromises—political, economic, and moral—the United States helped give Europe a generation of peace and a new and more favorable environment in which to confront the German question. Not long after leaving his position as High Commissioner, McCloy closed a series of lectures at Harvard University with this thought: "It is a lesson of American history that when we meet our responsibilities with minds open to new ideas and concepts, with determination, and with firm adherence to our traditions of tolerance and freedom, no challenge is too great for us." His words capture both the sense of triumph and the arrogance of achievement which his generation of American leaders experienced, believing as they did that America's power to shape world events was unlimited. But they also reflect the purpose and idealism, the certainty about progress and the improvement of the human condition, that infused men like McCloy.[26]

Abbreviations

Selected Bibliography

Notes

Index

Abbreviations

BA	Bundesarchiv
BA = MA	Bundesmilitärarchiv
DBPO	*Documents on British Policy Overseas*
FRUS	*Foreign Relations of the United States*
GPO	Government Printing Office
HICOG	The American High Commission in Germany
HMSO	Her Majesty's Stationery Office
MGFA	Militärgeschichtliches Forschungsamt
NARS	National Archives and Records Service
NARS-DB	National Archives and Records Service, Diplomatic Branch
NARS-MMB	National Archives and Records Service, Modern Military Branch
NL	Nachlass (Papers)
OED	Office of the Executive Director (HICOG)
PA-AA	Politisches Archiv des Auswärtiges Amts
PRO	Public Record Office
PSF	President's Secretary's Files
RAS-OPA	Reactions Analysis Staff, Office of Public Affairs
RG	Record Group
SPD	Social Democratic Party of Germany
StBKA	Stiftung Bundeskanzler-Adenauer-Haus
TSGR	Top Secret General Records

Selected Bibliography

United States

National Archives, Washington, D.C.

Record Group 43. Records of World War II Conferences and Records of the
Allied Control Commission
Record Group 59. Records of the Department of State
Decimal Files
Lot Files
Records of Charles Bohlen, 1942–1952
Records of the Office of the Executive Secretariat
Records of the Policy Planning Staff
Records of the Research and Analysis Branch and the
Bureau of Intelligence and Research
Record Group 107. Records of the Assistant Secretary of War
Record Group 218. Records of the Joint Chiefs of Staff
Record Group 286. Records of the Agency for International Development,
Federal Records Center, Suitland, Md.
Record Group 319. Records of the Army Staff
Record Group 330. Records of the Secretary of Defense
Record Group 466. Records of the High Commission, McCloy Papers, Federal
Records Center, Suitland, Md.

Collections of Personal Papers

Dean Acheson Papers. Harry S. Truman Library, Independence, Mo.
Dean Acheson Papers. Sterling Library, Yale University, New Haven, Conn.

Joseph and Stewart Alsop Papers. Manuscript Division, Library of Congress, Washington, D.C.

Eben Ayers Papers. Harry S. Truman Library, Independence, Mo.

David Bruce Papers. Virginia Historical Society, Richmond, Va.

William L. Clayton Papers. Harry S. Truman Library, Independence, Mo.

Clark M. Clifford Papers. Harry S. Truman Library, Independence, Mo.

John Foster Dulles Papers. Dwight D. Eisenhower Library, Abilene, Kans.

Dwight D. Eisenhower Papers. Dwight D. Eisenhower Library, Abilene, Kans.

George M. Elsey Papers. Harry S. Truman Library, Independence, Mo.

Felix Frankfurter Papers. Manuscript Division, Library of Congress, Washington, D.C.

Robert Garner Papers. Harry S. Truman Library, Independence, Mo.

Averell Harriman Papers. Manuscript Division, Library of Congress, Washington, D.C. (These were examined when they were still in Governor Harriman's possession.)

Paul Hoffmann Papers. Harry S. Truman Library, Independence, Mo.

Harry L. Hopkins Papers. Franklin D. Roosevelt Library, Hyde Park, N.Y.

Harold L. Ickes Papers and Manuscript Diary. Manuscript Division, Library of Congress, Washington, D.C.

Walter Lippmann Papers. Sterling Library, Yale University, New Haven, Conn.

John J. McCloy Papers. Amherst College Archives, Amherst, Mass. (These papers were examined when they were at the Council on Foreign Relations in New York.)

Eugene Meyer Papers. Manuscript Division, Library of Congress, Washington, D.C.

Henry Morgenthau Papers. Franklin D. Roosevelt Library, Hyde Park, N.Y.

Joseph Panuch Papers. Harry S. Truman Library, Independence, Mo.

Robert Patterson Papers. Manuscript Division, Library of Congress, Washington, D.C.

James Pollock Papers. University of Michigan, Ann Arbor, Mich.

Harry Price Papers. Harry S. Truman Library, Independence, Mo.

Eleanor Roosevelt Papers. Franklin D. Roosevelt Library, Hyde Park, N.Y.

John Snyder Papers. Harry S. Truman Library, Independence, Mo.

Henry L. Stimson Papers. Sterling Library, Yale University, New Haven, Conn.

Shepard Stone Papers. Privately held.

Maxwell D. Taylor Papers. National War College, Washington, D.C.

Charles Thayer Papers. Harry S. Truman Library, Independence, Mo.

Harry S. Truman Papers. Harry S. Truman Library, Independence, Mo.

James Warburg Papers. John F. Kennedy Library, Boston, Mass.

James Webb Papers. Harry S. Truman Library, Independence, Mo.

Oral Histories and Personal Interviews

Theodore Achilles (Truman Library)

Lucius Battle (Truman Library and personal interview)

Robert Bowie (Personal interview)
David Bruce (Truman Library)
Benjamin Buttenwieser (Columbia University and personal interview)
Henry Byroade (Personal interview)
Emilio Collado (Truman Library)
Donald Cook (Personal interview)
Eli W. Debevoise (Personal interview)
Benjamin Ferencz (Telephone interview)
Roswell Gilpatric (Personal interview)
Lincoln Gordon (Truman Library and personal interview)
W. Averell Harriman (Personal interview)
Perry Laukhuff (Truman Library)
Robert Lovett (Truman Library)
Ellen Z. McCloy (Personal interview)
John J. McCloy (Personal interview)
John J. McCloy II (Personal interview)
H. Freeman Matthews (Truman Library)
Drew Middleton (Personal interview)
Maurice Moore (Personal interview)
Jack Raymond (Personal interview)
Jacques J. Reinstein (Personal interview)
Benjamin Shute (Telephone interview)
Joseph Slater (Personal interview)
Shepard Stone (Personal interview)
Maxwell Taylor (Personal interview)
Telford Taylor (Personal interview)
John S. Zinsser (Personal interview)

Published Documents
(all published in Washington, D.C., unless otherwise indicated)

Documents on Germany, 1944–1985. Office of the Historian, Department of
State. 1986.
Foreign Relations of the United States, 1945. Volumes I and II, *The Conference of
Berlin (The Potsdam Conference).* 1960.
Foreign Relations of the United States, 1946. Volume V, *British Commonwealth;
Western and Central Europe.* 1969.
Foreign Relations of the United States, 1947. Volume III, *The British Common-
wealth; Europe.* 1972.
Foreign Relations of the United States, 1948. Volume II, *Germany and Austria.*
1973.
Foreign Relations of the United States, 1949. Volume III, *Council of Foreign Min-
isters; Germany and Austria.* 1974.
Foreign Relations of the United States, 1949. Volume IV, *Western Europe.* 1974.
Foreign Relations of the United States, 1950. Volume III, *Western Europe.* 1977.

Foreign Relations of the United States, 1950. Volume IV, *Central and Eastern Europe; The Soviet Union.* 1980.

Foreign Relations of the United States, 1951. Volume III, *European Security and the German Question,* parts I and II. 1981.

Foreign Relations of the United States, 1951. Volume IV, *Europe: Political and Economic Developments,* parts I and II. 1985.

Foreign Relations of the United States, 1952–1954. Volume V, *Western European Security,* parts I and II. 1983.

Foreign Relations of the United States, 1952–1954. Volume VII, *Germany and Austria,* parts I and II. 1986.

Public Papers of the President: Harry S Truman, 1949–1953. 1964.

Trial of the Major War Criminals before the International Military Tribunal, Volume I. Nuremberg, Germany, 1947.

Trials of War Criminals before the Nuremberg Military Tribunals under Control Council Law No. 10. Volume IX, *The Krupp Case.* 1950.

Congressional Documents

Convention on Relations with the Federal Republic of Germany and a Protocol to the North Atlantic Treaty. Hearings before the Committee on Foreign Relations, U.S. Senate, 82nd Congress, 2nd Session, June 1952.

Export Controls and Policies. Hearings before the Subcommittee on Export Controls and Policies of the Committee on Interstate and Foreign Commerce, U.S. Senate, 82nd Congress, 1st Session, 1951.

Extension of European Recovery. Hearings before the Committee on Foreign Relations, U.S. Senate, 81st Congress, 1st Session, February 1949.

Foreign Aid Appropriations for 1951. Hearings before the Committee on Appropriations, House of Representatives, 81st Congress, 2nd Session, Feb. 28, 1950.

Foreign Aid Appropriations for 1951. Hearings before the Committee on Appropriations, U.S. Senate, 81st Congress, 2nd Session, March 10, 1950.

International Bank for Reconstruction and Development. Hearings before the Committee on Banking and Currency, House of Representatives, 81st Congress, 1st Session, 1949.

Marketing of Securities of the World Bank. Hearings before the Subcommittee of the Committee on Banking and Currency, U.S. Senate, 81st Congress, 1st Session, June 10, 1949.

Supplemental Appropriations Bill for 1952. Hearings before Committee on Appropriations, U.S. Senate, 82nd Congress, 1st Session, 1951.

High Commission Reports and Historical Monographs

Gillen, J. F. J. *Labor Problems in West Germany.* Bonn and Bad Godesberg: HICOG, 1952.

———— *The Special Projects Program of the Office of the U.S. High Commissioner for Germany.* Bad Godesberg and Mehlem: HICOG, 1952.

———— *State and Local Government in West Germany, 1945–1953, with Special Reference to the U.S. Zone and Bremen.* Bad Godesberg and Mehlem: HICOG, 1953.

Lee, Guy A. *The Establishment of the Office of U.S. High Commissioner for Germany.* Bad Godesberg and Mehlem: HICOG, 1951.

———— ed. *Documents on the Field Organization of the Office of the U.S. High Commissioner for Germany, 1949–1951.* Bad Godesberg and Mehlem: HICOG, 1952.

McClaskey, Beryl R. *The History of U.S. Policy and Program in the Field of Religious Affairs under the Office of the U.S. High Commissioner for Germany.* Bad Godesberg and Mehlem: HICOG, 1951.

Office of the United States High Commissioner for Germany. (Monthly) *Information Bulletin,* 1949–1952.

———— *Quarterly Report on Germany.* Ten reports, Sept. 21, 1949–March 31, 1952. Bad Godesberg and Mehlem: HICOG, 1949–1952.

———— *Report on Germany, Sept. 21, 1949–July 31, 1952.* Bad Godesberg and Mehlem: HICOG, 1952.

Pilgert, Henry P. *Community and Group Life in West Germany.* Bad Godesberg and Mehlem: HICOG, 1952.

Plischke, Elmer. *The Allied High Commission for Germany.* Bad Godesberg and Mehlem: HICOG, 1953.

———— *Allied High Commission Relations with the West German Government, 1949–1951.* Bad Godesberg and Mehlem: HICOG, 1952.

———— *Berlin: Development of Its Government and Administration.* Bad Godesberg and Mehlem: HICOG, 1952.

———— *History of the Allied High Commission for Germany: Its Establishment, Structure, and Procedures.* Bad Godesberg and Mehlem: HICOG, 1951.

———— *Revision of the Occupation Statute, Sept. 21, 1949–March 7, 1951.* Bad Godesberg and Mehlem: HICOG, 1951.

———— *U.S. Information Programs in Berlin.* With Henry P. Pilgert. Bad Godesberg and Mehlem: HICOG, 1953.

———— *The West German Federal Government.* With H. J. Hille. Bad Godesberg and Mehlem: HICOG, 1952.

Federal Republic of Germany

Politisches Archiv des Auswärtiges Amts, Bonn

Record Groups and Collections, 1949–1954

Bundesarchiv, Koblenz

Ministry Records
  B102. Bundesministerium für Wirtschaft
  B136. Bundeskanzleramt
  B146. Bundesministerium für den Marshallplan

Bundes Militärarchiv, Freiburg

Records of Petersberg and EDC negotiations

Collections of Personal Papers

Konrad Adenauer Nachlass. Stiftung Bundeskanzler-Adenauer-Haus, Rhöndorf.
Herbert Blankenhorn Diary. Bundesarchiv, Koblenz.
Franz Blücher Nachlass. Bundesarchiv, Koblenz, and FDP Archive, Bonn.
Hans Böckler Nachlass. Deutsche Gewerkschaft Bund Archive, Düsseldorf.
Heinrich von Brentano Nachlass. Bundesarchiv, Koblenz.
Thomas Dehler Nachlass. FDP Archive, Bonn.
Ludwig Erhart Nachlass. Ludwig Erhart Stiftung, Bonn.
Fritz Heine Bestand. SPD Archive, Bonn.
Günther Henle Nachlass. Klöckner Archive, Duisburg.
Jakob Kaiser Nachlass. Bundesarchiv, Koblenz.
Robert Lehr Nachlass. Bundesarchiv, Koblenz.
Hermann Pünder Nachlass. Bundesarchiv, Koblenz.
Fritz Schäffer Nachlass. Bundesarchiv, Koblenz.
Carlo Schmid Bestand. SPD Archive, Bonn.
Kurt Schumacher Bestand. SPD Archive, Bonn.
Hans-Günther Sohl Nachlass. Thyssen AG Archiv, Duisburg.
Eberhard Wildemuth Nachlass. Bundesarchiv, Koblenz.

Political Party and Trade Union Archives

Deutsche Gewerkschaft Bund Archive, Düsseldorf, Protokolle, DGB Vorstand
FDP Archive, Friedrich Naumann Stiftung, Bonn, Vorstandsprotokolle and
  Fraktionsprotokolle
SPD Archive, Friedrich Ebert Stiftung, Bonn, Vorstandsprotokolle and Frak-
  tionsprotokolle

Personal Interviews and Oral Histories

Hermann Abs (Personal interview)
Bertoldt Beitz (Personal interview)
Kurt Birrenbach (Personal interview)

Herbert Blankenhorn (Personal interview)
Alexander Böker (Personal interview)
Wilhelm Grewe (Personal interview)
Fritz Hellwig (Personal interview)
Johann Adolf Graf von Kielmansegg (Personal interview)
Heinz Krekeler (Personal interview)
Ulrich de Maizière (Personal interview)
Erich Potthoff (Personal interview)
Gerhard Graf von Schwerin (Oral history, MGFA, Freiburg)
Hans-Günther Sohl (Personal interview)
Michael Thomas (Oral history, MGFA, Freiburg)
Eric Warburg (Personal interview)
Ludgar Westrick (Personal interview)

Published Documents

Enders, Ulrich, and Konrad Reisen, eds. *Die Kabinettsprotokolle der Bundes-regierung*, volumes I–V, 1949–1952. Boppard am Rhein: Harald Boldt Verlag, 1982–1989.
Kreikamp, Hans Dieter, ed. *Akten zur Vorgeschichte der Bundesrepublik Deutschland, 1945–1949*, volume V, January–September 1949. Munich: R. Oldenbourg, 1981.
Die Neuordnung der Eisen- und Stahlindustrie: Eine Bericht der Stahltreuhänderverein. Munich and Berlin: C. H. Beck, 1954.
von Schubert, Klaus, ed. *Sicherheitspolitik der Bundesrepublik Deutschland: Dokumente, 1945–1977.* Cologne: Verlag Wissenschaft und Politik, 1978.

Great Britain

Public Record Office, London

FO 371. General correspondence, Foreign Office
FO 1005. Records of the Allied High Commission
FO 1008. Records of the British High Commission

Published Documents

Documents on British Policy Overseas, Series II, Volume I, *The Schuman Plan, the Council of Europe, and Western European Integration, 1950–1952.* London: HMSO, 1987.
Documents on British Policy Overseas, Series II, Volume II, *The London Conference, Anglo-American Relations, and Cold War Strategy, 1950.* London: HMSO, 1987.

Documents on British Policy Overseas, Series II, Volume III, *German Rearmament*. London: HMSO, 1988.

Documents on Germany under Occupation, 1945–1954. Beate Ruhm von Oppen, ed. London: Oxford University Press, 1955.

Documents on International Affairs, 1949–1950. Margaret Carlyle, ed. London: Oxford University Press, 1953.

Documents on International Affairs, 1951. Denise Folliot, ed. London: Oxford University Press, 1954.

Documents on International Affairs, 1952. Denise Folliot, ed. London: Oxford University Press, 1955.

Interviews

Con O'Neill (Personal interview)
Lance Pope (Personal interview)
Sir Frank Roberts (Personal interview)

France

Personal Papers

Papers of Jean Monnet, Fondation Jean Monnet pour l'Europe (Monnet Archive), Lausanne, Switzerland

Oral Histories, Interviews, and Correspondence

Oral Histories (Monnet Archive)—George Ball, Robert Bowie, Bernhard Clappier, Stanley Cleveland, Kay Graham, John J. McCloy, René Pleven, Shepard Stone, Pierre Uri
Hervé Alphand (Personal interview)
Armand Bérard (Personal interview)
Jean Laloy (Private correspondence)
René Pleven (Personal interview)
Pierre Uri (Personal interview)

Notes

1. The Making of a High Commissioner

1. *Time,* June 20, 1949. Readers interested in more complete documentation of these points may refer to my doctoral dissertation, "From Occupation to Alliance: John J. McCloy and the Allied High Commission in the Federal Republic of Germany, 1949–1952" (Harvard University, 1985).

2. For this account of McCloy's life, I draw from personal interviews with McCloy and also from: Walter Isaacson and Evan Thomas, *The Wise Men* (New York: Simon & Schuster, 1986); Alan Brinkley, "The Most Influential Private Citizen in America," *Harper's,* February 1983, pp. 31–46; and Robert T. Swaine, *The Cravath Firm and Its Predecessors, 1819–1948,* II (New York: Ad Press, 1948), 467–468. I would like to thank Max Holland, who made available to me the first chapter of his projected biography of McCloy.

3. McCloy's comment on the relaxation provided by Greek poetry is in James Laughlin, "The Pleasures of Reading the Classics in Translation," *Antaeus,* 59 (Autumn 1987), 145, where Laughlin recalls encountering McCloy on the subway as he was reading the poems of Callimachus. My thanks to Edward J. Reilly for providing a copy of this article.

4. Robert Paul Browder and Thomas G. Smith, *Independent: A Biography of Lewis W. Douglas* (New York: Knopf, 1986), pp. 20–21. For a description of life at Amherst during this time, see Claude Fuess Moore, *Amherst: The Story of a New England College.* (Boston: Little, Brown, 1935).

5. J. S. Bixler, "Alexander Meiklejohn: The Making of the Amherst Mind," *New England Quarterly,* June 1974, pp. 179ff. For the *New Republic* statement and the Plattsburg movement, see John G. Clifford, *The Citizen Soldiers: The Plattsburg Training Camp Movement, 1913–1920* (Lexington: University of Kentucky Press, 1972), p. 195. For a more critical view, see Michael Pearlman, *To Make Democracy Safe for America* (Urbana and Chicago: University of Illinois Press, 1984), pp. 58–81.

6. John P. Finnegan, *Against the Specter of a Dragon: The Campaign for American Military Preparedness, 1914–1917* (Westport, Conn.: Greenwood, 1974), pp. 66–67. See also J. Garry Clifford and Samuel R. Spencer, Jr., *The First Peacetime Draft* (Lawrence: University Press of Kansas, 1986), pp. 200–234. Distinguished Plattsburg alumni who later served in government included not only McCloy and Douglas but also Robert Patterson, William J. Donovan, and Howard Petersen.

7. Letter from John J. McCloy to Dr. Priscilla Roberts, Nov. 10, 1982. My thanks to Dr. Roberts for making this available. Claude Fuess Moore, *The Amherst Memorial Volume* (Amherst, 1926), pp. 7, 188.

8. McCloy to Anna McCloy, June 27, 1917, McCloy Scrapbooks. When I read this letter, the papers were still in Mr. McCloy's office at the Council on Foreign Relations in New York. This letter will eventually become part of the collection of McCloy's personal papers in the Amherst College Archives.

9. John J. McCloy, "In Defense of the Army Mind," *Harper's*, April 1947, p. 341. On General Preston, see *Time*, June 20, 1949. Considering some of the subsequent controversies surrounding McCloy, it is ironic that his mentor, General Preston, had served in the Seventh Cavalry at the massacre of Indians at Wounded Knee.

10. David M. Kennedy, *Over Here: The First World War and American Society* (New York: Oxford University Press, 1980), pp. 220 (quotation), 205–218.

11. Isaacson and Thomas, *Wise Men*, p. 71. The authors note that a number of distinguished American leaders—among them Franklin Roosevelt, Woodrow Wilson, and Douglas MacArthur—have had mothers who accompanied them through their educational years. On Harvard Law School at the time, see David McLellan, *Dean Acheson: The State Department Years* (New York: Dodd, Mead, 1976), p. 12. McCloy entered with a class of 334 and graduated in a class of 196. John H. Muller of the Harvard Law School supplied these statistics.

12. Swaine, *Cravath Firm*, pp. 318–319.

13. Isaacson and Thomas, *Wise Men*, pp. 119–122.

14. Swaine, *Cravath Firm*, pp. 256–262, 300–304, 469.

15. Ibid., p. 265.

16. Isaacson and Thomas, *Wise Men*, p. 123.

17. On the Black Tom case, see Harland Manchester, "The Black Tom Case," *Harper's*, December 1939, pp. 60–69; W. Reginald Hall and Amos J. Peaslee, *Three Wars with Germany* (New York: Putnam's, 1944); and Henry Landau, *The Enemy Within* (New York: Putnam's, 1937). See also the most recent treatment: Jules Witcover, *Sabotage at Black Tom* (Chapel Hill: Algonquin Books, 1989).

18. Swaine, *Cravath Firm*, pp. 639–644.

19. Landau, *Enemy Within*, p. 136. McCloy told Harold Ickes that the Black Tom case had earned him $500,000. Diary of Harold Ickes, Aug. 20, 1944, Harold L. Ickes Papers, Library of Congress.

20. Diary of Henry L. Stimson, Sept. 16, 25, and Oct. 3 and 8, 1940, Papers of Henry L. Stimson, Microfilm edition, Yale University.

21. *Time,* June 20, 1949. McCloy to Acheson, Sept. 13, 1940, Folder 261, Box 21, Papers of Dean Acheson, Sterling Library, Yale University. To the extent McCloy had an ideology, he was a "corporate liberal" who sought a "noncoercive, self-disciplined, and harmonious corporate society [with limits on] the New Deal state . . . cooperative relations between business and government . . . social harmony and consensus at home, and . . . a stable and Western-oriented international order abroad." Robert Griffith, "Dwight D. Eisenhower and the Corporate Commonwealth," *American Historical Review,* 87 (February 1982), 97–100. On corporatism, see the debate between John Lewis Gaddis and Michael Hogan; John L. Gaddis, "The Corporatist Synthesis: A Skeptical View," *Diplomatic History,* 10 (Fall 1986), 357–362; and Michael Hogan, "Corporatism: A Positive Appraisal," *Diplomatic History,* 10 (Fall 1986), 363–372. On corporatism as a synthesis for recent diplomatic history, see Thomas J. McCormick, "Drift or Mastery? A Corporatist Synthesis for American Diplomatic History," *Reviews in American History,* 10 (December 1982), 318–330. Although the corporatist synthesis is intriguing, it is not always helpful in explaining McCloy's actions. McCloy's insistence on "objective" approaches to problems and "getting things done" required an essentially pragmatic response to policy questions, which, while hardly value-free or without class bias, was often affected as much by circumstances and external constraints as by any predetermined ideology.

22. Isaacson and Thomas, *Wise Men,* pp. 179–182. When McCloy received a Presidential citation after World War II, he noted that he stood in Stimson's office "under the steady gaze of Elihu Root. I felt a direct current running from Root through Stimson to me for if they were giants in the formulation of our national defense, I had benefitted by the work with the close association and help I have had through the years of the war with and from the General Staff." McCloy Diary, September 1945, John J. McCloy Papers, Amherst College Archives. Literature on the "Establishment tradition" is not voluminous. See Leonard S. Silk and Mark Silk, *The American Establishment* (New York: Basic Books, 1980). See also the excellent summary of this literature by one of the foremost students of the subject: Priscilla M. Roberts, "The American 'Eastern Establishment' and Foreign Affairs: A Challenge for Historians," *Society for Historians of American Foreign Relations, Newsletter,* 15 (March 1984), 8–18.

23. Henry L. Stimson and McGeorge Bundy, *On Active Service in Peace and War* (New York: Harper, 1947), p. 342. John J. McCloy, "Henry L. Stimson: Hero-Statesman," *Andover Bulletin,* 55 (Spring 1961), 14–17. Joseph P. Lash, *From the Diaries of Felix Frankfurter* (New York: Norton, 1975), p. 236.

24. Elting E. Morison, *Turmoil and Tradition* (Boston: Houghton Mifflin, 1960), p. 492; and *Time,* June 20, 1949.

25. McCloy, "German Sabotage in the United States," Nov. 16, 1940, Military Intelligence Division, RG 165, NARS. For the McCloy-Jackson exchange: Jackson, Memo for the President, April 29, 1941; Jackson, Memo for Patterson and McCloy, April 30, 1941; McCloy to Jackson, May 6, 1941; Jackson to McCloy, May 16, 1941; and McCloy to Jackson, May 19, 1941; all in Attorney

General Wiretapping Controversy, War Department Involvement, Box 94, Robert Jackson Papers, Library of Congress. I want to thank Francis MacDonnell, a Harvard graduate student completing the first study of the Fifth Column scare in the United States, for making these documents available to me.

26. John J. McCloy, "America's Present Military Strength: No Basis for Defeatism" (Address given to Amherst Alumni June 14, 1941, and distributed by The Fight for Freedom Committee, New York). Speech by McCloy, May 16, 1942, in Speeches, Mr. McCloy, Box 4, RG 218, Records of the United States Joint Chiefs of Staff, NARS-MMB; and *Amherst College Alumni News,* Commencement Issue, 1946, pp. 211–212.

27. Forrest C. Pogue, *George C. Marshall: Organizer of Victory, 1943–1945,* III (New York: Viking Press, 1973), 68–69. Marshall told Pogue that on civil affairs questions he generally took McCloy's advice. Morris J. MacGregor, Jr., *Integration of the Armed Forces, 1940–1965,* Defense Studies Series (Washington, D.C.: GPO, 1981), pp. 23, 34–35, 43, 57, 135, 157–158, 612–613.

28. Report of the Commission on Wartime Relocation and Internment of Civilians, *Personal Justice Denied* (Washington, D.C.: GPO, 1982), pp. 28–46, 67–86. See also Roger Daniels, *The Decision to Relocate the Japanese-Americans* (Malabar, Fla.: Robert E. Krieger, 1986), pp. 3–58; and Robert Dallek, *Franklin D. Roosevelt and American Foreign Policy, 1932–1945* (New York: Oxford University Press, 1979), pp. 334–335.

29. On the connection in McCloy's thinking between the Black Tom case and internment, see Peter Irons, *Justice at War* (New York: Oxford University Press, 1983), p. 15. A Japanese espionage network had been discovered on the West Coast before Pearl Harbor. For McCloy's belief in a Japanese fifth column, see Diary of Harold L. Ickes, Dec. 20, 1941, Library of Congress. The MAGIC dispatches may have contributed to his belief: see the article by Charles Mohr in the *New York Times,* May 22, 1983. For McCloy's comment on the Constitution, and the Gullion memo of Feb. 6, 1942, see Daniels, *Decision to Relocate,* pp. 87, 104. My views on the importance of "urgency" in McCloy's thinking come from his reaction to DeWitt's later report on the internment; see *Personal Justice Denied,* pp. 214–222. For Stimson's reaction, see Stimson Diary, Feb. 10, 1942. Although "wartime necessity" was invoked to justify internment, there was no widespread internment of Japanese-Americans on the Hawaiian Islands, where the military threat was far more immediate. The fact is that action against the small number of Japanese-Americans on the West Coast was *politically possible* rather than *militarily necessary.* A similar internment in Hawaii was not favored by the population or the military commanders, and it would have caused economic havoc. Nevertheless, Roosevelt constantly pressed for the internment of the Japanese-Americans in Hawaii. Elizabeth Anne Casey, "Fair Treatment: Why There Was No Large-Scale Internment of the Japanese in Hawaii during World War II" (Honors thesis, Harvard University, 1987), pp. 56–57, 63–64.

30. For McCloy's praise of the Army's handling of the program, see Daniels, *Decision to Relocate,* p. 56. See *Personal Justice Denied,* pp. 89–99 and 215–243,

on the Nisei soldiers. McCloy has also been accused of playing a major role in a legal "cover-up" to defend the internment decision before the Supreme Court. Irons, *Justice at War,* pp. 278–310. The basis of that charge was McCloy's suppression of a footnote in the government's brief in the *Korematsu* case. As originally written, the footnote indicated that the Justice Department no longer believed the 1942 Report by General DeWitt arguing for the "military necessity" of internment. The final version of the footnote was more ambiguous. The issues are complex, but McCloy's actions raise many troubling questions. See Aviam Soifer, "Lawyers and Loyalty," *Reviews in American History,* 12 (1984), 575–582.

31. The most detailed account is David S. Wyman, *The Abandonment of the Jews: America and the Holocaust, 1941–1945* (New York: Pantheon Books, 1984), esp. pp. 288–307, 323.

32. Martin Gilbert, *Auschwitz and the Allies* (New York: Holt, Rinehart and Winston, 1981), pp. 238, 248, 255–256, 303, 321, 327–328. See also Richard Breitman, "Auschwitz and the Archives," *Central European History,* 18 (1985), 365–373.

33. Wyman, *Abandonment of the Jews,* p. 323; and Richard W. Steele, "American Popular Opinion and the War against Germany: The Issue of a Negotiated Peace, 1942," *Journal of American History,* 55 (December 1978), 720. The most extreme charge leveled against McCloy was that the decision not to bomb Auschwitz reflected his pro-German and anti-Semitic bias. This accusation, which links the Auschwitz case with McCloy's later clemency toward Nazi war criminals, is neither a fair assessment of his career nor helpful in understanding either decision.

34. Stimson Diary, July 23, 1942; Lash, *Frankfurter Diaries,* May 28, 1943, pp. 222, 246; and Memorandum, McCloy to Eisenhower, March 1, 1943, Pre-Presidential Correspondence 16–52, Box 75, Papers of Dwight D. Eisenhower, Eisenhower Library, Abilene. Robert Murphy, who distrusted Monnet, recognized the Frenchman's influence on McCloy. Memorandum, Murphy to President Roosevelt, July 6, 1943, PSF-Diplomatic, Folder PSF France 1943, Box 42, Papers of Franklin D. Roosevelt, Roosevelt Library, Hyde Park, N.Y.

35. Robert E. Sherwood, *Roosevelt and Hopkins: An Intimate History* (New York: Harper & Row, 1948) pp. 667–697. Roosevelt's disdain for DeGaulle was strongly influenced by the advice he received from the French diplomat Alexis Léger, a man who enjoyed fame as a Symbolist poet and Nobel laureate. Léger, who despised DeGaulle, convinced Roosevelt that he possessed no legitimate right to speak in the name of France. Raoul Aglion, *Roosevelt and de Gaulle: Allies in Conflict* (New York: Free Press, 1988), pp. 35, 47–49, 188–190. Stimson Diary, Jan. 14 and Feb. 29, 1944. For McCloy's views on the importance of France, see Memorandum, McCloy to Eisenhower, March 8, 1943, Pre-Presidential Correspondence 16–52, Box 75, Papers of Dwight D. Eisenhower.

36. Memorandum for the Secretary of War from the President, Aug. 26, 1944, PSF, Folder PSF, War Department, 1944–1945, Box 104, Papers of Franklin D. Roosevelt, Roosevelt Library. Roosevelt had strong views on the Germans. "We have got to be tough with Germany, and I mean the German

people not just Nazis. We either have to castrate the German people or you have got to treat them in such manner so they can't just go on reproducing people who want to continue the way they have in the past." Quoted in Dallek, *Franklin D. Roosevelt and American Foreign Policy,* p. 472.

37. Morgenthau Diary, 1944, pp. 158–165, Box 768, Papers of Henry Morgenthau, Roosevelt Library.

38. Dinner meeting at the Secretary's Home, Sept. 4, 1944, Morgenthau Diary, p. 156, Box 768, Morgenthau Papers, Roosevelt Library; Stimson Diary, Sept. 7, 1944.

39. Dallek, *Franklin D. Roosevelt and American Foreign Policy,* pp. 474–477.

40. Stimson Diary, Sept. 7, 1944; John Morton Blum, *From the Morgenthau Diaries: Years of War, 1941–1945* (Boston: Houghton Mifflin, 1967), pp. 384–385. See also Paul Y. Hammond, "Directives for the Occupation of Germany: The Washington Controversy," in Harold Stein, ed., *American Civil-Military Decisions: A Book of Case Studies* (Birmingham: University of Alabama Press, 1963), p. 375; and Memorandum for the President, from John J. McCloy, April 26, 1945, PSF-Subject File, Germany folder #1, Box 178, Papers of Harry S. Truman, Harry S. Truman Library, Independence, Mo.

41. Walter Millis, ed., *The Forrestal Diaries,* with E. S. Ruffield (New York: Viking, 1951), pp. 11–12. John J. McCloy, "From Military Government to Self-Government," in Robert Wolfe, ed., *Americans as Proconsuls: United States Military Government in Germany and Japan, 1944–1952* (Carbondale: Southern Illinois University Press, 1984), pp. 119–120; and McCloy to John G. Winant, Jan. 19, 1945, Papers of Harry L. Hopkins, Sherwood Collection, Box 337, Roosevelt Library. See also Steven Rearden, "American Policy toward Germany, 1944–1946" (Ph.D. diss., Harvard University, 1974), pp. 51–52; and John Lewis Gaddis, *The United States and the Origins of the Cold War, 1941–1947* (New York: Columbia University Press, 1972), pp. 121–125.

42. McCloy Diary, April 16, 1945. See also Bradley F. Smith, *The Road to Nuremberg* (New York: Basic Books, 1981), pp. 92–93, 191, 248.

43. McCloy Diary, April 5, 7, and 10, 1945; and Memorandum for the President, from John J. McCloy, April 26, 1945, PSF-Subject File, Germany folder #1, Box 178, Truman Papers.

44. McCloy Diary, April 19, 1945.

45. Ibid., July 15, 16, and 17, 1945.

46. Ibid., July 17, 20, 23, 24, and 26, 1945. Isaacson and Thomas, *Wise Men,* pp. 288–313.

47. McCloy Diary, July 16, 20, 29, 1945; and Edward N. Peterson, *The American Occupation of Germany: Retreat to Victory* (Detroit: Wayne State University Press, 1977), p. 319.

48. John J. McCloy, "Personal Impressions of World Conditions," *Proceedings of the American Academy of Political Science,* 21 (January 1946), 558–561; and McCloy Diary, Aug. 15(?), 1945.

49. Daniel Yergin, *Shattered Peace* (Boston: Houghton Mifflin, 1978), pp. 196–201. For McCloy's support of Universal Military Training, see Michael S. Sherry, *Preparing for the Next War* (New Haven: Yale University Press, 1977), p. 83; and John J. McCloy, "American Occupation Policies in Germany," *Proceedings of the American Academy of Political Science*, 21 (January 1946), 91.

50. McCloy's speech is quoted in Sherry, *Preparing for the Next War*, p. 86. Bernard Weisberger, *Cold War, Cold Peace* (New York: American Heritage, 1985), pp. 68–69.

51. McCloy Diary, Aug. 11, 1945. Ickes Diary, Aug. 26 and Nov. 25, 1945, Papers of Harold L. Ickes. Francis Plimpton to Felix Frankfurter, June 19, 1945, Personal Correspondence, McCloy folder, Felix Frankfurter Papers, Library of Congress. McCloy to Acheson, Jan. 7, 1946, Under Secretary Correspondence, 1945–1947, Box 27, Papers of Dean Acheson, Truman Library.

52. McCloy Diary, July 21 and Aug. 7, 1945. McCloy tended to embellish the tale of his insistence that a warning be given to the Japanese in lieu of using the bomb. He wanted to avoid an invasion of Japan, and he was willing to compromise on the retention of the Emperor. But there is little evidence that he pressed this matter strongly. Isaacson and Thomas, *Wise Men*, p. 297; and Forrest C. Pogue, *George C. Marshall: Statesman, 1945–1957*, IV (New York: Viking, 1987) 1–25. McCloy to Frankfurter, Feb. 13, 1946, Correspondence, McCloy folder, Frankfurter Papers.

53. In one critic's view, McCloy's actions led to his appearing "as a man on horseback who would dictate to [the Bank] and ride roughshod over the executive directors—an entrance that to some extent clouded the whole of his administration." Edward S. Mason and Robert E. Asher, *The World Bank since Bretton Woods* (Washington: Brookings Institution, 1973), p. 50; and see John J. McCloy, "The Lessons of the World Bank," *Foreign Affairs*, July 1949, p. 560. See also Robert Pollard, *Economic Security and the Origins of the Cold War, 1945–1950* (New York: Columbia University Press, 1985), pp. 1–9.

54. McCloy to Truman, March 25, 1947, Folder 85-E Bretton Woods, Official File, Box 424, Truman Papers. Robert Garner, *This Is the Way It Was* (privately published, 1972), pp. 208–209, in Papers of Robert Garner, Box 3, Truman Library. The French loan was also a priority of the State Department. Under Secretary of State Robert Lovett telephoned McCloy on July 3, 1947, to urge action on the loan. Robert Lovett Phone Logs, Papers of Robert Lovett, New York Historical Society, New York.

55. McCloy to Douglas, June 10, 1947, enclosed in a letter of the same date to William L. Clayton, the Under Secretary of State for Economic Affairs, Folder McCloy, Papers of William L. Clayton, Box 65, Truman Library; and McCloy's testimony in Congress, in *International Bank for Reconstruction and Development*, Hearings before the Committee on Banking and Currency, House of Representatives, 81st Cong. 1st sess., 1949, p. 17; and Isaacson and Thomas, *Wise Men*, pp. 457–459.

56. *New York Times,* Sept. 30, 1948.

57. *New York Times Magazine,* May 29, 1949; and Robert Cutler, *No Time for Rest* (Boston: Little, Brown, 1966), p. 201.

2. Changing of the Guard

1. Dean Acheson, *Present at the Creation* (New York: W. W. Norton, 1969), pp. 249–250.

2. The detailed record of the Potsdam Conference is available in *FRUS 1945,* I and II. On Soviet policy in Germany, see Robert A. Slusser, ed., *Soviet Economic Policy in Postwar Germany: A Collection of Papers by Former Soviet Officials* (New York: Research Program on the USSR, 1953), pp. 14–17.

3. On the suspension of reparations deliveries, see *FRUS 1946,* V, 547–549. The literature on General Clay's years in Germany, which is extensive, is filled with debates over Clay's motivations as a Cold Warrior. The most recent and most comprehensive study is Wolfgang Krieger, *General Lucius D. Clay und die amerikanische Deutschlandpolitik, 1945–1949* (Stuttgart: Klett-Cotta, 1987). See also Lucius D. Clay, *Decision in Germany* (Garden City, N.Y.: Doubleday, 1950); John H. Backer, *Winds of History: The German Years of Lucius DuBignon Clay* (New York: Van Nostrand, 1983); John Gimbel, *The American Occupation of Germany, 1945–1949* (Stanford: Stanford University Press, 1968), and Edward N. Peterson, *The American Occupation of Germany: Retreat to Victory* (Detroit: Wayne State University Press, 1977); and Harold Zink, *The United States in Germany, 1944–1955* (Princeton: Van Nostrand, 1957).

4. The Byrnes speech is in a collection of documents issued by the Department of State, *Documents on Germany, 1944–1985* (Washington, D.C.: GPO, 1986), pp. 91–99.

5. *FRUS 1948,* II, 292.

6. Ibid., p. 467.

7. National Security Council Meeting, Oct. 22, 1948, President's Secretary's File, NSC Meetings, Box 220, Truman Library; and *FRUS 1948,* II, 1195. On the merger of the image of Nazis and Communists, see Les K. Adler and Thomas G. Paterson, "Red Fascism: The Merger of Nazi Germany and Soviet Russia in the American Image of Totalitarianism, 1930's–1950's," *American Historical Review,* 75 (1970), 1046–64.

8. J. Edward Smith, ed., *The Papers of Lucius D. Clay, 1945–1949,* I, xxviii, and II, 977. Some of the most prominent contemporary criticisms of military government were James Stewart Martin, *All Honorable Men* (Boston: Houghton Mifflin, 1950), which concerns decartelization; Delbert Clark, *Again the Goose Step* (Indianapolis: Bobbs Merrill, 1949), which predicted a resurgence of German militarism; and Freda Utley, *The High Cost of Vengeance* (Chicago: Henry Regnery, 1949), a scathing attack on the policy of dismantling.

9. For the statistics on German production, see Werner Abelshauser, *Wirt-*

schaftgeschichte der Bundesrepublik Deutschland, 1945–1980 (Frankfurt: Suhrkamp, 1983), p. 34.

10. Guy A. Lee, *The Establishment of the Office of U.S. High Commissioner for Germany* (Bad Godesberg and Mehlem: HICOG, 1951), p. 21. Acheson's uncertainty about Germany is highlighted in an excellent doctoral dissertation by Wilson Douglas Miscamble, "George F. Kennan: The Policy Planning Staff and American Foreign Policy, 1947–1950" (University of Notre Dame, 1980), p. 143. Memo of conversation, Jan. 24, 1949, Papers of Dean Acheson, Box 64, Truman Library. *FRUS 1949,* III, 87–89.

11. *Washington Post,* March 31, 1949. For Kennan's views on Germany, see *FRUS 1946,* V, 516–520; and for his "Program A," see *FRUS 1948,* II, 1325ff. The literature on George Kennan is voluminous and continues to grow. See John Lewis Gaddis, *Strategies of Containment* (New York: Oxford University Press, 1982), pp. 71–83; David Mayers, *George Kennan and the Dilemma of U.S. Foreign Policy* (New York: Oxford University Press, 1988), pp. 145–152; and Anders Stephanson, *Kennan and the Art of Foreign Policy* (Cambridge, Mass.: Harvard University Press, 1989), pp. 117–156.

12. *FRUS 1949,* III, 90–93; and paper of Feb. 14, 1949, in Records of the Policy Planning Staff, Folder Germany 1949, Box 15, RG 59, NARS-DB.

13. *FRUS 1949,* III, 102–105. See also Miscamble, "George F. Kennan," pp. 143–144, 169–170.

14. *FRUS 1949,* III, 94–96, 118–131.

15. Ibid., pp. 129–130. Murphy's reaction to Kennan's Program A also reflects an awareness of this transnational coalition. "The trouble with our good blueprints (Kennan's plan) often seems to be that they get bloody noses bumping into Russian, French, and at times British stone walls." *FRUS 1948,* II, 1320n.

16. *FRUS 1949,* II, 280–281, 317–318. On French policy see Jacques Fremeaux and Andre Martel, "French Defense Policy, 1947–1949," in Olav Riste, ed., *Western Security: The Formative Years* (Oslo: Norwegian University Press, 1985), pp. 95–97; Jean-Baptiste Duroselle, *France and the United States,* trans. Derek Coltman (Chicago: University of Chicago Press, 1978), pp. 175–186; and Krieger, *Clay,* pp. 492–498.

17. Memos of Conversation, March 15, 1949, Acheson Papers, Box 64, Truman Library.

18. *FRUS 1949,* III, 115–118; and Smith, *Clay Papers,* II, 1056–1058.

19. *FRUS 1949,* III, 142–155. The aim of the subcommittee's paper was to prevent the emergence of an autarchic and irredentist Germany.

20. Smith, *Clay Papers,* II, 1090.

21. *New York Times,* May 14, 1949; and Raymond Poidevin, "Die Neuorientierung der französischen Deutschlandpolitik, 1948–1949," in Josef Foschepoth, ed., *Kalter Krieg und Deutsche Frage* (Goettingen: Vandenhoeck & Ruprecht, 1985), pp. 143–144. Johnson to Acheson, May 14, 1949, CDF, 740.00119, Control (Germany), Box 189, NARS-DB; Smith, *Clay Papers,* II, 1148–1152;

and Douglas to State, May 11, 1949, London Embassy Files 1949, 350-Germany, RG 84, Box 189, NARS-Suitland.

22. Acheson, *Present at the Creation,* pp. 291–297.

23. Memorandum of Conversation, April 4, 1949, Acheson Papers, Box 64, Truman Library; *FRUS 1949,* III, 104; and Summary of Daily Meeting with the Secretary, March 28, 1949, Executive Secretariat Records, Box 4, NARS-DB.

24. McCloy had reacted enthusiastically to Acheson's appointment, stating in a letter that Acheson was certain to become a "great Secretary of State." McCloy to Acheson, Jan. 8, 1949, Folder 261, Box 21, Papers of Dean Acheson, Yale University.

25. McCloy's insistence on heading the ECA in Germany is recorded in his handwritten notes dated April 29, 1949, kept in his personal scrapbook. The scrapbook will eventually become part of the McCloy collection at Amherst.

26. Memo, Byroade to Webb, April 29, 1949, MDF, 740.00119, Control (Germany), Box 3794, RG 59, NARS-DB. Summary of Daily Meeting with the Secretary, May 4, 1949, 740.00119, Control (Germany), Box 189, RG 59, NARS-DB; and Memorandum of Conversation, May 5, 1949, Box 64, Acheson Papers, Truman Library. For Acheson's comment on McCloy's negotiation of his position, see Princeton Seminars, Box 74, p. 7, Acheson Papers, Truman Library.

27. Gaddis Smith, *Dean Acheson* (New York: Cooper Square, 1972), p. 103; *New York Times,* June 22 and July 1, 1949.

28. Lee, *Establishment,* pp. 67–72, 78; and Zink, *United States in Germany,* p. 49, which notes that McCloy was not successful in reducing HICOG's size until 1952. Criticisms of the McCloy takeover are contained in a series of letters by Joseph Panuch dated July 18, 25, 26, and 27, 1949, in Folder, "Military Government of Germany," Box 10, Papers of Joseph Panuch, Truman Library.

29. McCloy to Acheson, Sept. 16, 1949, D(49) 190, RG 466, McCloy Papers, NARS-Suitland. McCloy was concerned about Buttenwieser being in an "exposed position" because the Germans might make an issue of his Jewish background. Zink, *United States in Germany,* p. 52. Appropriations for public affairs activities actually increased under McCloy, when almost all other areas were being cut back. *Supplemental Appropriations for 1952, Hearings before the Senate Appropriations Committee,* 82nd Cong. 1951–52, XX, 309.

30. *FRUS 1949,* III, 319–340; and Webb to McCloy, Sept. 27, 1949, CDF, 740.00119, Control (Germany), Box 194, NARS-DB.

31. *FRUS 1949,* IV, 470–472; and *Boston Herald,* Sept. 18, 1949. Acheson's insistence on the need for French leadership was also motivated by the realization that Britain was not going to sacrifice its ties with the Commonwealth by joining any European Union. John W. Young, *Britain, France, and the Unity of Europe, 1945–1951* (Leicester: Leicester University Press, 1984), p. 126. Other Americans conveyed the same message to the Germans. Walter Lippman told the Chancellor's aide, Herbert Blankenhorn, that Germany "must direct its attention to Paris, not Washington." Blankenhorn Diary, Oct. 10, 1949, Herbert Blankenhorn NL 351/1b, p. 32, BA-Koblenz.

32. It was feared that a Continental federation without Britain would be dominated by Germany. Kennan was prepared to accept this possibility, once commenting that "what was wrong with Hitler's new order was that it was Hitler's." Kennan, quoted in John Lewis Gaddis, *The Long Peace* (New York: Oxford, 1987), pp. 68–70.

33. *Department of State Bulletin,* Aug. 22, 1949, p. 272; and McCloy press conference, Aug. 12, 1949, Box 68, Acheson Papers, Truman Library.

34. Theodore H. White, *In Search of History* (New York: Harper & Row, 1978), p. 410; and Drew Middleton, *Where Has Last July Gone?* (New York: Quadrangle, 1973), p. 173.

35. Elmer Plischke, "Denazification in Germany," in Robert Wolfe, ed., *Americans as Proconsuls: United States Military Government in Germany and Japan, 1944–1952* (Carbondale: Southern Illinois University Press, 1984), pp. 198–225 (numbers of Nazis on pp. 216–217). For one of the earliest and still most penetrating studies of denazification, see William E. Griffith, "Denazification in the United States Zone of Germany," *Annals of the American Academy of Political and Social Science,* 267 (January 1950), 68–76. See also Peterson, *Retreat to Victory,* p. 151. Peterson quotes the American political adviser Walter Dorn, who stated that it was "impossible for a minority to purge a majority." For example, although only 10 percent of Germans were members of the party, this constituted 29 percent of the adult population.

36. Christopher Simpson, *Blowback* (New York: Macmillan, 1988), provides an interesting, if somewhat exaggerated, account of the American recruitment of ex-Nazis. On Gehlen and his organization, see Reinhard Gehlen, *The Service: The Memoirs of General Reinhard Gehlen,* trans. David Irving (New York: World Publishing, 1972); and E. H. Cookridge, *Gehlen: Spy of the Century* (London: Hodder & Stoughton, 1971). For the policies of the other occupying powers, see Plischke, "Denazification," pp. 218–220; and Richard Barnet, *The Alliance* (New York: Simon & Schuster, 1983), pp. 27-30.

37. Griffith, "Denazification," pp. 68–70; and *New York Times,* Aug. 10, 1949.

38. *U.S. News and World Report,* Nov. 4, 1949; and Comment on "Renazification" in Germany, April 17, 1950, D(50) 1179, RG 466, McCloy Papers, NARS-Suitland; and Plischke, "Denazification," pp. 222–224. A number of German studies have portrayed the mixed results of denazification on the local level. See Justus Fürstenau, *Entnazifizierung: Ein Kapitel deutscher Nachkriegspolitik* (Neuwied, 1969); Wolfgang Krüger, *"Entnazifizierung!" Zur Praxis der politischen Säuberung in Nordrhein-Westfalen* (Wuppertal, 1982); and Lutz Niethammer, *Entnazifizierung in Bayern: Säuberung und Rehabilitierung unter amerikanischer Besatzung* (Frankfurt, 1972).

39. Plishchke, "Denazification," p. 223. On the fear of a revival of nationalism, see Office of Intelligence and Research (OIR), State Department, "The Present Strategy and Strength of German Nationalism," Report #4929, June 15, 1949, p. 39, RG 59, NARS-DB. President Truman was concerned about this

point. See his marking in the margin, "Discussion," in a report on the growth of nationalism. "Political Trends in Western Germany," July 22, 1948, Central Intelligence Reports, PSF, Box 255, Truman Library. White, *In Search of History,* p. 412.

40. Konrad Adenauer, *Memoirs, 1945–1953,* trans. Beate Ruhm von Oppen (Chicago: Henry Regnery, 1966), p. 180; White, *In Search of History,* p. 416; Charles W. Thayer, *The Unquiet Germans* (New York: Harper, 1957), pp. 119–120. Lewis J. Edinger, *Kurt Schumacher: A Study in Personality and Political Behavior* (Stanford: Stanford University Press, 1965), pp. 217–218, shows that Schumacher was known by more than half of the West Germans.

41. The best work is Hans Peter Schwarz, *Adenauer: Der Aufstieg, 1876–1952* (Stuttgart: Deutsche Verlag, 1986), the first part of a biography that will probably be considered definitive. See also Paul Weymar, *Adenauer: His Authorized Biography,* trans. Peter DeMendelssohn (New York: E. P. Dutton, 1957); Peter Koch, *Konrad Adenauer: Eine politische Biographie* (Reinbek: Rowohlt, 1986); Edgar Alexander, *Adenauer and the New Germany* (New York: Farrar, Strauss, and Cudaly, 1957); Terence Prittie, *Konrad Adenauer, 1876–1967* (London: Tom Stacey, 1971); and Charles Wighton, *Adenauer: Democratic Dictator* (London: Frederick Muller, 1963). On the importance of Cologne and the Rhineland in Adenauer's thinking, see Arnulf Baring, *Im Anfang war Adenauer* (Munich: Deutscher Taschenbuch, 1982), pp. 86–109.

42. Herbert Blankenhorn, *Verständnis und Verständigung* (Frankfurt am Main: Ullstein, 1980), p. 43. Blankenhorn was Adenauer's principal foreign policy adviser during the early years of his Chancellorship. Schwarz, *Adenauer,* pp. 212ff, treats the separatist charges in detail and with considerable sympathy for Adenauer's difficult position. See also Karl Dietrich Erdmann, *Adenauer in der Rheinlandpolitik nach dem Ersten Weltkrieg* (Stuttgart: Ernst Klett, 1966), esp. pp. 187–203. Baring argues that Adenauer's advocacy of separation from Prussia could easily be confused with separatism, but was actually quite different. Baring, *Im Anfang,* p. 97. Henning Koehler, *Adenauer und de Rheinische Republik* (Opladen: Westdeutscher Verlag, 1986), p. 274, argues that Adenauer put the interests of the Rhineland over the national interest. The French High Commissioner told McCloy that Adenauer was a separatist. McCloy to State Department, Aug. 22, 1949, 862.00, RG 59, Box 684, NARS-DB. For another discussion of the controversy, see Fritz Stern, "Adenauer in Weimar: The Man and the System," in *The Failure of Illiberalism* (Chicago: University of Chicago Press, 1971), pp. 162–192.

43. Schwarz, *Adenauer,* pp. 182–185, 343–424. The relationship between Adenauer's second wife and Ellen McCloy was brought to McCloy's attention by Adenauer. Adenauer to Ellen McCloy, June 13, 1949, in Adenauer Papers, Stiftung Bundeskanzler-Adenauer-Haus, Rhöndorf. The grandfather of Auguste Zinsser was a brother of Mrs. McCloy's grandfather. The families had lost contact, however.

44. Schwarz, *Adenauer*, pp. 427–616. A recent perceptive history of the CDU is Hans-Jürgen Grabbe, *Unionsparteien, Sozialdemokratie und Vereinigte Staaten von Amerika, 1945–1966* (Düsseldorf: Droste, 1983).

45. Schwarz, *Adenauer*, pp. 619–638. Jürgen W. Falter, "Kontinuität und Neubeginn," *Politische Vierteljahresschrift*, 22 (September 1981), 236–263. For American interest in a coalition government, see "Possible Consequences of the Forthcoming West German Elections," July 19, 1949, Central Intelligence Reports, PSF, Box 256, Truman Papers, Truman Library.

46. Konrad Adenauer, *Erinnerungen, 1953–1955*, II (Stuttgart: Deutsche Verlag, 1966), 63. (All translations are my own unless otherwise indicated.)

47. Adenauer, *Memoirs*, pp. 35–41, 78–79, 258–259; and *Die Kabinettsprotokolle der Bundesregierung, Band I, 1949*, ed. Ulrich Enders and Konrad Reisen (Boppard am Rhein: Harald Boldt, 1982), p. 138.

48. Blankenhorn, *Verständnis*, p. 47; and *Die Kabinettsprotokolle*, p. 328.

49. Office of the United States High Commissioner for Germany, *First Quarterly Report on Germany, September 21, 1949–December 31, 1949* (Bad Godesberg and Mehlem: HICOG, 1949), p. 7.

50. Edinger, *Schumacher*, pp. 175–185; Vincent Auriol, *Journal du Septennat*, vol. III (1949), ed. Pierre Nora and Jacques Ozouf (Paris: Armand Colin, 1970), pp. 455–456; and Alfred Grosser, *The Western Alliance*, trans. Michael Shaw (New York: Vintage Books, 1980), p. 107.

51. Edinger, *Schumacher*, pp. 9–12, 81; and Thayer, *Unquiet Germans*, p. 133. Edinger's biography is not well written, but it is still an essential work. Other biographies include the three-volume study edited by Arno Scholz and Walther Oschilewski, *Turmwächter der Demokratie: Ein Lebensbild von Kurt Schumacher* (Berlin: Arani, 1954); Waldemar Ritter, *Kurt Schumacher* (Hannover: Dietz, 1964); Willy Albrecht, *Kurt Schumacher: Ein Leben für den demokratischen Sozialismus* (Bonn: Neue Gesellschaft, 1985); and Günther Scholz, *Kurt Schumacher* (Düsseldorf: Econ, 1988).

52. Edinger, *Schumacher*, pp. 15–19.

53. Gordon D. Drummond, *The German Social Democrats in Opposition, 1949–1960: The Case against Rearmament* (Norman: University of Oklahoma Press, 1982), pp. 13–14.

54. Edinger, *Schumacher*, pp. 62–63, 99–100.

55. Ibid., p. 100; and Drummond, *German Social Democrats*, p. 13. An account of Schumacher's resistance to the forced merger of the KPD and SPD is in Henry Krisch, *German Politics under Soviet Occupation* (New York: Columbia University Press, 1974).

56. Edinger, *Schumacher*, pp. 169–170, 185; Smith, *Clay Papers*, II, 1077 and 1117. Schumacher to Adolf Hamburger, 24 Aug. 1949, Schumacher Bestand, Korrespondenz Q-23, Archiv der Friedrich Ebert Stiftung (SPD Archive), Bonn.

57. Edinger, *Schumacher*, p. 44; Drummond, *German Social Democrats*, p. 23; and Schumacher press conference, Oct. 27, 1949, Schumacher Bestand, Korres-

pondenz Q-23, SPD Archive, Bonn. Schumacher's views can also be studied in the excellent collection assembled by Willy Albrecht, *Kurt Schumacher: Reden-Schriften-Korrespondenzen, 1945–1952* (Berlin: Dietz, 1985).

58. Edinger, *Schumacher,* pp. 76–80, 236; Thayer, *Unquiet Germans,* p. 137; and Carlo Schmid, *Erinnerungen* (Bern: Scherz, 1979), p. 432.

3. Avoiding the Fate of Weimar: The Petersberg Protocols

1. Adenauer, *Memoirs,* p. 184; and Baring, *Im Anfang,* p. 117.

2. John J. McCloy, "Adenauer und die Hohe Kommission," in *Konrad Adenauer und seine Zeit,* ed. Dieter Blumenwitz et al. (Stuttgart: Deutsche Verlag, 1976), p. 424.

3. For French policy, particularly in terms of France's relationship with the United States, see Jean-Baptiste Duroselle, *France and the United States,* trans. Derek Coltman (Chicago: University of Chicago Press, 1978), pp. 169–211. On British policy, see John W. Young, *Britain, France, and the Unity of Europe, 1945–1951* (Leicester: Leicester University Press, 1984), esp. pp. 132–138.

4. Ivone Kirkpatrick, *The Inner Circle* (London: Macmillan, 1959), pp. 232–233; and Alan Bullock, *Ernest Bevin: Foreign Secretary, 1945–1951,* III (London, Heinemann, 1983), 90, 764.

5. On François-Poncet, the best short sketch is Franklin Ford, "Three Observers in Berlin: Rumbold, Dodd, and François-Poncet," in *The Diplomats, 1919–1939,* ed. Gordon A. Craig and Felix Gilbert (Princeton: Princeton University Press, 1953), pp. 460–474. See also F. Roy Willis, *France, Germany, and the New Europe, 1945–1963* (Stanford: Stanford University Press, 1965), pp. 59ff.

6. Ford, "Three Observers," pp. 462–470; and Anthony Adamthwaite, *France and the Coming of the Second World War, 1936–1939* (London: Frank Cass, 1977), pp. 152, 286. Adamthwaite is particularly critical of François-Poncet, noting that he was in favor of a German takeover of Czechoslovakia and reacted to Munich by saying, "Peace is saved . . . that is the main thing." Jean-Baptiste Duroselle, *La Decadence, 1932–1939* (Paris: Imprimerie Nationale, 1979) pp. 61–62, is also quite critical of François-Poncet, considering him too optimistic in his evaluation of Hitler. For his memoirs, see André François-Poncet, *The Fateful Years,* trans. Jacque LeClercq (New York: Harcourt, Brace, 1949).

7. Willis, *France, Germany, and the New Europe,* p. 60.

8. Meeting of the Allied High Commission, Sept. 29, 1949, FO 1005/1628, PRO, London. Schwarz, *Adenauer,* p. 676, describes the "poisonous" atmosphere that existed between François-Poncet and Adenauer in their first encounters.

9. Friedrich Jerchow, "Der Aussenkurs der Mark, 1944–1949," *Vierteljahrshefte für Zeitgeschichte,* 30 (1982), 287.

10. Karl Hardach, *The Political Economy of Germany in the Twentieth Century* (Berkeley: University of California Press, 1980), pp. 171–172, with tables on pp. 226–228.

11. Jerchow, "Der Aussenkurs," p. 288; and Memo, Lowell M. Pumphrey to McCloy, Sept. 20, 1949, D(49) 175–202A, Box 2, RG 466, McCloy Papers, NARS-Suitland; and *FRUS 1949*, III, 448–450.

12. Jerchow, "Der Aussenkurs," pp. 294–295. See also *FRUS 1949*, III, 451; and *FRUS 1949*, IV, 444.

13. Weekly Staff Conference, Oct. 11, 1949, File 6–14, Box 1, RG 466, McCloy Papers, NARS-Suitland. See also McCloy to Webb, Oct. 28, 1949, 862.00 Germany CDF, Box 685, RG 59, NARS-DB.

14. *FRUS 1949*, III, 448–450; and *Die Kabinettsprotokolle*, pp. 285–300, which is a stenographic record of the Cabinet meeting.

15. *Die Kabinettsprotokolle*, p. 299; and *FRUS 1949*, III, 450–452.

16. *Die Kabinettsprotokolle*, pp. 305–306; and *FRUS 1949*, III, 457.

17. McCloy to Acheson, Sept. 25, 1949, TS(49)15, Box 1, RG 466, McCloy Papers, NARS-Suitland. See also *FRUS 1949*, III, 459–460.

18. *Die Kabinettsprotokolle*, pp. 327–328. Adenauer's favorable impression of McCloy may have been influenced by the contrast with Clay, who could berate "the minister presidents of the German Länder like schoolboys when they did not observe American directives." Grosser, *Western Alliance*, p. 82.

19. McCloy to Webb, Oct. 28, 1949, 862.00 Germany CDF, Box 685, RG 59, NARS-DB; and *FRUS 1949*, III, 463–465. See also Buttenwieser's memorandum of the meeting, dated Sept. 26, 1949, D(49)227, Box 2, RG 466, McCloy Papers, NARS-Suitland.

20. McCloy to Acheson, Sept. 25, 1949, TS(49)8, Box 1, RG 466, McCloy Papers, NARS-Suitland. *FRUS 1949*, III, 460–462.

21. Memo of Conversation, Sept. 27, 1949, Box 64, Acheson Papers, Truman Library; and *FRUS* 1949, III, 466–467, 470.

22. *FRUS 1949*, III, 472–474. Despite German anger over the American solution, the most recent study of the devaluation concluded that it had worked in favor of the German export industry, forcing it to rationalize and become more competitive, and leaving the DM undervalued for most of the 1950s. Jerchow, "Der Aussenkurs," p. 297.

23. Weekly Staff Conference, Oct. 11, 1949, File 6–14, Box 1, RG 466, McCloy Papers, NARS-Suitland; and Weekly Intelligence Report—Office of Land Commissioner in West Baden, Oct. 5, 1949, 862.00 Germany, MDF, Box 6510, RG 59, NARS-DB.

24. Office of Intelligence and Research (OIR), State Department, "The Militarization of the German Police in Eastern Germany," Report #4798.3 (undated, but sometime between June and October 1949), NARS-DB. The report considered that the Bereitschaften was probably designed for internal security rather than external aggression. On Soviet policy toward East Germany, see Vojtech Mastny, "Stalin and the Militarization of the Cold War," *International Security*, 9 (Winter 1984–85), 109–129. See also Hans W. Gatzke, *Germany and the United States—A Special Relationship* (Cambridge, Mass.: Harvard University

Press, 1980), pp. 170–172. Among the studies of the DDR are J. P. Nettl, *The Eastern Zone and Soviet Policy in Germany, 1945–1950* (London: Oxford University Press, 1951); Wolfgang Leonhard, *Child of the Revolution,* trans. C. M. Woodhouse (London: Collins, 1957); L. H. Legters, ed., *The German Democratic Republic* (Boulder: Westview, 1978); and Martin McCauley, *The German Democratic Republic since 1945* (London: Macmillan, 1983).

25. *FRUS 1949,* III, 533–534. For a record of U.S. concern over the development of the DDR, see *FRUS 1949,* III, 505–545. Stalin's speech is in *Pravda,* Oct. 19, 1949, in *Soviet Press Translations* (Far Eastern Institute, University of Washington), V, 17. McCloy discussed the propaganda apppeals of East Germany in *FRUS 1949,* IV, 485–486.

26. Intelligence Report, Nov. 26, 1949, RG 43, Allied Control Council (Germany), NARS-DB. See also Ernest R. May, "Soviet Policy and the 'German Problem,'" *Naval War College Review,* 36 (September–October 1983), 22–26.

27. Gert Whitman to McCloy, Oct. 17, 1949, 862.00 Germany, NARS-DB; Meeting of the High Commission, Oct. 14, 1949, FO 1005/1628, PRO, London. For Adenauer's views of the Berlin issue, see Schwarz, *Adenauer,* pp. 679–681.

28. Briefs on Current German Situation, Oct. 19, 1949, World War II Conferences, Box 312, RG 43, NARS-DB; and Robert Pollard, *Economic Security and the Origins of the Cold War, 1945–1950* (New York: Columbia University Press, 1985), pp. 87–89. See also Bruce Kuklick, *American Policy and the Division of Germany* (Ithaca: Cornell University Press, 1972); and Manuel Gottlieb, *The German Peace Settlement and the Berlin Crisis* (New York: Paine Whitman, 1960). Although the United States did not take any of the industrial plants as reparations, it did remove from Germany both scientists and technical information valuable in industrial production. The exact value of this removal remains unclear, but there are enough cases to dispel the myth that the United States was the one nation that did not take reparations. John Gimbel, "Science, Technology, and Reparations in Postwar Germany" (Paper, University of Marburg, 1989). Gimbel notes that this program came to an end in 1947.

29. My account of Soviet policy is based on Vladimir Alexandrov, "The Dismantling of German Industry," in Robert Slusser, ed., *Soviet Economic Policy in Postwar Germany* (New York: Research Program on the USSR, 1953), pp. 14–17. This volume is a collection of articles by Soviet defectors describing in detail various aspects of Russia's German policy. Other important articles are those by Vladimir Rudolph and Vassily Yershov.

30. Hardach, *Political Economy,* pp. 94–95; and Alfred Grosser, *Germany in Our Time,* trans. Paul Stephenson (New York: Praeger, 1970), p. 60.

31. Concerning the German protests and their effect, see Edith Baade to Fritz Heine, June 19, 1949, Bestand Fritz Heine, #5, SPD Archive, Bonn. Raymond Stokes, *Divide and Prosper: The Heirs of I.G. Farben under Allied Authority, 1945–1951* (Berkeley: University of California Press, 1989), pp. 81–85.

32. *FRUS 1949,* III, 594.

33. Ibid., p. 596.

34. Personal interview with Eric Warburg, Hamburg, May 10, 1983; and *FRUS 1949*, III, 597.

35. *FRUS 1949*, III, 598.

36. Adenauer, *Memoirs*, p. 195. Adenauer to McCloy, Oct. 3, 1949, PA-AA 244.04, vol. I, Bonn. This volume contains a record of the dismantling controversy, compiled by Alexander Böker, an aide to Blankenhorn.

37. H. G. Sohl to Robert Lehr, Oct. 6, 1949, Robert Lehr NL 18, BA-Koblenz; and Adenauer to McCloy, Oct. 10, 1949, PA-AA 244.04, vol. I, Bonn. Adenauer sent a copy of the October 10 letter to the former mayor of Düsseldorf, Robert Lehr, a member of the board of directors of the August Thyssen works, and assured him, "I am doing what I can." Adenauer to Lehr, Oct. 14, 1949, Lehr NL 18, BA-Koblenz.

38. Meeting of the High Commissioners, Oct. 14, 1949, FO 1005/1628, PRO, London; and *FRUS 1949*, III, 292–293.

39. Justus D. Doenecke, *Not to the Swift* (Lewisburg, Pa.: Bucknell University Press, 1979), pp. 138–139. On the activities of the Cranes, and their relationship with Hans-Günther Sohl, see Joan Crane to H. G. Sohl, Oct. 24, 1949, Lehr NL 18, BA-Koblenz. Sohl forwarded most of his letters from the Cranes to Lehr, and Lehr often sent them on to the Chancellor and other political figures. See also the Crane's letters of Sept. 12, Oct. 2, Oct. 24, Oct. 30, and Nov. 9, 1949, to H. G. Sohl, in Lehr NL 18, BA-Koblenz. On the Cranes' success in Washington, see Joan Crane to Alexander Böker, Oct. 24, 1949, in PA-AA 244.04, vol. I, Bonn. On Hoffmann's concerns, see *FRUS 1949*, III, 608–609.

40. McCloy's newspaper interview is in PA-AA 244.04, vol. I, Bonn. See *New York Times*, Oct. 10, 1949; and *The Times*, Oct. 18, 1949.

41. Roger Stevens to Ivone Kirkpatrick, Oct. 18, 1949, FO 371/77140, PRO.

42. *FRUS 1949*, III, 615–618; and Memo of Conversation, Oct. 27, 1949, Box 64, Acheson Papers, Truman Library.

43. *Die Kabinettsprotokolle*, pp. 148–150, 165; Adenauer to Robertson, Nov. 1, 1949, in PA-AA 210.05, Bonn. For Adenauer's newspaper campaign, see *Die Zeit*, Nov. 3, 1949; a copy of the *Baltimore Sun* interview is in PA-AA 210.05, Bonn. Adenauer told his Cabinet that he had selected the *Baltimore Sun* because he knew Truman read it. He also told them that he had not given a specific figure for French capital, but that the confusion resulted from the fact that Vereinigte Stahlwerke constituted 40 percent of the German steel market. *Die Kabinettsprotokolle*, p. 193.

44. *FRUS 1949*, III, 618–621.

45. Ibid., pp. 621–623.

46. McCloy to HICOG (Frankfurt) for Acheson, Nov. 1, 1949, TS(49)27, Box 1, and "Brief on Dismantling" prepared by US HICOG Staff for Mr. McCloy for use at the Foreign Ministers' Conference, November 1949, D(49)338, RG

466, McCloy Papers, NARS-Suitland. For the State Department's position, see *FRUS 1949,* III, 295–304, 630.

47. Three Ministers' Talks, Nov. 9, 1949, World War II Conferences, Box 313, RG 43, NARS-DB; Dean Acheson, *Sketches from Life* (New York: Harper, 1959), pp. 22–23; and Ivone Kirkpatrick, *The Inner Circle* (London: Macmillan, 1959), pp. 216–217.

48. *FRUS 1949,* III, 309–310; and Acheson, *Sketches,* pp. 170–171.

49. *FRUS 1949,* III, 311.

50. Princeton Seminars, pp. 766–770, Box 75, Acheson Papers, Truman Library; and Acheson, *Present at the Creation,* pp. 341–342.

51. *FRUS 1949,* III, 312; Acheson, *Present at the Creation,* p. 341; and Princeton Seminars, pp. 767–768, Box 75, Acheson Papers, Truman Library.

52. *New York Times,* Nov. 12, 1949; and *Information Bulletin,* HICOG, December 1949, p. 40.

53. *FRUS 1949,* III, 314–316, 638–640.

54. Ibid., p. 316; and Adenauer, *Memoirs,* pp. 212–220. On November 30 Adenauer applied for membership in the Ruhr Authority, but he still did not want to accede to the agreement under the provisions of Article 31, the article which he considered gave the Allies a "blank check." The dispute lasted almost three weeks, leading to public irritation on the part of the Allies and the suggestion that Adenauer was trying to back out of the Petersberg Agreements. The Chancellor eventually relented, and Germany was admitted to the IAR under Article 31 without any special conditions. The dispute can be followed in a series of cables from December 2 to December 21, 1949, in 740.00119 Control (Germany) CDF, Box 196, RG 59, NARS-DB, and in Germany, PA-AA 243.01, vol. I, Bonn.

55. Meeting of the High Commission, Nov. 17, 1949, FO 1005/1628, PRO, London; Paul Weymar, *Adenauer: His Authorized Biography,* trans. Peter De-Mendelssohn (New York: E. P. Dutton, 1957), pp. 293–294.

56. Adenauer, *Memoirs,* pp. 214–215.

57. Schwarz, *Adenauer,* pp. 658–661; Meeting of the High Commission, Nov. 17, 1949, FO 1005/1628, PRO; and Terence Prittie, *Konrad Adenauer, 1876–1967* (London: Stacey, 1971), p. 200.

58. Adenauer, *Memoirs,* p. 221. Blankenhorn compared the agreement with the 1925 Locarno Treaty. Blankenhorn Diary, Nov. 17, 1949, NL 351/2, p. 42. Schwarz, *Adenauer,* p. 687, tends to minimize the achievement. In Thyssen's case, however, the reprieve came in the nick of time. Of 268,000 tons on the reparations list, 109,000 had been dismantled or scrapped. But the specific losses of modern machinery were even more damaging than a simple tonnage figure indicates. See the diagram in the history of the Thyssen works; Wilhelm Treue and Helmut Uebbing, *Die Feuer verlöschen nie* (Düsseldorf: Econ, 1969), pp. 151–153.

59. Meeting of the High Commission, Nov. 22, 1949, FO 1005/1628, PRO, London; Adenauer, *Memoirs,* pp. 221–222; and *New York Times,* Nov. 24, 1949.

The text of the agreement is in *FRUS 1949*, III, 343–348. For the Adenauer-Schumacher exchange, see Adenauer, *Memoirs*, pp. 222–230.

60. *FRUS 1949*, III, 353–354; and Adenauer, *Memoirs*, p. 230.

4. Monnet and the Schuman Plan

1. *FRUS 1950*, III, 639–640. Donovan describes this mood as a "vague sense of trouble . . . that the Soviet Union was getting the upper hand." Robert J. Donovan, *Tumultuous Years: The Presidency of Harry S Truman, 1949–1953* (New York: Norton, 1982), p. 176.

2. *DBPO*, ser. II, vol. III, *German Rearmament, 1950* (London: HMSO, 1988), no. 104, pp. 266–267. For McCloy's Congressional testimony, see *Foreign Aid Appropriations for 1951*, Hearings before the Committee on Appropriations, U.S. Senate, 81st Cong., 2nd sess., March 10, 1950, p. 68. Adenauer, *Memoirs*, p. 244; and the *New York Times*, April 3, 1950.

3. Adenauer to McCloy, Feb. 8, 1950. Adenauer Papers, StBKA-Rhöndorf. Some of Adenauer's letters, including this one, have been collected and published: Konrad Adenauer, *Briefe, 1949–1951*, ed. Hans Peter Mensing (Berlin: Siedler, 1985), pp. 170–171. For the McCloy-Adenauer conversation of April 12, 1950, I have used *FRUS 1950*, IV, 627–628; and the Blankenhorn Diary, April 13, 1950, NL 351/3, pp. 156–158, BA-Koblenz.

4. *FRUS 1950*, IV, 627–628.

5. Meetings of the High Commission, Jan. 12 and April 28, 1950, FO 1005/1126a, PRO.

6. Dehler's speech was covered in the *New York Times*, Jan. 25, 1950. For an account of the Bundestag incident involving the anti-Semitic deputy, Wolfgang Hedler, see *Time*, Feb. 27, 1950. For the confidential HICOG report, see "Nationalism in Western Germany," March 3, 1950, D(50) 605, Box 10, RG 466, McCloy Papers, NARS-Suitland. The resolution for a Congressional investigation can be found in the *Congressional Record*, 81st Cong. 2nd sess., April 17, 1950, 96(1), 5236–37.

7. *FRUS 1950*, IV, 927–934. See also Jacques Freymond, *The Saar Conflict, 1945–1955* (New York: Praeger, 1960), pp. 39–105.

8. Meetings of the AHC, March 2 and 22, 1950, FO 1005/1126a, PRO, London; *FRUS 1950*, III, 767–768, 817; and *New York Times*, April 3, 1950. For François-Poncet's frustration with Adenauer, see Armand Bérard, *Un Ambassadeur Se Souvient*, vol. II, *Washington et Bonn, 1945–1955* (Paris: Plon, 1978), p. 303.

9. Edinger, *Schumacher*, p. 153; *New York Times*, Jan. 2, 1950; and *FRUS 1950*, IV, 608–611. For the American perspective on the necessity for advocating reunification, see *FRUS 1950*, IV, 594, 623. Walter Lippmann emphasized this point repeatedly, arguing that it was a "far fetched" theory that the Germans would ever accept partition. *Boston Globe*, March 2, 1950.

10. Abelshauser, *Wirtschaftsgeschichte*, p. 64. For McCloy's testimony, see *Foreign Aid Appropriations for 1951*, Hearings before the Subcommittee of the

Committee on Appropriations, House of Representatives, 81st Cong., 2nd sess., Feb. 28, 1950, p. 465. The blunt description of Germany's problems by Robert Hanes, the ECA Mission Chief in Germany under McCloy, can be found in Benjamin J. Buttenwieser, Oral History, Columbia University, New York, p. 129. This pessimism was shared by Lincoln Gordon, one of Harriman's top assistants. Interview with Lincoln Gordon, Oct. 13, 1982. The statistics on unemployment are in a report assembled by HICOG for the meeting of American Ambassadors in March 1950: "Briefs on the Current German Situation," Harriman-HICOG, OSR, Central Secretariat, Country Subject Files, RG 286, NARS-Suitland, Box 3. The British assessment can be found in *DBPO,* ser. II, vol. II, *The London Conferences: Anglo-American Relations and Cold War Strategy, 1950* (London: HMSO, 1987), no. 31, p. 110. The majority of the refugees were coming into the British areas of Schleswig-Holstein and Lower Saxony, which accounts for Robertson's concern. Meeting of the Allied High Commission, March 2, 1950, FO 1005/1126a, PRO.

11. This subject will receive extensive treatment in my "European Integration and the 'Special Relationship'—Implementing the Marshall Plan in the Federal Republic of Germany, 1948–1951," in Charles S. Maier, ed., *The Marshall Plan and Germany,* (London: Berg, forthcoming). Ludwig Erhard, *Wohlstand für Alle* (Düsseldorf: Econ, 1957), p. 43; Erhard to Adenauer, Jan. 27, 1950, Schriftwechsel, 1949–50, Papers of Ludwig Erhard, Ludwig Erhard Stiftung, Bonn. A copy of the original German report, entitled "Memoranden der Bundesrepublik Deutschland zur Program 1950–1951 und 1951–1952," Dec. 15, 1949, is in the papers of Franz Blücher, NL/287, BA-Koblenz. On the fear of industrial espionage, see Memo, Schalfejew to Adenauer, Jan. 30, 1950, PA-AA 242.04, Bonn. Germany ranked third in total Marshall Plan assistance, behind France and Great Britain.

12. The American report which triggered the "memorandum war," dated Jan. 21, 1950, can be found in PA-AA 318.00, Bd. 3, Bonn. Adenauer to McCloy, Feb. 8 and 11, 1950, Adenauer Papers, StBKA-Rhöndorf. For Adenauer's comment about Brüning, see Meeting of the AHC, Feb. 16 and March 2, 1950, FO 1005/1126a, PRO. See also Heiner R. Adamsen, *Investitionshilfe für die Ruhr* (Wuppertal: Peter Hammer, 1981), p. 69. For American dissatisfaction with Adenauer's economic program, see Hanes to Harriman, April 21, 1950, Counterpart-Germany, OSR Central Secretariat, Country Subject Files, RG 286, Box 4, NARS-Suitland; and McCloy to Adenauer, May 29, 1950, PA-AA 318.00, Bd. 3, Bonn. There were political implications to the dispute as well, especially in view of the weakness of the Adenauer government; see "Political Aspects of West German Economic Difficulties," March 7, 1950, 762A.00/3-750, NARS-DB.

13. See Elmer Plischke, *Allied High Commission Relations with the West German Government* (Bad Godesberg and Mehlem: HICOG, 1952), pp. 35–42. McCloy to Acheson, April 5, 1950, 862A.11/4-550, and McCloy to Acheson, April 25, 1950, 862A.11/4-2550, in Germany, RG 59, Box 5212, NARS-DB.

The Bundestag never passed the luxury tax, but the deficit declined thanks to Germany's rapid economic growth.

14. HICOG Staff Conference, Jan. 31, 1950, Weekly Staff Conferences, Box 1, RG 466, McCloy Papers, NARS-Suitland; and "Briefs on the Current German Situation," HICOG, NARS-Suitland. The article in the *Frankfurter Allgemeine Zeitung* of April 1, 1950, entitled "Possibilities of German-Russian Talks," was reported to Washington in McCloy to Acheson, April 8, 1950, 862A.00/4-850, Germany, RG 59, Box 5180, NARS-DB. McCloy's comment to the British official is recorded in *DBPO,* ser. II, vol. II, no. 5, p. 17. For the comparison between trade with the East and the Marshall Plan, see HICOG Intelligence Report, Nov. 26, 1949, RG 43, ACC (Germany), Box 44, NARS-DB.

15. Alan S. Milward, *The Reconstruction of Western Europe, 1945–51* (Berkeley: University of California Press, 1984), pp. 367–372.

16. *Die Neuordnung der Eisen- und Stahlindustrie: Eine Bericht der Stahltreuhänderverein* (Munich and Berlin: C. H. Beck, 1954), pp. 15–19. This is the report of the Steel Trustees Association, which oversaw the restructuring of heavy industry.

17. Acheson to Paris Embassy, April 8, 1950, D(50)1125, Box 12, RG 466, McCloy Papers, NARS-Suitland; McCloy to Acheson, March 18, 1950, 762A.00/3-1850, Germany, RG 59, NARS-DB; and *FRUS 1950,* IV, 630, 634–635.

18. Raymond Poidevin, "Frankreich und die Ruhrfrage, 1945–1951," *Historische Zeitschrift,* 228, pt. 2 (1979), 318–329; and *New York Times,* Jan. 25, 1950.

19. *DBPO,* ser. II, vol. II, no. 5, p. 17. *New York Times,* April 5, 1950. Memo, McCloy to Acheson, May 10, 1950, D(50)1299, Box 13, RG 466, McCloy Papers, NARS-Suitland.

20. Acheson's speech before the Pilgrims Club, May 10, 1950, in Papers of James Webb, Box 20, Truman Library, printed in the *New York Times,* May 11, 1950.

21. John W. Young, *Britain, France, and the Unity of Europe, 1945–1951* (Leicester: Leicester University Press, 1984), p. 131. George W. Ball, *The Past Has Another Pattern* (New York: Norton, 1982), p. 83; and *FRUS 1950,* III, 62.

22. There is no full biography of Monnet, though John Gillingham is at work on one. Jean Monnet, *Memoirs,* trans. Richard Mayne (London: Collins, 1978), can be supplemented by Merry and Serge Bromberger, *Jean Monnet and the United States of Europe,* trans. Elaine P. Halperin (New York: Coward-McCann, 1969). This book must be used carefully because it contains a number of inaccuracies. See also Donald Cook, *Ten Men and History* (Garden City, N.Y.: Doubleday, 1981), pp. 98–123. For DeGaulle's views of Monnet, see Grosser, *Western Alliance,* p. 101; and Milward, *Reconstruction,* p. 129.

23. McCloy to Felix Frankfurter, Nov. 1, 1941, Frankfurter Papers. Frankfurter took McCloy's letter and quoted extensively from it in a letter he wrote to Lord Halifax on Nov. 14, 1941.

24. André Kaspi, *La Mission de Jean Monnet à Alger* (Paris: Richelieu, 1971), p. 227.

25. Richard F. Kuisel, *Capitalism and the State in Modern France* (Cambridge: Cambridge University Press, 1981), pp. 219–247, esp. pp. 226, 230, and 241. Theodore H. White, *In Search of History* (New York: Harper & Row, 1978), pp. 437–438, describes Monnet's views of planning.

26. Kuisel, *Capitalism,* pp. 232, 241; and Monnet, *Memoirs,* p. 270.

27. White, *In Search of History,* pp. 435–437. On Monnet's effectiveness with Americans, see the Oral Histories of John J. McCloy, Robert Bowie, and Stanley Cleveland in Fondation Jean Monnet pour l'Europe (Monnet Archive), Lausanne, Switzerland.

28. Monnet to Frankfurter, Feb. 13, 1948, Frankfurter Papers. Monnet, *Memoirs,* pp. 271–272. Monnet expounded his views to his increasingly wide circle of Eastern-establishment friends—the bankers Pierre-David Weill, George Murnane, Floyd Blair, and Dean Jay; the lawyer-diplomats Dean Acheson and George Ball; professors such as the Rostow brothers and McGeorge Bundy; publishers and journalists such as Phil and Kay Graham, Walter Lippmann, Eugene Meyer, Joseph Alsop, James Reston, and David Schoenbrun.

29. John J. McCloy, Oral History, Monnet Archive, Lausanne. Monnet expressed his beliefs about the transformation of capitalism in two letters to René Pleven, Sept. 3 and Oct. 21, 1950, AMI 4/3/46 and 4/7/3, Monnet Archive, Lausanne.

30. Ball, *Past Has Another Pattern,* pp. 82–83; Monnet, *Memoirs,* pp. 284–294.

31. Monnet, *Memoirs,* p. 293; and F. Roy Willis, "Schuman Breaks the Deadlock," quoted in John Gillingham, *Industry and Politics in the Third Reich* (New York: Columbia University Press, 1985), p. 166.

32. Monnet, *Memoirs,* pp. 294ff. For the text of the announcement of the Schuman Plan, see *FRUS 1950,* III, 693–694. Pierre Uri explained the difference between the Schuman Plan's approach and that of a cartel. Interview with Pierre Uri, Paris, May 19, 1983.

33. Gillingham, *Industry and Politics,* pp. 166–167.

34. Bernard Clappier, Oral History, Monnet Archive, Lausanne. The best biography of Robert Schuman is Raymond Poidevin, *Robert Schuman* (Paris: Imprimerie Nationale, 1986). The importance of Law 27 is made clear in Hays to Secretary of State, May 12, 1950, 850.33/5-1250, NARS-DB.

35. Paris Embassy to Secretary of State, June 20, 1950, 850.33/6-2050, NARS-DB. *FRUS 1950,* III, 698–699. See also Eckhard Wandel, "Adenauer und der Schuman Plan," *Vierteljahrshefte für Zeitgeschichte,* 20 (1972), 201.

36. Monnet, *Memoirs,* pp. 299–302; Acheson, *Present at the Creation,* pp. 382–383; and *FRUS 1950,* III, 694–695. See also Michael Hogan, *The Marshall Plan* (Cambridge: Cambridge University Press, 1987), p. 367.

37. The various reactions to the Schuman Plan can be found in Hogan, *Marshall Plan,* p. 367; *FRUS 1950,* III, 695, 702; Fulbright to Webb, and

Washington to HICOG, May 12, 1950, 850.33/5-1250, NARS-DB; and *Time,* May 22, 1950, and *Newsweek,* May 22, 1950.

38. *FRUS 1950,* III, 1016, 1026, 1047, 1089–92.

39. *FRUS 1950,* III, 706–708; and Transcript, May 23, 1950, AMG 2/3/8, Monnet Archive, Lausanne.

40. Bonn to Secretary of State, May 10, 1950, 850.33/5-1050, RG 59, NARS-DB; Monnet, *Memoirs,* p. 309; and Adenauer, *Memoirs,* pp. 257–263.

41. *New York Times,* May 23, 1950; *Saturday Evening Post,* April 15, 1950; and *New York Herald Tribune,* May 26, 1950.

42. Speech by John J. McCloy, June 16, 1950, in *Third Quarterly Report,* HICOG, pp. 85–90.

43. *New York Times,* June 17, 1950; and Stone to McCloy, July 14, 1950, D(50)1537, McCloy Papers, RG 466, Box 15, NARS-Suitland.

44. For Britain's "isolationism" and the "special relationship," see Bullock, *Bevin,* p. 761; Peter Boyle, "The 'Special Relationship' with Washington," in John W. Young, ed., *The Foreign Policy of Churchill's Peacetime Administration, 1951–55* (Leicester: Leicester University Press, 1986), pp. 36–38, 51. The quotation from Sargent can be found in *DBPO,* ser. I, vol. I, *The Conference at Potsdam, 1945* (London: HMSO, 1984), no. 102, p. 185.

45. *FRUS 1950,* IV, 591, 601–602; Bullock, *Bevin,* p. 757; and Young, *Britain, France, and the Unity of Europe,* pp. 142–143. In December 1951 Churchill noted that the Americans "would like us to fall into the general line of European pensioners which we have no intention of doing." *DBPO,* ser. II, vol. I, *The Schuman Plan, the Council of Europe, and Western European Integration, 1950–1952,* no. 413, p. 781, n. 3.

46. *FRUS 1950,* III, 1048; Douglas to Acheson, June 5, 1950, 850.33/6-550, and Sir Oliver Franks to Acheson, June 8, 1950, 850.33/6-850, NARS-DB.

47. McCloy to Acheson, June 29 and July 6, 1950, 850.33/6-2950 and 850.33/7-650, NARS-DB. David Bruce also suspected the British. Bruce Diary, June 3, 1950, Bruce Papers, Virginia Historical Society. Adenauer mentioned his doubts about the British in a conversation with Hans Schäffer, whom he hoped to appoint as German negotiator of the Plan. Wandel, "Adenauer und der Schuman Plan," p. 198. Monnet, *Memoirs,* pp. 316–317. Strachey's attack on the plan appeared in *The Observer,* July 2, 1950, and was reported to Washington. Douglas to Acheson, 850.33/7-750, NARS-DB.

48. *DBPO,* ser. II, vol. I, no. 129, pp. 239ff. For Schumacher's views, I have relied on the Protokolle, Sitzungen des Parteivorstand, April 19, May 19, and June 24, 1950, SPD Archive, Bonn; and Kurt Schumacher, *Bundestagsreden* (Bonn: AZ Studio, Pfattheicher & Reichardt, 1972), pp. 59–60.

49. Paris Embassy to Washington, May 13, 1950, 850.33/5-1350, NARS-DB. Carlo Schmid, *Erinnerungen* (Bern: Scherz, 1979), pp. 518–519. Brandt is quoted in Monnet, *Memoirs,* p. 319. Wilhelm Kaisen, *Meine Arbeit, mein Leben* (Munich: Paul List, 1967), p. 268.

50. Protokolle, Sitzungen des Parteivorstand, Jan. 5 and 6 and Feb. 4 and

5, 1950, SPD Archive. In one of his first talks with McCloy, Böckler said he would insist on the political independence of the unions. Protokolle, Geschäfts-führenden Vorstand der DGB, 3rd Meeting, Dec. 16 and 17, 1949, DGB Archive, Düsseldorf. For the DGB's views and its interaction with other European trade unionists, see Protokolle über der deutsch-französische Gewerkschaftsbesprech-ung, May 21, 1950, Vorsitzender-Böckler, 1949–1951, and Protokolle, DGB Bundesvorstand, June 13, 1950, DGB Archive, Düsseldorf.

51. Margaret Carlyle, ed., *Documents on International Affairs, 1949–1950* (London: Oxford University Press, 1953), pp. 360ff.

5. The Dilemmas of Rearmament

1. Frank A. Ninkovich, *Germany and the United States* (Boston: Twayne, 1988), p. 84.

2. Paul Nitze, "The Development of NSC 68," *International Security,* 4 (Spring 1980), 173. For Bradley's testimony, see *New York Times,* Oct. 16, 1949. Ernest R. May, "American Forces in the Federal Republic: Past, Current, and Future," in James Cooney et al., *The Federal Republic of Germany and the United States* (Boulder: Westview, 1984), pp. 159–160.

3. Samuel F. Wells, Jr., "Sounding the Tocsin: NSC 68 and the Soviet Threat," *International Security,* 4 (Fall 1979), 152–153; and Lawrence S. Kaplan, *A Community of Interests: NATO and the Military Assistance Program, 1948–1951* (Washington, D.C.: GPO, 1980), pp. 77–78. For a strong attack on the assump-tion of Soviet conventional superiority, see Matthew A. Evangelista, "Stalin's Postwar Army Reappraised," *International Security,* 7 (Winter 1982–83), 110–138. Some have argued that former German generals such as Reinhard Gehlen played "a very real role in shaping U.S. perceptions of the USSR during this pivotal period." Simpson, *Blowback,* p. 64. But Simpson's book greatly exaggerates Gehlen's influence and ignores the fact that almost all observers of Soviet behavior shared in these estimates of Soviet aggressive and threatening behavior. Soviet secretiveness made it very difficult if not impossible to be more skeptical about Soviet military strength.

4. Wells, "Sounding the Tocsin," p. 156. For a State Department assessment of Soviet policy in East Germany, see "The State of East Germany," Office of Intelligence and Research Report #5230, May 24, 1950, p. 9, NARS-DB. On Berlin, see *FRUS 1950,* III, 811; *FRUS 1950,* IV, 848; "Communist Youth Demonstrations in Berlin, May 26–30, 1950," and Memo, Byroade to Acheson, Feb. 28, 1950, 762.00/2-2850, TSF, NARS-DB; and Maxwell Taylor, Briefing, National Defense College, April 17, 1950, Papers of Maxwell Taylor, Box 3, National War College, Washington. Testimony of John J. McCloy, *Foreign Aid Appropriations,* Senate Hearings, March 10, 1950, p. 30.

5. Kaplan, *Community of Interests,* pp. 77–78; and Nitze, "NSC 68," p. 171.

6. May, "American Forces," p. 160; Kaplan, *Community of Interests,* pp. 85–86; and Kenneth Condit, *The Joint Chiefs of Staff and National Policy, 1947–1949,*

vol. II of *The History of the Joint Chiefs of Staff* (Wilmington, Del.: Glazier, 1979), p. 301. *New York Times,* April 3, 1950; and Nitze, "NSC 68," p. 171.

7. For a copy of NSC-68, see Thomas H. Etzold and John Lewis Gaddis, eds., *Containment: Documents on American Policy and Strategy, 1945–1950* (New York: Columbia University Press, 1978), pp. 383–442.

8. Bonn to Washington, Dec. 16, 1949, 862.00 MDF, 12-1649, RG 59, Box 6512, NARS-DB.

9. Adenauer, *Memoirs,* p. 268; Steel to A. G. Gilchrist, Dec. 31, 1949, FO 371/85048, PRO; and Meeting of the High Commission, Dec. 8, 1949, FO 1005/1628, PRO.

10. *New York Times,* March 22, 1950. For the Chancellor's comparison of his situation with Chiang's, see Bérard, *Washington et Bonn,* p. 298. For Schwerin's report, see Norbert Wiggershaus, "Zur Frage der Planung für die verdeckte Aufstellung westdeutscher Verteidigungskräfte in Konrad Adenauers sicherheits-politischer Konzeption 1950," in *Dienstgruppen und westdeutscher Verteidigungs-beitrag* (Boppard am Rhein: Harald Boldt, 1982), p. 37; and Roland G. Foerster, "Innenpolitische Aspekte der Sicherheit Westdeutschlands, 1947–1950," in R. G. Foerster et al., *Anfänge westdeutscher Sicherheitspolitik, 1945–1956,* I (Munich: Oldenbourg, 1982), 461–462.

11. *FRUS 1950,* IV, 687. The view of the British Chiefs can be found in "Military Aspects of United Kingdom Policy toward Germany," COS Report, 29 March 1950, FO 371/85048, PRO. For the American Army's unhappiness with the French, see General Thomas Handy to General J. Lawton Collins, June 4, 1950, General Bradley Files, CJCS, 091 France 1950, RG 218, Records of the Joint Chiefs of Staff, NARS-MMB; and Report on the Functioning of the French High Command, Oct. 26, 1950, 1951, in G-3 091 France TS (Section I) Cases 16 & 20, Entry 97, Army-Operations General Decimal File 1950–1951, Box 20, RG 319, Records of the Army Staff, NARS-MMB. For the Army's views of the Germans, see "U.S. Policy respecting the Disarmament and Demilitarization of the Federal German Republic," Jan. 23, 1950, G-3 091 Germany TS (Section I) Cases 1–20, Plans and Operations Division, Decimal File 1949-Feb. 1950, Box 538, RG 319, Records of the Army Staff, NARS-MMB. The best account of the debate within the U.S. Government is still Lawrence Martin, "The American Decision to Rearm Germany," in Harold E. Stein, ed., *American Civil-Military Decisions: A Book of Case Studies* (Birmingham: University of Alabama Press, 1963), pp. 645–663.

12. Robertson to Adenauer, March 8, 1950, and Adenauer to Robertson, March 21, 1950, PA-AA 244.04, Bd. 2, Bonn; and Robertson to Kirkpatrick, June 22, 1950, FO 371/85050, PRO. See also the exchange of letters between Dennis Allen and Christopher Steel in which they discuss Robertson's change of heart on rearmament. Steel to Allen, April 15, 1950, and Allen to Steel, April 18, 1950, FO 371/85048, PRO.

13. Robertson to Kirkpatrick, March 21, 1950, FO 371/85048, PRO. Robertson was worried that Adenauer might be listening to "wild and irresponsible

people like Manteuffel," a former general associated with right-wing and nationalist circles. For background on Schwerin, I have relied on an unpublished essay by Oberstleutnant G. Fischer, "Der Dienststelle Schwerin—Erste Institution zur Vorbereitung eines Beitrages der Bundesrepublik Deutschland für die westeuropäische Verteidigung," in MGFA, Freiburg. On American protests over the British involvement with Schwerin, see *FRUS 1950,* IV, 688–690.

14. "Report to the High Commissioner," Sept. 12, 1950, Papers of James Pollack, University of Michigan, Ann Arbor; and Hans Speier, *From the Ashes of Disgrace* (Amherst: University of Massachusetts Press, 1981), p. 97. I have also relied on the public opinion surveys compiled by McCloy's assistant, Shepard Stone. For example: "German Attitudes toward an Army and Military Training," Report #19, March 17, 1950, RAS-OPA, HICOG, Papers of Shepard Stone, privately held. For the State Department's views, see *FRUS 1950,* IV, 692. Schumacher's criticism of Adenauer's *Plain Dealer* interview is in the *Berliner Sozialdemokrat,* Jan. 8, 1950, Press Conferences, Schumacher Bestand, Q 14, SPD Archive. See also Drummond, *German Social Democrats,* p. 40.

15. Weekly Intelligence Report, HICOG, Dec. 20, 1949, Box 44, RG 43, Allied Control Council (Germany), NARS-DB; and Bruce to Acheson, Nov. 28, 1949, London Embassy Files 1949, Box 190, RG 84, 350 Germany, NARS-Suitland. About two-thirds of the French opposed German rearmament. George Gallup, *The Gallup Poll: Public Opinion, 1935–1971,* I (New York, 1972), 962.

16. Bullock, *Bevin,* p. 764. For British concerns about rearmament, see "Germany-Defense Questions," Draft Brief for the Secretary at Foreign Ministers' talks, April 1950, FO 371/85048, PRO.

17. *FRUS 1950,* III, 1077.

18. *FRUS 1950,* IV, 688–694. Memo from the President to the Secretary of State, June 16, 1950, NSC Meeting #60, PSF, Box 208, Truman Library. The memorandum is reprinted in *FRUS,* but without the President's handwritten addition.

19. Martin identified McCloy as an early supporter of rearmament, but he provides no evidence for this. Martin, "Decision to Rearm," p. 647. For McCloy's views, see Cyrus Sulzberger, *A Long Row of Candles: Memoirs and Diaries, 1934–1954* (Toronto: Macmillan, 1969), pp. 484–485; *New York Times,* Feb. 7, 1950; *FRUS 1950,* IV, 592, 595; and *New York Herald Tribune,* May 26, 1950. McCloy also opposed Adenauer's suggestion for fear that it would discourage the French from undertaking their own rearmament. Blankenhorn Diary, June 7, 1950, Blankenhorn NL 351/5, pp. 16–17, BA-Koblenz. McCloy to Stimson, June 28, 1950, Reel 123, microfilm edition, Stimson Papers, Yale University.

20. McCloy to Stimson, June 28, 1950, Reel 123, microfilm edition, Stimson Papers, Yale University. Like the State Department, the High Commissioner feared anything that smacked of a revival of centralized police forces resembling the Gestapo. He did not want any mixing of army and police forces, fearing the effect on Germany's fragile democracy. But McCloy also believed that "the lack of a Federal Agency for maintenance of law and order within Germany in emer-

gencies is a serious weakness." McCloy to Acheson, June 26, 1950, 762A.5/ 6-2650, NARS-DB. On the need for a united Europe, see *FRUS 1950*, IV, 635; and Blankenhorn Diary, June 7, 1950, Blankenhorn NL 351/5, pp. 16–17, BA-Koblenz.

21. Ernest R. May, *Lessons of the Past* (New York: Oxford University Press, 1973), pp. 82–83.

22. The reporter was Anne O'Hare McCormick, in *New York Times*, Sept. 18, 1950. After the Chinese intervention in Korea, General Handy, the Army commander in Germany, informed McCloy that the "JCS consider that the current situation in Korea has greatly increased the possibility of general war." Handy to McCloy, 8 Dec. 1950, TSGR, Box 3, Folder II, RG 466, McCloy Papers, NARS-Suitland.

23. Kirkpatrick to Foreign Office, July 4, 1950, FO 371-85049, PRO. For the East German threats, see Morgan (Berlin) to Acheson, Aug. 7, 1950, 762A.00/8-750, NARS-DB; and Norbert Wiggershaus, "Bedrohungsvorstell-ungen Bundeskanzler Adenauer nach Ausbruch des Korea-Krieges," *Militärge-schichtliche Mitteilungen*, 25 (1979), 103–104; and *FRUS 1950*, IV, 966. On the threat to Berlin, see General Handy (CINCEUR) to COS Army, Aug. 29, 1950, D(50)2067, Box 2, RG 466, McCloy Papers, NARS-Suitland. *DBPO*, ser. II, vol. III, no. 3, p. 12. Blankenhorn Diary, July 17, 1950, Blankenhorn NL 351/ 5, p. 55, BA-Koblenz. The French wanted to evacuate the Bonn government to Canada; Blankenhorn preferred Spain.

24. On the mood in Bonn, see "Repercussions in Western Germany of the Korean Conflict," Office of Intelligence, HICOG, Reports and Analysis Division, July 27, 1950, D(50)1860, Box 17, and HICOG Staff Meeting, Aug. 1, 1950, Staff Meetings, Box 1, RG 466, McCloy Papers, NARS-Suitland. For the British perspective, see Kirkpatrick to Foreign Office, Aug. 23, 1950, FO 371/85054, and Kirkpatrick to Gainer, July 15, 1950, FO 371/85049, PRO.

25. Blankenhorn Diary, July 10, 1950, NL 351/5, p. 49, BA-Koblenz. Thayer, *Unquiet Germans*, pp. 210–211. Thayer was prone to exaggerate, but it is interesting that years later he wrote to Blankenhorn about the Chancellor's request to purchase American firearms, telling him he wanted to use the story in his book. Blankenhorn refused permission, probably because of the political embarrassment it might have caused him. See the exchange of letters between Thayer and Blankenhorn, Jan. 8 and 29, 1958, Papers of Charles Thayer, Box 1, Truman Library. Martin, "Decision to Rearm," p. 663; and *FRUS 1950*, IV, 696–697.

26. *FRUS 1950*, IV, 698. Schwerin's memorandum can be found in FO 371/ 85050, PRO. I was not able to find the memo in the American records.

27. McCloy to Byroade, July 18, 1950, in G-3 091 Germany TS (Section I), Cases 1–20, Box 20, RG 319, Army Operations, NARS-MMB; and Acheson, *Present at the Creation*, p. 436.

28. The interview was broadcast on July 22, 1950, and is reprinted in *Information Bulletin*, HICOG, September 1950, pp. 59–60.

29. On the importance of German involvement in any "liberation" of the country, see General Handy to General Collins, July 19, 1950, G-3 091 Germany TS (Section I), Cases 1–20, Box 20, RG 319, Army Operations, NARS-MMB. Kaplan, *Community of Interests,* p. 110. The American representatives were reflecting the sharp change in public sentiment. Although in May 1950 a Gallup Poll had revealed that Americans opposed German rearmament by a 41 to 34 percent margin, by August that had changed dramatically, with 71 percent favoring rearmament. George H. Gallup, *The Gallup Poll: Public Opinion, 1935–1971,* vol. I (New York: Random House, 1972), p. 914.

30. Truman's question to Acheson was recalled by Henry Byroade in a conversation with Shepard Stone, McCloy's Public Affairs Chief. Notes on a conversation with Byroade, July 25, 1950, Shepard Stone Papers. The military's thinking is reflected in Handy to Collins, July 19, 1950, G-3 091 Germany TS (Section I), Cases 1–20, Box 20, RG 319, Army Operations, NARS-MMB. Summary of Daily Meeting with the Secretary, July 18, 1950, Box 4, Executive Secretariat Records, NARS-DB; and *FRUS 1950,* III, 151–159.

31. Byroade's reservations and his dealings with Acheson were expressed in his conversations with Stone. Notes on conversation with Byroade, July 25 and July 31, 1950, Stone Papers. See also Martin, "Decision to Rearm," p. 654. The idea of an international force was also in the air because of the United Nations approval of the American effort in Korea. *FRUS 1950,* III, 167–168.

32. *FRUS 1950,* III, 180–182.

33. Ibid.

34. Byroade's paper, "An Approach to the Formation of a European Army," can be found in G-3 091 Germany TS (Section I-C), Case 12, Book II, Sub. Nos. 11–20, Box 21, RG 319, Army Operations, NARS-MMB. G-3 also provides an analysis of the deficiencies of Byroade's proposal.

35. The final version of the Byroade proposal can be found in *FRUS 1950,* III, 211–219. For the way in which it was negotiated, see Memo for the Record, conversation between Byroade, Gerhardt, and General Schuyler, Aug. 10, 1950, G-3 091 Germany TS (Section I-C), Case 12, Book II, Sub. Nos. 11–20, RG 319, Box 21, Army Operations, NARS-MMB; and Gerhardt to McCloy, Aug. 12, 1950, D(50)1972, TS(50)85, Box 2, RG 466, McCloy Papers, NARS-Suitland.

36. McCloy's lobbying can be followed in *FRUS 1950,* III, 184, 190–192, 194–195, 205–207.

37. These quotations are drawn from an Addendum, dated Sept. 2, 1950, to a Report by Joint Strategic Survey Committee to Joint Chiefs of Staff on the Rearmament of Western Germany, July 27, 1950, CCS-092 Germany [5-4-49] (SCC.3), Box 19, RG 218, Records of the Joint Chiefs of Staff, NARS-MMB; and Memo for General Schuyler, Aug. 5, 1950, Conference re German rearmament, G-3 091 Germany TS (Section I-C), Case 12, Book II, Sub. Nos. 11–20, Box 21, RG 319, Army Operations, NARS-MMB. See also Kaplan, *Community of Interests,* p. 113.

38. Wiggershaus, "Bedrohungsvorstellungen," pp. 82–86; Hans Speidel, *Aus unserer Zeit: Erinnerungen* (Berlin: Ullstein, 1977), pp. 477–496; Wiggershaus, "Zur Frage," pp. 52–55; *FRUS 1950,* IV, 706–709; and *New York Times,* Aug. 18, 1950.

39. *FRUS 1950,* IV, 711–722. Adenauer confuses the issue even further in his memoirs by mixing up the August 17 meeting with the August 23 meeting. Adenauer, *Memoirs,* p. 277. The "Sicherheitsmemorandum" is reprinted in *Sicherheitspolitik der Bundesrepublik Deutschland: Dokumente, 1945–1977,* ed. Klaus von Schubert (Cologne: Wissenschaft und Politik, 1978), pp. 79–85. The compromise proposal on the "European defense force" can be found in *FRUS 1950,* III, 273–278. The fact that "European defense force" was not capitalized was a subtle indication that the military had prevailed. See also Martin, "Decision to Rearm," pp. 656–657.

40. McCloy to Harriman, Sept. 9, 1950, #3 Shaw-Walker, Drawer B, Folder-McCloy, Averell Harriman Papers, Library of Congress. McCloy to Louis Johnson, Sept. 5, 1950, CD 091.7 (Europe) 1950, Box 176, RG 330, NARS-MMB. *Washington Post,* Sept. 9, 1950; and *New York Times,* Sept. 10, 1950.

41. McCloy, "The Situation in Germany," Memorandum for the President, Sept. 10, 1950, PSF, Germany Folder 2, Box 178, Truman Library.

42. Martin, "Decision to Rearm," p. 658. For Acheson's account, see Acheson, *Present at the Creation,* p. 438. On the revolutionary aspect of the American commitment, see *FRUS 1950,* III, 317.

43. Bevin's memo, "German Association with Defense of the West," can be found in *FRUS 1950,* III, 265–266. For Bevin's hesitation about rearmament, a memo by R. Barclay dated July 22, 1950, provides the reasoning: "It is only on account of French and American susceptibilities that the [British] Secretary of State has felt that we must be so very cautious at the present moment about appearing ready even to contemplate measures of German rearmament." FO 371/85050, PRO. For a recent account of the decision making, see Young, *Britain, France, and the Unity of Europe,* pp. 168–169.

44. *FRUS 1950,* III, 297; and Acheson, *Present at the Creation,* p. 442. The Foreign Office's reservations can be found in their messages to Bevin, Sept. 14 and 15, 1950, FO 371/85053, PRO. Young, *Britain, France, and the Unity of Europe,* p. 170. The reservations expressed by William Strang about American policy were particularly pronounced. See Note by Strang, Sept. 15, 1950, FO 371/85054, PRO.

45. Kirkpatrick makes the argument for the police force in his memoirs. Kirkpatrick, *Inner Circle,* pp. 240–241. There is considerable evidence against his idea. Harvey to Foreign Office, Sept. 7, 1950, FO 371/85053, PRO; *The Times,* Sept. 7, 1950. Record of conversation between Lord Henderson and Kurt Schumacher, Sept. 23, 1950, FO 371/85055, PRO. Oliver Franks to FO, Sept. 9, 1950, FO 371/85053, PRO; *FRUS 1950,* III, 1204–05; and Gainer to Dixon, Oct. 12, 1950, FO 371/85056, PRO.

46. Acheson, *Present at the Creation,* p. 442. Schuman told Monnet that he

did not expect the rearmament issue to arise. Monnet, *Memoirs,* p. 341. But Monnet did warn Schuman that the subject was on the American agenda. See his notes to Schuman for early September 1950, AMI 4/4/1, 4/4/2, 4/4/3, and 4/4/4, Monnet Archive, Lausanne. On French views of German rearmament, see Annex D, U.S. and West European Views on German Rearmament, Aug. 17, 1950, FO 371/85050, PRO; and *FRUS 1950,* III, 297–298. For the French proposals on an integrated defense, see *FRUS 1950,* III, 220–224, 1381–82. For the fears of inflation and defense concerns, see *FRUS 1950,* III, 148–149, 154, 170–171. The French demand for massive support "upon the outbreak of hostilities" resembles the demand put forward by Kurt Schumacher in his criticism of Allied rearmament plans. In each case the fear of being occupied and then "liberated" is expressed.

47. *FRUS 1950,* III, 314–315. For background on Jules Moch, see the report prepared by G-3. Memo to Greunther from Bolte, Sept. 26, 1950, 1951, G-3 091 France TS (Section I), Cases 16 & 20, Entry 97, General Decimal File, 1950–1951, Box 20, RG 319, Army Operations, NARS-MMB. For Moch's views on German rearmament, see *FRUS 1950,* III, 172; and his own account of the crisis, Jules Moch, *Historie de réarmement allemand depuis 1950* (Paris: Robert Laffont, 1965), pp. 101–102.

48. *FRUS 1950,* III, 311–313, 322–332.

49. McCloy to Acheson, Sept. 20, 1950, Memo of Conversation, Acheson Papers, Box 65, Truman Library; and *FRUS 1950,* III, 336–337.

50. *FRUS 1950,* III, 338, 358, 364–365.

51. Ball, *Past Has Another Pattern,* p. 91; Monnet, *Memoirs,* p. 344; and *FRUS 1950,* III, 749. On German steel orders and the Ruhr, see *Newsweek,* Sept. 11, 1950, p. 38. Erhard thought Korea offered a golden opportunity, and urged Adenauer to speak to McCloy about eliminating the steel quota. Erhard to Adenauer, Aug. 3, 1950, Adenauer/Erhard Schriftwechsel, Erhard Papers, Bonn; Hays to Acheson, Oct. 19, 1950, 762A.00/10-1950, NARS-DB; and Monnet, *Memoirs,* p. 341.

52. Monnet to Pleven, Oct. 21, 1950, AMI 4/7/3, Monnet Papers, Lausanne. There were other reasons for compromise, including France's financial needs and the demands of war in Indochina. *FRUS 1950,* III, 354; and Schuman's telegram to Paris, Sept. 18, 1950, AMI 4/5/1, Monnet Papers, Lausanne. On the connection between France's financial needs, war in Indochina, and the need for a compromise on German rearmament, see Memo of conversation, Harriman and Petsche, Oct. 20, 1950, #2 Shaw Walker 1950–1953, Drawer A, Harriman Papers. Harriman told Petsche bluntly, "Our whole rearmament effort, the stationing of U.S. troops in Europe, the naming of a U.S. commander, and our large outlay of financial assistance, were all made with the idea of making it easier for France to bring Germany in."

53. *FRUS 1950,* III, 377–380, 384–385; and Monnet, *Memoirs,* pp. 346–347. Schuman and Pleven may have decided not to go beyond a promise of discussions once the Schuman Plan was approved. Acheson's cool reaction may have led them to be more concrete.

54. Carlyle, *Documents on International Affairs,* pp. 339–344. It is estimated that during this period some 60 percent of the French Foreign Legion were Germans. John Robert Young, *The French Foreign Legion: The Inside Story of the World-Famous Fighting Force* (New York: Thomas & Hudson, 1984), p. 208.

55. Edward Fursdon, *The European Defense Community: A History* (New York: St. Martin's Press, 1980), pp. 90–91; Acheson, *Present at the Creation,* p. 459; and *FRUS 1950,* III, 404–405.

56. Memo of conversation with Secretary Marshall, Oct. 27, 1950, Acheson Papers, Box 65, Truman Library; and *FRUS 1950,* III, 420. A. G. Gilchrist, Memo on conversation with M. Lebel of the French Embassy, Oct. 25, 1950, FO 371/85089, PRO.

57. *FRUS 1950,* III, 427–431; and telephone interview with Lincoln Gordon, Washington, D.C., Oct. 13, 1982.

58. Bruce Diary, Oct. 24, 1950, Virginia Historical Society, Richmond; *FRUS 1950,* III, 414; and McCloy to Byroade, Oct. 26, 1950, 762A.5/10-2650, NARS-DB.

59. Monnet, *Memoirs,* p. 348. Monnet's handwritten notes of the meeting, in English, are dated Oct. 27, 1950. AMI 5/2/2, Monnet Papers, Lausanne. McCloy's account of the meeting is in a cable to Byroade and Acheson, Oct. 28, 1950, 762A.5/10-2850, NARS-DB.

60. McCloy to Byroade, Oct. 28, 1950, 762A.5/10-2850, and McCloy to Acheson, Nov. 8, 1950, 762A.5/11-850, NARS-DB. Carlyle, *Documents on International Affairs,* p. 344. At the same time McCloy assisted Adenauer by calling Monnet and insisting that the Ruhr Authority be abolished after the Schuman Plan came into effect, a concession the French would later be forced to grant. McCloy-Monnet telephone conversation, Nov. 6, 1950, AMI 5/7/2, Monnet Archive, Lausanne.

61. A survey of August 1950 found 39 percent of Germans in favor of a West German army, with 50 percent opposed. "Germans View the Korean Outbreak," Report #33, Aug. 23, 1950, RAS-OPA, HICOG, Papers of Shepard Stone. McCloy to Spofford, Nov. 17, 1950, 762A.5/11-1750, NARS-DB; and Sir Con O'Neill to W. D. Allen, Nov. 22, 1950, FO 371/85057, PRO.

62. Drummond, *German Social Democrats,* pp. 45–48; and Schumacher Press Conference, Oct. 24, 1950, Schumacher Bestand, Q 14, SPD Archive. For a thoughtful discussion of Schumacher's concept of a strategic offensive and its relationship to German reunification, see Ulrich Buczylowski, *Kurt Schumacher und die deutsche Frage* (Stuttgart: Seewald, 1973), esp. pp. 102–112.

63. Conversation between Strang and Massagli, Oct. 19, 1950, FO 371/85089, PRO. Adenauer, *Memoirs,* p. 301; and Edinger, *Schumacher,* p. 230. On the election question, see McCloy to Acheson, Dec. 8, 1950, 762A.00/12-850, NARS-DB; and Erich Peter Neumann and Elisabeth Noelle, *Statistics on Adenauer* (Allensbach and Bonn: Verlag für Demoskopie, 1967), pp. 40–41.

64. Blankenhorn Diary, Aug. 31, 1950, Blankenhorn NL 351/5, p. 154, BA Koblenz; and Schwarz, *Adenauer,* pp. 766–767.

65. *FRUS 1950,* IV, 725–727, and III, 369.

66. The Schwerin case is discussed fully by Kirkpatrick, who had an inside view because of Schwerin's ties to the British. Kirkpatrick to D. Gainer, Oct. 31, 1950, FO 371/85057, PRO. There were a variety of explanations for Schwerin's firing. Adenauer claimed he had fired the General because he "was dabbling in politics" and that it would be "a good lesson for the others." Actually the former General had never had much support from other German officers, many of whom saw him as second-rate and even questioned his wartime record. They particularly disliked some of the early ideas he had worked out, such as using a "police force" to begin rebuilding an army. To these men, such ideas, which smacked of using German soldiers as "cannon fodder," were not worthy of consideration. In fact Schwerin had simply been overtaken by events. Initially called upon to plan a secret and slow rearmament process, his position was extremely vulnerable when the process came into the open. Schwerin's close ties to the British did not help either. When rearmament became an American initiative, the United States looked elsewhere for German military leadership.

67. U.S. Department of State, *Documents on Germany, 1944–1985* (Washington, D.C.: GPO, 1986), pp. 345–347; and Terence Prittie, *Konrad Adenauer, 1876–1967* (London: Stacey, 1971), pp. 244–245.

68. Meeting of the Allied High Commission, Nov. 16, 1950, FO 1005/1126b, PRO; and *FRUS 1950*, IV, 780–784.

69. *FRUS 1950*, IV, 784.

70. Meeting of the Allied High Commission, Dec. 1, 1950, FO 1005/1126b, PRO; and Erhard to Adenauer, Nov. 27, 1950, Adenauer/Erhard Schriftwechsel, Erhard Papers, Bonn.

71. *FRUS 1950*, III, 460–464. Emphasis in the last quotation is mine.

72. Ibid., pp. 460–464, 471, 479–480, 493.

73. Drew Middleton, *Where Has Last July Gone?* (New York: Quadrangle, 1973) p. 182.

74. *FRUS 1950*, III, 496–498 (my emphasis).

75. Ibid., pp. 499, 525–528; and Memo for Deputy Secretary of Defense from J. H. Burns, Dec. 5, 1950, Box 176, RG 330, CD 091.7 (Europe) 1950, NARS-MMB. The official history of the JCS notes that after the Spofford Compromise was approved, the Joint Chiefs removed their endorsement from the proposal to send a specified number of infantry divisions to Europe. Walter S. Poole, *The Joint Chiefs of Staff and National Policy, 1950–1952*, vol. IV of *The History of the Joint Chiefs of Staff* (Wilmington, Del.: Glazier, 1979), p. 218.

76. *FRUS 1950*, III, 579–582; and Notes on a Cabinet Meeting, Dec. 8, 1950, Papers of Matthew Connelly, Box 1, Truman Library. Schumacher's criticism of the Spofford Plan came in an interview in the *Frankfurter Allgemeine Zeitung*, Dec. 14, 1950, Schumacher Bestand, Q 7, SPD Archive. Adenauer, *Memoirs*, p. 307; and Adenauer to McCloy, Dec. 11, 1950, Adenauer Papers, StBKA, Rhöndorf.

77. Acheson, *Present at the Creation*, pp. 487–488; Memo, Charles Bolte to General Greunther, Dec. 7, 1950, RG 319, Army Operations, General Decimal

File 1950-51, .091 Germany, Folder G-3, Germany TS (Section II), Cases 21–40, Box 22, NARS-MMB; and *FRUS 1950,* III, 584–585. For the British perspective, see A. G. Gilchrist to Bevin, Nov. 21, 1950, FO 371/85057, PRO; Strang to Bevin, Dec. 5, 1950, FO 371/85058, PRO; and Ivo Mallet's comment on Pierson Dixon's analysis, Dec. 6, 1950, FO 371/85058, PRO.

78. Acheson, *Present at the Creation,* pp. 487–488; and *FRUS 1950,* IV, 808–811.

79. Adenauer's reassurances can be found in *FRUS 1950,* IV, 674–675. For McCloy's thinking, see *FRUS 1950,* IV, 791–792; and McCloy to Acheson, Nov. 29, 1950, 762.A.5/11-2950, NARS-DB.

80. McCloy to Acheson, Dec. 4, 1950, 762A.5/12-450, and McCloy to Acheson, Dec. 8, 1950, 762A.00/12-850, and McCloy to Spofford, Nov. 17, 1950, 762A.5/11-1750, NARS-DB; and "Trend in Opinion on West German Remilitarization," Report #45, Oct. 31, 1950, and "Germans View the Remilitarization Issue," Report #55, Dec. 28, 1950, RAS-OPA, HICOG, Stone Papers. Even a skeptical British observer noted the support for the European concept. Con O'Neill to W. D. Allen, Nov. 22, 1950, FO 371/85057, PRO.

81. *FRUS 1950,* IV, 802.

6. Dealing with the Past: Moral Integration

1. For the record of the original Nuremberg trial, see *Trial of the Major War Criminals before the International Military Tribunal,* vols. I & II (Nuremberg, Germany, 1947). For the record of the twelve other trials held by the United States, see *Trials of War Criminals before the Nuremberg Military Tribunals under Control Council Law No. 10,* 15 vols. (Washington, D.C.: GPO, 1949–1953). These crimes included, but were not limited to, involvement in the "Final Solution," the plundering of occupied countries, and the exploitation of slave labor. My summary of the Nuremberg trials is based on John Mendelsohn, "War Crimes Trials and Clemency in Germany and Japan," in Robert Wolfe, *Americans as Proconsuls* (Carbondale: Southern Illinois University Press, 1984), pp. 227–228. The Army carried out its own review of war crimes cases, and General Handy announced his decisions on clemency at the same time as McCloy. A recent work has made it clear that the German protests often referred to both sets of prisoners (Nuremberg and Dachau) without drawing any distinctions. Frank M. Buscher, *The U.S. War Crimes Trial Program in Germany, 1946–1955* (New York: Greenwood Press, 1989), pp. 160–164.

2. James T. Patterson, *Mr. Republican: A Biography of Robert A. Taft* (Boston: Houghton Mifflin, 1972), pp. 326–328; William J. Bosch, *Judgment on Nuremberg* (Chapel Hill: University of North Carolina Press, 1970), pp. 67–86; and Kennan, *Memoirs, 1925–1950,* p. 261. Kennan favored the British position of summary executions. Many lawyers objected to the new international procedures employed at Nuremberg which strayed from American practices. During the three years in which the trials were held, some procedures varied widely. A later study

indicated that the "policies regarding documents, as practiced by the tribunals in the SS and ministries cases . . . appear to belong to two different worlds." John Mendelsohn, "Trial by Document: The Problem of Due Process for War Criminals at Nuernberg," *Prologue,* 7 (Winter 1975), 234; and Mendelsohn, "War Crimes Trials," pp. 249–251. One cause of confusion was that the Nuremberg procedures combined aspects of both the Anglo-American and Continental legal systems. Although Telford Taylor defended this combination quite persuasively, there was a tendency over time to think that only American principles should apply to the cases. McCloy, for example, referred to his review as "justice American style." McCloy to Javits, May 10, 1951, reprinted in *Department of State Bulletin,* June 11, 1951, p. 941. For Taylor's defense, see Telford Taylor, "The Krupp Trial: Fact vs. Fiction," *Columbia Law Review,* 53 (February 1953), 204–205.

3. Allen W. Dulles, *Germany's Underground* (New York: Macmillan, 1947), p. 198. Clay is quoted in David Clay Large, "'A Gift to the German Future?' The Anti-Nazi Resistance Movement and West German Rearmament," *German Studies Review,* 7 (1984), 499–529. The "other Germany" was a favorite subject of conversation between McCloy and German political leaders as he sought to rebuild German political confidence. McCloy's son would later write his undergraduate honors thesis at Princeton on the German resistance to Hitler. Interview with John J. McCloy II, New York, May 13, 1981.

4. Smith, *Clay Papers,* II, 1038, 1062.

5. Marion Dönhoff, *Foe into Friend,* trans. Gabriele Annan (London: Weidenfeld & Nicolson, 1982), pp. 22–23. On the number of proceedings and executions, see Adalbert Rückerl, *NS-Verbrechen vor Gericht* (Heidelberg: C. F. Müller, 1982), pp. 95–99. On the Schlusstrich, see David Clay Large, "Reckoning without the Past: The HIAG of the Waffen-SS and the Politics of Rehabilitation in the Bonn Republic, 1950–1961," *Journal of Modern History,* 59 (March 1987), 79–113. Philip Jenninger, whose speech on the fortieth anniversary of Kristallnacht led to his resignation, said at one point in his talk: "That is why the call to 'finally put an end' to our past is senseless. Our past will not be quiet, it will not go away . . . " *New York Times,* Nov. 12, 1988.

6. McCloy to Acheson, Jan. 7, 1946, Under Secretary's Correspondence, 1945–1947, Box 27, Acheson Papers, Truman Library. In light of their later disagreement, it is interesting that McCloy admired the work of the American prosecutor Telford Taylor, whom he considered a "very energetic and highly intelligent young lawyer," and even appealed to him (unsuccessfully) to remain in Germany to serve under the High Commission. McCloy to Stimson, Dec. 30, 1948, Reel 121, Henry Stimson Papers, Yale University. McCloy to Adenauer, April 24, 1950, D(50)1228, Box 13, RG 466, McCloy Papers, NARS-Suitland, refers to Adenauer's letter of Feb. 28, 1950. Interview with Eric Warburg, Hamburg, May 10, 1983. Geiler came to see McCloy with a group of jurists, asserting that a new tribunal was necessary. They also asked McCloy to adopt a parole system. HICOG Staff Meeting, Nov. 30, 1949, Weekly Staff Conferences, Box 1, and Frings to McCloy, Nov. 17, 1949, D(49)440a, Box 5, RG 466, McCloy

Papers, NARS-Suitland. See also Buscher, *U.S. War Crimes Trial Program*, pp. 91–113.

7. McCloy to Adenauer, April 24, 1950, D(50)1228, Box 13, and McCloy to A. J. Muench, Jan. 11, 1950 D(50)57, Box 6, and "Power of the High Commissioner to Alter, after Confirmation, the Sentences Imposed by the Military Tribunals at Nuremberg," Office of the General Counsel, Oct. 11, 1949, D(49)278, Box 3, all in RG 466, McCloy Papers, NARS-Suitland. On the issue of time off for good behavior, see McCloy to Manfred George, Aug. 28, 1950, D(50)2065, Box 18, and Weekly Staff Conference, Aug. 29, 1950, Box 1, RG 466, McCloy Papers, NARS-Suitland. McCloy's good-conduct system made no distinction between lesser war criminals, who were not unlike ordinary criminals, and high-level war criminals, who were hardly a threat to prison discipline and whose early release conveyed the impression of excessive leniency.

8. McCloy to Acheson, Feb. 17, 1950, and Acheson to McCloy, Feb. 22, 1950, D(50)472, Box 9, RG 466, McCloy Papers, NARS-Suitland.

9. "Memorandum for Mr. McCloy—War Crimes Clemency Board," Jan. 19, 1950, D(50)113–145, Box 7, and McCloy to Manfred George, Aug. 28, 1950, D(50)2065, Box 18, RG 466, McCloy Papers, NARS-Suitland. The decision to provide for another review was criticized by Robert S. Marcus of the World Jewish Congress. McCloy responded by assuring him that "such a review should not be construed in any sense to constitute a reopening of the Nuremberg proceedings, a re-examination of the validity of the decrees or a departure from the principles upon which the sentences were predicated." McCloy to Robert S. Marcus, March 29, 1950, D(50)1023, Box 11, RG 466, McCloy Papers, NARS-Suitland.

10. McCloy to Acheson, Feb. 17, 1950, D(50)472, Box 9, and Acheson to McCloy, March 1, 1950, D(50)554-604, Box 9, and Byroade to McCloy, March 17, 1950, D(50)787-828, Box 11, and McCloy to Moran, Oct. 9, 1950, D(50)2063, Box 18, all in RG 466, McCloy Papers, NARS-Suitland, and McCloy to Henry Morgenthau, March 7, 1951, McCloy Papers, Amherst College.

11. Letter of transmittal, Aug. 28, 1950, in "Report of the Advisory Board on Clemency for War Criminals to the United States High Commissioner for Germany," Aug. 28, 1950, 71A-2100, Box 373, RG 84, NARS-Suitland (henceforth referred to as Advisory Panel Report).

12. Advisory Panel Report. The introduction to this report, which was included in the HICOG publication *Landsberg: A Documentary Report*, was reprinted in HICOG's *Information Bulletin*, February 1951, pp. 3ff.

13. Advisory Panel Report; and Benjamin B. Ferencz, *Less Than Slaves* (Cambridge, Mass.: Harvard University Press, 1979), p. 74.

14. Advisory Panel Report. Bowie to McCloy, Oct. 31, 1950, 321.6 War Criminals, OED, Box 28, RG 466, McCloy Papers, NARS-Suitland. Judge Peck's behavior was not that unusual; although they are enjoined not to review questions of fact, appellate judges often find ways to overturn verdicts which they consider unreasonable or faulty. See Charles Alan Wright, "The Doubtful Omniscience of

Appellate Courts," *University of Minnesota Law Review,* 41 (1957), 751–782. William Manchester argues that the Panel's actions were evidence of a Washington "conspiracy" to free such German war criminals as Alfried Krupp in return for German rearmament. William Manchester, *The Arms of Krupp* (New York: Bantam, 1970), p. 768. But the evidence for such coordinated action is not compelling. The "conspiracy" view of the Peck Panel's decisions neglects the obvious fact that McCloy set up the Panel, with its mix of personnel and loose directives, *before* the Korean War.

15. McCloy, "The Situation in Germany," Memorandum for the President, Sept. 10, 1950, PSF, Germany Folder 2, Box 178, Truman Library. McCloy's extreme defensiveness about rearmament is an indication that this issue played an important role in his thinking, although it influenced the atmosphere in which decisions were made more than it did specific cases. McCloy to Karl Lowenstein, March 22, 1951, D(51)94–134, Box 24, RG 466, McCloy Papers, NARS-Suitland.

16. For Adenauer's demand, see *FRUS 1950,* IV, 782. For the Schmid and Strauss statements, see *New York Times,* Jan. 10 and April 26, 1951. Schumacher's position was stated in *Die Neue Zeitung,* Jan. 30, 1951, Schumacher Bestand, Interviews, Q-7, SPD Archive. A rather heated debate about the SPD's position on the Landsberg cases is found in the Fraktionsprotokolle, Jan. 9 and Feb. 1, 1951, SPD Archive. Quite a few SPD members opposed Schumacher's position and wanted to see the Landsberg criminals executed. Neuhäusler to McCloy, Jan. 20, 1951, D(51)119, Box 24, RG 466, McCloy Papers, NARS-Suitland. On the military's threats, see Thayer, *Unquiet Germans,* p. 234; and Georg Meyer, "Zur Situation der Deutschen Militärischen Führungsschicht im Vorfeld des Westdeutschenbeitrages, 1945–1950/51," in Roland Foerster, et al., *Anfänge westdeutscher Sicherheitspolitik, 1945–1956,* I (Munich: Oldenbourg, 1982), 696–697. Even Mrs. McCloy was constantly implored to influence her husband. Princess von Isenburg, known as the "mother of the Landsberg defendants," asked her, "von Frau zu Frau," to plead with her husband for clemency. *Der Spiegel,* Jan. 31, 1951, p. 8. Kirkpatrick to Gainer, Feb. 3, 1951, FO 371/93536, PRO.

17. Acheson to McCloy, Nov. 16, 1950, D(50)2530, Box 21, RG 466, McCloy Papers, NARS-Suitland. Truman to Frank Land, Feb. 1, 1951, PSF, Foreign Affairs, Germany—Nazi War Criminals, Box 179, Truman Library. Truman was also convinced, as he put it, "that the German war criminals have had much better treatment than they would have had under their own government."

18. McCloy to Moran, Oct. 9, 1950, D(50)2063, Box 18, and "Meeting between Mr. McCloy and Delegation from the Bundestag," Jan. 9, 1951, D(51) 17/A, Box 24, RG 466, McCloy Papers, NARS-Suitland. McCloy met with several of the defendants, but not with Krupp. Manchester, *Arms of Krupp,* p. 758. Thayer, *Unquiet Germans,* p. 233. Jonathan Rintels to McCloy, June 9, 1952, McCloy Scrapbooks, McCloy Papers, Amherst College. Interviews with Benjamin Buttenwieser, New York, March 28, 1981, and with Robert Bowie, Washington, D.C., Oct. 12, 1982.

19. "Meeting between Mr. McCloy and Delegation from the Bundestag," Jan. 9, 1951, D(51)17/A, Box 24, RG 466, McCloy Papers. NARS-Suitland.

20. Ibid. This report, later given to the columnist Arthur Krock at the *New York Times*, was published April 26, 1951. Undoubtedly McCloy wanted Americans to understand better the pressures he faced in Germany.

21. McCloy to Peck, Feb. 5, 1951, D(51)126, Box 24, RG 466, McCloy Papers, NARS-Suitland; and McCloy to H. Morgenthau, March 7, 1951, McCloy Papers, Amherst College. Mendelsohn, "War Crimes Trials," pp. 250–251; and Large, "Gift to the German Future," p. 504. Although the presence of German military men in Allied prisons—3657 in 1950—was a constant source of dispute between the Germans and the Allies, it was not a more significant cause of delay in German rearmament than French intransigence or the larger movements of opposition in the Federal Republic. German military men, such as Reinhard Gehlen, liked to boast, "As long as a man like General Manstein is imprisoned at Werl, I shall not put on a uniform again." Hans Speier, *From the Ashes of Disgrace: A Journal from Germany, 1945–1955* (Amherst: University of Massachusetts Press, 1981), p. 208. And indeed Manstein, who was held by the British, was released before rearmament officially began in 1955, as were Reinhardt, List, and Kuntze. But the fact was that the process of rearmament did proceed before all the war criminals were freed, and that German military men showed a great willingness to cooperate with the Allies despite the imprisonment of their comrades-in-arms. This is not to say that there was no connection at all between McCloy's decisions and the willingness to assist in the rearmament policy. One of the generals McCloy freed, Wilhelm Speidel, was the brother of Hans Speidel, a key adviser to Adenauer.

22. Mendelsohn, "War Crimes Trials," pp. 250–251; and Manchester, *Arms of Krupp,* pp. 771–773.

23. McCloy to Morgenthau, March 7, 1951, McCloy Papers, Amherst College. McCloy also believed that Clay had some of the same doubts he had. General Clay had modified the confiscation order for Krupp's property, making the order subject to action by each "Zone Commander" rather than by the four-power Control Council for Germany. One reason for this was the fear that if the original decree was carried out, it "would have the effect of vesting title to the forfeited properties in the Control Council and would provide a legal basis for a Russian contention that the Soviet Government was entitled to a voice in the Ruhr properties." Keeping the Russians out of the Ruhr took priority over confiscating Krupp's property, especially as it was assumed that such property would be subject to Allied regulations and controls, such as Law 27 and, later, the Schuman Plan. "Confiscation of Properties," Memo, Bross to McLain, Jan. 19, 1950, D(50)125, Box 7, and McCloy to Senator James Murray, Feb. 24, 1950, D(50)710, Box 10, RG 466, McCloy Papers, NARS-Suitland.

24. "Review of German and Foreign Press Reaction to the Clemency Decisions on Landsberg War Crimes Cases" Feb. 10, 1951, D(51)126, Box 24, and "Analysis of Letters on Landsberg Decisions," March 9, 1951, in Shute to

McCloy, March 9, 1951, D(51)126, Box 24, RG 466, McCloy Papers, NARS-Suitland. For an analysis of public opinion, see "West German Reactions to the Landsberg Decisions," March 6, 1951, Report #63, RAS-OPA, HICOG, She-pard Stone Papers. Liaison Bonn to HICOG Frankfurt, March 7, 1951, 321.6 War Criminals, OED, Box 28, RG 466, McCloy Papers, NARS-Suitland. Coverage in the American press was more pessimistic; see *New York Times,* Feb. 15, Feb. 20, April 6, June 1, and June 10, 1951.

25. Manchester, *Arms of Krupp,* pp. 763–764. *New York Times,* Feb. 7 and 8, 1951. "Review of German and Foreign Press Reaction to the Clemency De-cisions on Landsberg War Crimes Cases," Feb. 10, 1951, D(51)126, Box 24, RG 466, McCloy Papers, NARS-Suitland.

26. *New York Times,* Feb. 2, 1951; *Washington Post,* Feb. 2, 1951; and Telford Taylor, "The Nazis Go Free," *Nation,* Feb. 24, 1951, pp. 170–172.

27. McCloy to Felix Frankfurter, July 11, 1951, Frankfurter Papers, Library of Congress; Meeting between Mr. McCloy and the Bundestag, Jan. 9, 1951, D(51)17/A, Box 24, and McCloy to Lowenstein, March 22, 1951, D(51)126, Box 24, RG 466, McCloy Papers, NARS-Suitland. "Political" is a dangerous word to use because it implies that McCloy ordered men executed who were in some sense innocent. That was not the case. He actually spared men who, in his view, were less guilty than those he ordered executed, and he spared them, at least in part, because of the appeal of German leaders.

28. McCloy to Cardinal Frings, March 15, 1951, D(51)126, Box 24, RG 466, McCloy Papers, NARS-Suitland.

29. McCloy to Eleanor Roosevelt, March 12, 1951, folder J. J. McCloy, Eleanor Roosevelt Papers, Box 3913, Franklin D. Roosevelt Library; and McCloy to Javits, May 10, 1951, in *Department of State Bulletin,* June 11, 1951, p. 941. On Krupp's conviction, see Taylor, "Krupp Trial," pp. 208–209. As Ferencz notes, in 1943 when Alfried Krupp became chairman, one of his first directives confirmed that "the owner of the family enterprise has the full responsibility for the direction of the entire enterprise." Ferencz, *Less Than Slaves,* p. 70.

30. McCloy to Morgenthau, March 7, 1951, McCloy Papers, Amherst Col-lege; and Taylor, "Nazis Go Free," p. 172. Peter Hayes, *Industry and Ideology: I. G. Farben in the Nazi Era* (Cambridge, Eng.: Cambridge University Press, 1987), pp. 380–381.

31. For the relatively light sentences given in the Farben and Flick cases, and the sentences in the Krupp case, see *Trials of War Criminals before the Nuremberg Military Tribunals under Control Council Law No. 10: VIII, U.S. v. Krauch* (Wash-ington, D.C.: GPO, 1953), 1205–08; VI, *U.S. v. Flick* (Washington, D.C.: GPO, 1952), 1223; and IX, *U.S. v. Krupp* (Washington, D.C.: GPO, 1950), 1444–46. The prosecution staff was outraged at the light sentences given in the Farben case. Joseph Borkin, *The Crime and Punishment of I. G. Farben* (New York: Free Press, 1978), pp. 154–55. Lersner to McCloy, Feb. 1, 1951, VST Presse, 500 03-I, Thyssen Archive, Duisburg. A British visitor reported that one industrialist, Hans-Günther Sohl of Vereinigte Stahlwerke, spoke "somewhat contemptuously

about Alfried Krupp as a somewhat insignificant person who could never have merited such a severe sentence." Dennis Wilson, comments on a trip to Germany, Feb. 6–16, 1951, FO 371/93376, PRO. Ferencz's book tells the depressing story of the refusal of most of the industrialists to pay restitution. He also stresses the important role McCloy played in gaining restitution from Krupp. Ferencz, *Less Than Slaves,* p. 189.

32. Acheson, *Present at the Creation,* p. 621. In December 1952 Adenauer emphasized that a "far-reaching gesture toward solution of war-criminals problem" would "favorably impress public opinion." *FRUS 1952–1954,* VII, 392. He brought up the issue of war criminals at his first meeting with President Eisenhower. *FRUS 1952–1954,* VII, 442. As his emissary, Hallstein also pressed the issue. MacArthur to Handy, Jan. 29, 1952, D(52)267, Box 36, and Heusinger to McCloy, May 19, 1952, D(52)1234, Box 41, RG 466, McCloy Papers, NARS-Suitland. On the Parole Boards, see Mendelsohn, "War Crimes Trials," pp. 253–254.

33. The subsequent story of the Krupp firm is told in an entertaining, if somewhat overdramatized, fashion by Manchester, *Arms of Krupp,* pp. 771ff.

34. "Current West German Views on the War Criminals Issue," Sept. 8, 1952, Report #153, ser. 2, RAS-OPA, HICOG, Shepard Stone Papers; Noelle and Neumann, *The Germans,* p. 315; and Tom Bower, *The Pledge Betrayed* (Garden City, N.Y.: Doubleday, 1982), pp. 364–392.

35. Mendelsohn, "War Crimes Trials" p. 259. In a comparative context, the policy in Germany was more successful than that in Japan, although one might argue that the scale of war crimes committed by the Germans invalidates such a comparison. Gotthard Jasper has recently argued that part of the price paid for the success of Adenauer's Western oriented policy was the silence about Nazi war criminals. He contends that Adenauer's reliance on right-wing and conservative parties in his coalition made it politically impossible for his government to act tougher on this issue, and the Western powers went along with this. The only problem with his argument is the assumption that the SPD would have conducted a more vigorous policy to hunt out war criminals. This is hard to accept. If anything, the SPD's hope to capture nationalist sentiment might have made it even more cautious. Gotthard Jasper, "Wiedergutmachung und Westintegration: Die halbherzige justizielle Aufarbeitung der NS-Vergangenheit in der frühen Bundesrepublik," in *Westdeutschland, 1945–1955,* ed. Ludolf Herbst (Munich: Oldenbourg, 1986), pp. 183–202.

36. McCloy, "Remarks," Conference on the Future of Jews in Germany, D(49)36-71, Box 1, RG 466, McCloy Papers, NARS-Suitland. Sharett is quoted in Lily Gardner Feldman, *The Special Relationship between West Germany and Israel* (Boston: Allen & Unwin, 1984), p. 56. See also Nicholas Balabkins, *West German Reparations to Israel* (New Brunswick, N.J.: Rutgers University Press, 1971).

37. The skepticism about the American role, and specifically McCloy's activities, on behalf of Wiedergutmachung can be found in Michael Wolffsohn, "Globalentschädigung für Israel und die Juden? Adenauer und die Opposition in der

Bundesregierung," in Ludolf Herbst and Constantin Goschler, *Wiedergutmachung in der Bundesrepublik Deutschland* (Munich: Oldenbourg, 1989), pp. 180–181. Wolffsohn also argues that Germany's treaty with Israel was of little consequence in influencing Western public opinion: M. Wolffsohn, "Die Wiedergutmachung und der Westen—Tatsachen und Legenden," *Aus Politik und Zeitgeschichte,* 16–17 (1987), 19–29. He also argues that the treaty had little importance in influencing the action of major governments: M. Wolffsohn, "Das Deutsch-Israelische Wiedergutmachungsabkommen von 1952 im Internationalen Zusammenhang," *Vierteljahrshefte für Zeitgeschichte,* 36 (1988), 691–731. For a different view, see Kai von Jena, "Versöhnung mit Israel? Die Deutsch-Israelischen Verhandlungen bis zum Wiedergutmachungsabkommen von 1952," *Vierteljahrshefte für Zeitgeschichte,* 34 (1986), 457–480. On the question of public opinion, Norbert Frei has written an effective rebuttal to Wolffsohn's arguments: Norbert Frei, "Die deutsche Wiedergutmachungspolitik gegenüber Israel im Urteil der öffentlichen Meinung der USA," in Herbst and Goschler, *Wiedergutmachung,* pp. 215–230. The percentage of Germans favoring "restitution to German Jews who are still alive" in August 1949 was 54 percent. But to the more specific question "Do you think Germany should make restitution to Israel in the form of 3000 million Marks' worth of goods, or do you feel it is unnecessary?" 44 percent answered that they felt it unnecessary, 24 percent expressed agreement but felt the amount was too high, and only 11 percent expressed unqualified agreement. Noelle and Neumann, *The Germans,* p. 188.

38. McCloy, "Remarks," Conference on The Future of Jews in Germany, D(49)36-71, Box 1, RG 466, McCloy Papers, NARS-Suitland; and *New York Times,* Aug. 9, 1949.

39. Nahum Goldmann, *The Autobiography of Nahum Goldmann,* trans. Helen Sebba (New York: Holt, Rinehart & Winston, 1969), pp. 251–253. Telephone interview with Benjamin Ferencz, New York, Oct. 28, 1981. Ferencz felt McCloy's position on the restitution program was "perfect, absolutely perfect." "Minutes of Meeting with the High Commissioner," April 10, 1950, D(50)1129, Box 11, and Memo, Hanes to McCloy, "Jewish Restitution Successor Organization: Proposal re bulk settlement of JRSO claims," Aug. 11, 1950, D(50)1967, Box 17, and Ferencz to McCloy, Sept. 25, 1951, D(51)1487, Box 32, and McCloy to Kaisen, March 25, 1952, D(52)768, Box 39, all in RG 466, McCloy Papers, NARS-Suitland. McCloy also insured that the laws of restitution in the American zone, which were the most liberal, were extended to the rest of the Federal Republic. At a meeting of the JRSO in November 1951 the organization adopted a resolution "expressing gratitude and appreciation to Mr. John J. McCloy . . . for his invaluable assistance and cooperation, particularly in connection with bulk settlements, without which many of the achievements during this past year would have been impossible." Goldwater to McCloy, Nov. 20, 1951, D(51)1967, Box 33, RG 466, McCloy Papers, NARS-Suitland. On JRSO's administrative costs, see Ferencz to McCloy, April 30, 1952, D(52)1062, Box 40, RG 466, McCloy Papers, NARS-Suitland. Ferencz later stated that one of the ways he had con-

vinced McCloy to cover JRSO's administrative costs was to point out, "You've just given back a convicted war criminal [Krupp] about three billion marks in assets, I owe you three million. If you insist I'll pay it back, but it's got to come out of the pockets of the victims, and I don't think it's fair to ask the victims to pay back the expenses of what it took to get back part of what was stolen from them." McCloy was persuaded. Interview with John J. McCloy and Benjamin Ferencz, April 24, 1984, McCloy Project, Council on Foreign Relations, McCloy Papers, Amherst College.

40. Adenauer's speech is quoted in *Der deutsch-israelische Dialog,* ed. Rolf Vogel, I (Munich: K. G. Saur, 1987), p. 45. See also Balabkins, *West German Reparations,* pp. 96-118.

41. Schwarz, *Adenauer,* pp. 897–906, provides a sympathetic portrait of Adenauer's motives. Frei quotes the *St. Louis Post-Dispatch*: "If Chancellor Adenauer truly spoke for the German people when he promised reparations to Israel for wrongs inflicted on the Jews by the Nazis, then the new Germany has advanced far beyond the unspeakable racism of Hitler's day." Frei, "Wiedergutmachungspolitik," p. 219.

42. Goldmann, *Autobiography,* pp. 258–261; and Jena, "Versöhnung," pp. 465–467. The best account of the opposition to Adenauer's commitments can be found in Wolffsohn, "Globalentschädigung," pp. 162–172.

43. The State Department's message is quoted in "Memorandum to Mr. McCloy on Israel-German negotiations: from Benjamin Ferencz, April 4, 1952, D(52)833, Box 39, RG 466, McCloy Papers, NARS-Suitland. On the attempt by Abs to engineer a postponement, see London to Acheson, March 3, 1952, and Acheson to London, March 7, 1952, D(52)427, Box 37, RG 466, McCloy Papers, NARS-Suitland. McCloy to Goldmann, March 11, 1952, D(52)571-621, Box 38, RG 466, McCloy Papers, NARS-Suitland. For Adenauer's comments at the Cabinet meeting, see Ulrich Enders and Konrad Reisen, eds., *Die Kabinettsprotokolle der Bundesregierung,* V (Boppard am Rhein: Harald Boldt, 1988), 132–133; and the notation by Hans-Christoph Seebohm in Wolffsohn, "Globalentschädigung," p. 165.

44. London Embassy to Washington, March 31, 1952, D(52)675-720, Box 38, RG 466, McCloy Papers, NARS-Suitland.

45. Acheson to McCloy, April 4, 1952, D(52)859, and Memo, Ferencz to McCloy, April 4, 1952, D(52)833, Box 39, RG 466, McCloy Papers, NARS-Suitland.

46. Wolffsohn, "Globalentschädigung," p. 168. Acheson to McCloy, April 22, 1952, D(52)859c, Box 39, and McCloy to Acheson, April 28, 1952, D(52)958, Box 40, RG 466, McCloy Papers, NARS-Suitland.

47. Jena, "Versöhnung," p. 471; and Goldmann, *Autobiography,* pp. 263–264. For the opposition of Schäffer and Abs, see Wolffsohn, "Globalentschädigung," pp. 171–174. For Blankenhorn's fears about a failure of the negotiations, see Wolffsohn, "Globalentschädigung," p. 174.

48. Goldmann to Adenauer, May 19, 1952 (copy) and Goldmann to McCloy,

May 20, 1952, D(52)1259-1299, Box 42, RG 466, McCloy Papers, NARS-Suitland; and Goldmann, *Autobiography,* pp. 265–266.

49. McCloy to Acheson, May 15, 1952, D(52)1212, Box 41, RG 466, McCloy Papers, NARS-Suitland. Jena, "Versöhnung," pp. 473–475. Goldmann, *Autobiography,* pp. 265–268. See Bonn (Liaison) to Acheson, May 21, 1952, D(52)1253, and May 23, 1952 D(52)1254, Box 41, RG 466, McCloy Papers, NARS-Suitland, for reports on the consternation in Bonn political circles over the resignations of Böhm and Küster, and the realization of the "bad effect on US and world opinion of suspicion that FedRep unwilling to atone for crimes of the past."

50. *FRUS 1952–1954,* VII, 103.

51. Reber to McCloy, June 11, 1952, D(52)1413, Box 42, RG 466, McCloy Papers, NARS-Suitland. For the June 17 Cabinet meeting, *Die Kabinettsprotokolle,* 5 (1952), 394–398; and Wolffsohn, "Globalentschädigung," p. 179. For McCloy's telegram of July 15, 1952, see Blankenhorn NL 351/13, p. 98, BA-Koblenz.

52. Wolffsohn, "Globalentschädigung," pp. 180–181, disputes Jena's contention that McCloy was sympathetic to Jews, citing as evidence McCloy's role in the decision not to bomb Auschwitz. He argues that in a special search of the archives of the American Jewish Committee he could not support the argument that McCloy had a "judenfreundliche" (friendly-to-Jews) attitude. One need not maintain, however, that McCloy was "judenfreundlich" to recognize that McCloy's words and actions conveyed the message to German leaders that Germany's relationship to Israel and the Jews was a "test" of the Federal Republic's commitment to democracy, and that American attitudes and policy would be affected by this.

7. Ties That Bind: Economic Integration

1. *FRUS 1950,* IV, 674; and McCloy to Acheson, Dec. 27, 1950, 762A.00/12-2750, NARS-DB.

2. McCloy, "The Situation in Germany," Memorandum for the President, Sept. 10, 1950, PSF, Germany, Folder 2, Box 178, Truman Library. How seriously McCloy lobbied or intervened with German politicians to bring this about is unclear, but the evidence suggests that he did not use very much pressure.

3. Daily Meetings of the Secretary, Dec. 28, 1950, Records of the Office of Executive Secretary, Box 4, NARS-DB; and *FRUS 1951,* IV, 98–100.

4. *FRUS 1951,* IV, 103.

5. Ibid., pp. 87–89; and William J. Diebold, *The Schuman Plan* (New York: Harper, 1959), pp. 363ff. The defense of the combined economy, made by Hermann Kellermann of the Arbeitskreis für Fragen der Neuordnung, is quoted in Leah Zell, "The Politics of Reconstruction in the Ruhr, 1945–1952," (Ph.D. diss., Harvard University, 1979), pp. 469, 474. Zell's dissertation is the most detailed and thorough investigation of this topic. She notes that although the

steelmakers were committed to the combined economy, the coal industry and the unions were so skeptical that they forced concessions from the steel industry before they would back its plan.

6. Bowie's remark, made during negotiations with Erhard, Jan. 2, 1951, is in PA-AA 243.05, Bd. 2, Bonn. The British referred to Bowie as the "mad mullah of decartelization." A. D. Wilson to D. B. Pitblade, Feb. 27, 1951, FO 371/93693, PRO. Their views on Law 27 are in Memorandum on Organizational Structure of Steel Unit Companies, March 1951, FO 371/93693, PRO. For the French position, see Monnet to Schuman, Jan. 22, 1951, AMG 11/1/9, Monnet Archive, Lausanne; and *FRUS 1951,* IV, 88.

7. *FRUS 1951,* IV, 88.

8. Diebold, *Schuman Plan,* pp. 380–382.

9. A. D. Wilson to D. B. Pitblade, Feb. 27, 1951, FO 371/93693, PRO; and McCloy to Secretary of State, Sept. 27, 1950, 850.33/9-2750, NARS-DB. For Monnet's arguments to Schuman against the DKV, see Monnet to Schuman, Dec. 22, 1950, AMG 20/5/5, Monnet Archive, Lausanne. Bowie's comments on the DKV can be found in his talks with Erhard, Jan. 2, 1951, PA-AA 243.05, Bd. 2, Bonn; and in *FRUS 1951,* IV, 89.

10. For the meetings in question, I have used British and German sources: Meeting of Jan. 2, 1951, FO 371/93688, PRO; Meeting of Jan. 2, 1951, PA-AA 243.055, Bd. 2, Bonn; Aktienvermerk, Jan. 17, 1951, PA-AA 243.03, Bd. 2, Bonn; and Vermerk, Jan. 15, 1951, PA-AA 221.40, Bd. 6, Bonn.

11. Meeting of Jan. 2, 1951, FO 371/93688, PRO; and Meeting of Jan. 2, 1951, PA-AA 243.055, Bd. 2, Bonn. For Erhard's problems, see Heiner R. Adamsen, *Investitionshilfe für die Ruhr* (Wuppertal: Peter Hammer, 1981), p. 56; and Kirkpatrick to Foreign Office, March 13, 1951, FO 371/93765, PRO. Adenauer could be a harsh critic of Erhard. Adenauer to Erhard, March 19, 1951, Schriftwechsel, Erhard Papers, Erhard Stiftung, Bonn.

12. *Die Neuordnung Eisen- und Stahlindustrie* (Munich: C. H. Beck, 1954), pp. 447–454.

13. The conversation between Bowie and Erhard is recorded in Aktienvermerk, Jan. 17, 1951, PA-AA 243.03, Bd. 2, Bonn. The British actually opposed a fixed percentage agreement. Notes of a Meeting at the Foreign Office, Jan. 26, 1951, FO 371/93690, PRO.

14. Henle to Erhard, Dec. 21, 1950, Schuman Plan Korrespondenz 1950–1952, Henle Nachlass, Klöckner Archiv, Duisburg. For Henle's complaints about Law 27, see Henle to McCloy, Dec. 20, 1950, and Jan. 9, 1951, Schuman Plan Korrespondenz 1950–1952, and Henle to Gert Whitman, Jan. 25, 1951, AHK Korrespondenz 1945–1955, both in Henle Nachlass, Klöckner Archiv, Duisburg. On the importance of Sohl in the resistance to Law 27, see Lersner to Sohl, Jan. 20, 1951, Lersner/Sohl Korrespondenz, VST Presse 500-03-I, Thyssen Archiv, Duisburg. The British also thought that Vereinigte Stahlwerke (Vestag) "had not given up its prewar expansionist ambitions." Record of conversation, Hon. M. Layton with A. E. Teare, March 14, 1951, FO 371/93694, PRO. Vestag brought

in the New York law firm of Shearman, Sterling, and Wright, who pleaded the German case on grounds of the "security of the United States." For this and Zangen's comment, see Zell, "Politics of Reconstruction," pp. 479–480.

15. The suspicions about the Ruhr industrialists can be found in Walter Lippmann's articles in the *New York Herald Tribune,* March 5, 1951, and the *Washington Post,* March 6, 1951. McCloy to Henle, Jan. 27, 1951, Henle NL, Schuman Plan Korrespondenz 1950–1952, Klöckner Archiv, Duisburg; and H. G. Sohl, Memorandum of conversation, Feb. 9, 1951, Lehr NL 20, BA-Koblenz.

16. McCloy to Adenauer, Feb. 12, 1951, PA-AA 242.19, Bd. 5, Bonn.

17. Kirkpatrick to Morrison, March 21, 1951, FO 371/93357, PRO. On the crisis in the German economy, see Werner Abelshauser, "Ansätze 'Korporativer Marktwirtschaft' in der Korea Krise der Früheren Fünfzige Jahre," *Vierteljahrshefte für Zeitgeschichte,* 30 (1982), 715–756. Adenauer pushed the industrialists hard for an agreement on codetermination. Zell, "Politics of Reconstruction," pp. 459–461. For another account of Adenauer's role in the resolution of the codetermination controversy, see Horst Thum, *Mitbestimmung in der Montanindustrie* (Stuttgart: Deutsche Verlag, 1982), pp. 79–86. Henle encouraged Adenauer's intervention by playing on his distrust of Erhard and insisting that Erhard and the Schuman Plan negotiators had given too much to the Americans. Henle also implied that McCloy, though secretly sympathetic, was trapped by the "anti-trust complex" of such men as the fanatical Bowie. Henle to Adenauer, Feb. 13, 1951, Henle NL, Korrespondenz mit Bundeskanzler, September 1949–September 1953, Klöckner Archiv, Duisburg. Adenauer's intervention is in Adenauer to McCloy, Feb. 15, 1951, PA-AA 242.19, Bd. 5, Bonn.

18. *FRUS 1951,* IV, 91–93. That McCloy's suspicions were correct is shown by an examination of Henle's correspondence, sometimes channeled through Adenauer's close friend Robert Pferdmenges. Henle to Pferdmenges, Jan. 31, 1951, and Feb. 20, 1951, Henle NL, Allgemeine Korrespondenz 1945–1955, Klöckner Archiv, Duisburg. For the McCloy-Monnet conversation, see Notes on a conversation with McCloy, Feb. 19, 1951, AMG 12/3/6, Monnet Archive, Lausanne.

19. Adenauer to McCloy, Feb. 20 and 28, 1951, PA-AA 242.19, Bd. 5, Bonn. The Chancellor also requested a 75 percent "global" coverage, rather than just meeting the needs of individual firms. If such a plan yielded surpluses of coal for some steel companies, Adenauer proposed that they should "voluntarily" allow the Schuman Plan's High Authority to dispose of the surpluses. He also proposed a two-year delay before the liquidation of the DKV, which would put off the problem until after the next elections.

20. *FRUS 1951,* IV, 97; and McCloy to Adenauer, March 11, 1951, PA-AA 242.19, Bd. 5, Bonn.

21. On the Patterson trip, see Zell, "Politics of Reconstruction," pp. 481–482; and McCloy to Acheson, Feb. 28, 1951, D(51)255, Box 25, RG 466, McCloy Papers, NARS-Suitland. Some writers mistakenly give Patterson credit for successfully convincing the American High Commission to restore the coal and steel industry to private ownership. Thum, *Mitbestimmung,* p. 112.

22. McCloy to Acheson, Feb. 28, 1951, D(51)255, Box 25, RG 466, McCloy Papers, NARS-Suitland; and Patterson to McCloy, Feb. 28, 1951, General Correspondence, Box 41, Papers of Robert Patterson, Library of Congress. Patterson rather immodestly claimed to have "broken the deadlock." *New York Times,* March 5, 1951. For the Germans' investment of $15,000, and their resulting anger at Schmid, see Küster to Henle, Feb. 15, 1951, Henle NL, Gesetz 27 Schriftwechsel, Klöckner Archiv, Duisburg; and Zell, "Politics of Reconstruction," pp. 486–487.

23. *FRUS 1951,* IV, 97–98; and Zell, "Politics of Reconstruction," pp. 488–489.

24. This account of the March 3, 1951, meeting is based on a memorandum dated May 15, 1951, prepared by the Correspondence Control Unit, D(51)286, Box 25, RG 466, McCloy Papers, NARS-Suitland. This document is actually a translation of a German record of the meeting. McCloy's agreement with Monnet is recorded by Bowie in a Memorandum by Robert Bowie, March 4, 1951, D(51)289, Box 25, RG 466, McCloy Papers, NARS-Suitland. McCloy gave his own account of the meeting in an Executive Session of the High Commission. Kirkpatrick to Foreign Office, March 8, 1951, FO 371/93693, PRO. The trade-union leaders did not feel as though they had given way on their basic objections; they understood that McCloy was willing to allow a replacement organization to assume the "technical" functions of the DKV. Protokolle DGB Bundesvorstand, March 11 and 12, 1951, DGB Archiv, Düsseldorf. This led to later misunderstandings. *FRUS 1951,* IV, 130–135.

25. The account of McCloy's meeting with the industrialists is based on a record kept by Sohl, dated March 5, 1951, in Lehr NL 20, BA-Koblenz. McCloy even told the industrialists that cooperation with the Schuman Plan would also influence the level of Marshall Plan assistance, an important consideration because of Germany's balance-of-payments crisis.

26. The liaison was Fritz Oppenheimer, whose memorandum for Bowie, dated March 6, 1951, can be found in D(51)289, Box 25, RG 466, McCloy Papers, NARS-Suitland. Kirkpatrick to Foreign Office, March 8, 1951, FO 371/93693, PRO. Adenauer's March 14, 1951, letter is reprinted in *Die Neuordnung der Eisen- und Stahlindustrie,* pp. 455–457. Zell notes some of the technical problems created by the proposal. Zell, "Politics of Reconstruction," pp. 489–490. Following a brief flurry over the status of the Saar, an exchange of letters was attached to the treaty in which the German government declared that by signing the treaty it did not recognize the final status of the Saar. Diebold, *Schuman Plan,* pp. 76–77.

27. Oliver Harvey to Morrison, May 4, 1951, FO 1008/1, PRO; Byroade to Acheson, March 20, 1951, 850.33/3-2051, NARS-DB; and *Le Monde,* March 16–22, 1951 (weekly edition), quoted in Diebold, *Schuman Plan,* p. 75.

28. Adenauer, *Memoirs,* pp. 354–355; and *Department of State Bulletin,* Aug. 13, 1951, p. 263, and July 9, 1951, p. 65.

29. "The Effectiveness of Recent Informational Efforts on the Schuman Plan," May 30, 1951, RAS-OPA, HICOG, Stone Papers. The FDP's "plot" against

Adenauer and its failure was reported by Thayer. Bonn Liaison (Thayer) to Secretary of State, April 7, 1951, 762A.00/4-751, and April 16, 1951, 762A.00/4-1651, Box 3851, RG 59, NARS-DB.

30. Schumacher's statements about the Schuman Plan can be found in: the SPD Fraktion in the Bundestag, May 8, 1951, in B136/24775, BA-Koblenz; his speech of May 25, 1951, Schumacher Bestand, Q-17, SPD Archive, Bonn; *FRUS 1951,* IV, 105; and Liaison Bonn to Frankfurt, May 9, 1951, D(51)609, Box 27, RG 466, McCloy Papers, NARS-Suitland. For the reaction of industrialists, see Zell, "Politics of Reconstruction," p. 491; as well as Sohl to Pferdmenges, April 6, 1951, VST-Volkswirtschaft 400-03, Thyssen Archiv, Duisburg; Henle to F. Stallworth, March 28, 1951, Henle NL, Korrespondenz USA/Reise 1949–1951, Klöckner Archiv, Duisburg; and McCloy to Adenauer, March 22, 1951, PA-AA 221.40, Bd. 6, Bonn.

31. Harvey to Bevin, 2 March 1951, *DBPO,* II/I, no. 222, p. 419; and Morrison to Harvey, 12 March 1951, *DBPO,* II/I, no. 227, p. 431. See also Discussion in the Foreign Office, June 29, 1951, FO 371/93379, PRO; and Morrison to Kirkpatrick, March 17, 1951, FO 371/93693, and March 27, 1951, FO 371/93694, PRO. The British did hold up the ratification of the Schuman Plan until they got a guarantee from the Germans for their supplies of scrap steel. *DBPO,* II/I, no. 341, p. 645.

32. The British did insist, however, that the High Commissioners ask the Chancellor whether he intended to pose the question of the nationalization of heavy industry to the Bundestag. Adenauer replied that he did not, and that in his opinion there was no majority in favor of it. Meeting of the Allied High Commission, April 5, 1951, FO 1005/1124, PRO.

33. Zell, "Politics of Reconstruction," p. 512; Diebold, *Schuman Plan,* p. 357; Alan S. Milward, *The Reconstruction of Western Europe, 1945–1951* (London: Methuen, 1984), p. 411; and Volker R. Berghahn, *The Americanisation of West German Industry* (Leamington Spa: Berg, 1986), p. 286.

34. *FRUS 1951,* IV, 130–135. For the delay in the DKV dissolution, see McCloy to Acheson, July 1, 1952, 850.33/7-152, NARS-DB; and Diebold, *Schuman Plan,* p. 380.

35. Berghahn, *Americanisation,* pp. 286–287.

36. Ibid., pp. 284–285.

37. In her otherwise distinguished work, Zell underemphasizes the role of American intervention in helping Adenauer overcome the resistance of groups such as the Ruhr industrialists to European cooperation. Zell, "Politics of Reconstruction," p. 549. Milward, *Reconstruction,* p. 418.

38. Milward, *Reconstruction,* p. 429; and Michael Hogan, *The Marshall Plan,* (Cambridge, Eng.: Cambridge University Press, 1987), p. 355. On the EPU, see William Diebold, *Trade and Payments in Western Europe* (New York: Harper and Row, 1952), pp. 87–110; and Hogan, *Marshall Plan,* pp. 295–335. The Germans could not settle their October deficit with the EPU in dollars because their reserves totaled only $200 million—"just peanuts," in the words of Hubert Havlick, the

U.S. Representative on the Managing Board of the EPU. Hubert Havlick, Oral History, p. 188, Truman Library.

39. Benjamin Buttenwieser, Oral History, Columbia University, pp. 71–74; Acheson to Katz, Nov. 2, 1950, Germany-1951, OSR, Central Secretariat, Country Subject Files, Box 4, RG 286, NARS-Suitland; and Riddleberger to Katz, Oct. 23, 1950, Germany-Trade, OSR, Country Subject Files, Box 3, RG 286, NARS-Suitland.

40. Hogan, *Marshall Plan,* pp. 357–358; Milward, *Reconstruction,* pp. 431–432; and Diebold, *Trade and Payments,* pp. 111–117.

41. Hanes to Erhard, Oct. 13, 1950, B102/12627, BA-Koblenz; and Erhard to Adenauer, Dec. 6, 1950, Schriftwechsel, Erhard Papers, Erhard Stiftung, Bonn. On the social implications of restricting the economy in order to deal with the balance-of-payments problem, see "Report on Internal Financial Stability of the Federal Republic," Marshall Plan Ministry, May 1951, B146/224, BA-Koblenz.

42. For Katz's protest over German policies, see *FRUS 1951,* III, 1618–1620. His angrier comments were made to Sir Edmund Hall-Patch, March 13, 1951, FO 371/93766, PRO. See also Diebold, *Trade and Payments,* pp. 120–121; Hogan, *Marshall Plan,* p. 357.

43. The British saw the friction between the German ministries as the reason for the ineffectiveness of the German response to these economic problems. Kirkpatrick to Foreign Office, 13 March 1951, FO 371/93765, PRO. Vocke to Adenauer, Feb. 26, 1951, from the BDL Archive, Ludwig Erhard Stiftung, Bonn. On Blücher's concerns, see Karl Albrecht, *Das Menschliche hinter dem Wunder* (Düsseldorf: Econ, 1970), pp. 156–160. McCloy to Acheson, March 6, 1951, 862A.00/3-651, Box 5181, RG 59, NARS-DB. For a copy of McCloy's letter to Adenauer, see Abelshauser, "Ansätze 'Korporativer Marktwirtschaft,'" pp. 734–738.

44. For Adenauer's reply, see Abelshauser, "Ansätze 'Korporativer Marktwirtschaft,'" pp. 739–752. For Erhard's protest over Blücher's appointment, and Adenauer's response, see Erhard to Adenauer, March 2, 1951, and Adenauer to Erhard, March 19, 1951, Schriftwechsel, Erhard Papers, Erhard Stiftung, Bonn.

45. On the grain shortage, see McCloy to Acheson, March 3, 1951, 850.33/3-51, RG 59, NARS-DB. For Adenauer's reaction to McCloy's letter, see Kirkpatrick to FO, March 13, 1951, FO 371/93765, PRO.

46. *FRUS 1951,* III, 1623–1629; and Hogan, *Marshall Plan,* p. 363.

47. See Bode (for McCloy) to Frankfurt (HICOG), March 22, 1951, D(51)373, and ECA's reply, Foster to Frankfurt, March 27, 1951, D(51)394, Box 26, RG 466, McCloy Papers, NARS-Suitland. For the German record, see Vermerk, March 23, 1951, conversation between Cattier, Bode, and Adenauer, B-102/12581(2), BA-Koblenz. See also McCloy to Acheson, March 9, 1951, 862A.0033/3-951, Box 5238, and April 11, 1951, 862A.0033/4-1151, Box 5181, RG 59, NARS-DB.

48. Abelshauser, "Ansätze 'Korporativer Marktwirtschaft,'" pp. 715–733. Despite his earlier resistance, Erhard was already coming to the conclusion that

some controls would be necessary to adapt the German economy to the American defense effort. Erhard to Adenauer, March 12, 1951, Schriftwechsel, Erhard Papers, Erhard Stiftung, Bonn.

49. In July Erhard noted that "with the exception of iron and steel, supplies of raw materials for the export industries are sufficiently adequate so that no priority list is needed." McCloy to Acheson, July 5, 1951, 862A.00/7-551, Box 5182, RG 59, NARS-DB. Foster to ECA (Paris), Sept. 12, 1951, D(51)1378, Box 3, RG 466, McCloy Papers, NARS-Suitland.

50. McCloy to Acheson, April 11, 1952, D(52)916, Box 40, RG 466, McCloy Papers, NARS-Suitland. The East-West trade issue was a source of contention between the Americans and the Germans, but it never reached the passions of the conflict between the Germans and the British. For a fuller treatment of this issue, see Thomas Schwartz, "European Integration and the 'Special Relationship': Implementing the Marshall Plan in the Federal Republic of Germany, 1948–1951," in Charles S. Maier, ed., *The Marshall Plan and Germany* (London: Berg, forthcoming).

8. The Skeleton Key: Military Integration

1. Among the earlier treatments of the EDC are Daniel Lerner and Raymond Aron, eds., *France Defeats EDC* (New York: Praeger, 1957); Robert McGeehan, *The German Rearmament Question: American Diplomacy and European Defense After World War II* (Urbana: University of Illinois Press, 1971), which relies rather too heavily on the memoirs of Jules Moch and other French opponents of the EDC; and Edward Fursdon, *The European Defense Community: A History* (New York: St. Martin's Press, 1980). See also Hans-Erich Volkmann and Walter Schwengler, *Die Europäische Verteidigungsgemeinschaft: Stand und Probleme der Forschung*, vol. VII, *Militärgeschichte seit 1945* (Boppard: Harald Boldt, 1985).

2. For the argument of this chapter in shorter form, see Thomas A. Schwartz, "The 'Skeleton Key'—American Foreign Policy, European Unity, and German Rearmament, 1949–1954," *Central European History*, 19 (1986), 369–385. I want to thank the journal for permission to reproduce part of the article.

3. Attlee's speech of Feb. 12, 1951, is in Denise Folliot, ed., *Documents on International Affairs, 1951* (London: Oxford University Press, 1954), p. 105; and in Kirkpatrick to Foreign Office, Feb. 19, 1951, FO 371/93376, PRO. For a recent and perceptive study of the British policy toward German rearmament, see Saki Dockrill, "Britain and a West German Contribution to NATO, 1950–1955" (D. Phil. diss., King's College, London, 1988), esp. pp. 129–148. French reservations on the subject of German rearmament are clear in the record of the Truman-Pleven talks of Jan. 30, 1951, folder Truman-Pleven talks, PSF, Box 165, Truman Library; and in the Memorandum by Paul Leroy-Beaulieu, the French Chairman of the Finance and Economics Board in NATO, Jan. 23, 1951, AMI 5/7/6, Monnet Archive, Lausanne.

4. The record of the Petersberg talks can be found in *FRUS 1951*, III, 990–

1047. The figure of 100,000 men was used for purposes of discussion, but the Germans ultimately proposed a larger force. Ibid., p. 992. For the position of the Joint Chiefs, see Memo for the Secretary of Defense from General Bradley, Feb. 28, 1951, CD 091.7 (Europe), Folder #1, Entry 199, Box 175, RG 330, NARS-MMB.

    5. Fursdon, *EDC*, p. 107.

    6. Not only was it illegal to discuss or plan rearmament, but the Germans told the Allies that the Russians could impose the death penalty on any German soldiers they captured. *FRUS 1951*, III, 994, 997–998. On the October 1950 meetings at the Himmeroder monastery, see Hans-Jürgen Rautenberg and Norbert Wiggershaus, "Die 'Himmeroder Denkschrift,' vom October 1950," *Militärgeschichtliche Mitteilungen*, 1 (1977), 166–190; and Donald Abenheim, *Reforging the Iron Cross* (Princeton: Princeton University Press, 1988), pp. 47–63. Abenheim's book, an excellent account of the creation of the Bundeswehr, focuses primarily on the reform of the internal structure of the army rather than on whether it would exist within the EDC or NATO. For the German discussion of tactics, see *FRUS 1951*, III, 999–1001. The specific breakdown of the proposed German force of 150,000 was as follows: twelve combat teams of 10,000 men, totaling 120,000; service units totaling 30,000 men; tactical air force and coastal force units totaling 65,000; reinforcing troops, such as artillery, armor, and engineers, 20,000 men; and the remainder, 15,000 divided among staffs, territorial units, and administrative personnel. *FRUS 1951*, III, 1017. For the German suspicions of the Pleven Plan, see *FRUS 1951*, III, 994–995, 1024. For German worries about the American attitudes, see Niederschrift über die Bespechung über den Pleven-Plan, Feb. 20, 1951, pp. 13–15, BW9/3066, BA-MA, Freiburg. There is also a German transcript of the Petersberg talks in BW9/3092, BA-MA, Freiburg.

    7. *FRUS 1951*, III, 1032–1033, 1045–1046.

    8. For the final Petersberg report, see *FRUS 1951*, III, 1044–1047. For the U.S. Army's preference for the Petersberg solution, see Memo for Admiral Wright from Col. J. K. Woolnough, June 19, 1951, G-3, 092 Germany (Section III-C) (case 48 only) (Book I) (Sub. nos. 1), Box 23A, RG 319, Records of the Army Chief of Staff, NARS-MMB. For Adenauer's complaints, see *FRUS 1951*, III, 1026–1027. According to HICOG's intelligence sources, the Chancellor viewed the French ban on the German political party in the Saar very seriously. What irritated him most was that Schuman had taken the action without informing or consulting him. "Background of the Saar Crisis," June 12, 1951, Office of Intelligence, HICOG, 762.00/6-1251, RG 59, NARS-DB. For his letter, see Adenauer to McCloy, June 7, 1951, Adenauer Papers, StBKA, Rhöndorf.

    9. Adenauer to McCloy, June 7, 1951, Adenauer Papers, StBKA Rhöndorf; and Adenauer, *Memoirs*, pp. 336–368. In this letter, which Adenauer expected McCloy to take to the United States, the Chancellor also argued that the United States should not look only at military concerns in building strength, but must address social and economic problems of European countries, especially Germany.

Financial burdens, including the refugees and the homeless, had to be considered when deciding on Germany's contribution to Western defense. Such concerns reinforced McCloy's view that the financial weakness of Europe was another reason to adopt a European Army approach.

10. The preliminary talks on the European Army were reported by Bruce in *FRUS 1951*, III, 755–798, esp. 775–777. For the French concerns, see McCloy to Acheson, March 20, 1951, 762A.5/3-2051, Box 3897A, RG 59, NARS-DB; and *FRUS 1951*, III, 782.

11. Adenauer's comment is in *FRUS 1951*, III, 771. Speidel's comment can be found in the Niederschrift über die Bespechung über den Pleven-Plan, June 5, 1951, p. 67, BW9/3066, BA-MA, Freiburg. For Acheson's views, see Acheson to the U.S. Ambassador to The Hague, Feb. 10, 1951, TS(51)28, D(51)187, Box 4, RG 466, McCloy Papers, NARS-Suitland; and David S. McLellan, *Dean Acheson: The State Department Years* (New York: Dodd, Mead, 1976), p. 348. In April 1951 the Senate passed, 48 to 41, a resolution favoring the use of German, Spanish, and other troops in Western European forces. See "The Great Debate and the Troops to Europe," p. 12, Box 73, Acheson Papers, Truman Library.

12. Acheson's cable of June 28, 1951, is in *FRUS 1951*, III, 803. My presentation of this issue has benefited from Martin F. Herz, *David Bruce's "Long Telegram" of July 3, 1951* (Lanham, Md.: University Press of America, 1986). This short pamphlet, written by a diplomat stationed in Paris during this period, emphasizes Bruce's important role in persuading Washington to back the EDC.

13. For a description of the SRP, see Large, "Gift to the German Future," p. 514. For German attitudes toward the SRP, see "The Present Status of Neo-Nazism in West Germany," Jan. 10, 1952, RAS-OPA, HICOG, Report #118, Stone Papers. There is a useful collection of SRP documents in B-104, BA-Koblenz. When the British received word that one of Adenauer's coalition partners, the German Party, was considering allowing the SRP to join the government in Lower Saxony, they insisted that Adenauer firmly rebuke his partner. Report, T. W. Garvey to Foreign Office, June 14, 1951, FO 1008/14, PRO.

14. Acheson's comments on German neutrality can be found in the Truman-Pleven talks, PSF, Box 165, Truman Library. On the strength of neutralist sentiment, see "The West German People View Defense Participation, Neutrality, and Related Issues," March 29, 1951, Report #88, RAS-OPA, HICOG, Stone Papers; and "Current Thinking on West German Defense Participation," July 6, 1951, Report #69, Stone Papers.

15. *FRUS 1951*, III, 1482–1485; and "The Views of the West Germans on the Defense of Western Europe," Aug. 27, 1951, Report #94, and "A Note on the Communist Projected Plebiscite on West German Defense Participation," April 2, 1951, both in RAS-OPA, HICOG, Stone Papers. It was still unclear whether a constitutional amendment would be necessary before rearmament could be approved in Germany, but McCloy operated on the premise that even if it was not necessary, rearmament must have a "sizable majority" of the Bundestag behind it.

16. Con O'Neill to W. D. Allen, Nov. 22, 1950, FO 371/85057, and O'Neill to Allen, Dec. 4, 1950, FO 371/85058, PRO.

17. For the French dealings with McCloy, and his reaction, see *FRUS 1951,* III, 779–781, 785–786, 1482. It was also reported at the time that the French wanted McCloy to repeat the role he had played in the Schuman Plan negotiations. *New York Times,* March 20, 1951. McCloy held a news conference when he returned to the United States which presented the basic conclusions of the Petersberg report. This had the effect of a "veritable bomb" on Paris and led the French to consider new ways to win support for the European Army. Raymond Poidevin, *Robert Schuman,* (Paris, 1986), p. 319.

18. McCloy to Sir Arthur Salter, March 21, 1951, Eyes Only (51)33, McCloy Papers, NARS-Suitland. *FRUS 1951,* III, 802, 806.

19. Stephen E. Ambrose, *Eisenhower,* I (New York: Simon and Schuster, 1982), 500–509.

20. For McCloy and Eisenhower's compliments, see McCloy to Eisenhower, Nov. 24, 1945, and Eisenhower to McCloy, Nov. 27, 1945, Pre-Presidential Correspondence 16-52, Folder McCloy, Box 75, Eisenhower Library. The two men remained in frequent contact after the war, and their correspondence was warm and friendly. When Eisenhower became President of Columbia University, he invited McCloy to the inauguration ceremony. McCloy responded quickly, but noted that he had not received a card of admission. Ike instructed his secretary to check into this oversight "at once," writing, "Jack McCloy is an important and dear friend." Eisenhower's written comment is on this letter: McCloy to Eisenhower, Sept. 17, 1948, Pre-Presidential Correspondence 16–52, Folder McCloy, Box 75, Eisenhower Library. For the ideological beliefs of both Eisenhower and McCloy, see Robert Griffith, "Dwight D. Eisenhower and the Corporate Commonwealth," *American Historical Review,* 87 (1982), 97–100.

21. *FRUS 1951,* III, 401–402. For background on the issue of the German soldier's "honor," see Hans-Jürgen Rautenberg, "Zur Standortbestimmung für künftige deutsche Streitkräfte, in Roland Foerster et al., *Anfänge westdeutscher Sicherheitspolitik 1945–1956* (Munich: Oldenbourg, 1982), pp. 698–701. In his book *Crusade in Europe* (New York: Doubleday, 1948), p. 147, Eisenhower explained that his refusal to speak to captured German officers was rooted in his ideological view of the war. For the meeting with Eisenhower, see Hans Speidel, *Aus unserer Zeit: Erinnerungen* (Berlin: Ullstein, 1977), *FRUS 1951,* III, 446; and Eisenhower Press Conference, Jan. 20, 1951, Pre-Presidential Correspondence 16–52, Folder McCloy, Box 75, Eisenhower Library. Although Eisenhower's statements about the German Army scored some political points, they were not historically accurate. The argument that the Wehrmacht fought the honorable fight while the SS committed atrocities has been effectively demolished by historians. Wehrmacht complicity in and acquiescence toward Nazi atrocities has been well established, though much of the proof of such behavior was not brought out until the 1960s. For examples, see Jürgen Förster, "The Wehrmacht and the War of Extermination against the Soviet Union," *Yad Vashem Studies,* 14, (1981),

7-34; and Volker R. Berghahn, "Wehrmacht und Nationalsozialismus," *Neue Politische Literatur,* 1 (1970), 44–52. The July 20 plot against Hitler, with which Speidel was associated, provided the basis for the rehabilitation of German soldiery, which suppressed some unpleasant realities. Large, "Gift to the German Future," pp. 499–529.

22. McCloy to Eisenhower, Jan. 31, 1951, Pre-Presidential Correspondence 16-52 (PPC, 16-52), Folder McCloy, Box 75, Eisenhower Library. For Eisenhower's views in mid-March, see Memorandum of Conversation at SHAPE Headquarters, March 22, 1951, TSGR, Box 4, RG 466, McCloy Papers, NARS-Suitland; and *FRUS 1951,* III, 1030–1032.

23. *FRUS 1951,* III, 1032.

24. Eisenhower to Secretary of Defense George Marshall, May 18, 1951, PPC, 16-52, Folder George Marshall, Box 80, Eisenhower Library. Cyrus Sulzberger, *A Long Row of Candles: Memoirs and Diaries, 1934–1954* (Toronto: Macmillan, 1969), p. 615, records a conversation with Eisenhower on March 6, 1951. See also Meeting of President Truman and General Eisenhower, Nov. 5, 1951, Papers of Eben Ayers, Folder EDC and Contractuals, Box 6, Truman Library. For Eisenhower's frustrations in Europe, see Eisenhower to Averell Harriman, April 2 and May 12, 1951, PPC, 16-52, Folder Averell Harriman, Box 55, Eisenhower Library.

25. Eisenhower Diary, entry June 11, 1951, DDE Diary Series, Eisenhower Library.

26. Immediately after the signing of the Schuman Plan treaty, a number of discussions took place in Paris on the idea of European federation and even on the calling of a constitutional convention. Bruce Diary, entries April 21, April 22, April 24, and May 12, 1951, Virginia Historical Society, Richmond.

27. McCloy to Eisenhower, undated but either June 9 or 10, 1951, Pre-Presidential Correspondence 16-52, Folder McCloy, Box 75, Eisenhower Library.

28. Monnet, *Memoirs,* pp. 358–359.

29. Fursdon, *EDC,* p. 119; and Speech before the English Speaking Union, July 3, 1951, Pre-Presidential Correspondence 16-52, Box 163, Eisenhower Library.

30. McCloy's meetings at the Pentagon are recorded in Memo from General J. Lawton Collins, for Assistant Chief of Staff, G-3, Subject: Notes on Conference with Mr. McCloy reference German Participation in the Defense of Western Europe, June 19, 1951, G-3, 092 Germany (Section III-C) (case 48 only) (Book I) (Sub. nos. 1), Box 23A, RG 319, Records of the Army Chief of Staff, NARS-MMB; and Memo of Conversation, June 26, 1951, Subject—Relationship of European Army to German Remilitarization, CD 091.7 [Europe], Folder #2 from May 7, 1951, to July 31, 1951, Box 226, RG 330, Records of the Office of the Secretary of Defense, NARS-MMB.

31. Memo for Admiral Wright from Col. J. K. Woolnough, June 19, 1951, G-3, 092 Germany (Section III-C) (case 48 only) (Book I) (Sub. nos. 1), Box 23A, RG 319, Records of the Army Chief of Staff, NARS-MMB; and Memo for

the Director, Joint Staff, Joint Chiefs of Staff, June 20, 1951, CD 091.7 [Europe], Folder #2 from May 7, 1951, to July 31, 1951, Box 226, RG 330, Records of the Office of the Secretary of Defense, NARS-MMB. The Army also argued that because the Military Development Assistance Plan was based on a bilateral approach to assistance, Congress might balk at giving money to this experimental and untested arrangement involving a bloc of nations. Memo for the Deputy Secretary of Defense from Col. R. E. Beebe, June 21, 1951, CD 091.7 [Europe], Folder #2 from May 7, 1951, to July 31, 1951, Box 226, RG 330, Records of the Office of the Secretary of Defense, NARS-MMB.

32. *FRUS 1951,* III, 1150; Alexander Werth, *France, 1940–1955* (Boston: Beacon Press, 1956), pp. 540–542; and Jean-Pierre Rioux, *La France de la Quatrième République,* I, *L'ardeur et la nécessité* (Paris: Editions du Seuil, 1980), 210–234.

33. *FRUS 1951,* III, 801–805. My interpretation of the Acheson telegram relies on Herz, *David Bruce's "Long Telegram,"* pp. 6–7. Herz suggests that McCloy may have played a role in writing the telegram. In my view he probably contributed the suggestion that a merger of the two approaches, Petersberg and Paris, offered the best plan for German rearmament.

34. McCloy's office in Bonn interpreted Acheson's message as Bruce did. "Finally if Germany is permitted to organize a national military force on an equality with other NATO states, one may be confident that Germany's willingness to merge such a force into an European Army, possibly under a French general, will be considerably less than at present when no national force exists." Bonn (Thayer) to Reber, July 3, 1951, TS(51)98, D(51)887, TSGR, Box 5, RG 466, McCloy Papers, NARS-Suitland.

35. *FRUS 1951,* III, 805–812, 815.

36. McCloy speech, June 26, 1951, *Department of State Bulletin,* July 9, 1951, pp. 63–65; *New York Times,* July 4, 1951; and McCloy to Secretary of State, July 6, 1951, #11, 762.5/7-651, Box 3853, RG 59, NARS-DB.

37. Speidel, *Erinnerungen,* pp. 292–293; and McCloy to the Secretary of State, July 7, 1951, 762A.00/7-751, Box 3858, RG 59, NARS-DB. When McCloy argued that the Petersberg and Paris approaches could be "reconciled," the SPD leader ridiculed the suggestion and told reporters: "You have never seen an American who was wrong." *New York Times,* July 14, 1951. Relations between the two grew even worse when, at the end of August 1951, McCloy cited HICOG polls indicating that German support for rearmament was again increasing. Schumacher claimed this demonstrated McCloy's "extraordinary disrespect for the German people." Schumacher, Presse Konferenz, Aug. 24, 1951, Schumacher Bestand, Q-17, Schuman Plan, SPD Archive, Bonn. See also *New York Times,* Aug. 25, 1951.

38. *FRUS 1951,* III, 1487–1489; and Adenauer, *Memoirs,* pp. 354–357.

39. *FRUS 1951,* III, 824–826, 844.

40. McCloy to Harriman, July 9, 1951, #3 Shaw-Walker, Drawer B, DDE Diary, entry July 2, 1951, Harriman Papers, Eisenhower Library; Memo by Mr.

McCloy, July 17, 1951, D(51)981, Box 28, RG 466, McCloy Papers, NARS-Suitland; and *FRUS 1951,* III, 838–839.

41. *FRUS 1951,* III, 820.

42. Ibid., pp. 837, 843–846, 903–905, 937–938, 1269. The other result of adopting the EDC was to end the Brussels restrictions on the size of the German forces. This was not immediately commented upon. The restriction—that Germans could constitute only 20 percent of the total NATO forces—was no longer in effect, at least in American and German eyes. This allowed the Germans to plan on a force equal to the French, or 500,000 men, which the Americans had long preferred.

43. *FRUS 1951,* III, 843–846.

44. Ibid., pp. 839–842.

45. Ibid., pp. 818–819, 835–837, 849–852.

46. Ibid., pp. 869–870.

47. Ibid., pp. 874–877, 1519. Both McCloy and Eisenhower emphasized the economic advantages of the EDC. With the burden of defense weighing heavily on each nation, only a united Europe seemed to offer the hope of sustaining a large land army. Supporters of the EDC presumed that economies of scale would operate in defense production just as the single market of the Schuman Plan would help expand coal and steel production.

48. Memorandum by Jean Monnet on the German contribution to European defense, undated but probably July 1951, drafted by Bowie and Tomlinson, AMI 12/4/1, Monnet Archive, Lausanne. (The possible date given in the Monnet papers is September 1951, but this is too late.) There was some optimism about the EDC as well. Bidault told Bruce that French deputies would vote in favor of the Schuman Plan and the EDC. "They commit many stupidities, but few crimes against the national interest." Bruce Diary, Aug. 30, 1951, Virginia Historical Society, Richmond. For DeGaulle's criticism, see Ball, *Past Has Another Pattern,* p. 92. Moch told Alphand that he would deny the paternity of the European Defense Community. Moch, *Historie,* p. 279.

49. Memorandum by Mr. McCloy, Sept. 4, 1951, Documents Files EO, D(51)67-99, Box 1, RG 466, McCloy Papers, NARS-Suitland. But McCloy could perceive from the French reaction to his appeal that Robert Schuman, the Foreign Minister who had been instrumental in guiding previous measures of European integration, was no longer politically strong enough to "take bold measures" in respect to Germany.

9. How Free Should the Germans Be? Political Integration

1. Meeting of the Allied High Commission, Dec. 21, 1950, FO 1005/1126b, PRO.

2. *FRUS 1952–1954,* VII, 81.

3. *FRUS 1951,* III, 1457, 1461, 1466.

4. "Die Umgestaltung des Besatzungsregimes," Jan. 27, 1951, and "Betrac-

tungen zur Frage 'obersten Gewalt,'" PA-AA 241.27, vol. I, Bonn; Aufzeichnung, April 5, 1951, PA-AA 241.26, vol. I, Bonn; and Bonn Liaison (Thayer) to Frankfurt, May 8, 1951, D(51)608, Box 27, RG 466, McCloy Papers, NARS-Suitland. See also Wilhelm Grewe, *Rückblenden, 1976–1951* (Frankfurt: Propylaen, 1979), p. 134.

5. The 39 points are mentioned in *FRUS 1951,* III, 1464. For quotations I have relied on the Aide-Memoire, dated Feb. 27, 1951, found in PA-AA 241.26, vol. I, Bonn.

6. The Auswärtiges Amt was reestablished in March 1951 after the Bundestag accepted German responsibility for the debts of the former German Reich. Adenauer became the first Foreign Minister. The observation about the "red flag" was made by Wilhelm Grewe. Grewe, *Rückblenden,* pp. 134, 139–140; and Vermerk, July 6 and June 22, 1951, PA-AA 241.30, vol. II, Bonn. For the British observation, see Con O'Neill to Andrew Gilchrist, May 11, 1951, FO 371/93380, PRO. Grewe came under attack for taking too pragmatic a view on the supreme authority question. E. Kaufmann to Dittmann, July 14, 1951, PA-AA 241.30, vol. I, and Grewe's reply dated July 18, 1951, PA-AA 241.30, vol. IV, Bonn.

7. Memo, Henry Kellermann to H. Byroade, July 9, 1951, 762A.00/7–951, RG 59, NARS-DB. The difference among the Allies are apparent in the final report, dated Aug. 9, 1951, in *FRUS 1951,* III, 1501–11. The Germans were informed of these disagreements by Allied officials, in an attempt to draw them into the process of designing politically acceptable agreements. Aufzeichnung, Dittmann, May 10, 1951, PA-AA 241.26, vol. I, Bonn; Aufzeichnung, Dittmann to Grewe, June 19, 1951, PA-AA 241.30, vol. I, Bonn; and Vermerk, Grewe, July 19, 1951, PA-AA 241.30, vol. II, Bonn.

8. *FRUS 1951,* III, 1520–21. For the German background on Bürgenstock, see Grewe, *Rückblenden,* pp. 138–145.

9. *FRUS 1951,* III, 1175–79, 1192–95; and Meeting of the Allied High Commission, Aug. 9, 1951, FO 1005/1105, PRO. At one point McCloy referred to this guarantee as a "Monroe doctrine for democracy," an expression which must have brought smiles to Europeans, whose understanding of the Monroe Doctrine had little to do with protecting democracy

10. *FRUS 1951,* III, 1270. Acheson qualified his endorsement of the EDC by adding: "At the same time this attitude was consistent with the view that if after all possible effort had been made the project was not feasible, then it would be necessary to review policy and see what else could be done." Harvey to Morrison, May 4, 1951, FO 1008/1, PRO; and Dockrill, "Britain and a Western German Contribution," pp. 168–171.

11. Acheson, *Present at the Creation,* pp. 559–560; and Lawrence S. Kaplan, *NATO and the United States* (Boston: Twayne, 1988), pp. 58–59. On British and French concerns, see Dockrill, "Britain and a West German Contribution," p. 166; *FRUS 1951,* III, 1288–90; and Kaplan, *Community of Interests,* p. 162.

12. *FRUS 1951,* III, 1273–74. The editors of this volume of *FRUS* thought that Acheson was referring to Max Reimann, the head of West Germany's Com-

munist party, rather than to ex-General Remer of the SRP; many forget that the internal threat in Germany was seen as a resurgent right-wing nationalism rather than left-wing communism. Acheson's treatment of this issue in his memoirs is misleading because it underemphasizes the concerns about German political reliability. Acheson, *Present at the Creation*, pp. 556–557.

13. *FRUS 1951*, III, 1528–34. For the instructions to the High Commissioners and the original draft of the General Agreement, see *FRUS 1951*, III, 1197–1214. For the early Allied drafts of the Treaty on the Rights and Obligations of Foreign Forces, see Oct. 30, 1951, PA-AA 241.27q, Bonn.

14. Adenauer, *Memoirs*, pp. 370–372; *FRUS 1951*, III, 1525–28; and Kirkpatrick, *Inner Circle*, p. 244.

15. *FRUS 1951*, III, 1537; and Schwarz, *Adenauer*, pp. 884–885. For the evaluation of the SPD's strength, see "Briefs on Germany, November 1951," D(51)1865, Box 33, RG 466, McCloy Papers, NARS-Suitland. For the public opinion polls, see "The Current State of German-American Relations," Oct. 12, 1951, Report #103, RAS-OPA, HICOG, Stone Papers. For the FDP's increasing independence, see *New York Times*, Sept. 9, 1951; and FDP Resolutions on Foreign Policy, Sept. 20, 1951, folder 231, FDP-Bundesparteitag, Munich, FDP Archive, Bonn.

16. For the text of the Grotewohl speech, see *Documents on International Affairs, 1951*, p. 275. I have relied heavily on an outstanding dissertation, Paul Raymond Willging, "Soviet Foreign Policy in the German Question, 1950–1955" (Ph.D. diss., Columbia University, 1973), pp. 116–118.

17. *FRUS 1951*, III, 1522–26, 1787–1827.

18. Ibid., pp. 1536–37, 1175–79.

19. Ibid., pp. 1538–40. Why McCloy thought Washington was leaking to the SPD is not clear, but it indicates how bad his relationship with Schumacher had become.

20. Byroade to McCloy, Oct. 26, 1951, D(51)1709, Box 32, RG 466, McCloy Papers, NARS-Suitland.

21. *FRUS 1951*, III, 1540–44.

22. Ibid., p. 1546; and Kirkpatrick to Foreign Office, Oct. 4, 1951, FO 371/93400, PRO. The French were particularly insistent on the subject of supreme authority. Cable, François-Poncet to Paris, Sept. 29, 1951, AMI 12/1/2, Monnet Archive, Lausanne.

23. Kirkpatrick to Foreign Office, Oct. 4, 1951, FO 371/93400, PRO; and *FRUS 1951*, III, 1540–47.

24. *FRUS 1951*, III, 1547, 1592–93.

25. Ibid., pp. 1531, 1566. In the various subcommittees concerned with the contractuals, the American representative, Samuel Reber, continually repeated the formula that under no circumstances would the Allies limit their rights to station and protect their forces. Niederschrift, Hauptausschuss-Truppenvertrag, Oct. 24, 1951, PA-AA 241.27q, Bonn. For the military's concern about its rights in an emergency, see *FRUS 1951*, III, 1588. Kirkpatrick also detected that the U.S.

Army was pressuring McCloy on this issue. Kirkpatrick to Foreign Office, Nov. 4, 1951, FO 371/93405, PRO.

26. Adenauer's desire to ease the situation of Allied forces in Germany was expressed by Hallstein in a meeting of the German advisory committee on the Status of Forces Agreement. This committee also concerned itself with comparing the German forces agreement with the NATO treaties, and it was advised on McCloy's views. See the reports on the following meetings: Niederschrift, Beratende Ausschuss, Truppenabkommen, Sept. 18, Nov. 5, Nov. 13, and Nov. 19, 1951, PA-AA 241,27q, Bonn. See also *FRUS 1951,* III, 1588–89. For the addition of Article IV on the mission of the Allied forces, see *FRUS 1951,* III, 1558–59. On the question of troops from other countries being brought into the FRG, see Adenauer to McCloy, Nov. 9, 1951, Adenauer Papers, StBKA, Rhöndorf.

27. *FRUS 1951,* III, 1564–67.

28. On the Oder-Neisse issue, see *FRUS 1951,* III, 1580–82, 1585. Konrad Adenauer, *Erinnerungen, 1953–1955,* II (Stuttgart: Deutsche Verlag, 1966), 63ff; and Schwarz, *Adenauer,* pp. 827–850. The Oder-Neisse issue produced controversy in Germany during the summer of 1989 after Professor Karl Kaiser, the head of Germany's leading foreign policy institute, stated that Adenauer had signed away any German claim to the disputed territory. Kaiser could not produce the documentary evidence, but he did document that Adenauer would not ask the Western allies to support German claims to the disputed territory, a very important concession that reduced the significance of Germany's claims. *Die Zeit,* Sept. 29, 1989, pp. 49–50.

29. Acheson, *Present at the Creation,* pp. 584–585; and *FRUS 1951,* III, 1610.

30. *FRUS 1951,* III, 1609–11, 1732.

31. Bérard, *Washington et Bonn,* p. 387. *FRUS 1951,* III, 1732; and McCloy to Frankfurter, Feb. 4, 1952, Frankfurter Papers, Library of Congress.

32. Pierre Melandri, "France and the Atlantic Alliance, 1950–1953: Between Great Power Policy and European Integration," in *Western Security: The Formative Years,* ed. Olav Riste (Oslo: Norwegian University Press, 1985), pp. 272–273. Alexander Werth, *France, 1940–1955,* rev.ed. (Boston: Beacon Press, 1966), p. 561. For the designation "satellite," see Jean-Baptiste Duroselle, *France and the United States,* trans. Derek Coltman (Chicago: University of Chicago Press, 1978), pp. 187–188. For a thorough description of the political divisions in France in late 1951, which begins by saying (echoing Caesar), "All France is divided into six parts," see David Bruce's cable in *FRUS 1951,* IV, 463–473.

33. Acheson, *Present at the Creation,* p. 551. Bidault is quoted in Melandri, "France and the Atlantic Alliance," p. 278. Melandri draws too sharp a distinction between those pursuing "Great Power" policy and those striving for European integration. Although the difference in outlooks between a de Gaulle and a Monnet was wide, the majority of French politicians and citizens fell somewhere in between and wanted both policies pursued.

34. Bruce to Acheson, December 29, 1951, TS(51)191, D(51)2110, TSGR, Box 5, RG 466, McCloy Papers, NARS-Suitland; and *FRUS 1952–1954*, V, 15.

35. On French resentment toward the U.S.–British special relationship, see René Massigli, *Une comédie des erreurs* (Paris: Plon, 1978), p. 299; and Melandri, "France and the Atlantic Alliance," pp. 275–276.

36. On France and Indochina, see George Herring, *America's Longest War*, 2nd ed. (New York: Knopf, 1986), pp. 19–20. Memo, Tomlinson to Monnet, Nov. 7, 1951, AMI 15/1/4, Monnet Archive, Lausanne; *FRUS 1951*, IV, 455–459; and *FRUS 1952–1954*, V, 610–611. For Churchill's perspective, see Martin Gilbert, *Winston S. Churchill*, vol. VIII, *Never Despair, 1945–1965* (Boston: Houghton Mifflin, 1988), pp. 681–682.

37. Progress in the EDC negotiations is recorded in an undated report in *FRUS 1952–1954*, V, 597–604; and in Bickel to McCloy, Jan. 13, 1952, D(52)78, Box 35, RG 466, McCloy Papers, NARS-Suitland. Dockrill makes the point that these "voluminous agreements in principle" were achieved by putting off the settlement of many important details until after the treaty was signed. Dockrill, "Britain and a West German Contribution," pp. 209–210. For the Schuman letter, see *FRUS 1952–1954*, V, 7–11. Schuman's letter revealed how suspicious the French were of Germany's conversion to the West. Many believed that "the only nation that is strong enough to face a German-Russian coalition is the United States." François-Poncet, quoted in Memorandum by Mr. McCloy, Jan. 16, 1952, D(52)139, Box 35, RG 466, McCloy Papers, NARS-Suitland.

38. Acheson, *Present at the Creation*, p. 615; and *FRUS 1952–1954*, V, 18–23. On the French move in the Saar, see *FRUS 1952–1954*, V, 9; and McCloy to Bowie, March 13, 1952, D(52)661, Box 38, RG 466, McCloy Papers, NARS-Suitland. For Hallstein's reaction and the Budestag resolution, see Denise Folliot, ed., *Documents on International Affairs, 1952* (London: Oxford University Press, 1955), p. 77. On the German meeting with McCloy in Munich, see *FRUS 1952–1954*, VII, 1403–05.

39. Adenauer, *Memoirs*, p. 405; *FRUS 1952–1954*, V, 16; *FRUS 1952–1954*, VII, 1407–08, 1413–14; and McCloy to Acheson, March 20, 1952, 762.022/3-2052, RG 59, NARS-DB. Moderate French officials were gratified by McCloy's efforts to temper the German response. Guy Le Roy de la Tournelle, the Director General for Political and Economic Affairs in the Quai, told the Paris Embassy that McCloy had been a "helpful influence on Adenauer" in defusing the problem. Bonsal to Acheson, March 17, 1952, 762.022/3-1752, RG 59, NARS-DB.

40. On the security issue and German arms manufacturing, see *FRUS 1952–1954*, V, 91. McCloy himself favored allowing the Federal Republic to produce some military hardware and ammunition. *New York Herald Tribune*, Nov. 26, 1951. For Adenauer's concerns about discrimination and McCloy's suggestion of a "special undertaking," see *FRUS 1951*, III, 1740–1741.

41. *FRUS 1952–1954*, V, 67–77, 83–84, 165–167.

42. Ibid., pp. 48–49, 60–62, 77, 81.

43. Ibid., pp. 78–80.

44. Dockrill, "Britain and a West German Contribution," pp. 180–182. For Churchill's views of the EDC, see *FRUS 1951,* III, 971; Gilbert, *Churchill,* pp. 666, 684; and Acheson, *Present at the Creation,* p. 598.

45. Anthony Eden, *Full Circle* (Boston: Houghton Mifflin, 1960), pp. 39–49. The British made it clear to the Americans that they were considering alternatives. Acheson to McCloy, Dec. 12, 1951, TS(51)161, D(51)2029, TSGR, Box 5, RG 466, McCloy Papers, NARS-Suitland. Dockrill, "Britain and a West German Contribution," pp. 202–204, notes the British fear of being accused by the United States of sabotaging the EDC, the same kind of fear they had had during the Schuman Plan negotiations. The British perception that there was no alternative to present policies is expressed by Frank Roberts to Sir W. Strang, Jan. 31, 1952, FO 1008/98, PRO.

46. For Acheson's comments, see *FRUS 1951,* III, 970, 977. Eisenhower also urged the British to take a stronger position on the EDC. *FRUS 1951,* III, 974–975. Dockrill, "Britain and a West German Contribution," pp. 212–215, 220–221, discusses the dispute surrounding the British guarantee of the EDC.

47. Whitman to McCloy, Jan. 15, 1952, D(52)99, Box 35, and McCloy to Acheson, Feb. 11, 1952 D(52)388, Box 37, RG 466, McCloy Papers, NARS-Suitland. Germany's defense contribution posed a problem for the French, because influence in the EDC was related directly to the financial contribution. Eventually this was solved by giving each country the same votes.

48. *FRUS 1952–1954,* V, 84.

49. For the original estimate of DM 13 billion, see Memo, Buttenwieser to McCloy, Oct. 29, 1951, Folder Germany, Shaw-Walker Drawer C, Harriman Papers; and Decision on German Financial Contribution to Defense, Nov. 27, 1951, D(51)1906–2019, Box 33, and McCloy to Acheson, Feb. 1, 1952, D(52)295, Box 36, RG 466, McCloy Papers, NARS-Suitland. For McCloy's comment on Schäffer and Adenauer's role in the success of the London and Lisbon talks, see McCloy to Bowie, March 13, 1952, D(52)661, Box 38, RG 466, McCloy Papers, NARS-Suitland. Acheson's appeal to Adenauer is in *FRUS 1952–1954,* V, 260; Adenauer's reply, in German, is the cable, Adenauer to Acheson, Feb. 27, 1952, 762.00/2-2752, RG 59, NARS-DB.

50. On the "grand slam," see *FRUS 1952–1954,* V, 175–176; and Kaplan, *Community of Interests,* pp. 164–166. A conventional build-up to 96 divisions was projected for 1954. On Indochina, see *FRUS 1952–1954,* V, 273–277; and Herring, *America's Longest War,* p. 22.

51. Lord Ismay, *NATO: The First Five Years, 1949–1954* (Paris: NATO Information Service, 1955), p. 38. On the post-Lisbon disappointments, see Acheson, *Present at the Creation,* pp. 615, 641.

52. McCloy to Bowie, March 13, 1952, D(52)661, Box 38, RG 466, McCloy Papers, NARS-Suitland. The human rights issue is discussed in *FRUS 1952–1954,* VII, 35–38. Acheson was concerned about the preamble to the General Convention, in which the Federal Republic stated that it "shares with the three powers a determination to abide by the principles of the universal Declaration of Human

Rights." The Senate Foreign Relations Committee disliked similar language in the Japanese Peace Treaty, because of the implied commitment of the United States to the United Nations Declaration. Acheson was afraid that this could cause problems in the Senate, though he admitted to McCloy how uncomfortable he felt "going to the Germans and asking them to remove or modify the clause in which they express their intention of respecting human rights, because of a strong political opposition in the United States to anything which remotely appears to suggest that the United States itself is committed to the observance of human rights."

53. *FRUS 1952–1954*, VII, 24–25. The Germans did indeed raise the question of allowing the contractuals to go into force before the EDC. Ibid., pp. 62, 73. The Allies agreed that after the four parliaments had ratified the contractuals, they would consult with the Chancellor "to determine those parts of the contractual arrangements which [could] be put into effect without disturbing provisions of EDC treaty." Acheson sent a message to all the European foreign ministers proposing the deadline of May 9, 1952. *FRUS 1952–1954*, V, 641–642.

54. Gilbert, *Churchill,* p. 690. The Stalin Note can be found in U.S. Department of State, *Documents on Germany, 1944–1985* (Washington, D.C.: GPO, 1986), pp. 361–364. McCloy described the Note as appealing "to everybody— the Nazis, the Generals, the Neutralists, the Ruhr Industrialists, the Unificationists, and the do-gooders." McCloy to Bowie, March 13, 1952, D(52)661, Box 38, RG 466, McCloy Papers, NARS-Suitland.

55. *FRUS 1952–1954*, VII, 176.

56. The debate over the Stalin Note has become more intense in recent years, particularly because of the contribution of Rolf Steininger, who has argued forcefully that the Note was a serious offer. See Rolf Steininger, *Eine Chance zur Wiedervereinigung?* (Bonn: Neue Gesellschaft, 1985), which contains a collection of relevant documents; and Steininger, *Eine vertane Chance: Die Stalin-Note vom 10. März 1952 und die Wiedervereinigung* (Bonn: Dietz, 1985). For a different point of view, see Hermann Graml, "Die Legende von der Verpassten Gelegenheit," *Vierteljahrshefte für Zeitgeschichte,* 29 (1981), 307–341.

57. Willging, "Soviet Foreign Policy," pp. 146–148. Soviet views on this issue are strikingly close to the French reasons for not wanting the Germans in NATO. The French believed, however, that the Russians would perceive a difference between the EDC and NATO.

58. Willging, "Soviet Foreign Policy," pp. 130–137. Willging also cites evidence from some years later to show that the East German leaders believed the Soviet Union was prepared to "sacrifice" their party and rule over the GDR. Ibid., pp. 139–142.

59. Follow-up Study of German Views on the Contractual Agreement vs. Russian Unity Proposal, May 21, 1952, D(52)1291, Box 42, RG 466, McCloy Papers, NARS-Suitland. The study did show, however, that most Germans thought the Russian proposals were propaganda rather than a serious offer to negotiate. For further treatment of the neutrality issue, see Hans Peter Schwarz,

"The West Germans, Western Democracy, and Western Ties in the Light of Public Opinion Research," in James A. Cooney, Gordon A. Craig, Hans Peter Schwarz, and Fritz Stern, eds., *The Federal Republic of Germany and the United States: Changing Political, Social, and Economic Relations* (Boulder: Westview Press, 1984), p. 73. For the German reluctance to take any action, see the report by McCloy's Public Affairs Department, April 21, 1952, in *FRUS 1952–1954,* VII, 336. On Adenauer's popularity, see Elisabeth Noelle and Erich Peter Neumann, *The Germans: Public Opinion Polls, 1947–1966* (Allensbach and Bonn: Verlag für Demoskopie, 1967), pp. 256–257; and McCloy to Acheson, March 29, 1952, in Steininger, *Eine Chance,* p. 176.

60. For the perception of Soviet strategy, see Note by W. D. Allen, Foreign Office, FO 371/97877, in Steininger, *Eine Chance,* pp. 116–117. The French attitude can be found in "The Attitude of the Quai d'Orsay," Note by Frank Roberts, March 14, 1952, FO 371/97878, in Steininger, *Eine Chance,* p. 136. Eden's notation is handwritten on this document. For the PPS's views, see Memo by J. H. Ferguson for Dean Acheson, March 18, 1952, in Steininger, *Eine Chance,* pp. 157–159. The CIA did not believe the Soviet Union "would so relax its control over East Germany as to affect the foundations of Soviet authority." Review of Probable Soviet Courses with Respect to Germany during 1952, in the Light of Recent Soviet Moves, National Intelligence Estimate, May 1, 1952, PSF, Truman Papers, Independence.

61. Eden, *Full Circle,* pp. 50–51; and Acheson, *Present at the Creation,* pp. 630–631. The reference to Schumacher is in a Note by Frank Roberts for Anthony Eden and William Strang, March 15, 1952, FO 371/97879, in Steininger, *Eine Chance,* p. 142. For Eden and Schuman's insistence on including a number of issues in the Western reply, see Ambassador Dunn's cable to Acheson, March 20, 1952, *FRUS 1952–1954,* VII, 186. A copy of the Western reply is in *Documents on Germany, 1944–1985,* pp. 364–365. Schuman's views are captured in his letter to Anthony Eden, May 6, 1952, FO 371/97883, in Steininger, *Eine Chance,* pp. 244–245.

62. McCloy to Bowie, March 13, 1952, D(52)661, Box 38, RG 466, McCloy Papers, NARS-Suitland; and Acheson to Truman, March 11, 1952, Truman Papers, Confidential File, State Department Correspondence, Folder 30, Box 39, Truman Library, Independence. For McCloy's view of the Soviet note, see McCloy to Acheson, April 15, 1952, Folder 261, Box 21, Papers of Dean Acheson, Yale University. McCloy angrily and unfairly denounced Walter Lippmann for suggesting that the Allies negotiate the Soviet offer. Lippmann's articles, McCloy noted, were giving "comfort to the enemy." For Lippmann's incriminating article, see *New York Herald Tribune,* April 5, 1952. For McCloy's earlier insistence that the Germans must choose, see *FRUS 1951,* III, 1522–24; and McCloy's suggestion of "goodwill measures," Speech at Bernkastel, May 10, 1952, reprinted in *Department of State Bulletin,* June 2, 1952, p. 858.

63. Adenauer's view of the Stalin Note as expressed to McCloy is in McCloy to Acheson, March 20, 1952, 762.022/3-2052, RG 59, NARS-DB, and in *FRUS*

1952–1954, VII, 182–183. On the necessity of consultation with Adenauer, see *FRUS 1952–1954*, VII, 177-178. The American proposal on the second note as well as McCloy's views can be found in *FRUS 1952–1954*, VII, 222–224. Adenauer's opposition can be seen in McCloy's cable to Acheson, May 3, 1952, in Steininger, *Eine Chance*, p. 241. Adenauer was not the only one who opposed such a meeting. Acheson explained the change in the proposal in his Memorandum to the President, May 9, 1952, *FRUS 1952–1954*, VII, 238. As he put it, the proposal was left out because of "unanimous opinion of Mr. Eden, Mr. Schuman, Chancellor Adenauer, and Mayor Reuter that so definite a proposal would raise the danger in many quarters in Germany and elsewhere in Europe of postponing the signing of the EDC treaty and the contractual relations with Germany until such a meeting were held."

64. For Adenauer's concerns, see Adenauer, *Erinnerungen*, II, 91; Kirkpatrick to Foreign Office, March 12, 1952, FO 371/97877, in Steininger, *Eine Chance*, p. 119; and Hays to Acheson, March 17, 1952, *FRUS 1952–1954*, VII, 182–183, 186–188.

65. McCloy to Acheson, March 29, 1952, in Steininger, *Eine Chance*, p. 177. For Steininger's bitter attack on Adenauer on this issue, see Steininger, *Eine vertane Chance*, pp. 126–127. The SPD's attitude can be found in McCloy to Acheson, April 18, 1952, 762.00/4-1852, RG 59, NARS-DB. Schumacher's public letter, dated April 22, 1952, challenging Adenauer's policy, is in Folliot, *Documents on International Affairs, 1952*, pp. 94–95. At a press conference Schumacher rejected McCloy's notion that Germany must make a choice: "The assumption that Germans must side either with West or East is nothing but empty propaganda formula propagated by both East and West in order to commit Germans even prior to negotiations." Bonn (Liaison) to Washington, Jan. 4, 1952, D(52)1363, Box 42, RG 466, McCloy Papers, NARS-Suitland.

66. The Soviet note of May 24, 1952, is in *Documents on Germany, 1944–1985*, pp. 374–378. As the signing of the treaties neared, McCloy worried that the Soviets might take some action in Berlin. An attack on a French aircraft flying to Berlin in late April appeared to be the beginning of an attempt "to terrorize the West Germans and embarrass the Allies." Memo, Bendetsen to Lovett, May 13, 1952, Records of the Office of the Secretary of Defense, CD 091.7 Europe 1952, RG 330, NARS-MMB. The events in East Germany are recorded in *FRUS 1952–1954*, VII, 1555–57; and in S. Reber to Dean Acheson, June 2, 1952, in Steininger, *Eine Chance*, p. 274. For the viewpoint that this was Stalin's intention all along, see Hermann Graml, "Die Legende von der Verpassten Gelegenheit," *Vierteljahrshefte für Zeitgeschichte*, 29 (1981), 307–341. On British and French views, see Anthony Eden to Oliver Harvey, June 9, 1952, FO 371/97884, quoted in Steininger, *Eine Chance*, p. 276; and Eden to Harvey, May 27, 1952, FO 371/97849, in Steininger, *Eine Chance*, p. 258. Adenauer was very angry that the Allies considered opening four-power talks after the contractual agreements had been signed. He feared that the Soviet Union might accept such an offer, and that this would delay ratification "indefinitely." Blankenhorn Diary, June 30, 1952, NL 351/10, p. 12, BA-Koblenz.

67. The German debate over the Stalin Note also tends to ignore the fact that German unity had not been destroyed by the Allies, but by Hitler and his disastrous war of aggression.

68. McCloy to Acheson, April 7, 1952, D(52)862, Box 40, RG 466, McCloy Papers, NARS-Suitland; and Acheson, *Sketches,* pp. 177–178. For the "painful ordeal" of the talks, see Kirkpatrick, *Inner Circle,* pp. 244–245. On the German sense of a change in atmosphere, see Grewe, *Rückblenden,* pp. 147–148; and Niederschrift, Harris Gruppe, Truppenabkommen, April 16, 1952, PA-AA 241.27g, Bonn. Acheson and McCloy's comments can be found in Acheson, *Present at the Creation,* p. 640.

69. The Allied list of concessions, dated May 9, 1952, was translated by the Auswärtiges Amt, July 23, 1952, and can be found in B 126/12493, BA-Koblenz. McCloy's comment, often thought to be simply an exaggeration, is in Paul Weymar, *Adenauer: His Authorized Biography,* trans. Peter DeMendelssohn (New York: Dutton, 1957), p. 434. McCloy noted that the pressure of time required that "we may have to give on one or two fairly important points." McCloy to Acheson, May 7, 1952, D(52)1130, TS(52)55, TSGR, Box 6, RG 466, McCloy Papers, NARS-Suitland. For McCloy's trading of concessions, see Gegenstand und Ergebnis der Verhandlungen, March 11 and 12, 1952, PA-AA 241.27a, Bonn.

70. The uncertainty over what was covered in the defense contribution is apparent in the negotiations of the subcommittee charged with its determination. Niederschrift, Ausschuss für Finanzabkommen, March 24, 1952, PA-AA 241.27g, Bonn. On Schäffer's behavior in the negotiations, see McCloy to Acheson, April 7, 1952, D(52)862, Box 40, and McCloy to Acheson, May 16, 1952, D(52)1195, Box 41, RG 466, McCloy Papers, NARS-Suitland; and *FRUS 1952–1954,* VII, 23–24, 48–53.

71. For Lovett's concerns about expenditures, and McCloy's rejoinder, see *FRUS 1952–1954,* VII, 33–34. See also Summary of Daily Meeting, April 18, 1952, Records of the Office of the Executive Secretariat, Box 5, NARS-DB. Schäffer accused the Allies of breaking their word by increasing occupation costs. Schäffer to Michael Harris, April 18, 1952, D(52)936, Box 40, and Schäffer to McCloy, May 3, 1952, and McCloy's reply, McCloy to Schäffer, May 13, 1952, D(52)1090, Box 41, RG 466, McCloy Papers, NARS-Suitland. Adenauer's bitter complaint can be found in Adenauer to McCloy, May 1, 1952, FO 371/100031, along with Schäffer's prediction of a spending orgy, Kirkpatrick to Foreign Office, May 15, 1952, FO 371/100032, PRO.

72. The problem of Allied extravagance is discussed in Harold Zink, *The United States in Germany, 1944–1955* (Princeton: Van Nostrand, 1957), pp. 127–130. The strain of the occupation was apparent in a poll that found some 34 percent of Germans convinced that the Allies remained in Germany in part because they "like the soft life here." The Current State of German-American Relations, Oct. 12, 1951, Report #103, RAS-OPA, HICOG, Stone Papers. Schäffer stressed this continuously, as seen in Memo, R. G. Leonard to McCloy, July 19, 1951, D(51)1000, Box 28, RG 466, McCloy Papers, NARS-Suitland. On how this

debate appeared to the Army, see Memo, Post-Treaty disposition of Allied-held Private Property in Germany not Essential for Military Purposes, Sept. 14, 1951, Folder 091, Germany case 16-46, Box 640, RG 319, Records of the Army Staff, NARS-MMB. For the Army's attempt to make any reductions a tripartite matter, see Memo for General Hull from Assistant Secretary Karl R. Bendetsen, April 21, 1952, Folder 091, Germany case 16-46, Box 640, RG 319, Records of the Army Staff, NARS-MMB. For Parker's use of publicity, see *Baltimore Sun,* April 8, 1952; and *New York Times,* April 4 and 5, 1952. For the Army's angry reaction to the criticism, see Memo, Major General Jenkins for Lt. Col. Tyler, April 12, 1952, Folder 091, Germany case 16-46, Box 640, RG 319, Records of the Army Staff, NARS-MMB. McCloy defended himself angrily against charges that the cuts endangered the forces: "Most anxious to resolve this issue for as long as it is in suspense, feelings are aroused. Representations to the effect that we are in any way interfering with defense capacity of troops here is utterly false." McCloy to Acheson, April 15, 1952, 762A.5/4-1552, RG 59, NARS-DB. For the Army's concession, see *FRUS 1952–1954,* VII, 43–44; and *New York Times,* May 4, 1952.

73. On British concerns about the financial consequences of rearmament, see Dockrill, "Britain and a West German Contribution," p. 172; and W. Strang comment on Minute by Frank Roberts, April 28, 1952, FO 371/100029, PRO. Britain's concerns about providing for its expenses in Germany are also expressed in R. S. Crawford to Eric Roll, April 17, 1952, FO 371/100028, PRO. The British did get the attention they wanted from American officials. See Memo of Conversation, Acheson and Sir Oliver Franks, May 9, 1952, Box 67, Acheson Papers, Truman Library.

74. The three powers had agreed at London to a 10 percent cutback, but this was only a "suggestion" for the High Commission. For the British acceptance of the cutback, see Kirkpatrick to Foreign Office, May 5, 1952, FO 371/100030, and the "obsession with maids," May 15, 1952, FO 371/100032, PRO. On the "rigid" British position, see McCloy to Acheson, May 17, 1952, D(52)1224, Box 41, RG 466, McCloy Papers, NARS-Suitland; and *FRUS 1952–1954,* VII, 79–80. On German insistence on an equal division of costs, and the pessimism about a compromise, see Kirkpatrick to Foreign Office, May 18, 1952, FO 371/100032, PRO.

75. The original compromise McCloy worked out called for a distribution of DM 474 million to the Allies and DM 376 million to the Germans. This was modified in the final agreement to DM 511 million and DM 339 million respectively for the first six months. *FRUS 1952–1954,* VII, 79–81, 144–145. For Washington's request that London be more flexible, see Acheson to Eden, May 17, 1952, D(52)1224, Box 41, RG 466, McCloy Papers, NARS-Suitland. For the British hope that the Germans would not be given preference in the struggle for American military aid, see Kirkpatrick to Foreign Office, May 16, 1952, FO 371/100032, PRO. Both Blank and Schäffer suggested that spending begin on Germany's rearmament before the agreements were ratified. For the recognition that this would mean a slowdown in the Lisbon plans, see Eden to Kirkpatrick,

May 17, 1952, FO 371/100032, and Sir Frank Roberts, Draft Cabinet Paper, May 27, 1952, FO 371/100033, PRO.

76. The problem of the "preemergency measures" is discussed in *FRUS 1952–1954,* VII, 21–22, 28–30. The final text of Article 5 is in *FRUS 1952–1954,* VII, 115–116. The Germans emphasized that the differences between themselves and the Allies often turned "not on questions of substance but on questions of form." Hallstein explained to Americans that the concept of "fortress town" was "well-established in German law and provides basis for special military power in sensitive areas." His concern, however, was political. He wanted to see Allied requirements fulfilled through the German government rather than by Allied soldiers directly. Acheson to McCloy, March 17, 1952, D(52)675, Box 38, RG 466, McCloy Papers, NARS-Suitland.

77. *FRUS 1952–1954,* VII, 39–41, 53–54. The British were more sympathetic. Kirkpatrick to Foreign Office, April 17, 1952, FO 1008/100, PRO. Baring, *Im Anfang,* pp. 439–446, discusses these political developments in detail. One of Adenauer's major concerns was that the FDP in Baden-Württemberg had formed its governing coalition with the SPD, and that this might be done on the federal level.

78. *FRUS 1952–1954,* VII, 45–47, 55–56, 63.

79. For the original wording of the Binding Clause, see *FRUS 1951,* III, 1595–96; Adenauer's interest in it can be found on pp. 1566 and 1586, and the State Department's disapproval on p. 1574. The Bundestag members' objections are in *FRUS 1952–1954,* VII, 46. Philip Jessup saw the problem with the Binding Clause as soon as the Allies drafted their first response to the Soviets. Summary of Meeting with the Secretary, April 9, 1952, Records of the Office of the Executive Secretariat, Box 5, NARS-DB. For Acheson's compromise, see Acheson, *Present at the Creation,* pp. 644–646; and *FRUS 1952–1954,* VII, 106–108.

80. On the question of a guarantee for the EDC, see *FRUS 1952–1954,* V, 677–679. McCloy to Bowie, 27 May 1952, D(52)1320, Box 42, RG 466, McCloy Papers, NARS-Suitland. David Bruce gave McCloy much of the credit for the successful completion of the agreements. "As was the case also in the Schuman Plan, without your guidance, wisdom, courage, increasing attention and participation, these last two arrangements would have been utterly impossible." Bruce to McCloy, May 31, 1952, D(52)1321, Box 42, RG 466, McCloy Papers, NARS-Suitland.

81. Acheson, *Present at the Creation,* p. 647. On the relative German apathy toward the agreements, see "German Views on the Contractual Agreement following Initialing and Publication," July 8, 1952, Report #144, RAS-OPA, HI-COG, Stone Papers. Baring, *Im Anfang,* pp. 272–273, details the opposition to Adenauer's plans for a celebration. Young Henry Kissinger, who was in Germany when the contractuals were signed, called the reaction "hysterical." He noted that the agreements "led to an outburst of anti-American feeling totally out of proportion to the specific criticism advanced." Notes on Germany, Memo, William Elliott to Raymond B. Allen, July 11, 1952, Psychological Strategy Board, 091 Germany, Truman Papers, Truman Library. A record of the protests is contained

in PA-AA 241.27, Bonn. See also *Newsweek,* June 30, 1952; and Schumacher, Interview, May 23, 1952, Schumacher Bestand, Q-7, SPD Archive, Bonn. Adenauer remembered Schumacher's comment as "ceases to be a *good* German." Adenauer, *Erinnerungen,* II, 90.

82. For the record of Senate consideration, see *Convention on Relations with the Federal Republic of Germany and a Protocol to the North Atlantic Treaty,* Hearings before the Committee on Foreign Relations, U.S. Senate, 82nd Cong., 2nd sess., June 1952. McCloy's comments on Schumacher are on p. 77 of this Senate document. For the Senate's praise of the agreement, see *New York Times,* June 12, 1952. For the critical view of one contemporary, see James A. Warburg, *Germany: Key to Peace* (Cambridge, Mass.: Harvard University Press, 1953), pp. 247ff. For Schumacher's criticism, see Schumacher, Interview, June 20, 1952, Schumacher Bestand, Q-7, SPD Archive, Bonn.

83. McCloy's statement is in *Department of State Bulletin,* June 2, 1952, p. 858; and in McCloy's Press Conference, July 16, 1952, D(52)1674, Box 43, RG 466, McCloy Papers, NARS-Suitland. Adenauer's request can be found in McCloy to Acheson, June 18, 1952, D(52)1460, TS(52)73, TSGR, Box 6, RG 466, McCloy Papers, NARS-Suitland. For McCloy's reputation among the Germans, see "The Current State of German-American Relations," Oct. 12, 1951, Report #103, RAS-OPA, Stone Papers. For the press reaction, see *Information Bulletin,* HICOG, July 1952, p. 27; *Frankfurter Neue Presse,* June 30, 1952; *Time,* July 28, 1952; and *New York Times,* July 18, 1952.

10. The New Look: Eisenhower and Dulles, 1953–1955

1. Acheson, *Present at the Creation,* pp. 632–633; and *FRUS 1952–1954,* V, 693–702. For McCloy's appeal, see McCloy to Eisenhower, Dec. 14, 1952, Ann Whitman File, Administration Series, Folder John J. McCloy, Box 28, Eisenhower Library. In this letter McCloy enclosed a translation of a December 1, 1952, letter which he had received from Chancellor Adenauer.

2. John Lewis Gaddis, *Strategies of Containment,* (New York: Oxford University Press, 1982), p. 152; and *FRUS 1952–1954,* V, 712, 765. For Dulles's views on Germany before he became Secretary of State, see Ronald W. Preussen, *John Foster Dulles: The Road to Power* (New York: Free Press, 1982), pp. 337–344.

3. For Dulles's use of McCloy as an intermediary with Adenauer, see McCloy to Adenauer, Jan. 9, 1953, Subject Series, Classified Material, Papers of John Foster Dulles, Eisenhower Library. On the problems with Robert Murphy, see Memo of Conversation with McCloy, Dec. 23, 1952, and Memo of Conversation with Dulles, Dec. 24, 1952, Box 67a, Acheson Papers, Truman Library. On the appointment of Conant, which McCloy had sought to engineer as early as 1951, see James Conant, *My Several Lives* (New York: Harper & Row, 1970), pp. 534–537. McCloy, who wanted Conant even though the Harvard president had expressed some reservations about German rearmament, told the Germans that the

appointment of such an outstanding man was a great "compliment" to Germany. Krekeler to Riesser, Jan. 10, 1953, PA-AA 241.27a, vol. I, Bonn. Bowie played a key role in Task Force C of Project Solarium, which reconsidered America's security policy. The task force concluded, "Our minimum objective, however, is a rearmed West Germany associated with the West." *FRUS 1952–1954,* II, 416–419.

4. *FRUS 1952–1954,* V, 1783; Stephen E. Ambrose, *Eisenhower the President,* II (New York: Simon & Schuster, 1984), 70–71, 119–121; and Gaddis, *Strategies,* pp. 133–135.

5. For Fulbright's comment, see *Convention on Relations with Federal Republic of Germany,* p. 99. On the change in Soviet policy after Stalin's death, see William Taubman, *Stalin's American Policy* (New York: Norton, 1982), p. 231.

6. Churchill's interest in a summit can be followed in his exchange of letters with Eisenhower, beginning with his letter of March 11, 1953, in Steininger, *Eine Chance,* pp. 296-308, and in Gilbert, *Churchill,* pp. 827–833. See also Josef Foschepoth, "Churchill, Adenauer und die Neutralisierung Deutschlands," *Deutschland Archiv,* 17 (December 1984), 1286–1301.

7. Gilbert, *Churchill,* p. 828; and Taubman, *Stalin's American Policy,* p. 232. Eisenhower reassured Adenauer, who had been disconcerted by Churchill's views, that he would be consulted about potential four-power talks. When Adenauer's personal representative, Herbert Blankenhorn, visited the United States in early June 1953, Eisenhower asked him to tell the Chancellor that "U.S. policy with respect to Germany was based on (1) West Germany becoming an integrated part of Western Europe and (2) on the ultimate unification of Germany." *FRUS 1952–1954,* VII, 469–470. On the change in Soviet policy toward East Germany, the "new course," see Willging, "Soviet Foreign Policy," pp. 165–201; and M. Steven Fish, "After Stalin's Death: The Anglo-American Debate over a New Cold War," *Diplomatic History,* 10 (1986), 337–339.

8. Willging, "Soviet Foreign Policy," pp. 201–215. For the American reaction to the June 17 uprising, see High Commissioner Conant's letter to Dulles, June 25, 1953, in *FRUS 1952–1954,* VII, 480. Eisenhower's letter to Adenauer, dated July 23, 1953, is in *FRUS 1952–1954,* VII, 491–494. Eisenhower's musings about the Soviets' inability to hold Germany militarily are found in a letter to the British Field Marshall, Bernard Montgomery, dated July 2, 1953, and quoted in Ninkovich, *Germany and the United States,* p. 102. These musings about revolution in East Germany brought a quick visit from the French Ambassador, who feared that the President might rely on violence rather than negotiations to bring about a German settlement. Memorandum of a Conversation with the Secretary of State, July 29, 1953, in *FRUS 1952–1954,* VII, 498. For the Eisenhower Administration's interest in a demilitarized zone, see Hermann-Josef Rupieper, "Deutsche Frage und europäische Sicherheit: Politisch-strategische Überlegungen, 1953–1955," in *Zwischen Kaltem Krieg und Entspannung,* ed. Bruno Thoss and Hans Erich Volkmann (Boppard am Rhein, 1966), pp. 181–190.

9. NSC 160/1, dated Aug. 17, 1953, is in *FRUS 1952–1954*, VII, 510–520. One of the potential difficulties of a unified neutral Germany was raised by General Collins: "We could scarcely expect the French to accept six American divisions . . . Where would these forces go, and how would we defend Germany against a Russian advance?" Ibid., p. 505.

10. Noelle and Neumann, *The Germans*, pp. 256–257. On Germany's dynamism and its consequences for Europe, see *FRUS 1952–1954*, VII, 355–359, and V, 809.

11. *FRUS 1952–1954*, VII, 540–543, 868.

12. Ibid., V, 796, 867, 888–889.

13. On the rise of nuclear weapons, see Thomas H. Etzold, "The End of the Beginning . . . NATO's Adoption of Nuclear Strategy," in Riste, *Western Security*, pp. 290–295; Gaddis, *Strategies*, p. 167; and *FRUS 1952–1954*, V, 511–512. On the important role of the British in persuading the United States and NATO to rely on nuclear weapons, see Robert A. Wampler, "From Lisbon to M.C. 48: The United States, Great Britain, and the 'New Look' in NATO, 1952–1954" (Paper given at Conference on the United States and West European Security, Harvard University, December 1987).

14. For the French insistence on four-power talks, see *FRUS 1952–1954*, V, 1617 and 870. The Eden Plan can be found in *FRUS 1952–1954*, VII, 1177–80. For the arguments of Dulles, see *FRUS 1952–1954*, VII, 899–900, 933–934.

15. Dulles felt that the Soviets could have exploited even more effectively the issue of a reunited Germany's right to leave the EDC. Dulles to President Eisenhower, Feb. 5, 1954, *FRUS 1952–1954*, VII, 962; for Molotov's proposals, see pp. 956–957.

16. On the Soviet bureaucracy and the shift in Soviet policy, see Ernest May, "Soviet Policy and 'The German Problem,'" *Naval War College Review*, 36 (1984), 25–27. For the Soviet preference for a divided Germany, see Dockrill, "Britain and a West German Contribution," p. 304. In March 1954 the Soviet Union announced, in advance of any Western move, that it would grant the German Democratic Republic its sovereignty. This shift in policy may have been related to the overthrow of Beria and his associates by Soviet leaders sympathetic to the East German Communist Walter Ulbricht. Beria, the head of Stalin's secret police, was in favor of liberalizing conditions in East Germany and being willing to sacrifice the East German Communists for a neutral Germany. Willging, "Soviet Foreign Policy," pp. 165–201.

17. Dulles came away from the Berlin conference believing that the Soviet Union could not act on German reunification because it was afraid of losing power in Eastern Europe. He told Adenauer that with the increasing unification and strengthening of Western Europe, the Soviets would be forced "to reanalyze their policy toward the satellite states and give them some form of semi-autonomous character." This would transform those countries into "buffer states," perhaps with a status similar to Finland's. Such a change would eventually lead

the Soviets to loosen their "iron grip" on East Germany, and this might allow East Germany to "join" West Germany. *FRUS 1952–1954,* VII, 1208–15. For Eisenhower's reassurances on the EDC, see *FRUS 1952–1954,* V, 888, 975, 984.

18. *FRUS 1952–1954,* V, 1113; on the ouster of Schuman and the new French demands, see V, 702–708, and on the issue of the Saar, VII, 1444. The French allowed this issue to disappear from the discussions in 1954, when it was overshadowed by Indochina. Eventually they agreed to allow the Saar to choose between "Europeanization" and returning to Germany. After having rejected Europeanization, the Saar was incorporated into the Federal Republic on January 1, 1957.

19. On the increasing American involvement in Indochina, and the strains it created with the French, see Herring, *America's Longest War,* pp. 26–42. For the proposals of Mendès-France and the American reaction, see *FRUS 1952–1954,* V, 1023–43.

20. *FRUS 1952–1954,* V, 1029–30.

21. For the State Department's view of the lessons of the EDC, see *FRUS 1952–1954,* V, 1170–77. For Dulles's reaction and his desire to be "cagey" at the conference, see p. 1383. For the record of the London Conference, see pp. 1294–1369. For Adenauer's unilateral declaration, which said that the Germans could not manufacture such weapons without the approval (by a two-thirds majority) of the Brussels Council of Ministers and on the recommendation of the NATO Supreme Commander, see p. 1325. On French resignation to the inevitable, see p. 1387.

22. On the need for revisions in the agreements, see *FRUS 1952–1954,* V, 1167–1170, 1174; on Adenauer's need for a "concrete achievement," see p. 1379. For a limited comparison of the treaties, see the 1952 agreements in *FRUS 1952–1954,* VII, 112–168, and the final version in *Documents on Germany, 1944–1985,* p. 425–438.

23. *FRUS 1952–1954,* V, 1381–82.

24. For Dulles's prediction of Soviet behavior, see *FRUS 1952–1954,* V, 1383. For the Soviet initiatives, see *Documents on Germany, 1944–1985,* pp. 438–443.

25. The concern about Adenauer's position was expressed by Cecil Lyon in January 1955, quoted in Rupieper, "Deutsche Frage," p. 192. Eisenhower's reaction to the French Assembly's action is in *FRUS 1952–1954,* V, 1520–22.

26. For an excellent discussion of the German question at the Geneva Conference, see Rupieper, "Deutsche Frage," pp. 193–209. For the interesting comparison Dulles made between German and Austrian neutrality, see *Documents on Germany, 1944–1985,* p. 448.

Conclusions

1. *FRUS 1950,* IV, 634. The comparison with Weimar also justified what was essentially a strategy of "appeasement" toward Germany at a time when that

word was out of fashion. For the original statement of the comparison, see Fritz René Allemann, *Bonn ist nicht Weimar* (Cologne: Kiepenheuer & Witsch, 1956).

2. Melvyn P. Leffler, *The Elusive Quest: America's Pursuit of European Stability and French Security, 1919–1933* (Chapel Hill: University of North Carolina Press, 1979), pp. 82–83. Charles S. Maier, "The Politics of Productivity," in Peter S. Katzenstein, ed., *Between Power and Plenty: Foreign Economic Policies of Advanced Industrial States* (Madison: University of Wisconsin Press, 1978), pp. 23–49. For the argument that excessive reparation payments damaged Weimar's domestic political legitimacy in the 1920s, see Peter Krüger, "Das Reparationsproblem der Weimarer Republik in fragwürdiger Sicht," *Vierteljahrshefte für Zeitgeschichte,* 29 (January 1981), 34–40. For a treatment of the reparations issue more in sympathy with the French position, see Steven Schuker, *The End of French Predominance in Europe* (Chapel Hill: University of North Carolina Press, 1976); and Marc Trachtenberg, *Reparation in World Politics* (New York: Columbia University Press, 1980). Charles Maier has argued that "Weimar falls and Hitler's disastrous foreign policy triumphs because, within the ranks of both industry and the military, progressive forces could stalemate simple reaction, but did not have the strength to impose moderation, decency, and internationalism." Charles S. Maier, "The Vulnerabilities of Interwar Germany," *Journal of Modern History,* 56 (March 1984), 99. In the postwar period American assistance would be vital in helping progressive forces succeed. See also Maier's article, "The Two Postwar Eras and the Conditions for Stability in Twentieth Century Western Europe," *American Historical Review,* 86 (April 1981), 327–352. On the role of American capital in the 1920s, see William C. McNeil, *American Money and the Weimar Republic* (New York: Columbia University Press, 1986), pp. 271–280; and Frank Costigliola, "The United States and the Reconstruction of Germany in the 1920s," *Business History Review,* 50 (Winter 1986), 477–502. The concept of analogies in decision making is explored in Richard E. Neustadt and Ernest R. May, *Thinking in Time: The Uses of History for Decision-Makers* (New York: Free Press, 1986). An earlier book on the subject is Ernest R. May, *Lessons of the Past* (New York: Oxford University Press, 1973).

3. Jon Jacobsen, "Is There a New International History of the 1920s?" *American Historical Review,* 88 (June 1983), 629–630.

4. George Ball, *Past Has Another Pattern,* pp. 81–83; and McCloy Press Conference, June 26, 1952, D(52)1530, Box 43, RG 466, McCloy Papers, NARS-Suitland.

5. Hogan, *Marshall Plan,* pp. 427–430, emphasizes the importance of European integration in American thinking. Milward, *Reconstruction,* pp. 400–420, diminishes the American role and argues that such proposals as the Schuman Plan were a "defeat" for American policy. Lawrence Kaplan, the dean of NATO historians, also tends to underestimate the importance of American sentiment for European integration. See his *United States and NATO: The Formative Years* (Lexington: University of Kentucky Press, 1984), pp. 57–58.

6. The connection between the failure of denazification and concerns about

German reliability is also seen in Mary Fulbrook, "The State and the Transformation of Political Legitimacy in East and West Germany since 1945," *Comparative Studies in Society and History,* 29 (1987), 223. Berghahn, *Americanisation,* p. 328, noted the "slowness" with which the attitudes of the industrial elites changed. Both Ninkovich, *Germany and the United States,* pp. 82–106, and Wolfram Hanrieder, *Germany, America, Europe* (New Haven: Yale University Press, 1989), pp. 30–31, use the term "double containment" to describe American policy, but "dual" better captures the connection between the two policies.

7. Fulbrook argues quite sensibly that "elite commitment perhaps held the key to political stability; popular loyalty to and support of the system developed as a result of that stability, and was not in itself an important causal factor." The increasing support for democracy during the 1950s came as the result of economic improvements, as the system "delivered the goods." Fulbrook, "State and Transformation," pp. 227–240. George Kennan put this in a different light when he noted in 1947, "There is a little bit of the totalitarian buried somewhere, way down deep, in each and every one of us . . . It is only the cheerful light of confidence and security which keeps this evil genius down . . . If confidence and security were to disappear, don't think that he would not be waiting to take their place." Quoted in John Lewis Gaddis, *The Long Peace* (New York: Oxford University Press, 1987), p. 43. Geir Lundestad, "Empire by Invitation: The United States and Western Europe," *Newsletter of the Society of Historians of American Foreign Relations,* 15 (September 1984), 1–21.

8. Most of the recent German treatments of this topic assume that a reunited Germany would have developed in a fashion similar to that of the Federal Republic, lacking only its military tie to NATO. This type of counterfactual argument is stimulating, but it ignores all the other elements in the equation that would have changed if Germany had not been linked to the Western alliance. It also ignores the fact that the German people in the early 1950s were hardly reliable believers in democracy. In October 1948, for example, 57 percent still believed that National Socialism was "a good idea that was badly put into practice." Steininger, *Eine vertane Chance,* pp. 123–129; and Noelle and Neumann, *The Germans,* p. 197.

9. Fritz Stern, "Conclusion: German-American Relations and 'The Return of the Repressed,'" in Cooney, et al., *Federal Republic and the United States,* p. 238.

10. Josef Joffe, "Europe's American Pacifier," *Foreign Policy,* 54 (Spring 1984), 83. On the "destruction" of the European unification movement, see Joseph Bernard Egan, "The Struggle for the Soul of Faust: The American Drive for German Rearmament, 1950–1955," (Ph.D. diss., University of Connecticut, 1985), p. 463. Egan's work is well documented but lacks an understanding of the complexities of the European viewpoint.

11. Gaddis, *The Long Peace,* p. 57.

12. Alan Brinkley, "The Most Influential Private Citizen in America: Minister without Portfolio," *Harper's,* February 1983, p. 33.

13. Charles Maier, "The Making of 'Pax Americana'" (Paper presented at Diplomatic History Workshop, Harvard University, October 1988), pp. 3–4. Hogan, *Marshall Plan*, pp. 427–445, also discusses the historical perceptions of these elites. McCloy's speech about the impossibility of isolationism is in the *Department of State Bulletin*, July 9, 1951, p. 66.

14. Maier, "The Making of 'Pax Americana,'" p. 4. Maier refers to the transnational elite's shared ideas as part of a larger "Atlantic culture." For an earlier use of the concept of an "Atlantic community" to explain shifts in American thinking on foreign policy, see the outstanding essay by Ernest R. May, *American Imperialism: A Speculative Essay* (New York: Atheneum, 1968), May's challenge to American historians to investigate the interplay between American elites and opinion movements and their counterparts in other nations has not been fully met. But for an excellent example of this approach in the realm of intellectual history, see James T. Kloppenberg, *Uncertain Victory: Social Democracy and Progressivism in European and American Thought, 1870–1920* (New York: Oxford University Press, 1986).

15. Maier, "The Two Postwar Eras," p. 350.

16. Alexander Böker, "Die amerikanischer Einstellung gegenüber Deutschland," Jan. 15, 1950, PA-AA 210.01/80, vol. I, Bonn. Böker also insisted on the need to cultivate American Jewish opinion, noting that "every act of restitution, every gesture of good will is of significance." For the attempt to cultivate McCloy, see Pferdmenges to Henle, Feb. 10, 1954, Allgemeine Korrespondenz 1945–1955, Henle NL, Klöckner Archive, Duisburg. Pferdmenges relayed a letter from McCloy indicating that the Chase Bank—of which McCloy was president—was interested in helping Klöckner build a steel mill in Brazil. Pferdmenges reminded Henle, who had fought with McCloy over the vertical integration issue, that it would be "interesting for every German concern to have friendly relations with a figure of the stature of Mr. McCloy."

17. Stern, "German-American Relations," p. 238.

18. John J. McCloy, *The Challenge to American Foreign Policy* (Cambridge: Mass.: Harvard University Press, 1953), p. 65.

19. Stern, "German-American Relations," p. 238.

20. Ernest R. May, "The American Commitment to Germany, 1949–55," *Diplomatic History,* 13, 4 (1989), 459.

21. Henry Brandon, *Special Relationships* (New York: Atheneum, 1988), p. 43. Brandon was the *Sunday Times* correspondent in Washington, and he interviewed Kennan in April 1949. Lippmann to Bernard Berenson, Aug. 9, 1949, Folder 208, Box 56, Papers of Walter Lippmann, Sterling Library, Yale University.

22. A. W. DePorte, *Europe between the Superpowers* (New Haven: Yale University Press, 1979), pp. 162–165, offers an assessment similar to the one presented here. Ernest May notes that American leaders, seeing a number of signs of European weakness, came to believe that "it might be safer at the margin for Europeans to see the United States as inflexible rather than flexible." Ernest R.

May, "The Cold War," in Joseph S. Nye, *The Making of America's Soviet Policy* (New Haven: Yale University Press, 1984), p. 226.

23. Herring, *America's Longest War,* p. 23.

24. C. Wright Mills, *The Power Elite* (New York: Oxford University Press, 1956), p. 356; and the review article by Douglas Little, "Crackpot Realists and Other Heroes: The Rise and Fall of the Postwar American Diplomatic Elite," *Diplomatic History,* 13, no. 1 (1989), 99–111.

25. David C. Large, "Reckoning without the Past: the HIAG of the Waffen SS and the Politics of Rehabilitation in the Bonn Republic, 1950–1961." *Journal of Modern History,* 59 (1987), 80; Tom Bower, *The Pledge Betrayed* (Garden City, N.Y.: Doubleday, 1982), pp. 379–392; and Brinkley, "Most Influential Private Citizen," p. 38.

26. McCloy, *Challenge to American Policy,* p. 81.

Index

Abelshauser, Werner, 208
Abs, Hermann, 62–63, 179–180, 181, 182
Acheson, Dean, 1, 10, 26, 42, 302; as Secretary of State, 29, 34; view of Kennan's Program A, 36, 39; and occupation policy, 37, 38, 40, 84, 240, 250, 255, 303–304; support for JJM as High Commissioner, 41; and French reaction to German restoration, 45, 251; and devaluation crisis, 64–65; and dismantling of German industry, 70, 71, 73, 74, 75, 76–77; visit to Bonn, 78–80; and Saar region, 88, 254; and German recovery, 93–94, 197, 242; and German role in Europe, 95, 103; and Schuman Plan, 104–105, 106, 110, 186; and American military strength, 116; and German rearmament, 120, 122, 128, 129, 135–136, 137, 139, 140, 141, 142, 143, 151–152, 153, 154, 155, 216, 217, 226–227, 231–232, 241, 256, 257–258; and Nazi war criminals, 161, 166, 174; and restitution, 180–181, 182, 183; and German balance of payments, 204; and EDC negotiations, 253–254, 275, 277, 279; and occupation costs, 258–260; and Allied negotiations, 261, 269; and Stalin Note, 262, 265; and 1952 presidential election, 279; influence of Monnet, 342n28
Acheson-Lilienthal Committee, 26
Adenauer, Emma Weyer, 50
Adenauer, Gussie Zinsser, 50

Adenauer, Konrad: background, 49–53; opposition to, 55, 56, 146, 147, 217, 296; and Occupation Statute, 57; and devaluation crisis, 63, 64, 65; political instability, 66, 244, 264, 274, 298; and Berlin, 67; and German industrialization, 70, 71–73, 75, 80–83, 85–87, 88–89, 187, 192–194, 195–196, 197, 200–201; conciliatory attitude, 78–79, 264, 266, 304; and German equality, 85; and German economic recovery, 91–92, 206–208, 239–240; and Schuman Plan, 107, 112; and German rearmament, 117, 119–120, 123, 124, 127, 133–134, 136, 137, 144–145, 147, 148–149, 152, 153, 155, 192, 212, 213–214, 215, 228–229, 232–233, 252, 255–256, 291; and Nazi war criminals, 159, 160, 165, 173–174, 256; and reconciliation with Israel, 178; and restitution, 178–180, 181, 182–184, 304, 306; and German reunification, 185, 246, 267, 283; support for, 199, 284, 292, 298–299, 300; and German surrender, 235, 236, 237, 239, 242–243, 245, 246–249, 255; and Saar region, 254; and occupation costs, 258–260, 270–271, 273; and Stalin Note, 266–269; and Bonn-Paris treaty negotiations, 269, 275–276; and EDC, 280
Advisory Board on Clemency for War Criminals (Peck Panel), 160, 162–165, 168, 169, 172, 174
Allen, Dennis, 345n12

All-German Constitutional Council, 148
Allied Control Commission, 30, 31
Allied Control Council, 68
Allied High Commission (AHC), 56, 57, 60, 61, 63, 65, 91, 94
Allied Maritime Transport Executive, 97
Alphand, Hervé, 218
Alsop, Joseph, 342n28
American Council on Germany, 304
American High Commission in Germany (HICOG): policy directive, 43–44, 106; report on German nationalism, 87; and economic policy, 92; and Schuman Plan, 106, 108, 186; and German rearmament, 120; and control of Germany, 238, 245
Amherst College, 3, 4, 25
Appeasement, 389n1
Arbeitsgemeinschaft der Schutzvereinigung für Wertpapierbesitz, 194
Article IV of General Agreement, 248
Atlantic High Council for Peace (proposed), 96, 104, 110, 251
Atlantic Pact treaty, 37, 113
Atomic energy policy, 26
Atomic weapons, 25, 26, 114, 118, 286, 290
Attlee, Clement, 211, 241, 272
August-Thyssen steel plant, 69, 71, 72, 73, 77, 78, 140, 190, 192, 201
Auriol, Vincent, 53
Auschwitz, bombing of, 17–18, 362n52
Austria, 294
Auswärtiges Amt, 238

Ball, George, 96, 342n28
Baltimore Sun, 75
Bank Deutscher Länder, 63
Barbie, Klaus, 47
Barth, Karl, 148
Bauer, Walter, 192
Bech, Joseph, 140
Beitz, Bertoldt, 174
Bérard, Armand, 60, 211, 250
Bereitschaften, 66, 114, 125, 126
Berlin: as Twelfth Land, 67; Soviet policy in, 114–115; Allied control of, 235, 236, 237, 238, 239, 246, 247; German expenses for, 258; Western support in, 305
Berlin Airlift, 32

Berlin Blockade, 28, 32, 35, 39, 84, 115
Berlin Wall, 306
Bethlehem Steel, 6, 9
Bevin, Ernest, 37, 40, 55, 59, 71, 75–76, 77, 106, 109–110, 120, 121, 126, 136, 152
Bidault, Georges, 96, 104, 110, 226, 251
Biddle, Francis, 15
Black, Eugene, 27, 41
Black Tom case, 8–9
Blair, Floyd, 342n28
Blair and Company, 7, 97
Blank, Theodor, 148, 211–212, 228, 229
Blankenhorn, Herbert, 126, 144, 330n31, 332n42, 387n7
Blobel, Paul, 164
Blücher, Franz, 190, 206, 207
Blum, Leon, 10
Böckler, Hans, 82, 112
Bohlen, Charles, 279
Böhm, Franz, 181, 182
Bonnet, Henri, 142
Bonn-Paris treaties, 269–278
Bowie, Robert, 43, 130, 131, 144, 164–165, 187, 189–190, 192, 195, 265, 276, 281, 303
Bradley, Gen. Omar N., 39, 114, 225
Brandt, Willy, 111, 306
Brauer, Max, 111
Bretton Woods agreement (1944), 26
Brinkley, Alan, 302
Bross, John, 166
Bruce, David, 63, 100, 105, 109, 129, 132, 140, 143, 151, 186, 215, 216, 219, 226, 227, 231, 232, 281, 303, 385n80
Brüderschaft, 87
Brüning, Heinrich, 91
Brussels Pact treaty, 290–291
Bullock, Alan, 109
Bundy, McGeorge, 342n28
Bureau of German Affairs (U.S. State Department), 43, 109, 122, 129, 240, 245
Buttenwieser, Benjamin, 43
Byrnes, James, 23, 24, 31, 68
Byroade, Col. Henry, 128, 129, 130, 131, 133, 134, 240, 245

Cadwalader, Wickersham, and Taft (law firm), 6
Cairncross, Sir Alec, 205

Chamberlain, Neville, 57
Chase Bank, 279
Chicago, Milwaukee, and St. Paul Railroad, 6
China, 84, 94, 113, 129, 205
Christian Democratic Union (CDU), 40, 48, 49, 50–51, 85, 146, 185, 277, 284
Churchill, Sir Winston, 20, 98, 253, 256–257, 262, 282
Clappier, Bernard, 103
Clark, Grenville, 3
Clark, Gen. Mark, 40
Clay, Gen. Lucius: as Military Governor, 21, 30, 41, 158; and occupation policy, 24, 30, 31, 32, 34, 38, 39–40, 55; and defense of Western Europe, 37; and denazification program, 47; and Nazi war trials, 157, 158–159, 166; and German resistance, 158; and restitution, 177; personality, 335n18
Cleveland Plain Dealer, 117, 120, 121
Collado, Emilio, 26, 27
Collins, Gen. J. Lawton, 224, 225, 231, 388n9
Committee to Defend America by Aiding the Allies, 10
Communism: French, 37, 52, 96, 121, 138, 226, 251; Italian, 52; and Hitler's opposition to Bolshevism, 218, 282, 308
Conant, James, 280
Containment policy, 35, 299
Corporatism, 323n21
Council of Ambassadors, 242, 246, 248, 249
Council of Europe, 86, 88–89, 111, 112
Council of Foreign Ministers (CFM), 37, 38, 39
Crane, Joan, 73
Crane, John, 73
Cravath, Henderson, and deGersdorff (later Cravath, Swaine, and Moore) (law firm), 6–9, 25
Cravath, Paul, 7
Cuban missile crisis, 306
Currency reform: and Operation Bird Dog, 32; and devaluation, 61–65, 87
Czechoslovakia, 266, 285

Dachau, 54
Darlan, Adm. Jean, 18

de Gaulle, Gen. Charles, 18–19, 60, 96, 98, 226, 233, 307
Degoutte, Gen. Jean-Marie-Joseph, 59
Dehler, Thomas, 87
de Lattre de Tassigny, Gen. Jean, 252
Denmark, 205
Deterrence, atomic, 114, 115, 125
Deutscher Kohlen-Verkauf (DKV), 188–189, 190, 192, 196, 200, 201
Dewey, Thomas, 10
DeWitt, Gen. John, 15, 16
DGB, 111–112, 199
Die Zeit, 75
Dodd, William, 59
Dönhoff, Marion, 159
Donovan, Col. William ("Wild Bill"), 5, 322n6
Dorn, Walter, 331n35
Douglas, Lewis W., 3, 4, 8, 40, 41, 109, 132, 143
Douglas, Peggy, 8
Dulles, Allen W., 158
Dulles, John Foster, 97, 105, 280–294 passim, 302, 307

Economic Cooperation Administration (ECA), 34, 37, 41–42, 64, 90, 92, 206, 207; Industrial Advisory Committee, 69
Economic Problems of Socialism in the U.S.S.R. (Stalin), 263
Eden, Sir Anthony, 183, 257, 258, 264, 265, 268, 288, 290
Eden Plan, 287, 288, 293
Eisenhower, Gen. Dwight D., 18, 21, 150, 153, 216, 219–224, 227, 229–231, 241, 261, 279–294 passim, 308
Emergency, state of, 237, 239, 246, 248–249, 273–274, 291–292
English Speaking Union, 224
Erhard, Ludwig, 50–51, 55, 61, 62, 63, 91, 92, 112, 149, 189–190, 191, 192, 204, 205, 206, 207, 208
European Coal and Steel Community, 203, 230, 281, 298, 303
European Command (EUCOM), 271, 272, 273
European Defense Community (EDC), 210, 216, 230–234, 241, 251–252, 256–258, 264–265, 275–276, 277, 279–280, 281, 285, 286–291, 292, 299, 301, 303

European Defense Council, 232
European Defense Force (EDF), 130, 132, 135, 142, 230
European Ministry of Defense, 141
European Payments Union (EPU), 204, 205, 206, 208, 209
European Security Force (ESF), 130, 132
Export-Import Bank, 99

Farben, I. G., 163, 169, 173
Federal Republic of Germany (FRG), creation of, 113. *See also* Germany
Federation of German Industry, 208
Ferencz, Benjamin, 177, 181
Finland, 266, 388n17
Flick, Friedrich, 160, 163, 169, 173
Fontaine, André, 96
Forrestal, James, 21
Fort Ethan Allen (Vermont), 4–5
Four-Power Agreements on Germany, 153, 198
France: occupation policy, 30, 31, 44, 45, 52, 57, 58, 60–61, 67, 69, 102; Communist party, 37, 52, 96, 121, 138, 226, 251; steel industry, 62, 93, 94, 101–102, 104, 187, 189, 202; role in Europe, 95–96, 251; opposition to German rearmament in, 120–121, 140, 143–144, 214–215, 218, 226–227, 229, 233, 289; and access to German markets, 204–205
Franco, Francisco, 122
François-Poncet, André, 53, 57, 59–60, 63, 64, 65, 67, 72, 88, 89, 121, 126, 235
Franc-Tireur, 170
Frankfurt Economic Council, 63
Frankfurter, Felix, 6, 11, 12, 26, 98, 171, 250
Frankfurter Allgemeine Zeitung, 92
Frankfurter Neue Presse, 277
Franks, Sir Oliver, 110, 142
Free Democratic Party (FDP), 51, 193, 199, 244, 274
Freie Deutsche Jugend, 114
French Committee of National Liberation, 18, 98
French Modernization and Investment Plan, 99, 100
Frings (cardinal of Cologne), 159, 171
Fulbright, J. William, 105, 281

Gaddis, John Lewis, 280, 301
Gehlen, Gen. Reinhard, 47, 344n3, 357n21
Geiler, Kurt, 159
Gelsenberg-Benzin plant, 71
Gemeinschaftsorganisation Ruhrkohle (GEORG), 201
General Claims Law, 177
Gentleman's Agreement (1908), 15
George VI (king of England), 255
Gerhardt, Col. Al, 130, 131, 221
German-American Mixed Claims Commission, 9
German Basic Law, 39, 159, 167, 169, 192, 243
German Communist Party (KPD), 54
German Democratic Republic (GDR), founding of, 66. *See also* Germany
German National Assembly, 244
German Party (DP), 51, 274, 370n13
Germany: sabotage in U.S. by, 8–9, 12–13; economic recovery, 19, 20, 21, 23, 27–28, 30–31, 34, 47, 89–94, 174, 196, 203–204, 258, 284, 305; American occupation policy, 19–21, 23, 29–42 passim, 43–44, 106, 107; denazification, 20, 21, 24, 30, 34, 45–48; French occupation policy, 30, 31, 44, 45, 52, 57, 58, 60–61, 67, 69, 102; Soviet occupation policy, 30–31, 32, 40, 66, 67, 68, 86, 92, 114–115, 282–283, 286–288, 292–293, 336n29; British occupation policy, 31, 45, 58, 70, 108–111; currency reform, 32, 61–65, 87; partition, 35, 36, 66, 288; reunification, 36–37, 39, 40, 45, 52, 66, 67, 89, 148, 236, 244, 246, 247, 249, 262, 263, 264, 268, 275, 282, 283–284, 287, 293, 300, 306; American military government, 41–42; political rebirth, 48–56, 235–278 passim, 306; role in Europe, 57, 84–95, 217, 231, 237, 252, 269; dismantling of industry, 68–83 passim, 87, 92–94, 102, 149; civil service reform, 78, 81–82, 270, 298; in Council of Europe, 86, 88–89, 111, 112; neutrality, 86, 217, 237, 264, 265, 284, 290, 293, 300; censorship in, 87, 266; free elections, 89, 244, 266, 267, 284, 287; income tax law, 91–92; membership in NATO, 111, 117, 124, 211,

213, 249, 253, 254, 255, 256, 263,
268, 291, 292, 293–94, 295; trade
unions, 111–112, 188, 193, 196, 201,
208; rearmament, 113–155 passim, 185,
210–234 passim, 236, 241, 262, 285,
291, 357n21; moral integration, 156–
184 passim; trade balance, 203–209;
arms production, 255–256, 262, 291;
Americanization, 300–301
Germany's Underground (Dulles), 158
Giraud, Gen. Henri-Honoré, 18, 98
Globke, Hans, 81
Goldmann, Nahum, 17, 179, 180, 182–
183
Goldschmidt, Theodore, 108
Göring, Hermann, 9, 157, 170
Graham, Kay, 342n28
Graham, Phil, 342n28
Great Britain: occupation policy, 31, 45,
58, 70, 108–111; devaluation of pound,
61; and German rearmament, 121, 272;
and access to German markets, 205
Greece, 240, 260
Grewe, Wilhelm, 238
Grotewohl, Otto, 244, 265
Gruenther, Gen. Alfred, 224, 292
Gullion, Gen. Allen, 15

Hallstein, Walter, 107, 192, 254
Handy, Gen. Thomas, 127, 353n1
Harriman, Averell, 34, 40, 42, 64, 105,
129, 134, 229, 241
Harvard Law School, 4, 5–6
Havlick, Hubert, 366n38
Hayes, Peter, 173
Hays, Gen. George, 126, 127, 211, 221
Heinemann, Dannie, 50
Heinemann, Gustav, 140, 146–147, 148,
284
Henle, Günther, 191, 199, 392n16
Hess, Rudolf, 9, 157
Heusinger, Gen. Adolf, 165, 212, 220,
228
Heuss, Theodor, 70
HICOG. *See* American High Commission
in Germany (HICOG)
High Authority, 103, 107, 112, 194, 196,
201. *See also* Schuman Plan
Himmeroder Memorandum, 212
Hirsch, Etienne, 103
Hiss, Alger, 43, 94

Hitler, Adolf: JJM's acquaintance with, 9;
seizure of power, 50, 54; and German
nationalism, 56, 87, 121; and François-
Poncet, 59, 60; plot to assassinate, 82,
216; and German industrialization, 93,
108, 169, 170, 171; and fear of German
rearmament, 138; German resistance to,
158; and persecution, 175; and German
expansionism, 214; and opposition to
Bolshevism, 218, 282, 308; successes,
296, 303; destruction of German unity,
383n67
Hoffmann, Paul, 42, 73
Hogan, Michael, 204, 297
Holland, 205
Hoover, Herbert, 11, 31, 185
Hopkins, Harry, 19, 98
Horowitz, David, 178
Hoth, Hermann, 168
Hull, Cordell, 18, 19, 20
Hydrogen bomb, 116

Ickes, Harold, 25
Indochina, French war in, 121, 211, 241,
251, 252–253, 260, 289–290, 307,
350n52
Inter-Governmental Study Group (ISG),
106
Interim Mixed Parole and Clemency
Board, 174
Inter-Ministerial Coordinating Committee,
207
International Authority for the Ruhr
(IAR), 27–28, 31–32, 69, 74, 75, 78,
80, 82, 94, 104, 146, 149, 188, 197,
205, 351n60
International Bank for Reconstruction and
Development. *See* World Bank
International Court (The Hague), 9
Internationalism: "Founding Fathers," 1;
and global problems, 24, 25
Isolationism, American, 86, 261, 285–286.
See also Neo-isolationism
Israel, restitution to, 156, 175–184
Italy, Communist Party, 52

Jackson, Robert, 13, 15, 169
Jacobssen, Per, 205
Japanese-Americans, internment of, 15–17
Jay, Dean, 342n28
JCS 1067, 21, 24, 30

Jenninger, Philip, 354n5
Jessup, Philip, 37, 275
Jewish Claims Conference, 180
Jewish Restitution Successor Organization
(JRSO), 177–178
Johnson, Louis, 41, 116, 135, 139
Johnson, Lyndon B., 308

Kaisen, Wilhelm, 111
Kaiser, Jakob, 267
Kaiser, Karl, 377n28
Kaspi, André, 98
Katz, Milton, 204, 205–206, 207
Kellerman, Hermann, 362n5
Kennan, George, 35–36, 37, 38, 39, 116,
157, 302, 306, 391n7
Kennedy, John F., 305
Kennedy, Joseph, 185
Khrushchev, Nikita, 288
Kiesinger, Kurt, 127
Kim-Il-Sung, 124
Kirkpatrick, Sir Ivone, 58, 77, 166, 200,
243, 249, 269
Kissinger, Henry, 306, 385n81
Kohl, Helmut, 300
Korean War, 116, 124–126, 128, 140,
150, 152, 188, 202, 204, 205, 219,
240, 282, 295, 299
Krock, Arthur, 357n20
Krupp, Alfried, 169, 170, 171, 172–173,
174, 175
Krupp, Gustav, 169, 172
Kubowitzki, Leon, 17–18
Kuhn, Ferdinand, 135
Kuntze, Gen. Walter, 168
Küster, Otto, 181, 182

Labour party, British, 110–111, 170, 257
Lackawanna Steel Company, 6
Law for the Safeguarding of the Economy,
207
Law 27: 93, 104, 108, 112, 186, 187,
189–197, 198, 199, 200–201, 202, 208
Law 75: 93, 94
League of Nations, 7, 97
Leahy, Adm. William D., 24
Le Figaro, 60, 170
Léger, Alexis, 325n35
Lehr, Robert, 39, 140, 337n37
Le Monde, 96, 113
Lend-Lease program, 12, 20

Le Roy de la Tournelle, Guy, 378n39
Lincoln, Abraham, 82
Lippmann, Walter, 15, 105, 306, 330n31,
342n28, 381n62
List, Wilhelm, 168
London Conference (June 1948), 32, 34,
36
London Times, 74, 170
Lovett, Robert, 12, 29, 225, 271, 272,
327n54
Lundestad, Geir, 299
Lusitania, sinking of, 4
Luxembourg Treaty (1952), 178, 183–
184

MacArthur, Gen. Douglas, 5, 125, 222,
223, 322n11
McCarthy, Joseph, 34, 94, 158
McCloy, Anna May Snader (mother), 1–2,
5, 8
McCloy, Ellen Zinsser (wife): marriage to
JJM, 8; German ancestry, 41, 50
McCloy, John J.: appointed High Commissioner, 1, 21, 40–45, 58, 80; birth
and family, 1–2; interest in sports, 2, 3,
5, 7; education, 2–3, 4, 5–6; military
service, 3, 4–5; early employment, 6–8;
personality, 7–8, 28; marriage, 8; and
Black Tom case, 8–9, 12; as Assistant
Secretary of War, 10–25 passim; as lawyer with Milbank, Tweed, 25–26; as
president of World Bank, 26–28, 99; influence on Germans, 61; and devaluation
crisis, 62–65; views on founding of
GDR, 66–67; and dismantling of German industry, 70–82 passim; and Soviet
initiative in Germany, 84, 86; and role
of Germany in Europe, 85–86, 95, 155,
269; and Saar region, 88; on German
reunification and redevelopment, 89, 90,
91–92, 94; influence of Monnet, 96, 97,
98, 100, 101, 102, 105, 106; and Schuman Plan, 106, 107–108, 186, 187,
189–197, 198, 201, 202, 203, 206–
207, 209; and Allied control of Germany, 107, 235, 236, 240, 244–245,
246, 247–249; and German rearmament, 116, 117, 123–124, 126, 127–
128, 130–135, 139, 143–144, 145,
147, 149, 153–154, 186, 216–221,
223–225, 227–230, 231–234; and resti-

tution, 156, 175–184; and war criminals, 156–175 passim, 308; threats on life, 166; and Law 27 negotiations, 189, 191–192; and German trade balance, 203–209; and occupation, 235, 237; and delays in Allied negotiations, 261, 265–266; and Stalin Note, 265–266; and Bonn-Paris treaty negotiations, 269, 269–278; return to private life, 279, 304; importance, 302–303, 304–305, 308

McCloy, John Jay (father), 1–2
McCloy, William (brother), 2
McCloy Committee (Advisory Committee on Negro Troop Policies), 14
McKinley, William, 11
Maier, Charles, 299, 302
Malmedy massacre case, 34, 157, 158
Malone, George, 73
Manchester Guardian, 170
Maplewood School, 2
Marcus, Robert S., 355n9
Marshall, Gen. George, 5, 14, 16, 18, 29, 139, 230, 241
Marshall Plan, 27, 31–32, 34, 40, 41, 63, 69, 74, 77, 84, 90, 91, 92, 99–100, 101, 112, 203, 205, 206, 227, 297, 305
May, Ernest, 305
Mayer, René, 289
Meikeljohn, Alexander, 3
Meiser, Hans, 160
Mendelsohn, John, 175
Mendès-France, Pierre, 289–290, 291
Merchant, Livingston, 284
Meyer, Eugene, 26, 342n28
Milbank, Tweed, Hope, and Hadley (law firm), 25–26
Military Development Assistance Plan, 115
Military Security Board (MSB), 78, 82, 91, 202
Military training, universal, 11, 25
Mills, C. Wright, 307–308
Milward, Alan, 96
Mitbestimmung (parity codetermination) controversy, 192–193
Mixed Parole and Clemency Board, 174
Moch, Jules, 138, 141, 143, 221, 226, 233
Mollet, Guy, 288
Molotov, V. M., 23, 287–288
Monnet, Jean: influence on JJM, 7, 12, 18, 41, 100, 303; and occupation policy, 95–105; importance, 96, 100; background, 96–99; and French industrialization, 99, 101–105, 186, 188–189, 193; and Schuman Plan, 104–105, 106–107, 110, 112, 140, 186, 193, 196, 198, 202, 298; and German rearmament, 140, 143, 144; and German role in Europe, 199, 306; influence on Eisenhower, 223–224; and EDC negotiations, 233; on Executive Committee of TCC, 241; and role of France, 251; and war in Indochina, 253; and Robert Murphy, 281; influence on Dean Acheson, 342n28

Monnet Plan, 102, 202
Monroe Doctrine, 375n9
Montgomery, Bernard, 387n8
Moran, Frederick A., 162
Morgenthau, Henry, 19, 20
Morgenthau Plan, 19–20, 21, 68
Morrison, Herbert, 200
Murnane, George, 342n28
Murphy, Robert, 36–37, 280, 325n34

Nathan, Robert, 99
Nation, 171
National security, as interest of JJM, 11, 13–14, 24–25
National Security Council (NSC), 12, 35, 131
Nazi war criminals: execution, 19, 21, 159, 165, 167, 170, 171; trials, 20, 21–22, 46–47, 149, 157, 158, 308; in Landsberg prison, 156–175 passim; clemency for, 160–164, 166, 167–168, 169–171, 172, 256
Neo-isolationism, 45, 185. *See also* Isolationism, American
Neo-Nazism, 145
Neuhäusler (bishop of Munich), 165
New Deal, 10–11, 220
New Look policies, 280, 281
New Republic, 3–4
Newsweek, 73, 105
New York Daily News, 73
New York Times, 87, 134, 170, 179, 278
Nicholson, Ralph, 43
Niemöller, Martin, 89, 147, 148
Nitze, Paul, 115, 129, 280
North Atlantic Alliance, 113

North Atlantic Treaty, 34, 38
North Atlantic Treaty Organization
(NATO), 134; as guarantee against
aggression, 38, 113, 115, 128, 138,
152; success of, 84, 222; German membership, 111, 117, 124, 211, 213, 249,
253, 254, 255, 256, 263, 268, 291,
292, 293–294, 295; forces under, 114,
125, 129, 131, 132–133, 136, 150,
153, 154, 213, 219, 232, 248, 252,
260; Military Production and Supply
Board, 131; founding, 136; and German
exports, 206; and German rearmament,
216, 218; Greece and Turkey as members of, 240, 260; American commitment to, 285; and use of atomic
weapons, 286; strengthening of, 307
North Atlantic Union, 95
Norway, 204
NSC-68, 116, 124, 125
NSC-115, 232
NSC 160/1, 283, 285
NSC 162/2, 286
Nuclear weapons. See Atomic weapons
Nuremberg trials. See Nazi war criminals

Occupation Statute, 32, 38, 39, 44, 57,
58, 82, 106, 146, 148, 150, 238, 273
Office of Political Affairs (HICOG), 48
Office of War Mobilization, 99
Ohlendorf, Otto, 164
Ollenhauer, Erich, 284
Olson, Culbert, 15, 16
O'Neill, Con, 218
Operation Bird Dog, 32
Organization for European Economic Co-
operation (OEEC), 101, 204, 205, 208

Pace, Frank, 224
Pacifism, 145
Paris Presse, 170
Parker, Chauncey, 43, 272
Patterson, Robert, 12, 194–195, 322n6
Peck, David W., 162
Peck Panel. See Advisory Board on Clem-
ency for War Criminals
Peddie Preparatory School, 2
Pentagon, construction of, 12
Pepper, George Wharton, 6
Pershing, Gen. John J., 5

Petersberg Protocols, 82, 84, 85, 93, 112,
117, 121, 190, 199, 296
Peterson, Howard, 322n6
Pferdmenges, Robert, 191, 364n18,
392n16
Plant, John, 3
Plattsburg movement, 3–4
Pleven, René, 141, 144, 145, 152, 211,
217, 226, 233, 251, 253
Pleven Plan, 141–143, 144, 150, 151,
154, 211, 212, 228, 230, 233, 241, 252
Plowden, Sir Edmund, 241
Poison gas, 118
Poland, 67, 90, 146, 285
Policy Planning Staff (U.S. Department of
State), 264, 281
Potsdam Conference (July 1945), 23–24,
26, 29, 30–31
Potsdam Treaty, 68
Pound, Roscoe, 6
Preparedness for war, 13–14
Preston, Gen. Guy H., 5, 322n9
Prisoners of war, German, 266
Program A, 35–36, 37, 38, 39–40
Progressivism, 3, 4
Prohibited and Limited Industries (PLI)
plan, 69, 74, 80, 197

Quebec Conference (September 1944), 20,
21
Queille, Henri, 63, 64

Reber, Samuel, 376n25
Reconstruction Finance Corporation, 62
Regimental Combat Teams (RCT), 131,
150, 215, 230
Reimann, Max, 375n12
Reinecke, Hermann, 168
Reinhardt, Hans, 168
Remer, Gen. Otto, 216, 242
Reparations, 30
Restitution, to German victims, 156, 175–
184, 270
Reston, James, 342n28
Reuter, Ernst, 111, 244
Reuter, Paul, 103
Reynaud, Paul, 252
Robertson, Gen. Brian, 58, 72, 80, 81,
106, 119
Roosevelt, Eleanor, 172

Roosevelt, Franklin D., 97; and labor, 10–11; and Executive Order 9066, 16, 17; and de Gaulle, 18–19; and Morgenthau Plan, 20; and appointment of High Commissioner, 21; death, 29; influence of Monnet, 98; education, 322n11

Roosevelt, Theodore, 11

Root, Elihu, 3, 11, 302, 323n22

Ruhr Agreement, 71

Ruhr Authority. *See* International Authority for the Ruhr (IAR)

Saar region, 87–89, 104, 146, 254, 289, 365n26

Sargent, Sir Orme, 109

Schäffer, Fritz, 179, 182, 183, 190, 258, 259, 269, 270–271, 273

Schäffer, Hans, 343n47

Schaukelpolitik (seesaw policy), 86, 130, 265, 295

Schmid, Carl Christian, 194

Schmidt, August, 76

Schmidt, Helmut, 306

Schoenbrun, David, 342n28

Scholl, Inge, 165

Schumacher, Kurt: background, 49, 53–56; and German industrialization, 70, 82–83; nationalism, 78, 79–80; opposition to Adenauer, 86, 120, 243, 256, 296; and Schuman Plan, 88, 111–112, 199; and German reunification, 89, 185, 244, 265, 276; and German rearmament, 137, 145–146, 228, 239, 349n46; and German equality, 152, 154; and Nazi war criminals, 165; and restitution, 179; relationship to JJM, 245; death, 277

Schuman, Robert, 77, 298; and occupation policy, 37–38; American support for, 45; and Franco-German reconciliation, 60, 121, 254; and devaluation crisis, 64–65; and German industrialization, 71, 76, 87, 88, 93, 101, 103–104, 122; and German rearmament, 137, 139–141, 142, 144, 151, 153, 233; political role, 138, 226; and EDC treaty negotiations, 253, 276; and German security controls, 260; and Soviet negotiations, 268; ouster, 289

Schuman Plan, 178; support for, 84, 105–112, 154; and German industrialization, 104, 123; opposition to, 108–112, 120, 173; impact, 113, 197–203; as model for other solutions, 129, 141, 144, 151; impact of Korean War, 140; problems with, 186–189; as focus of Allied negotiations, 236; and European federation, 372n26

Schwerin, Gen. Gerhard Graf von, 118, 120, 127–128, 136, 147

Seebohm, Hans-Christoph, 87

Selective Service Act (1940), 10

SFIO (French Socialists), 138

Sharett, Moshe, 176

Shinwell, Emmanuel, 142

Smith, Walter Bedell, 32

Snader, Lena, 2

Snader, Sadie, 2

Snow, Conrad E., 162

Social Democratic Party (SPD), 40, 48, 51, 53–56, 58, 80, 82–83, 85, 89, 111, 112, 120, 137, 145–146, 152, 154, 179, 185, 188, 199, 217, 243, 244, 267, 276, 284

Socialist Unity Party, 47

Sohl, Hans-Günther, 73, 191, 196, 197, 358n31

Soviet Union: American cooperation with, 20, 22–23, 24, 30–31; occupation policy, 30–31, 32, 40, 66, 67, 68, 86, 92, 114–15, 282–283, 286–288, 292–293, 336n29; atomic test by, 84, 113; American fear of, 113–116; and Stalin Note, 261–269; and occupation of Central Europe, 282–283

Soziale Marktwirtschaft (social market economy), 50

Sozialistische Reichspartei (SRP), 172, 216

Speer, Albert, 157

Speidel, Gen. Hans, 165, 212, 215, 220, 228, 357n21

Speidel, Gen. Wilhelm, 357n21

Spofford, Charles, 132, 150

Spofford Plan, 150–153, 212, 213, 230, 253

Stalin, Joseph, 35, 66, 114, 124, 133, 157, 171, 262–269, 281, 307

State-War-Navy Coordinating Committee, 12

Steel, Christopher, 345n12
Stern, Fritz, 305
Stimson, Henry: in Plattsburg movement, 3; as Secretary of War, 10, 11–12, 14, 16, 18, 19–20, 21–22, 23, 25; influence on JJM, 46, 123, 302
Stone, Shepard, 43, 346n14
Strachey, John, 110
Strauss, Franz-Josef, 165
Strong, Gen. Kenneth, 22
Sulzberger, Cyrus, 222
Supreme authority, concept of, 235, 236, 237, 238, 239, 242, 246, 247, 271
Supreme Headquarters of Allied Powers in Europe (SHAPE), 221, 227, 230, 241
Swaine, Robert, 25
Swatland, Donald, 6

Tactical nuclear weapons, 286
Taft, Robert, 157, 185, 261, 285
Taft, William Howard, 11
Task Force C of Project Solarium, 386n3
Taylor, Telford, 171, 173, 354n6
Temporary Council Committee (TCC), 241–242, 258, 271
Teppichpolitik (carpet policy), 57
Thayer, Charles, 126, 238
Thompson, Frederick, 3
Time, 105, 278
Tito (Josip Broz), 35
Tomlinson, William, 100, 303
Transnational coalition, 37, 45, 236
Transnational political elites, 302–303
Truman, Harry S: JJM's impressions of, 23–24; appointments, 25, 29, 41, 42; and German reparations, 68; support for Acheson, 75; and German industrialization, 77; and Schuman Plan, 105; and defense spending, 115, 116, 118, 124; and German rearmament, 120, 122, 129–130, 135, 139, 165, 232; response to Soviet aggression, 124; and American forces in Germany, 133, 185, 218–219; and Nazi war criminals, 166; and restitution, 176; and coalition government in Germany, 185; and 1952 election, 261, 279, 280
Turkey, 240, 260

Ulbricht, Walter, 125, 388n16
United Nations, 244, 262, 266, 267
Universal Declaration of Human Rights, 261
Uri, Pierre, 103, 342n32
U.S. Army, racial segregation in, 14
U.S.–Japanese Peace Treaty, 239

Verbundwirtschaft (combined economy), 187, 192, 193, 196, 201, 202
Vietnam. *See* Indochina
Vinson, Fred, 162
Vocke, Wilhelm, 206

Wall Street Journal, 73
Warburg, Eric, 70, 159
War Crimes Modification Board, 160
Ward, John, 211
War of the memoranda, 91
War Production Board, 99
Warren, Earl, 15
Washington Agreements on Germany, 38–40, 63, 69, 74–75
Washington Conference, 240–243
Washington Post, 171, 179
Watenstedt-Salzgitter plant, 78
Webb, James, 41
Weill, Pierre-David, 342n28
Weimar Republic, 50, 51
White, Austin, 307
White, Theodore, 46, 48
White, William Allen, 10
White Rose resistance movement, 165
Williston, Samuel, 6
Willkie, Wendell, 10
Wilson, Woodrow, 322n11
Wood, Leonard, 3
World Bank, 26–28, 41
Wurm, Theophil, 160

Yank, 307
Yergin, Daniel, 24

Zangen, Wilhelm, 191
Zentrum, 49, 50
Zinsser, Hans, 8